Bedford Cultural Editions

ALEXANDER POPE

The Rape of the Lock

Bedford Cultural Editions

ALEXANDER POPE
The Rape of the Lock

EDITED BY
Cynthia Wall
University of Virginia

BEDFORD BOOKS   BOSTON ✿ NEW YORK

For Bedford Books

President and Publisher: Charles H. Christensen
General Manager and Associate Publisher: Joan E. Feinberg
Managing Editor: Elizabeth M. Schaaf
Developmental Editor: Alanya Harter
Editorial Assistant: Aron Keesbury
Production Editor: Tony Perriello
Project Manager: Ann Knight
Production Assistant: Deborah Baker
Copyeditor: Kathryn Daniel
Cover Design: Susan Pace
Cover Art: William Hogarth, *Marriage à la Mode,* Plate IV, etched
and engraved from a painting, third state, June 1745.

Library of Congress Catalog Card Number: 97–74968

Manufactured in the United States of America.
1   0   9   8
f   e   d   c   b

For information, write: Bedford Books, 75 Arlington Street, Boston,
MA 02116 (617–426–7440)

ISBN: 0–312–11569–5 (paperback)
      0–312–12799–5 (hardcover)

Published and distributed outside North America by:
MACMILLAN PRESS, LTD.
Houndmills, Basingstoke, Hampshire RG21 2XS and London
Companies and representatives throughout the world.
ISBN: 0–333–69097–4

Acknowledgments

About the Series

The need to "historicize" literary texts — and even more to analyze the historical and cultural issues all texts embody — is now embraced by almost all teachers, scholars, critics, and theoreticians. But the question of how to teach such issues in the undergraduate classroom is still a difficult one. Teachers do not always have the historical information they need for a given text, and contextual documents and sources are not always readily available in the library — even if the teacher has the expertise (and students have the energy) to ferret them out. The Bedford Cultural Editions represent an effort to make available for the classroom the kinds of facts and documents that will enable teachers to use the latest historical approaches to textual analysis and cultural criticism. The best scholarly and theoretical work has for many years gone well beyond the "new critical" practices of formalist analysis and close reading, and we offer here a practical classroom model of the ways that many different kinds of issues can be engaged when texts are not thought of as islands unto themselves.

The impetus for the recent cultural and historical emphasis has come from many directions: the so-called new historicism of the late 1980s, the dominant historical versions of both feminism and Marxism, the cultural studies movement, and a sharply changed focus in older movements such as reader response, structuralism, deconstruction, and psychoanalytic theory. Emphases differ, of course, among schools and individuals, but what these movements and approaches have in common is a commitment to explore — and to have students in the classroom study interactively — texts in their full historical and cultural dimensions. The aim is to discover how older texts (and those from other traditions) differ from our own assumptions and expectations, and thus the focus in teaching falls on cultural and historical difference rather than on similarity or continuity.

The most striking feature of the Bedford Cultural Editions — and the one most likely to promote creative classroom discussion — is the inclusion of a generous selection of historical documents that contextualize the main text in a variety of ways. Each volume contains works (or passages from works) that are contemporary with the main text: legal and social documents, journalistic and autobiographical accounts, histories, sections from conduct books, travel books, poems, novels, and other historical sources. These materials have several uses. Often they provide information beyond what the main text offers. They provide, too, different perspectives on a particular theme, issue, or event central to the text, suggesting the range of opinions contemporary readers would have brought to their reading and allowing students to experience for themselves the details of cultural disagreement and debate. The documents are organized in thematic units — each with an introduction by the volume editor that historicizes a particular issue and suggests the ways in which individual selections work to contextualize the main text.

Each volume also contains a general introduction that provides students with information concerning the political, social, and intellectual context for the work as well as information concerning the material aspects of the text's creation, production, and distribution. There are also relevant illustrations, a chronology of important events, and, when helpful, an account of the reception history of the text. Finally, both the main work and its accompanying documents are carefully annotated in order to enable students to grasp the significance of historical references, literary allusions, and unfamiliar terms. Everywhere we have tried to keep the special needs of the modern student — especially the culturally conscious student of the turn of the millennium — in mind.

For each title, the volume editor has chosen the best teaching text of the main work and explained his or her choice. Old spellings and capitalizations have been preserved (except that the long "s" has been regularized to the modern "s") — the overwhelming preference of the two hundred teacher-scholars we surveyed in preparing the series.

Original habits of punctuation have also been kept, except for occasional places where the unusual usage would obscure the syntax for modern readers. Whenever possible, the supplementary texts and documents are reprinted from the first edition or the one most relevant to the issue at hand. We have thus meant to preserve — rather than counter — for modern students the sense of "strangeness" in older texts, expecting that the oddness will help students to see where older texts are *not* like modern ones, and expecting too that today's historically informed teachers will find their own creative ways to make something of such historical and cultural differences.

In developing this series, our goal has been to foreground the kinds of issues that typically engage teachers and students of literature and history now. We have not tried to move readers toward a particular ideological, political, or social position or to be exhaustive in our choice of contextual materials. Rather, our aim has been to be provocative — to enable teachers and students of literature to raise the most pressing political, economic, social, religious, intellectual, and artistic issues on a larger field than any single text can offer.

J. Paul Hunter, University of Chicago
William E. Cain, Wellesley College
Series Editors

About This Volume

Alexander Pope's *The Rape of the Lock* is a dazzlingly visual and witty poem, and this edition is not the first to suggest that its imagery and wit are rendered far more powerful when positioned within the cultural contexts of its own time and place. I have been deeply inspired by Clarence Tracy's *The Rape Observ'd* (1974) and William Kinsley's *The Rape of the Lock: Contexts Series: Selected Literary Works in Their Historical Settings* (1979), both unfortunately out of print. These editions elegantly contextualize *The Rape of the Lock*, Tracy's with "numerous pictures, from contemporary sources, of the people, places, and things mentioned," as its subtitle declares, and Kinsley's with facsimiles of contemporary literary sources and texts on genre theory and practice. My edition combines and updates aspects of each, employing historical and literary materials that show the intimate formal and cultural relations between Pope's poem and his world.

The documents included here are designed to contextualize the poem first, within Pope's life and career, and second, within eighteenth-century poetic traditions and innovations, social habits and assumptions, historical events and political implications. The publication and reception of *The Rape of the Lock* had a powerful effect on Pope's career and offer us an index to his early theories of poetry and attitudes toward life. Letters and essays by Pope and others discussing the technical demands and rewards of the now somewhat alien forms of mock-epic and heroic couplets open up the poem as an endlessly varied balancing of oppositions, paradoxes, contradictions — rhetorical, linguistic, imaginative, psychological, social, political. The poem as such represents and in a way tries to reshape the poetic, social, and political world as Pope saw it. Understanding how that world perceived the characters of men and women, in their socially constructed differences and similarities, helps the reader recognize the double edge of Pope's satire, its subtle equating of men and women, and its admiration as well as contempt for the life of the idle, beautiful rich. The documents in the section on the political world situate the poem's images within the wider historical and ideological context of England's corrupt judicial system and its fast-growing trading empire. It is my hope that these choices of contextual material will better enable modern readers to see and hear the literary, social, and political implications that Pope packs so carefully and yet so lightly into his delicate, dangerous images.

ACKNOWLEDGMENTS

It has been such a pleasure to work with so many helpful and interested people in putting together this edition of *The Rape of the Lock*. The project started at the suggestion of Paul Hunter, to whom, as always, I give my warmest thanks. I also acknowledge my great indebtedness to the works of other Pope scholars, particularly Helen Deutsch, Ian Gordon, Roger Lonsdale, Maynard Mack, Pat Rogers, Valerie Rumbold, Patricia Meyer Spacks, and Howard Weinbrot.

I began work on the project at Vassar College and remain indebted to my colleagues and students there, particularly Robert DeMaria, Noel Burton Jackson, Amos Katz, and Vanessa Magnanini. Many University of Virginia colleagues have been generous with their time and their knowledge; I particularly want to thank Martin Battestin, Gordon Braden, Clare Kinney, Patricia Meyer Spacks, and David Vander Meulen. My research assistants have been breathtakingly competent and inventive: (in order of appearance) Caroline Breashears, Aliza Lamdan, Evelyn Ch'ien, Joseph Walsh, and Megan Raymond.

Various reviewers and readers helped me with both my concepts and my writing. Bedford chose the outside readers well; the manuscript improved immensely from the criticisms and suggestions of Helen Deutsch, Christopher Fox, Dustin Griffin, Patricia Meyer

Spacks, and David Vander Meulen. And *thank you* to my many informal readers and consultants, most especially Catherine Ingrassia, Shef Rogers, Laura Rosenthal, Carolyn Russell, Kathryn Temple, and Howard Weinbrot. The staff at various libraries have been indispensable: The British Library, Alderman Library, Houghton Library, Henry E. Huntington Library, William Andrews Clark Memorial Library, and last but (for me) always first, The Newberry Library.

It has been a delight to work with the people at Bedford Books. Kathy Retan and Alanya Harter have been wonderful editors — visionary, sensible, and eminently tactful. Thanks also to other Bedford staff: Margaret Hyre, who cleared permissions for illustrations; Aron Keesbury, who did various necessary huntings and gatherings; and Tony Perriello, who handled production so well. Kathryn Daniel was a scrupulous copyeditor. I am very grateful to Chuck Christensen and Joan Feinberg for including me in the Bedford Cultural Editions series.

Cynthia Wall
University of Virginia

Contents

Illustrations

Bedford Cultural Editions

ALEXANDER POPE

The Rape of the Lock

Part One

The Rape of the Lock
The Complete Text

Introduction:
Cultural and
Historical Background

The Rape of the Lock has a certain timeless, placeless, enchanted quality in the satirical delicacy of its self-sufficient world. Its very genesis might be told as a story or fable, beginning "Once upon a time . . .": Once upon a time young Lord Petre crept up behind Mistress Arabella Fermor at a party and snipped off one of her ringlets. She was not amused, and a distinct coldness developed between their two families. Lord Petre's cousin and tutor, John Caryll, thought it in the best interests of all concerned — particularly since all were members of England's small (and persecuted) Roman Catholic community — to try to reconcile the families. As Pope recorded,

> The stealing of Miss Belle Fermor's hair was taken too seriously, and caused an estrangement between the two families, though they had lived long in great friendship before. A common acquaintance and well-wisher to both [John Caryll] desired me to write a poem to make a jest of it, and laugh them together again. It was in this view that I wrote my *Rape of the Lock,* which was well received and had its effect in the two families. (Spence 1: 44)

The two-part ("-canto") version was published in a collection of *Miscellanies* (1712) put together by the bookseller Bernard Lintot. Although the poem seemed to do the trick socially, Pope couldn't quite put it down. As with everything else he wrote, he subjected the *Rape* to numerous revisions, in 1714 publishing a five-canto version

3

with the additional "machinery" of sylphs and gnomes and illustrated with six engravings (included in this edition). In 1717 he had the character Clarissa offer a "moral." The poem promptly became one of the favorite and most widely read poems in English literature.

But this poem and the story behind it drew much more from the world in which they appeared than simply a narrative plot. Although the poem has been read beautifully on its own, as a shimmering example of art for art's sake, it is also a poem emphatically situated within and commenting on a particular place and time. On the one hand it reveals Pope at a critical juncture in both his life and his career, when he was still vying to be a player within his world rather than simply a satiric judge of it, and when perhaps the power of his art could perform personal as well as social miracles. On the other hand, the poem's formal structure, rhetorical art, and particular content embody as well as critique the beauty, the triviality, the power, the conflicts, and the ambivalences of Pope's culture. The biographical and historical contexts of *The Rape of the Lock* enrich our reading of it precisely because the poem partly shapes and partly takes shape from that culture; the more sensitively we can situate ourselves in that world, seeing and hearing and experiencing it, the more our reading of the poem will resonate. Pope, in his early career, had faith in the power of poetry to restructure a world. With this collection of contemporary documents — maps, engravings, portraits, caricatures, newspaper articles, advertisements, letters, biographies, and other writers' poems, satires, and critiques — this edition hopes to *recreate* one.

The poem watches the heroine, the belle Belinda, awaken from sweet sexy dreams ("That ev'n in Slumber caus'd her Cheek to glow" [I.24]) on a late luxurious morning, attended by her favorite dog and mysteriously beautiful sylphs who hover protectively over her mental and sexual chastity. She "arms" herself for amorous battle, mustering perfume, cosmetics, and dress, and sets out with her friends on a gloriously sunny day for a boat trip up the Thames River to Hampton Court, one of the queen's palaces, to spend the day playing cards and drinking coffee. But after Belinda wins at the card game of ombre, and perhaps gloats a little too blatantly, the Baron plots revenge, coveting her glossy ringlets. With the aid of Clarissa, who hands him her pocket scissors (and who will, later in the poem, speak its "moral"), the Baron cuts off one of the locks as Belinda bends over her coffee; her chief sylph, Ariel, flies impotently away when he discovers "an earthly lover lurking at her heart." The Baron flaunts the prize of the "rape" — the lock functions throughout the poem as a symbol of virginity — and Belinda plunges into the dark psychological corners of anger, shame, and depression in the Cave of Spleen. The last canto describes the apocalyptic "battle" as all the young people take sides; the poem ends with the apotheosis of the lock as it becomes a star seen only by "quick, poetic eyes."

The contemporary texts and illustrations that constitute Part Two of this edition will situate the players in the poem — including the poet, who closes the poem with himself and Muse foregrounded, inscribing "midst the stars . . . *Belinda*'s name" — within the cultural contexts of early-eighteenth-century England. In the first chapter of Part One, "The Poetic World," we will see how the factors that shaped Pope's life — his Catholicism, his physical deformity, his education, his temperament — also shaped his poetry. Included are some early *hostile* responses to the *Rape*; a suspicious literary "establishment" forced Pope to struggle to define himself as a poet. This first chapter also supplies literary contexts — what Pope's contemporaries would have known about epics, mock-epics, heroic couplets, and visual allusions. The second chapter in Part Two, "The Social World," pieces together documents and illustrations that show how men and women perceived themselves in relation to the universe, how they thought about each other, how they looked, what they played, and where they went. The fact that men wore make-up and perfume in the early eighteenth century, for example, and that social critics of the day were concerned that the boundaries between men's and women's appearances and actions seemed to be blurring, complicates the apparent gender differences *within* the poem. And Chapter 3, "The Political World," brings to the surface the implications beneath the poem's brief but telling allusions to the monarchy, the British Empire, British trade, and the judicial system. Knowing how prevalent, how profitable, and how powerful Britain's world trade was at this time adds significant interpretive weight to the tortoiseshell combs and Arabian perfumes on Belinda's dressing table.

Through all of these materials I suggest a way of reading the *Rape* that combines its poetic structures with its cultural assumptions — although at the same time, I hope to show that one of the great poetic as well as cultural powers of the *Rape* lies in the various formal, rhetorical, and historical ways it *eludes* interpretive fixtures and *invites* interpretive battle. *The Rape of the Lock,* based on a real event in Pope's life, marks a delicate, decisive intersection of a social, political, and aesthetic place and time, a representation and a definition, a satire and a celebration, a portrait and a prescription, an effect and a cause. From the pervasive sense of *things* in this poem — preparations for and products of trade and conquest, both economic and sexual (puffs, powders, patches; coffee cups and snuffboxes; playing cards and lunar treasures) — to the equally pervasive anxiety over things-that-are-*not* (thoughts, vows, hearts, promises, prayers, vapors, steams, spleens, shrieks, "the Fate of *Louis,* and the Fall of *Rome*") — the form and imagery of the *Rape* reveal and re-enact the sexual, social, political, and poetic energies, and the efforts to control and contain them, in early-eighteenth-century England.

HISTORICAL CONTEXTS

> What Tears has *Albion* shed,
> Heav'ns! what new Wounds, and how her old have bled?
> She saw her Sons with purple Deaths expire,
> Her sacred Domes involv'd in rolling Fire,
> A dreadful Series of Intestine Wars,
> Inglorious Triumphs, and dishonest Scars.
> At length great *ANNA* said — Let Discord cease!
> She said, the World obey'd, and all was *Peace!*
> Rich Industry sits smiling on the Plains,
> And Peace and Plenty tell, a *STUART* reigns.
> — *Windsor-Forest* (1713)

Published between the two versions of *The Rape of the Lock,* Pope's poem *Windsor-Forest* sets out to describe, celebrate, and sustain a moment of national peace and prosperity. *The Rape of the Lock* is a witty and enchanting satire on the early-eighteenth-century fashionable world, but its light political and religious allusions glance toward a context of precarious stability and implicit threat.

Against a historical backdrop of regicide, civil war, plague, and the Great Fire in the seventeenth century — not to mention previous centuries of tyrants, deforestation, poverty, and brutality — Queen Anne ascended to the throne in 1702 and seemed to calm (at least for a time) all sorts of political, religious, and cultural anxieties about the stability of the Protestant monarchy. England began to secure its trading empire, and new materials and luxuries poured in from around the world. Financial success seemed within the grasp of far more people. From some angles, things were looking up.

The seventeenth century had been a time of enormous political and social upheaval. Charles I was beheaded in 1649, after a philosophical battering of political and religious assumptions about the divine right of kings. Oliver Cromwell and then his son governed the Puritan Commonwealth until Charles II was urged home from his exile in France in 1660. Following the restoration of the monarchy, the theatres reopened and portrayed, as well as encouraged, a new social climate charged with verbal wit and sexual energy — a climate still redolent in the air of *The Rape of the Lock*. In the midst of this first decade of social and political reconstruction, the plague of 1665 and the Great Fire of 1666 successively destroyed much of the population ("with purple Deaths") and then much of the original city of London ("in rolling Fire"). Architectural reconstruction began promptly and for the most part sensibly, and London re-emerged like a phoenix from its ashes, as Londoners were tirelessly fond of saying. The rebuilding of the city roughly corresponded with some decisive naval victories over the French and Dutch that positioned England at the vanguard of an expanding network of world exploration, trade, and colonization. The quick profits of trade, the economic boom of rebuilding, and the concomitant rise in urban population (with people from all over the country pouring into London after those quick profits) meant that a wider number of Londoners outside the traditional aristocratic circles assumed more voice and more power in economic and social affairs. As social periodicals such as *The Spectator* and economic treatises such as Defoe's *Review* often insisted, not only did conditions seem more stable, they seemed to be *progressing*.

However, when Charles died in 1685 and his Roman Catholic brother James II ascended the throne, a lingering uneasiness surfaced. When James's queen, Mary of Modena, gave birth to a son and heir, uneasiness turned to panic. The "papists" seemed a greater enemy to the political and religious structure of England than the Stuart line seemed a blessing — "popery" was traditionally associated in the minds of many Protestant English with arbitrary government and bloody persecution. James and Mary fled to France and the so-called Glorious Revolution of 1688 was engineered to usher in William of Orange from the Dutch provinces and his wife Mary, the elder daughter of James, as the new Protestant rulers. When William and Mary died without heirs, Mary's younger sister Anne assumed the throne. Anne also died without heirs and the English throne went to the Hanoverian (German) George I in 1714 and his descendants.

During this time, England was not a particularly green and pleasant land for those who, like Pope, did *not* belong to the Church of England. Beginning with the Act of Uniformity in 1662 and later the Test and Corporation Acts, everyone (or rather everyone male) was required by law to swear an Oath of Allegiance to the Church of England and to conform to its basic practices. Anyone who refused to do so — and most Catholics and Protestant Dissenters such as Presbyterians, Quakers, and Anabaptists did refuse to change their faith — was prohibited from holding office, attending university, entering most professions, and in some cases owning land or title. Neighbors watched each other suspiciously; informers broke up the Dissenters' meetinghouses and betrayed Catholic sympathizers. "Papists" had been blamed for setting the Great Fire in order to distract the English from winning the sea battles against Roman Catholic France and Spain, and were still being tried on those charges in the 1670s.

Yet despite the anti-Catholic legislation passed during William and Mary's reign (in reaction to the relaxed enforcement under Charles and James), actual religious tolerance increased to some extent under both William and Anne.[1] A Toleration Act allowing Dissenters to attend their own meetinghouses was passed immediately after the Revolution. But the Test Act was still in effect, which meant that a number of Dissenters and Catholics took communion once a year in the Church of England, in compliance with the law, and the rest of the year went their own religious ways. But such "occasional conformity," as it was called, rankled some, and the very thought of toleration infuriated a few religious figures into a frenzy:

> If therefore We have any Concern for Our *Religion,* any True Allegiance for Our *Sovereign* or Regard to the Safety and Honour of Our *Country,* We must Watch against These Crafty, Faithless, and Insidious Persons, who can *Creep* to Our Altars, and partake of Our Sacraments, that They may be *Qualify'd,* more Secretly and Powerfully to Undermine Us. (Sacheverell, *Political Union* 61)

In 1688 — the year of Pope's birth — those crafty, insidious persons were exiled too far to creep: Catholics were prohibited by the

---

[1] Linda Colley cautions against supposing that "intolerance of this kind receded rapidly in the face of growing rationalism and literacy" and reminds us of what would have been painfully obvious to Pope, particularly in the anti-*Rape* rhetoric: "Catholics could still encounter personal abuse and physical injury at the hands of Protestants" (Colley 22; see Part Two, Chapter 1, in this book).

Ten Mile Act from living within ten miles of London. Thus a visible spatial barrier was inserted into the lives of those who would not conform to the state church, geographically confirming their pre-existing political, religious, and social displacement. Sacheverell's opinions were shared by many of Pope's enemies, and similar anti-Catholic rhetoric would shape much of the hostile response to the *Rape*, as well as Pope's satiric response to such paranoia in *The Key to the Lock*.

Added to these religious controversies and divisions was a series of political shifts and frictions that in time produced England's modern two-party system. In the Exclusion Crisis of 1679–1681, in which attempts were made to dislodge James from the succession, the Exclusionists were called "Whigs" after the anti-Catholic "whiggamores" in Scotland; those who supported James's succession were labeled "Tories" by their enemies in allusion to the highway robbers in Ireland (Downie 7ff). In the decades that followed, the Whigs tended to draw members from the city — merchants, traders, and those whose wealth depended less on land than on stocks — who in the reign of Anne supported the wars and resisted peace efforts based on compromises that relinquished English territorial conquests. The Tories, on the other hand, tended to be the landowners, conservatives who were ready to purchase peace to preserve what they already had. Party strife became a hallmark of government in the years of Anne and George I, and for a while England saw its monarchs effectively replaced in active rule by strong-willed prime ministers such as Robert Harley and Robert Walpole. Pope's fortunes as well as his sympathies (and those of his friends Jonathan Swift, John Gay, Lord Bolingbroke, Bishop Atterbury, and others) depended almost entirely on which party was in power. Pope and Swift were for the most part Tories — though Pope often claimed political neutrality (see Part Two, Chapter 1) — and enjoyed some political persuasion under Anne, but at her death the Whig party, spearheaded by Walpole, assumed power, and Pope and Swift were back in the margins outside political power. *The Rape of the Lock* was written and first published in the years when Pope seemed closest to achieving a real voice in the political arena.

The Rape of the Lock, like Pope's poetry in general, captures both obvious and subtle ambivalences and contradictions in his culture. The sense of progress competes with the sense of peril; opportunity means risk; credit implies debt; causes have consequences. Pope rarely voiced outright any clear-cut religious, political, or moral positions; he was far too aware of the undersides of things, of other competing stories. *Windsor-Forest,* for example, in which the submerged political contexts in *The Rape of the Lock* surface, seems an uncharacteristically overt and perhaps naively optimistic rendering of the political present and future. But like much of Pope's poetry, *Windsor-Forest* is less a documentary than a prescription, encouraging what could or ought to be rather than what is:

> The Time shall come, when free as Seas or Wind
> Unbounded *Thames* shall flow for all Mankind,
> Whole Nations enter with each swelling Tyde,
> And Seas but join the Regions they divide;
> Earth's distant Ends our Glory shall behold,
> And the new World launch forth to seek the Old. . . .
> Oh stretch thy Reign, fair *Peace!* from Shore to Shore,
>   Till Conquest cease, and Slav'ry be no more. (lines 397–408)

Even as a descriptive utopiad, the poem is tinged with inherent darknesses and the constant intrusive presence of other points of view. When the poem describes England (*"Albion"*) sending her "eager Sons to War" until "high in Air *Britannia's* Standard flies," it does so from the sharply poignant perspective of the hunted pheasant:

> See! from the Brake the whirring Pheasant springs,
> And mounts exulting on triumphant Wings;
> Short is his Joy! he feels the fiery Wound,
> Flutters in Blood, and panting beats the Ground. (111–14)

The pheasant represents "Some thoughtless Town, with Ease and Plenty blest" (107) that doesn't see the "closing Lines" of the trap, the invasion, the conquest. The celebration of England's present and future power is not unilateral; the perspective is bifocal. And in this sense, Pope's poetry *is* documentary in its ambivalence, its recording of tension and dissonance and alternate points of view, which creep more subtly into the *Rape* itself. Beneath its overtly exultant rhetoric, Pope's poetry never quite loses sight of the fact that Anne's reign, with its political disruptions and religious persecutions, was *not* such a peaceful plane of existence.

Thus the historical background of Pope's poetry was characterized by paradoxical impulses of division and union, by boundaries and boundary crossings, by instability and order. Religiously, persecution was embodied in laws that enforced social, political, and geographical separation, that demanded and emphasized displacement, that sent nonconformists to the symbolic and literal margins of the London world. Yet the laws bent to accommodate "occasional conformists"; legal space and regal precedent permitted tolerance, and many enjoyed it. Politically, the dominant figures in government lined up in permanently opposing parties split, remarkably, by a common cultural concern for political unity, stability, and a settled monarchic succession. Yet the two parties' differences disguised even wider discrepancies between the haves and have-nots; these battles were waged in the upper stratosphere, with the nation, as always, at stake — a "nation" for the most part defined by and limited to those privileged to engage in the debate: landowning Protestant men. Still, economically speaking, the debates about war and trade, conquest and treaty, succession and authority, were helping to shape the changing mercantile climate, in turn enriching and empowering greater numbers of the middle classes and loosening social boundaries along with economic constraints. It was a world of great flux, and consequently a world greatly interested in order. *The Rape of the Lock,* as we will see, presents in miniature such a world of war and trade, conquest and authority, boundaries and confusions.

POPE'S LIFE: THE BUSINESS OF POETRY

> He considered poetry as the business of his life, and however he might seem to lament his occupation, he followed it with constancy: to make verses was his first labour, and to mend them was his last.
> — Samuel Johnson, *Life of Pope*

Alexander Pope was situated on the uncertain periphery of a particular social world, politically isolated by his Catholicism and personally marginalized by physical deformity. Poetry was "the business of his life" partly because he believed in its power to effect real change. He so carefully crafted his poetry — making and mending his verses — in part to reshape his world: he wanted to define and occupy literary and social *centers,* not edges. He was twenty-four when the first version of the *Rape* appeared. He had worked his way into the prominent literary circles of London and had acquired some substantial fame through the publication of his early poems in Tonson's *Miscellanies* in 1709 and of the *Essay on Criticism* in 1711. His observations were sharp, his humor quick, his hopes high, his faith in the power of poetry fresh. *The Rape of the Lock* was to be a poem that would mark and secure the *beauty* of this world as well as its follies; that would tighten the social solidarity in the Catholic circles of Pope's friends; and that would validate his growing reputation by its poetical and social success. The shape of the poem may thus stand out more clearly within the contexts of Pope's life.

Alexander Pope was born in London on May 21, 1688, the year that William and Mary came to England and sent the Catholics packing. Pope's parents, in their forties, were devout Catholics; Pope's father, until then a successful linen merchant, was forced to retire. In 1700 new anti-Catholic legislation meant that Pope could not inherit his father's property. Subsequently the Popes put their property in the names of sympathetic Protestant or oath-taking Catholic friends and relatives and moved to Binfield, in Windsor Forest, Berkshire. There, if we can trust Pope's poetic recreations of the place and anecdotes told to Joseph Spence (Part Two, Chapter 1), he was happy, exploring his poetic gifts in a setting he imagines in *Windsor-Forest* as almost Edenic — historically, nationally, and culturally emblematic of the true heart of England, and aesthetically a true measure of natural balance. He describes its landscape in rich colors and soft motions, visualizing all the pleasant elements of the countryside poised in a satisfying, fluid balance "where, tho' all things differ, all agree" — a phrase that captures Pope's early faith in poetry and optimism in life.

Pope was twelve when his family left London; before this time he had attended an excellent school for Catholic boys, but had been expelled for writing a satire ridiculing one of his teachers. From Binfield on he was largely self-educated, a fact that would later earn him some contempt from the literary establishment when he came to translate Latin and Greek poetry; such accomplishments were traditionally reserved for those classically educated at Oxford and Cambridge, an option not available to Catholics. But Pope was determined not to remain on the geographical or social fringes of London. About 1705 or so, when he was seventeen, Pope began to work his way into the literary circles — through the relatively new institution of the "coffee house."

Early Success: The Coffee House and the Poet

London's literati of the early eighteenth century congregated at either Will's or Button's coffee shop. Pope told Spence "it was Dryden who made Will's Coffee-House the great resort for the wits of his time" (Spence 1:29). Those "wits" included the playwright William

Congreve, the actor Thomas Betterton, the poet Samuel Garth, the critic William Walsh, and the now-elderly poet and dramatist William Wycherley, who enthusiastically sponsored the young Pope (see Part Two, Chapter 1, for a letter from Pope thanking Wycherley for his praise and asking for his advice. Through Wycherley, "Pope could make imaginative contact with the literary lions of the past age . . . [and] hear anecdotes of the conversations at Will's and similar places of resort" (Mack 89). By 1713, Pope was spending a great deal of time in London (studying, among other things, painting with Charles Jervas), and he became a frequent visitor at the rival coffee house, Button's. There, the literary circle centered around a group of Whig writers headed by Joseph Addison, who with Richard Steele would later publish the *Spectator* and *Tatler* periodicals. Addison was an early supporter (though a later enemy) of Pope, whose "Receipt to Make an Epick Poem" (Part Two, p. 252) first appeared in *The Spectator*.[2] For a time Pope was able to cross literary boundaries of different cliques, although his first and fastest allegiances were to Wycherley and Walsh. That such a young man was welcomed in such disparate and well-established literary groups testifies to the power of Pope's early experiments and to the willingness of the literary elite to recognize that power.

The coffee house was no small institution in the literary and social milieu of the early eighteenth century. The kind of public dialogue and exchange of poetic and political views that Pope experienced at Will's and Button's was part of the growing professionalization and democratization of literature, which was gradually moving out of the realm of the aristocracy, from under the shades of patronage, and into a more public and publicized world. Literacy was expanding, print technology was improving, and booksellers rather than politicians were beginning to assume control over publishing and printing. The coffee house, which arose to accommodate the enormous demand for that exotic, relatively new drink (Part Two, Chapter 2), offered a new kind of social space in which people — mostly but not entirely men — from a wide range of professions and classes gathered

---

[2] Addison was to prove a treacherous friend from Pope's point of view. Addison publicly supported the plainly inferior *Pastorals* of Ambrose Phillips; Pope believed his motives were suspect in discouraging the addition of the "machinery" in the 1714 edition of the *Rape;* and Pope would finally characterize Addison as the jealous, underhanded Atticus in the *Epistle to Arbuthnot* (1735), who would "Damn with faint praise, assent with civil leer, / And without sneering, teach the rest to sneer" (ll. 201–02).

to drink coffee, and "not only . . . hear the latest gossip but also . . . read the most recent newspaper, newsletter, pamphlet, or manuscript poetry collection" (Pincus 833) and argue about politics, religion, and literature. Steve Pincus argues that the coffee houses were "not limited to the metropolis, not gender or class exclusive, and not defended or used exclusively by Whig ideologues." Instead, they were "ubiquitous" and part of "a new conception of political and social space" that acknowledged "the value of public opinion" (811). Pope heard his work read, praised, criticized, and debated in the "modern" public spaces of the coffee house.

London was a city divided, both geographically and socially, by class. Politicians and aristocrats occupied the city of Westminster and the west end of London; merchants, tradesmen, and apprentices inhabited the old central "City" (see the map, p. 373). Gradually in the late seventeenth and early eighteenth centuries, the topographical spaces between east and west — the "Town" — drew people from all over to the newly opened theaters and newly established coffee houses. Both theatre and coffee house thus became places in which social boundaries were at least temporarily relaxed, if never forgotten. Literary careers often began and ended in these public places as people sorted themselves or were sorted by others into various categories of "wits" and "hacks," poets and scribblers. The arena was not for the faint-hearted, according to Pope:

> I believe, if any one, early in his life should contemplate the dangerous fate of authors, he would scarce be of their number on any consideration. The life of a Wit is a warfare upon earth; and the present spirit of the learned world is such, that to attempt to serve it (any way) one must have the constancy of a martyr, and a resolution to suffer for its sake. (Preface to *Works*)

The battle for literary territory was fierce and public; a writer's personal life was considered fair game for attacking his or her literary productions; and Pope experienced early on — and with increasing bitterness and intensity through his career — the brutal personal and public penalties of life as a poet.[3]

---

[3] See Part Two, Chapter 1, for some of the vindictive personal criticism Pope received, at the hands of John Dennis in particular.

Early Difficulties: Catholicism

Pope's position in the literary arena was complicated by his Catholicism. Though Pope was hardly as overtly devout a Catholic as his parents, he never considered becoming Anglican or even simply taking the Oath of Allegiance, which would have made life much easier. Some of his friends seemed to think the ideal opportunity arrived when his father died in October 1717, but Pope disagreed:

> Whether the change would be to my spiritual advantage, God only knows: this I know, that I mean as well in the religion I now profess, as I can possibly ever do in another. Can a man who thinks so, justify a change, even if he thought both equally good? To such an one, the part of *Joyning* with any one body of Christians might perhaps be easy, but I think it would not be so to *Renounce* the other. (*Correspondence* 1: 453)

Pope was never dogmatic in his religious beliefs, but he was loyal to the Catholic community. Both the Petres and the Fermors were prominent, wealthy, aristocratic Catholic families, as was John Caryll and Sir George Brown, "Sir Plume" in the poem. Although Pope, as son of a linen draper, occupied a much lower social position than the players in the poem, he still identified with the small, anxious community — and, as he wrote to John Caryll on March 20, 1716, he believed at this time that social disputes "may be softened some degree, by a general well-managed humanity among ourselves." Caryll thus easily coaxed Pope to write the little poem that would laugh the parties together again (Spence 1:46), and in manuscript at least the poem seems to have done so. But after Pope published the piece, what had been a charming private affair was now public, figuring easily identifiable characters in acts of mischief, childishness, and lewdness, as many of the anti-*Rape* treatises (some of which are included in Part Two, Chapter 1) take great pains to show.[4] Some of this inappropriate and vulgar sexuality, they seem to imply, comes directly from Pope's nasty mind; some seems obscurely connected to Roman Catholicism in general. The Fermors and Petres were now offended, and Pope made some efforts to repair the damage by dissociating Arabella from Belinda in everything "but beauty" in the Epistle

---

[4] "In May of 1716 alone the newspapers attacked Pope, his politics, and his religion so often that on 20 June he complains to Swift that 'I suffer for my Religion in almost every weekly paper'" (*Correspondence* 1: 342; Weinbrot 24).

Dedicatory, though as Howard Weinbrot notes, "[The families'] embarrassment probably meant little to ambitious Alexander Pope. The occasion already was behind him and the characters given immortal life in the immortal poem that helped to establish his reputation as England's greatest young poet" (17).

Pope responded to the anti-Catholic readings of the poem in his pseudonymous *The Key to the Lock,* which offers a scrupulous pseudo-paranoiac reading of religious and political subversion in every line of the *Rape.* As Pope knew first-hand from invective he would suffer throughout his life, the best defense is a shrewdly satirical offense; *The Key to the Lock* appropriates the voices, vocabularies, and vexations of the enemy before the enemy is scarcely aware of it. The willful exaggeration on the part of the *Key's* "author," the Dutch apothecary Esdras Barnivelt (both apothecaries and the Dutch were suspect to the English), is meant to reground the *Rape* in the social sphere where it belongs. And so, too, is this mention of the Catholic contexts of the *Rape;* as Weinbrot argues, although the Catholic contexts shape the poem and its reception, the poem "above all is a poem, one by a young man able brilliantly to transform his own and others' lives into art" (26).

Early Difficulties: Disease and Desire

Personally as well as socially, Pope would make it the business of his poetry to transform his life into art. Pope's political and religious difficulties were exacerbated by an early and life-shaping illness. Sometime shortly after the family moved to Binfield, Pope contracted a tubercular disease of the bone that permanently disfigured him, leaving him small (as a grown man he was barely 4 feet 6 inches) and chronically frail, with a hunched back. As Samuel Johnson outlines in the *Life of Pope,* his perpetual illness contributed to his irascibility, his odd appetites, and the daily difficulties of what he would term in the *Epistle to Arbuthnot* "this long Disease, my Life." His friends described his fine eyes, Roman nose, handsome mouth; his enemies called him toad, spider, ape.

Figuratively as well as literally, Pope's physical appearance shaped his poetry. He is always concerned to find or create the beautiful, and particularly beauty in asymmetry; he is equally interested in the forms and meanings of ugliness. Much of his poetry, both early and late, tries to anticipate and rewrite a real or imagined response to his deformity, and to transform that deformity into some sort of reconfigured power. Much as his enemies would equate his misshapen body with a misshapen mind, Pope tried to read and write the unusual as the blessed rather than the cursed. But either way, he saw and eventually had to accept that his physical afflictions placed him permanently outside a normal social world.

His perception of this displacement figured poignantly, in the years surrounding *The Rape of the Lock,* in Pope's early relationships with women. During his time in Binfield Pope became friends with two women who would in important ways influence his outlook, his hopes, his life, and his poetry. Teresa and Martha ("Patty") Blount, sisters in a well-placed but not wealthy Catholic family, both about Pope's age, were for a time very much a part of his romantic imagination (see Part Two, Chapter 2). Teresa, his own age, was the more outgoing, perhaps the more striking woman, but Martha became one of Pope's dearest lifelong friends and the real-life symbol of a good woman and a good person; she is the "Lady" in *Epistle to a Lady* and the subject of many later poems. He watched over her financially throughout her life. Some contemporaries speculated about a secret marriage between them, although later biographers have found no evidence to support such speculation. Still, the fact that their relationship was so romanticized testifies to its contemporary strength.

During these years (1712–1720) Pope flirted conspicuously in his letters to women, indulging in what was called "epistolary gallantry" in imagining and creating a number of romantic scenarios. With the modest Martha he was the most circumspect; with Teresa he verged on the naughty; with Lady Mary Wortley Montagu, he grew rhapsodic. Consider, for example, the sexually punning couplet he sent (undated) to Teresa about a young country couple who were struck by lightning while curled up in a haystack:

> Here lye two poor Lovers, who had the mishap
> Tho very chaste people, to die of a Clap.

His version to Lady Mary, a well-educated and witty woman of great literary talents herself, just off to Turkey with her nondescript ambassador husband in 1716, becomes a romantic elegy, a poetic monument following a respectful narrative (for both, see Part Two, pp. 116, 122–25).

Pope's epistolary gallantry with Lady Mary would intensify during her years in Turkey, taking on a literary life of its own. He increasingly fantasized about a relationship in which the beloved woman obligingly overlooks her lover's infirmities and consummates the difficulties with pleasure, and without *any* attempt on his part "to make the Ugly a little less hideous"; in all respects his self-representation will be "most Horribly Like" (August 18, 1716). His seduction will be through his words; his power will spring from his poetry. He sometimes seems to see sexuality as an equation (text *as* sex) and sometimes as an exchange (sex *for* text):

> [Y]ou have all I am worth, that is, my Workes. . . .
>   (to Lady Mary Wortley Montagu, June 1717)

> I am at this instant placed betwixt Two such Ladies [Martha and Teresa] that in good faith 'tis all I'm able to do, to keep my self in my Skin. . . . How gladly wou'd I give all I am worth, that is to say, my *Pastorals* for *one* of their Maidenheads, & my *Essay* for the other? I wou'd lay out all my *Poetry* in *Love;* an *Original* for a *Lady,* & a *Translation* for a *Waiting Maid!*
>   (to Henry Cromwell, December 21, 1711)

And sometimes, Pope would see his poetry as the agent of change itself, with the power to change appearances, to change responses, to change the shape of the man, of the world. In his correspondence with Lady Mary he enacts a literary metamorphosis, first descriptively placing his twisted body before her eyes, with no flaw hidden or excused, and implying that the distance between them is not merely geographical but corporeal; then suggesting that in such exotic lands as Lady Mary is visiting the men of his make are particularly cherished as lovers; and finally transposing that distance into myths of goddesses and mortals, princesses and dwarfs, princesses and *poets*.

But sometimes, even early on, the fantasy doesn't work. In her response to his elegy to the country couple killed by lightning, for example, Lady Mary acerbically rewrites the John and Sarah story and insists on preferring to be his "stupid, *living,* humble servant, than to be *celebrated* by all the pens in Europe" (Part Two, p. 127).[5] Sometimes Pope's world refused to be rewritten. As Pope admitted to his friend John Caryll, he was all too aware that he was not "the great Alexander Mr Caryll is so civil to, but that little Alexander the women laugh at" (Part Two, p. 112). As the years passed, his hopes

---

[5] Lady Mary would later become an outspoken enemy of Pope's. Biographers are uncertain about the source of the enmity, but no one could remain unclear about its intensity. Pope would characterize Lady Mary as the slovenly Sappho in *Epistle to a Lady* (1735): "Sappho at her toilet's greasy task. / [agrees as ill] With Sappho fragrant at an ev'ning Mask: / So morning Insects that in muck begun, / Shine, buzz, and flyblow in the setting-sun" (ll. 25–28).

for a normal emotional and sexual relationship dwindled, and his enemies stepped up the discourse of deformity. He was not immune to such discourse, according to his eighteenth-century biographer Samuel Johnson, who notes in his *Life of Pope* that

> He pretends insensibility to censure and criticism, though it was observed by all who knew him that every pamphlet disturbed his quiet, and that his extreme irritability laid him open to perpetual vexation; but he wished to despise his criticks, and therefore hoped that he did despise them. (Johnson 209).

Early Career: Self-Fashioning

The difficulties Pope encountered never thwarted his poetic art, although they conspicuously shaped it. Perhaps they even spurred and sustained the energy of his attempts to rewrite the patterns or remake the fixtures of his world. Helen Deutsch has recently argued for the *productive* ways in which Pope "despised" his critics: "In Pope's literary self-fashioning ... deformity and poetic form create the ultimate couplet, guaranteeing the author, if not possession of his text, at least a kind of patent on it. ... [A]n ability to anticipate and manipulate such responses [informs] Pope's career-long strategies of self-authorization" (6). Certainly his early years were rich in explorations of poetic forms and traditions, as he tried different poetic voices to achieve different poetic ends. In first exploring the history of English poetry, he "imitated" (that is, explored the cultural sensibilities and poetic structures of) a wide range of poets: Geoffrey Chaucer, Thomas À Kempis, Edmund Spenser, Edmund Waller, Abraham Cowley, and John Dryden. He "corrected" some poems of Wycherley at Wycherley's request (if not with his undying gratitude). His *Pastorals* (1709) transfigured an old form and pattern of images into a new version of poetic autobiography and self-fashioning, at a point when poems were generally directed more publicly:

> Let other Swains attend the Rural Care,
> Feed fairer Flocks, or richer Fleeces share;
> But nigh yon' Mountain let me tune my Lays,
> Embrace my Love, and bind my Brows with Bays.
> That Flute is mine which *Colin*'s tuneful Breath
> Inspir'd when living, and bequeath'd in Death;
> He said; *Alexis*, take this Pipe. . . . ("Summer," lines 35–41,
> *The Second Pastoral, or Alexis* [1709])

Alexis, the young narrator,[6] wants a space apart from the other shepherds, a room of his own, so to speak, with world enough and time to sing his poetry and earn his fame; he accepts the poetic legacy — the "flute" — from "Colin," the figure for the great sixteenth-century poet Edmund Spenser, thus early positioning himself as a rightful heir to the laurels of the English poets.

Some of the voices of Pope's early poetry speak for and even *as* women trapped in and by pain, oppression, exclusion. In *Eloisa to Abelard* (1717), for example, Eloisa closes her own grieving epistolary poem to Abelard envisioning a powerfully sympathetic poet (who of course actually *is* writing Eloisa's lament):

> And sure if fate some future Bard shall join
> In sad similitude of griefs to mine,
> Condemn'd whole years in absence to deplore,
> And image charms he must behold no more,
> Such if there be, who loves so long, so well;
> Let him our sad, our tender story tell;
> The well-sung woes will sooth my pensive ghost;
> He best can paint 'em, who shall feel 'em most. (359–66)

In *The Rape of the Lock* it is the poet who counsels Belinda:

> Then cease, bright Nymph! to mourn thy ravish'd Hair
> Which adds new Glory to the shining Sphere! . . .
> When those fair Suns shall sett, as sett they must,
> And all those Tresses shall be laid in Dust;
> *This Lock*, the Muse shall consecrate to Fame,
> And 'midst the Stars inscribe *Belinda*'s Name! (V.141–42, 147–50)

On the one hand, of course, we could argue that in claiming to speak *for* the woman, Pope as male poet simply usurps her voice and has her repeat what he'd like her to say, perhaps even having her reinscribe *herself* into a position of submission; on the other, we could claim that Pope's position on the outside looking in in some measure experientially authorized him to voice the pain of oppression and exclusion.

Success — and More Difficulties

Whichever way we interpret the "voice" of the early Pope, it remains clear that he saw poetry as his chief source of strength and his only possibility for power. And his optimism was not just wishful

---

[6] Pope claims to have written the *Pastorals* in 1704, when he was sixteen.

thinking; fairly early on, his poetry earned him financial independence. Until 1714 Pope *almost* enjoyed a taste of political influence, becoming fast friends with Jonathan Swift, John Gay, and Dr. Arbuthnot, who together had formed the Scriblerus Club to satirize the academic pomposities of the day. The prime minister, Robert Harley, occasionally dropped by to contribute. But the death of Queen Anne in 1714 and the subsequent fall of Harley's Tory ministry blasted all hopes of court preferment. Pope had recently published proposals for translating Homer's *Iliad* in October 1713; he would now spend the next six years in painstaking, even haunting, care[7] to bring the power, violence, and heroism of the men and women, gods and goddesses, of ancient Greece, and the beauty and strength of Homer's poetry, into the poetic patterns and cultural sensibilities of his own day — at the very time he was also articulating the patterns and sensibilities of his culture in *The Rape of the Lock*, often borrowing from his epic to shape his mock-epic. Pope's translation brought him literary security and remained standard well into the nineteenth century. It also secured him economic independence for the rest of his life, earning him the equivalent of what would now be about $1.5 million (see Gordon 16). He leased a small villa in Twickenham, on the banks of the Thames River west and slightly south of London, where he spent the last twenty-five years of his life. His financial security freed him from the necessity of political or royal patronage; he had no need to court favor or fear retaliation. He was free to think and say what he liked, and he even turned down two government pensions to preserve that freedom: "But (thanks to *Homer*) since I live and thrive, / Indebted to no Prince or Peer alive" (*Imitation of Horace* II.ii.68–69).

Being free to say whatever one likes, and having much to say, can put one in a good position to be disliked, and Pope had already started a career at making and keeping enemies. Some of these enemies, like John Dennis, seemed to spring from nowhere and initiate the hostilities; others, Pope's own sharp tongue provoked. In 1725 Pope published an edition of Shakespeare, which the scholar Lewis Theobald shortly and with some justice discredited, for as Ian Gordon notes: "By modern standards Pope was not a particularly good editor, tending to correct and improve rather than restore and

---

[7] He told Joseph Spence: "In the beginning of my translating the *Iliad* I wished anybody would hang me, a hundred times. It sat so heavily on my mind at first that I often used to dream of it, and so do sometimes still" (Spence 1:84).

preserve" (18). Theobald became the chief Dunce in Pope's first versions of *The Dunciad* (1728, 1729), and many years passed — centuries, in fact — before Theobald's scholarly reputation recovered.

In the 1730s Pope published a series of satiric *Epistles* (excerpts from *Epistle to Cobham* are included here in Part Two, pp. 311–21) as well as the highly acclaimed *An Essay on Man* (1733–1734). Because by this time he had made so many nasty enemies, Pope published the *Essay on Man* anonymously. He wanted to see how a major poem of his would be received without all the incessant *ad hominem* racket. The poem was so well received for its elegant philosophy that when his authorship became known, his enemies were discomfited and silenced, at least for a moment. The end of the 1730s found Pope "imitating" Horace, speaking ever more authoritatively about the fate and faults of his world.

Self-shaping and world-shaping are two of the most fundamental characteristics of Pope's life and works, and they are essential to the understanding of his poetry. In 1735 Pope rather deviously tricked the notorious bookseller Edmund Curll into publishing an "unauthorized" edition of his correspondence (a disguised figure dropped the manuscript bundle on Curll's doorstep); with righteous indignation Pope loudly stepped forward with the true, correct, and authorized version in 1737, sidestepping charges of arrogance in the name of authenticity. The authorized correspondence had been carefully restructured to present the best possible image of the poet as loyal friend, tender son, dutiful citizen, and morally responsible poet. Certain original letters were re-edited and redirected to more famous correspondents, such as the letter to William Walsh about poetic practices and the letter to Addison about the fickle April weather of the human soul (see Part Two, Chapter 1). When all this tampering and duplicity came to light in the nineteenth century, Pope's reputation plummeted. But it is important to recontextualize much of Pope's project and methods here. One of the assumptions in the early eighteenth century was that the spontaneous word or gesture is not necessarily the truest or most authentic. Art *clarifies* nature; time spent polishing an image discovers rather than destroys its reality. Time and effort and revision give us a chance to say best what we truly think; something we toss off in an angry or passionate moment is as likely to be an accident, an exaggeration, a misdirection, a bit of froth, as a true indicator of self. So much for the larger cultural beliefs. Add to this Pope's particular idiosyncrasy in his love of secrecy — Samuel Johnson called it his "great delight in artifice," noting that he "hardly drank tea without a stratagem" (p. 100). It's impossible to say how much this delight was shaped by his peculiar difficulties; there is so much that he could *not* pursue in a straightforward way. As he says himself, "all other ambitions, my person, education, constitution, religion, &c. conspir'd to remove far from me" (letter to John Gay, October 1730; *Correspondence* 3: 138). As with his physical handicaps, Pope made a virtue of necessity. Yet to be a poet is also *by definition* to delight in artifice in some sense, to play with words, to sort and rank and choose among them, to test effects, to work with light and shade and surface and depth, the obvious and the obscure, to synthesize structure and meaning and at the same time refuse the possibility of fixed interpretations. Pope's deviousness, as well as his deformity and displacement, was part of the package of his poetry.

The last years of Pope's life were increasingly saddened and embittered as his close friends died, his enemies grew legion, and the literary world seemed spinning into moral darkness. The difference in tone from *The Rape of the Lock* to the later poetry is marked. Far from the "I sing" opening of the *Rape*, his *Epistle to Dr. Arbuthnot* begins with a complaint: "Shut, shut the door, good *John!* fatigu'd I said, / Tye up the knocker, say I'm sick, I'm dead." All the hopeful writers and hostile critics in the universe seemed toward the end of his life to be pounding at his door, demanding or denouncing, insisting or insulting. The 1742 version of the *Dunciad* ends with an added fourth book that depicts the fulfillment of what had been merely prophecy in 1728 — the final conquest by the goddess Chaos:

> Thus at her felt approach, and secret might,
> *Art* after *Art* goes out, and all is Night. . . .
> Nor *public* Flame, nor *private*, dares to shine;
> Nor *human* Spark is left, nor Glimpse *divine!*
> Lo! thy dread Empire, CHAOS! is restor'd;
> Light dies before thy uncreating word:
> Thy hand, great Anarch! lets the curtain fall;
> And Universal Darkness buries all. (IV: 639–56)

But some of the "Universal Darkness" that Pope felt was swallowing his world was to a certain extent his own doing. The market for literature had burst open in the early eighteenth century; it became possible to make a living by writing; booksellers and politicians hired writers (sometimes derogatorily known as "hacks") to publish propaganda or romance or anything that would make a profit; hungry readers were snatching at the press's outpourings. Pope and Swift and their friends — as well as enemies such as Addison and Lady Mary — were simultaneously excited, empowered, and threatened by the new possibilities of pen and print. They transformed the energies of this newly modern world and its newly modern forms into art of their own. Much of the literature of this period — *The Rape of the Lock* included — is almost obsessively local, fastened on the streets and strategies of London itself, on the ordinary minutiae of this singular time and place. At the same time, the new forms and the energies of their satires seemed to inject new form and energy into the very world they were trying to curb. Pope's *Dunciad*s, Swift's *Battel of the Books* and *A Tale of a Tub,* John Gay's *Trivia,* Lady Mary's *Eclogues*: All define and reinforce the contours of a world shared with the so-called hack writers Ned Ward, Richard Blackmore, Daniel Defoe, and Eliza Haywood. Pope died and left this world in May 1744, but in spite of his dissatisfactions with it — or perhaps because of them — it was very much a world he had helped to shape. The cultural landscape he left may not, finally, have been quite as splendid as *The Rape of the Lock,* but it had supplied the contexts. Our own world seems even more different from Pope's, but it still contains his poem, and through the poem, his world.

FORMAL STRUCTURES AND SOCIAL CONTEXTS

The world of the *Rape,* like the poem itself, was glittering, contradictory, trivial, and powerful. To understand the depth of its superficiality, so to speak, the artifice of its power, its fixtures and its instabilities, it helps to understand first, what the poem *is,* how it is put together, how it represents the world within it; and second, how it reflects the world it lies within. How did Pope's society understand "human nature"? How rigidly defined and restricting were categories of gender? What did people look like, how did they dress, and how did those outward appearances relate to philosophical conceptions? And, since *The Rape of the Lock* is, among many other things, a poem of a world of pleasure, what *were* those pleasures, and how did they relate to the forms of power? Competing cultural attitudes toward women are complicated by anxieties about men; celebrations of leisure evoke satires on idleness; and the literal topography of early-eighteenth-century London appears not only as boundlessly energetic and extravagantly beautiful, but also as morally corrupt and physically disgusting. Together, the cultural and literary contexts suggest a three-dimensional impression of this world in which the real and the fictive characters of *The Rape of the Lock* lived and moved and had their being.

Mock-Epics and Heroic Couplets

Both the poetic genre of mock-epic and the poetic form of heroic couplets of this poem emphasize paradox, inversion, an ironic slippage between appearance and reality, and a tension between containment and escape that influence all levels of thematic interpretation. A mock-epic or "heroi-comical" poem, as Pope described it, the *Rape* employs absurd contrasts to create poetic frictions, ostensibly in this case to soothe social ones. Its patterns, conventions, and language would all have resonated within contemporary readers' intimate knowledge of Homer's *Iliad* and *Odyssey,* Virgil's *Aeneid,* and Milton's *Paradise Lost.* About this time Pope had begun working on his own translation of the *Iliad* and was almost daily immersed in the great acts of heroism and violence, in the elevated language and imagery of Homer's ancient Greece, where acts of rape (in the older sense of the Latin *rapere,* "to carry away") were as much a part of the violence of man against man, god against man, and nation against nation, as rape was a crime of man against woman. The grandeur of epic poetry looms over the small stakes and trivial concerns of Belinda and the Baron. A world and a convention that invoke the greatness of gods, but that are peopled by impotent, genderless sylphs who serve a very mortal, very human "goddess," render the present figures ludicrous against their absent allusive ones. The allusions to the great universe of the past underscore the belittled sphere of the present: "What mighty Contests rise from trivial Things" (I.2). The world is *miniaturized:*

Unnumber'd Treasures ope at once, and here
The various Off'rings of the World appear;
From each she nicely culls with curious Toil,
And decks the Goddess with the glitt'ring Spoil.
This Casket *India*'s glowing Gems unlocks,
And all *Arabia* breathes from yonder Box.
The Tortoise here and Elephant unite,
Transform'd to *Combs,* the speckled and the white. (I.129–36)

The spoils of English trade are reduced to ivory combs and jewel boxes; the conquests are social, in card games and flirtations; the rape is not *really* sexual, only symbolically so.

Yet a mock-epic is rarely a simple satiric reduction of the epic. The idealized past and the disillusioning present *exchange* energies and effects. The power of the poetry and the carefully chiseled beauty of the poem's interior visions and structure lend a modern, culturally situated grace, power, and celebration to its satirized content. And the idea of miniaturization itself in the eighteenth century is paradoxically powerful. In 1818 William Hazlitt commented about the *Rape:* "It is like looking through a microscope, where every thing assumes a new character and a new consequence, where things are seen in their minutest circumstances and slightest shades of difference; where the little becomes gigantic, the deformed beautiful, and the beautiful deformed" (Hazlitt 4: 142). In the early eighteenth century the microscope was just beginning to become popularized; ladies wore miniature microscopes on their wrists and amateur scientists or "virtuosos" — male and female — were frequently satirized in poems and plays.[8] Both the simple act of looking through the microscope and its larger implications for use in research showed that to be miniaturized in the eighteenth century was not merely to be reduced. On the contrary, the miniature became magnified.[9] Thus, we can look at the same things in the poem through two different lenses at once: Japan, China, Arabia are all employed to produce a cup of coffee; a cup of coffee calls up all the East. Moreover, that coffee imports miracles: "COFFEE arrives, that Grave and wholesome Liquor, / That heals the Stomack, makes the Genius quicker, / Relieves the Memory, Revives the Sad, / And chears the Spirits, without making Mad" (Part Two, Chapter 2, in this book). From one interpretive point of view, the mock-epic form of the poem reduces the whole world to the clutter of Belinda's toilette; from another, her toilette very literally implies vast worlds. As we will continually see, this poem always *is* and *is not* what it appears to be.

---

[8] The invention of the microscope is variously attributed to the Dutch spectacle-maker Zacharias Janssen in 1590 and to Galileo, who announced it in 1610. In 1656 the English philosopher Thomas Hobbes noted with wonder: "There are now such Microscopes . . . that the things we see with them appear a hundred thousand times bigger, than they would do if we looked upon them with our bare Eyes" (Hobbes 1: 445). Thomas Shadwell and Susannah Centlivre are two early playwrights who popularize as well as satirize the notion of the microscope opening up the secrets of the universe.

[9] The telescope — "*Galileo's* eyes" (V.138) — was also a popular lens through which the human world seemed proportionately miniaturized.

The metrical form of the poem employs similar strategies of opening up meanings while simultaneously appearing to close things down. The poem is written entirely in heroic couplets, which means that every line's rhythm is iambic pentameter — that is, five metrical feet of two syllables each, with the stress normally on the second syllable — and each pair of lines rhymes. The result is an apparently rigid, inflexible structure of containment:

> Love in these Labyrinths his Slaves detains,
> And mighty Hearts are held in slender Chains. (II. 23–24)

But this very couplet on chains illustrates a larger general rule for Pope about the difference between simply *following* rules and *mastering* them; as he had said earlier in *An Essay on Criticism*: "True Ease in Writing comes from Art, not Chance, / As those move easiest who have learn'd to dance" (II.362–63). The immediate paradox is obvious: A woman's curls reduce a man to the slavery of lust; the "mighty heart" of the hero is captured by the delicate filament of hair. "Love" in the *Rape* couplet receives the uttered emphasis in the first line, and in fact the stress is almost held captive by that emphasis on "love" until the end of the clause, and matches up with emphasis on "Chains" in the next line, the two words thus holding the rest of the line between them. During the course of the poem we observe that the "love" that holds the chains belongs not so much to the owner of the hair as to the owner of desire (who hopes "By force to ravish, or by fraud betray"); in a sense Belinda becomes trapped in the slender chains of her own hair (and her attitudes toward it), as well as by the force and fraud of the Baron's "love." Both Belinda and the Baron are thus simultaneously caught in the form and imagery of the couplet. Knowing the rules so well — learning the dance — allows the strict metrical form to become supple, graceful, energetic, powerful, able to resist looking down at its feet.

In one of the most famous passages of *An Essay on Criticism* — a poem in which Pope distills the legacy of critical precepts about English poetry and in which he often imitates bad poetry in order to show what *not* to do — Pope instructs:

> But most by *Numbers* judge a Poet's Song,
> And *smooth* or *rough*, with them, is *right* or *wrong*; . . .
> These *Equal Syllables* alone require,
> Tho' oft the Ear the *open Vowels* tire,
> While *Expletives* their feeble Aid *do* join,
> And ten low Words oft creep in one dull Line. (337–47)

"Equal Syllables," or constant patterns of stress, can so easily render heroic couplets metrically monotonous; unvaried emphases, repetitive vowel patterns, unnecessary padding, stretched rhymes, thin clichés, and overly symmetrical syntax bore the reader and kill the poem. (See *The Spectator* 253 and Pope's letter to William Walsh in Part Two, Chapter 1, pp. 224–27, 234–38, for more on this subject.) The good couplet is one that deftly poises rather than strictly balances its elements, that springs grammatical surprises on the reader, that keeps one eye open when it appears to close:

> What dire Offence from am'rous Causes springs,
> What mighty Contests rise from trivial Things,
> I sing — This Verse to *Caryll,* Muse! is due;
> This, ev'n *Belinda* may vouchsafe to view:
> Slight is the Subject, but not so the Praise,
> If She inspire, and He approve my Lays. (*Rape,* I.1–6)

The first two lines seem parallel, but the operating verb moves from the end ("springs") to the middle ("rise"), pushing the "trivial Things" to the dominant position at the end of the line, elevating "things" over actions — until the next line, when the poet jumps in authoritatively: "I sing." Punctuation disturbs this line in three places, pointing to attentive control and minute placement, and wedges the dedicatee firmly in the center, surrounded by the poet's verse and his Muse — inscribed, like Belinda's lock at the end of the poem, by the poet's insistent self-reference. And just as the poet's *Lays* (lyrics, or sung narrative) firmly close this stanza, his *Muse* takes credit for the final future fame of Belinda's lock and name. For Pope the couplet is a bold signature.

Within those insistent couplet containers, Pope manipulates the imagery of his poem in equally unsettling ways. The balance between the imagery of containment and escape, built into the structure of the couplet, which itself balances oppositions and resists resolution, creates a poem that has lent itself to nearly three centuries of wildly varied interpretations. Half of the poem seems constantly to be escaping, to be half-formed, half-spoken, half-answered. In Canto I, Ariel speaks in whispers, and then only "said, or seem'd to say" (I.26); he recounts the genesis of sylphs through "soft Transitions" among various genders until they now "assume what Sexes and what Shapes they please" (I.47, 70). Those soft transitions include expiring, retiring, yielding, gliding, sinking, and fluttering. Female chastity *seems* to be preserved only through the precarious balance of competing interests, and those competing interests are men self-reduced to metonymic objects of adornment — the *persons* become *things*: "Wigs with Wigs, with Sword-knots Sword-knots strive" (I.101); actually, "the *Sylphs* contrive it all" (I.104). Thus what guards the "purity of melting Maids" shifts from interior vanity to exterior temptation and then to the sylphs, transformations of the original female vanities not lost with "transient Breath" — therefore back to a deeper sense of interior female vanity. The flitting visual imagery of the poem joins with its overt statements on women to suggest their inconstancy and shallowness.

Form and content indict the men as well. In Canto II, the sense of dissolution and fragmentation is distributed among the male characters with nearly equal devastating effect. The Baron builds an altar to Love, but it is as cluttered and unconsciously revealing as Belinda's own dressing table: "There lay three Garters, half a Pair of Gloves; / And all the Trophies of his former Loves" (II.39–40). The punishment for this half-formed altar is a half-answered prayer: "The rest, the Winds dispers'd in empty Air" (II.46). The account of the Baron's unfinished private life is immediately followed by dazzling descriptions of the sylphs, who seem to shimmer in and out of existence grammatically as well as visually. As Ian Gordon notes: "Pope establishes . . . transience . . . through the momentariness encapsulated in the use of present participles. Things are constantly 'trembling,' 'floating,' 'waving,' 'fluttering,' 'shining,' 'sparkling,' 'mingling,' 'melting,' and, above all, 'glittering'" (165). The sylphs are

> Transparent Forms, too fine for mortal Sight,
> Their fluid Bodies half dissolv'd in Light.
> Loose to the Wind their airy Garments flew,
> Thin glitt'ring Textures of the filmy Dew;
> Dipt in the richest Tincture of the Skies,
> Where Light disports in ever-mingling Dies,
> While ev'ry Beam new transient Colours flings,
> Colours that change whene'er they wave their Wings. (II.61–68)

The sylphs have taken on male shapes as if to confirm that these shifting spirits are no *more* mutable and fluttering than their human charges; in the previous canto, after all, it is 'Wigs with Wigs' and 'Sword-knots with Sword-knots' who strive with each other for female attention — the male dandy as identified with various sartorial vanities as Belinda with her locks. In short, the entire shifting landscape of the poem offers new layers of interpretation with every changing color, every changing verb.

Canto III is obscured by the fumes of coffee (III.118) as it clouds the politician's vision and overstimulates the Baron; the scope begins to widen and the political backdrop of the poem becomes as much a construction of the airy, dissolving, uncontainable word as the poem itself. As a 1680s poetry commonplace book claims: "Coffee politicians does create" (quoted in Pincus 821). Ariel winks out of existence as he spies the "earthly Lover lurking" in Belinda's heart (readers disagree on whether this image is the Baron); the sylph is snipped by scissors — "(But airy substance soon unites again)" — the lock is severed, the air is rent with lightning, screams, and shrieks. The wisps of the uncontainable have now burst the bounds; the world seems uncontained.

Canto IV explores the murkiest corners of all, opening with a series of negatives (not, not, not) and sinking into an image of the human mind shrouded in mist and darkness, confusion and grotesqueries; of "unnumbered Throngs" of shape-changers, boundary-crossers, label-dodgers: "Men prove with Child, as pow'rful Fancy works, / And Maids turn'd Bottels, call aloud for Corks" (IV.53–54). Screams, sighs, laments pour forth from torn bags, broken vials, dishevelled maids; at the same time the Cave of Spleen is self-enclosed, self-entrapped, like the "close recesses of the Virgin's thought" (III.140): "No chearful Breeze this sullen Region knows . . . . / Here, in a Grotto, shelter'd close from Air, / And screen'd in Shades from Day's detested Glare" (IV.19, 21–22). The forms do not protect, they ensnare. Thalestris's long discourse on the containing powers of Belinda's female sphere — the bound locks, "the tort'ring Irons," the corsets, the hoopskirts — highlights their essential flimsiness, the symbolic fragility of female self-protection. The Baron has succeeded "By Force to ravish [*and*] by Fraud betray" (II.32). Belinda seems complicit: The earthly lover chased the sylphs away; the steel of the scissors is "unresisted"; Belinda's last lament is *please* to substitute the hidden for the visible: "Oh hadst thou, cruel! been content to seize / Hairs less in sight, or any Hairs but these!" (IV.175–76). The sexual implications were just as apparent in Pope's time: John Dennis blames Pope for creating a lady more interested in preserving the appearance of chastity than the reality; and Giles Jacob's *The Rape of the Smock* extends the sexual metaphor even more openly (see Part Two, p. 203).

Canto V opens with the audience melting in tears; the battle is rejoined along gendered and sexual lines, with the men rising at the smiles and falling on the bodies of the women; snuff vanquishes the Baron; and the lock disappears into the lunar sphere with all the lost bits and fragments of the social world. With the snuff boxes and tweezer cases, broken vows and insincere gestures, the lock loses its material reality and becomes a symbol of the world that both produced and destroyed it. The shorn lock ends apotheosized — transformed, released, deified — as a "sudden Star," but it is still a fragment, a thing, a lock. In the act of immortalizing a piece of the world, the mock-epic glorifies the contingent and eternalizes the momentary. Pope preserves and celebrates his world as he laughs at it.

Thus the world, the language, and the form of the poem are constricting: mock-epic, heroic couplet, containers, jars, circles, corsets, expectations. But the world, the language, and the form of the poem are at the same time *uncontainable*: vows, promises, prayers; mists, vapors, rainbows; shifting lenses and unresolved oppositions. The poem as a whole offers a tensioned balance that resists resolution: Its careful metrical structures emphasize order, measure, hierarchy, and stability, but its images sabotage that order with chaos, uncertainty, unfulfillment, instability.

Identity and Gender

Part of the poem's sense of conflict between order, hierarchy, and fixity on the one hand, and chaos, instability, and fluidity on the other, draws on wider intellectual and cultural contexts in which ideas about human nature and the relation of human beings to the universe were in flux. In the early eighteenth century, the idea of personal identity, of what constituted the essence of a human being, was poised for change, hovering between an older, spiritually grounded sense of an eternal soul that maintained its identity from embryo to corpse and beyond, and a newer, empirically destabilized skepticism about the provable existence or even the *experience* of such inherent continuity. In 1694 John Locke had insisted that "*Socrates* waking and sleeping is not the same Person";[10] fifty years later David Hume fully articulated the problem: "I never can catch *myself* at any time without a perception, and never can observe any thing but the perception. . . . [Human beings] are nothing but a bundle or collection of

---

[10] John Locke, *An Essay Concerning Human Understanding*, 342. The first edition was published in 1690; the chapter on personal identity was added to the second edition in 1694 (see Fox 9).

different perceptions, which succeed each other with an inconceivable rapidity, and are in a perpetual flux and movement."[11] Both "question" and "answer" appear within Pope's lifetime and philosophically exhume the incompatible tensions between the literary concepts of Ben Jonson's "humours" — human nature conceived in terms of settled "characters," dominant characteristics, "ruling passions" — and the strikingly pervasive imagery from Restoration drama through mid-eighteenth-century novels of masks and disguises and their implications of shifting, mutable identities.[12] Belinda waking and sleeping is not quite the same person; the psychological Cave of Spleen, with its constant vapors, living teapots, walking pipkins, sighing jars, and talking goose-pies, is virtually a Humean bundle of perceptions and confused expressions of self.

Some of Pope's other poetry articulates these changing and competing notions of identity and links them to gender. His *Epistle to a Lady* (1735), excerpted in Part Two, Chapter 2, opens with an allusion to Martha Blount:

> Nothing so true as what you once let fall,
> 'Most Women have no Characters at all'.
> Matter too soft a lasting mark to bear,
> And best distinguish'd by black, brown, or fair. (1–4)

The poem then explores a gallery of female characters whose only consistency is in their chief affectation. The model woman at the end of the poem "Charms by accepting, by submitting sways, / Yet has her humour most, when she obeys" (263–64) and thus is "at best a Contradiction still" (270).

Belinda lives in a society that diligently prescribes, circumscribes, and trivializes women's lives, fostering their reputation for psychological inconstancy and behavioral contradiction. As *The Spectator* 79 contends, "*A Woman seldom writes her Mind but in her Postscript*" — figuratively marginalizing women's minds to a postscript. Swift's "Progress of Beauty" (lines 1–6; see pp. 296–97 in this book) watches the physical and by implication the spiritual woman slide in and out of artificial order; of her mind, he notes,

---

[11] David Hume, *A Treatise of Human Nature* (1739–40), 252.

[12] One critic has in fact labeled the early eighteenth century as the Age of Disguise (Maximillian Novak, *English Literature in the Age of Disguise*), and Terry Castle has written a wonderful study of identity and disguise in *Masquerade and Civilization*.

> A Set of Phrases learn't by Rote;
> A Passion for a Scarlet-coat;
> When at a Play to laugh, or cry,
> Yet cannot tell the Reason why:
> Never to hold her Tongue a Minute;
> While all she prates has nothing in it.

Some writers of the time, such as Daniel Defoe and Judith Drake — and occasionally Pope — argue that a woman's education *produces* such a fickle, shallow product because it *prohibits* anything sensible or challenging. Judith Drake argues in *An Essay in Defence of the Female Sex* (pp. 301–308) that

> [I]f we [women] be naturally defective, the defect must be either in Soul or Body. In the Soul it can't be, if what I have heard some learned Men maintain, be true, that all Souls are equal, and alike, and that consequently there is no such distinction, as Male and Female Souls; that there are no innate *Ideas*, but that all the Notions we have, are deriv'd from our External Senses, either immediately, or by Reflection.

The argument is thus that *if* women seem characteristically different from men — more changeable, more mutable — those differences are culturally produced. The social "containers" prohibit natural growth, and the human spirit struggles to escape.

Clarissa's speech in *The Rape of the Lock,* added in 1717, can be read as an indictment of women's self-entrapping, self-effacing, self-inflicted marginality; by concentrating as well as depending too much on beauty and artifice, women keep themselves within the circles of dance and dress, thus perpetuating their own stereotypes:

> How vain are all these Glories, all our Pains,
> Unless good Sense preserve what Beauty gains:
> That Men may say, when we the Front-box grace,
> Behold the first in Virtue, as in Face!
> Oh! if to dance all Night, and dress all Day,
> Charm'd the Small-pox, or chas'd old Age away;
> Who would not scorn what Huswife's Cares produce,
> Or who would learn one earthly Thing of Use? . . .
> But since, alas! frail Beauty must decay,
> Curl'd or uncurl'd, since Locks will turn to grey,
> Since painted, or not painted, all shall fade,
> And she who scorns a Man, must die a Maid;
> What then remains, but well our Pow'r to use,
> And keep good Humour still whate'er we lose? . . .

> Beauties in vain their pretty Eyes may roll;
> Charms strike the sight, but Merit wins the Soul. (V.15–34)

These lines have sparked nearly all of the controversy over Pope's views of women. On the one hand, Clarissa seems to be talking common sense and pushing for a moral depth to female behavior. Her poetic authority is *authorized* in some ways by the fact that her speech is modeled on Glaucus's speech to Sarpedon in the *Iliad* (from Pope's translation; see Part Two, Chapter 1), in which Glaucus recommends the heroism of eternity over the transience of the moment. For women, according to Clarissa, good sense, good humor, virtue, and merit ought to be the foundation for thought and action, if not for their inherent value, then more practically speaking because "frail beauty" is so short-lived.

But Clarissa counsels resignation, reinforcing a status quo that punishes a woman who scorns a man or rejects a lord — by definition denying her the ability and the right to choose. The poem itself, many critics argue (from John Dennis to Laura Brown), portrays Belinda as a vain, empty, artificial, sensual and sexual object, her beauty dependent on art, her temper dependent on getting her own way. As in *Epistle to a Lady*, Felicity Nussbaum argues in summarizing the critical debate that "women divide themselves into prudes and coquettes; they are inconstant and changeable; they pursue pleasure and power; they worship themselves at the expense of others" (139). The poem draws heavily upon "commonplace assumptions about women which may be derived from the native English tradition" (Nussbaum 138).

How is the poem finally weighted? Toward or against women? Clarissa's speech is received with "no Applause" (V.35). To what exactly were her audience mutely objecting — the attitude, the moral, or even possibly the bleak implications? Nussbaum concludes that neither *The Rape of the Lock* nor *Epistle to a Lady* "is finally misogynist, but each is ambiguous and complex in its use of eighteenth-century conventions and commonplaces about the sex" (140). Another more culturally contextual way of putting it is that *The Rape of the Lock* is ambiguous and complex in its *use* of gender commonplaces precisely because the culture was ambiguous and complex in its *creation* of them, and that the categories of identity and gender were in their own intellectual and social flux.

The cultural documents provided here on the status of men help to clarify as well as complicate interpretations of women in the poem. The men in this poem get little sympathy; if a hero emerges, it's only for a moment. The Baron snipes, in a devastating line, at the snuffling, inarticulate defense of Sir Plume: "It grieves me much (reply'd the Peer again) / Who speaks so well shou'd ever speak in vain" (IV. 131–32). But the Baron/rapist is already contextualized by a sort of impotence: His prayers, as we have seen, are only half-answered: "The rest, the Winds dispers'd in empty Air" (II.46). In the *Epistle to Cobham* — "Of the Knowledge and Characters of Men" — Pope writes: "That each from other differs, first confess; / Next, that he varies from himself no less: . . . / Our depths who fathoms, or our shallows finds, / Quick whirls, and shifting eddies, of our minds?" (II.19–20; 29–30). Although there is no effacing the gender distinctions and discriminations in the early eighteenth century, the boundaries are not *always* as clear as they might sometimes seem.[13]

A number of periodicals and advertisements, for example (see Part Two, Chapter 2), suggest that many people were anxious about the apparently increasing blurriness of gendered sartorial boundaries: Men and women looked much too much alike for a traditionally hierarchical world. Men's coats swirled out from a narrow waist with the luxuriance of a woman's skirt (in fact their coats were *called* skirts) and displayed shapely calves set off by elegantly buckled shoes; men applied patches and whitened their complexions with the same lead-based make-up; they liberally used perfumes and curled their wigs; in manners they imported French sensibilities that corresponded with "feminine" delicacy. Likewise, the women, according to an outraged *Spectator* essay, found that riding habits that rendered some masculine liberation of movement permitted corresponding liberation in manners, habits, and perhaps outlook. The fashions in clothing and mannerisms of both sexes seemed to some to foretell social decline in gendered collapse. The visual representations should emphasize the ambiguity of some of the gender boundaries in the poem. In the end, the poem concludes *outside* the social sphere of men and women and *inside* the lunar sphere marked by "quick poetic eyes" of the Muse-inspired poet — the figure who creates, defines,

---

[13] Christopher Fox, in his important work *Locke and the Scriblerians,* a study of the response of Pope and his literary contemporaries to the philosophical debate over personal identity, writes about the *Epistle to Cobham* that its opening section emphasizes "the transience, fluidity, and inscrutability of the human personality" while the closing section "introduces the ruling passion to argue that beneath these fluctuations there is an observable consistency at the core" (Fox 121). In other words, Fox, too, sees Pope trying to balance competing beliefs, but sees him pushing poetically for resolution rather than sustaining tension.

and blurs those boundaries as the poetic form demands.[14] That this figure is a poetic version of Pope, a man who even in these years of youth and hope was fully aware of his marginal sexual status, situates the poem squarely in its biographical as well as social contexts.

Things and Power

Alongside the social and sexual satires at play and at war in this poem are the political tensions and confusions of the time. The mad astrologer predicts "The Fate of *Louis*, and the Fall of *Rome*" (V.140) — in other words, impending seismic shifts in the political and religious structures of Europe, and so in the financial and spiritual contours of Pope's world. As Hazlitt notes about the poem: "The balance between the concealed irony and the assumed gravity, is as nicely trimmed as the balance of power in Europe. The little is made great, and the great little. You hardly know whether to laugh or to weep" (143). A constant but subtle presence is the larger world of war, conquest, trade, and wealth, implied in each item on Belinda's dressing table, in the rituals of coffee, in the passions of ombre, in the guest appearances of Queen Anne and her merchants and judges refreshing themselves in the social world as the British Empire busily — and in some ways terribly — expands. The poem's balance is delicate and powerful, mirroring greater stakes: What this glittering world was predicated on, its role as both cause and consequence of massive shifts in world economy and power — all embedded within the paradoxical forms of mock-epic and structures of heroic couplet — help further negotiate the tricky Popean voices of celebration and satire.

These tensions of celebration and satire emerge clearly and tightly in the lines on Belinda's dressing table quoted earlier (I.129–38). I focus here on the same passage to underscore the layers of interpretation that the *Rape* offers with a contextual reading. The power of England is implied positively and negatively in "Off'rings" and "Spoil": India and Arabia seem to donate their tribute (and tortoises and elephants their body parts) in honor of Belinda's personal beauty and cultural power. But as Laura Brown argues, in the last line — "Puffs, Powders, Patches, Bibles, Billet-doux" — these items accumulate on a young woman's dressing table, a clutter of fetishized com-

---

[14] The Muse is always a woman; male poets frequently figured themselves as impregnated by the Muse, with the offspring poem struggling to be born of the poet — a long, long tradition of the poet blurring gender boundaries.

modities in a list that despite its "air of indiscriminacy" is "carefully structured in sound and rhythm," in a way that "stands in diametrical opposition to the random relationship of things in the passage. The list does not distinguish 'Bibles' from 'Billet-doux,' a failure that in this poem indicates an implicit moral irresponsibility or disorder operating in contradiction to the poetic order of the line" (10–11). The power of the "Off'rings" is partially upset and partially underscored by their fate on a cluttered dressing table among a heap of trivialities. But the poem also recognizes that the "Off'rings" *are* "Spoil" — by definition, both the "rightful" prizes of conquest and the stolen goods of exploitation. And Pope of course was no stranger to political and economic oppression; the lines in *Windsor-Forest* discussed earlier reveal a vivid, poignant ability to understand the point of view of the blasted pheasant, the violence against other forms of cultural beauty.

The brief walk-on of Queen Anne in Canto III spotlights this intricate intersection of power and triviality, of prosperity and its implicit violence. Pope was not the first to couple tea and queens; Edmund Waller, in "Of Tea Commended by her Majesty" saw in "the best of Queens, and best of Herbs" the sign of England's growing mercantile power and the exhilarating acquaintance with distant cultures. In one of the famous zeugmas of the poem, Pope's Great Anna does "sometimes Counsel take, and sometimes Tea" — signifying both the branching of power and pleasure, and their momentary cultural interdependence. Tea is trivial; tea is ceremony; tea is health and prosperity; the Queen takes her tea from cup and country, simultaneously exercising the active as well as passive properties of the verb "to take" — which does she aggressively take, and which passively receive? Tea as "Spoil" is both taken (from elsewhere) and received by Britain. And some of the cultural ambivalence toward a female monarch may turn on "sometimes": sometimes this queen takes advice — but perhaps sometimes she doesn't.

The game of ombre in Canto III becomes an extended metaphor for the larger political implications and allusions of the poem:

> The *Club*'s black Tyrant first her Victim dy'd,
> Spite of his haughty Mien, and barb'rous Pride:
> What boots the Regal Circle on his Head,
> His Giant Limbs in State unwieldy spread?
> That long behind he trails his pompous Robe,
> And of all Monarchs only grasps the Globe? (III.69–74)

The club is a "black Tyrant," but he's also a victim, and *almost* seen from within, like the pheasant in *Windsor-Forest*. His power seems secure, his majesty intact; yet there's a rape here as well in the giant limbs unwieldy spread; his grasp of the world is short-lived in the hands of these English players. This scene both precedes and provokes the rape of the lock itself. The poem will not allow us to assign stable national or cultural identities to the characters; the luckless, lockless Belinda, who has been figured as the object and end of English trade, is here identified with the "black Tyrant" first as victor, then — as the Baron's Amazon moves in — as victim. England too is both victor and victim in this global game. And we should not forget that *all* the players here are disenfranchised Catholics. Thus a number of symbolic rapes are enacted in this poem.

The world in which *The Rape of the Lock* is culturally produced and which it poetically reproduces is a world of frightening, exhilarating change, of possibilities for personal and national improvement, for personal and national corruption. In spite of the advertisement for the Earl of Castlemaine's new globe (see Part Two, pp. 433–34), the "English Globe" was *not* a "fix'd and immoveable one." "*Restore the Lock!*" cries Belinda, and "all around / *Restore the Lock!* the vaulted Roofs rebound" (V.103–104). Restore what was stolen; put things back the way they were. But, of course, the lock is lost; it disappears into the heavens, marked by the Muse's eye and the poet's art, observed and tracked and enfamed — but not restored. The literary and cultural contexts of this world show its inhabitants watching the world change, some cheering the Baron, some demanding restitution, but no one quite knowing where it's all going to go.

Chronology of
Pope's Life and Times

1678

The Popish Plot, an alleged plan to murder Charles II (1630–1685) and re-establish Roman Catholicism in England, stirs a wave of anti-papism that results in the hanging of five Catholic lords and the passage of the Papists' Disabling Act.

John Dryden (1631–1700), *Macflecknoe.* John Bunyan (1628–1688), *Pilgrim's Progress.*

1679–81

The Exclusion Crisis unfolds; Whigs attempt to exclude the Catholic James II (1633–1701) from succession.

1681

Dryden, *Absalom and Achitophel,* a poem about the Exclusion Crisis.

1685

February: Charles II dies; James II ascends the throne.

June: James Scott, duke of Monmouth (the Absalom of Dryden's poem), illegitimate son of Charles II, stages a rebellion against James II. He is defeated and beheaded.

1688

May 21: Alexander Pope is born in London, son of a Catholic linen draper.

The Glorious Revolution forces James II to flee to France and brings William of Orange (1650–1702) to England.

1689

William III and Mary II (daughter of James II) (1662–1694) ascend the throne; the Oath of Allegiance is put into effect, requiring everyone to swear loyalty to the Church of England and conform to its basic practices. Many Catholics and Dissenters refused.

1690

The institution of penal laws legitimizes the persecution of Catholics, which continues until 1698.

John Locke (1632–1704), *An Essay Concerning Human Understanding*.

1694

December 28: Mary II dies.

The Bank of England is established.

1695

The Licensing Act expires and censorship eases.

1698

Jeremy Collier (1650–1726), *A Short View of the Immorality of the English Stage*.

1700

Pope's family moves to Windsor Forest, outside London, probably to comply with anti-Catholic Ten Mile Law that prohibited Catholics from owning property within ten miles of London. Martha Blount (1690–1763) and her sister Teresa, Pope's close friends, live ten miles away at Mapledurham.

May: John Dryden dies.

William Congreve (1670–1729), *The Way of the World*.

1701

June: The Act of Settlement provides for Protestant succession; Louis XIV of France recognizes "the [Old] Pretender" (James's son) as king of Great Britain and Ireland; England is at war with France.

1702

March: William III dies; Anne (sister of Mary II) (1665–1714) ascends the throne.

England enters the War of the Spanish Succession.

1704

John Churchill, Duke of Marlborough (1650–1722), defeats the French at Battle of Blenheim.

1705

Pope begins to enter literary circles of William Wycherley (1641–1715), Joseph Addison (1672–1719), and other London coffee-house wits.

1707

May: The Act of Union joins Scotland and England under the name Great Britain.

1708

October: Marlborough and Sidney Godolphin (1645–1712) are in power; Tory leader, Robert Harley, Earl of Oxford (1661–1724), is dismissed as prime minister.

1709

May: Pope's first published works, including his *Pastorals*, appear in Tonson's *Miscellanies;* begins a friendship with Catholic John Caryll (1625–1711).

The Copyright Act; Richard Steele (1672–1729) starts *The Tatler*.

1710

Jonathan Swift (1667–1745) publishes *The Examiner*.

1711

May: Pope's *An Essay on Criticism* is praised by Addison in *The Spectator* and criticized by John Dennis (1657–1734).

Addison and Steele create *The Spectator*.

1712

May: Pope's *Messiah* appears in *The Spectator;* the first version of the *Rape* included in Lintot's *Miscellany;* Pope begins his acquaintances with Swift, John Gay (1685–1732), Thomas Parnell (1679–1718), John Arbuthnot (1667–1735); together they form the Scriblerus Club.

1713

March: Pope writes a prologue for Addison's *Cato*, publishes *Windsor-Forest*, contributes to Steele's *Guardian*; submits proposals for translations of the *Iliad*; takes lessons in painting from Charles Jervas (1675?–1739).

England and France negotiate peace and ratify the Treaty of Utrecht.

1714

March: Pope expands the *Rape,* adding three more cantos.

August: Anne dies; George I (1660–1727) ascends the throne.

Sir Robert Walpole (1676–1745) replaces Harley as prime minister.

Henry St. John, Viscount Bolingbroke (1678–1751) flees to the Pretender's Court in France.

1715

February: Pope publishes *The Temple of Fame.*

June: Pope publishes the *Iliad,* Volume I; soon followed by attacks.

Pope begins friendship with Lady Mary Wortley Montagu (1689–1762).

1716

March: Volume II of the *Iliad* is published; bookseller Edmund Curll publishes unauthorized *Court Poems;* Pope administers emetic to Curll.

April: Pope's house at Binfield in Windsor Forest is sold. Pope moves to Chiswick near Lord Burlington.

July: Lady Mary travels to Turkey. Pope begins correspondence of "epistolary gallantry" with her.

1717

January: Pope adds Clarissa's speech to the *Rape;* publishes *Three Hours after Marriage* (with Gay and Arbuthnot).

June: Volume III of the *Iliad,* collected *Works* with *Eloisa to Abelard* and *Verses to the Memory of an Unfortunate Lady* are published.

October: Pope's father dies.

1718

June: Volume IV of the *Iliad* published.

Pope and his mother move to Twickenham, where Pope builds his villa, grotto, and gardens.

1719

Addison dies.

Daniel Defoe (1660–1731) publishes *Robinson Crusoe.*

Eliza Haywood (1693?–1756) publishes *Love in Excess.*

1720

May: Volumes V and VI of the *Iliad* are published.

September: The South Sea Bubble bursts (a rush of speculative investing in the South Sea Company); many people, including Pope, lose money, banks collapse.

1721

Walpole becomes Lord Treasurer.

1722

Defoe, *Journal of a Plague Year, Moll Flanders.*

1723

Pope serves as a witness at Francis Atterbury's (1662–1732) trial for his part in the alleged Jacobite plot; Atterbury is banished to France.

Bernard Mandeville (1670–1733), *Fable of the Bees* (revised).

1724

March: Pope publishes a six-volume edition of Shakespeare.

April: Volumes I–III of the *Odyssey* appear; "Grub Street" attacks Pope.

Bolingbroke returns from exile in France.

1726

March: Lewis Theobald's (1688–1734) *Shakespeare Restored* appears as a corrective to Pope's edition.

June: Pope publishes Volumes IV and V of the *Odyssey.*

Swift visits Pope; Pope begins friendship with Joseph Spence (1699–1768).

1727

June: Volumes I and II of Pope's and Swift's *Miscellanies* appear; Swift visits Pope again.

George I dies; George II (1683–1760) ascends the throne.

1728

May: Pope publishes the *Dunciad* with Theobald as "hero"; receives more angry attacks from Grub Street.

Gay, *Beggar's Opera.*

1729

April: Pope publishes *The Dunciad Variorum,* incorporating most of the Grub Street attacks verbatim.

Swift, *A Modest Proposal.*

1730

James Thomson (1700–1748), *The Seasons.*

1731

December: Pope publishes *Epistle to Burlington* (Moral Essay IV).

1732

October: *Miscellanies* Volume III is published.

December: Gay dies.

1733

January: Pope publishes *Epistle to Bathurst* (Moral Essay III).

February: The first *Imitation of Horace* appears.

February–May: Pope publishes *An Essay on Man,* Epistles I–III.

June: Pope's mother dies.

The Excise Crisis causes London to explode in anti-tax riots and nearly topples Walpole.

Swift, *On Poetry.*

1734

January: Pope publishes *Epistle to Cobham* (Moral Essay I), *An Essay on Man,* Epistle IV.

July: Pope publishes *Imitation of Horace.*

December: Pope publishes *Sober Advice from Horace.*

1735

January: *Epistle to Arbuthnot* is published.

February: *Of the Characters of Women* (Moral Essay II) is published.

April: Volume II of *Works* is published.

May: Curll's (unauthorized) edition of Pope's letters appears.

Bolingbroke returns to France.

Thomson, *Liberty.*

1737

April: Pope publishes more *Imitations of Horace.*

May: Pope's "authorized" edition of his letters is published.

French philosopher J. P. de Crousaz (1663–1748) attacks *An Essay on Man.*

Theatrical Licensing Act censors new plays.

Henry Fielding (1707–1754), *Historical Register.*

1738

January to March: Pope produces more *Imitations of Horace.*

May–July: Pope publishes *Epilogue to the Satires.*

November: Crousaz's attack translated into English.

William Warburton (1698–1779) begins response to Crousaz's attack on the *Essay on Man,* defending Pope's philosophy in six monthly published letters.

Bolingbroke visits Pope.

1739

England is at war with Spain.

1740

April: Pope meets Warburton.

Samuel Richardson (1689–1761), *Pamela.*

1742

March: Pope's *The New Dunciad* (i.e., Book IV) is published.

After mismanaging the war with Spain and losing the confidence of the Commons, Walpole falls from political favor.

1743

October: *The Dunciad,* in four books, is published; Colley Cibber (1671–1757) replaces Theobald on the throne because of his appointments as Poet Laureate in 1730, despite lack of poetic talent, and his self-aggrandizing autobiography *Apology* (1740).

1744

May 30: Pope dies.

Britain enters the War of the Austrian Succession (1740–48).

1745

Jacobite Rebellion attempts to restore the Stuarts ("Bonnie Prince Charlie") to the throne; routed April 1746.

October: Swift dies.

Notes on the Text
and Engravings

THE TEXT

The Rape of the Lock has been reprinted (with gratitude) from the Twickenham Edition of *The Poems of Alexander Pope*, published by Methuen and Yale University Press. The text comes from the third edition of Volume II (1962), a revision of the editions of 1940 and 1954, edited by Geoffrey Tillotson. Tillotson incorporates all of Pope's 1715, 1717, and 1736 revisions of the poem, including the addition of Clarissa's speech in 1717. Students should see the Twickenham Edition for a thorough textual history as well as comprehensive annotations of the poem. I have added notes to the text to explain references to events, objects, people, places, and language that might be unfamiliar to modern readers. On occasion I have reprinted some of Tillotson's annotations, courtesy of Yale University Press; those notes are credited [T]. Other abbreviations include [OED] (Oxford English Dictionary) and [Johnson] (Samuel Johnson's *Dictionary of the English Language*, 1755). Pope added his own notes in 1736 and 1751; all of those reproduced here are in quotation marks, followed by [P].

Wherever possible, the documents in Part Two are from the original or early editions or the most authoritative scholarly editions. Original spelling, punctuation, and emphasis — often very different from what modern readers expect — have been retained, although the long *s* has been modernized where it appears.

Many thanks to Oxford University Press and Routledge for their kind permission to reproduce so many of the important documents in Part Two.

THE ENGRAVINGS

As Robert Halsband argues in his wonderful study of the history of the illustrations of *The Rape of the Lock:* "Illustrations that appear with a literary work on its first publication are particularly significant, for they elucidate, modify, and supplement the meaning of the verbal text, particularly if the illustrations were drawn to the author's specifications or were subject to his approval" (vi). Halsband persuasively argues that Pope probably did consult with the engraver over the illustrations. It was rare for separately printed poems to be illustrated at all; David Foxon counts only six poems illustrated out of eleven hundred printed between 1704 and 1713 (Halsband 4; citing Foxon, *English Verse 1701–1750,* II). In any case, the bookseller Bernard Lintot thought highly enough of Pope's poem to spend the extra money. And the success of the poem justified Lintot's expenditure: three thousand copies sold in the first four days; second and third editions were printed in the same year, with a fourth edition in 1715, a fifth in 1718, and a sixth in 1723. By the fifth edition the copperplate engravings needed retouching (Halsband 3).

The artist, Louis Du Guernier (1687–1716), was born in Paris and emigrated to England in 1708. His early biographer thought little of his abilities, classifying him as a hack: "His labours were chiefly confined to the booksellers; and it is possible they might procure him much more profit, than credit" (Strutt 1:357). Perhaps confirming Strutt's sneer that "he never acquired any tolerable mastery of the point or the graver," he only designed the illustrations for the *Rape;* Claude Du Bosc (fl. 1714) actually executed the copperplate engravings (see the reference to "Du Bosse" in the advertisement in the *Daily Courant,* p. 178).

The Latin motto on the title page is from Ovid's *Metamorphoses,* Book VIII, about Scylla, daughter of King Nisus, who for love of Minos plucked out a purple hair from her father's head (on which the safety of Nisus and his kingdom depended). Minos was disgusted and after his victory sailed away; Scylla was turned into a bird. The last line translates: "[she] takes this name from the shorn lock of hair" (Loeb Classical Library ed., Ovid, *Metamorphoses,* vol. 1, p. 417).

Frontispiece (above) and title page (right) for the first printing of the five-canto version of *The Rape of the Lock* (1714). The engraving's backdrop features the East Front of the Christopher Wren royal palace at Hampton Court (see Part Two, Chapter 2, p. 382). In the foreground, sturdy sylphs cavort with cards, point toward the rising lock, and assist the cosmetic preparations of a barelegged Belinda.

THE

RAPE of the *LOCK*.

AN

HEROI-COMICAL

POEM.

In FIVE CANTO'S.

Written by Mr. *POPE*.

——*A tonſo eſt hoc nomen adepta capillo.*
OVID.

LONDON:

Printed for BERNARD LINTOTT, at the
Croſs-Keys in *Fleetſtreet.* 1714.

The Rape of the Lock:

An Heroi-Comical Poem
in Five Cantos

TO
Mrs. *ARABELLA FERMOR.*

MADAM,

It will be in vain to deny that I have some Regard for this Piece, since I Dedicate it to You. Yet You may bear me Witness, it was intended only to divert a few young Ladies, who have good Sense and good Humour enough, to laugh not only at their Sex's little unguarded Follies, but at their own. But as it was communicated with the Air of a Secret, it soon found its Way into the World. An imperfect Copy having been offer'd to a Bookseller, You had the Good-Nature for my Sake to consent to the Publication of one more correct: This I was forc'd to before I had executed half my Design, for the *Machinery* was entirely wanting to compleat it.

The *Machinery*, Madam, is a Term invented by the Criticks, to signify that Part which the Deities, Angels, or Dæmons, are made to act in a Poem: For the ancient Poets are in one respect like many modern Ladies; Let an Action be never so trivial in it self, they always make it appear of the utmost Importance. These Machines I determin'd to raise on a very new and odd Foundation, the *Rosicrucian* Doctrine of Spirits.

I know how disagreeable it is to make use of hard Words before a Lady; but 'tis so much the Concern of a Poet to have his Works understood, and particularly by your Sex, that You must give me leave to explain two or three difficult Terms.

The *Rosicrucians*[1] are a People I must bring You acquainted with. The best Account I know of them is in a French Book call'd *Le Comte de Gabalis,* which both in its Title and Size is so like a *Novel,* that many of the Fair Sex have read it for one by Mistake. According to these Gentlemen, the four Elements are inhabited by Spirits, which they call *Sylphs, Gnomes, Nymphs,* and *Salamanders.* The *Gnomes,* or *Dæmons* of Earth, delight in Mischief; but the *Sylphs,* whose Habitation is in the Air, are the best-condition'd Creatures imaginable. For they say, any Mortals may enjoy the most intimate Familiarities with these gentle Spirits, upon a Condition very easie to all true *Adepts,* an inviolate Preservation of Chastity.

As to the following Canto's, all the Passages of them are as Fabulous,[2] as the Vision at the Beginning, or the Transformation at the End; (except the Loss of your Hair, which I always mention with Reverence.) The Human Persons are as Fictitious as the Airy ones; and the Character of *Belinda,* as it is now manag'd, resembles You in nothing but in Beauty.

If this Poem had as many Graces as there are in Your Person, or in Your Mind, yet I could never hope it should pass thro' the World half so Uncensured as You have done. But let its Fortune be what it will, mine is happy enough, to have given me this Occasion of assuring You that I am, with the truest Esteem,

Madam,
Your Most Obedient
Humble Servant.
A. POPE.

---

[1] *Rosicrucians:* A religious sect first appearing in Germany in the early seventeenth century.

[2] *Fabulous:* Celebrated in fable; unhistorical, legendary, incredible, absurd, exaggerated [OED].

Canto 1.

Lud.Du Guernier inv.   C.Du Bose sculp.

Plate for Canto I, illustrating the sleeping Belinda, Ariel at her ear and Shock at her side.

Canto I

What dire Offence from am'rous Causes springs,
What mighty Contests rise from trivial Things,
I sing — This Verse to *Caryll*, Muse! is due;°
This, ev'n *Belinda* may vouchsafe to view:
Slight is the Subject, but not so the Praise,   5
If She inspire, and He approve my Lays.°
   Say what strange Motive, Goddess! cou'd compel
A well-bred *Lord* t'assault a gentle *Belle*?°
Oh say what stranger Cause, yet unexplor'd,
Cou'd make a gentle *Belle* reject a *Lord*?   10
In Tasks so bold, can Little Men engage,
And in soft Bosoms dwells such mighty Rage?
   Sol° thro' white Curtains shot a tim'rous Ray,
And op'd those Eyes that must eclipse the Day;
Now Lapdogs° give themselves the rowzing Shake,   15
And sleepless Lovers, just at Twelve, awake:
Thrice rung the Bell the Slipper knock'd the Ground,
And the press'd Watch return'd a silver Sound.°
Belinda still her downy Pillow prest,
Her Guardian *Sylph* prolong'd the balmy Rest.   20
'Twas he had summon'd to her silent Bed
The Morning-Dream that hover'd o'er her Head.
A Youth more glitt'ring than a *Birth-night Beau*,°
(That ev'n in Slumber caus'd her Cheek to glow)

---

3. *I sing:* In epic poetry, the poet traditionally invokes the muse ("poet's inspiring goddess, poet's genius" [OED]) or some other supernatural assistant. In this case, the muse that "inspired" Pope was his friend John Caryll (see Part Two, Chapter 1).

6. *Lays:* Short lyric or narrative poem, usually — though obviously not in this case — meant to be sung.

8. *Belle:* The reigning beauty; a fair lady.

13. *Sol:* The sun personified.

15. *Lapdogs:* Small dogs were fashionable pets; Belinda's is named Shock (I.115), derived from *shough,* "a kind of lap-dog thought to have been brought to England from Iceland" [T].

18. *Thrice rung the Bell, the Slipper knock'd the Ground:* The order of events here has been debated, but it seems that, after the sun peeps into her window, Belinda rings a handbell for her maid, and then knocks her slipper against the floor, and then checks her watch, which when pressed would chime to the nearest hour and quarter-hour. She appears to sink back into sleep — or at least a dozing daydream — in the next line.

23. *Birth-night Beau:* A "beau" is the matching male term for "belle"; the birthdays (birth-nights) of royalty would be celebrated lavishly at Court.

Seem'd to her Ear his winning Lips to lay,   25
And thus in Whispers said, or seem'd to say.°
   Fairest of Mortals, thou distinguish'd Care
Of thousand bright Inhabitants of Air!
If e'er one Vision touch'd thy infant Thought,
Of all the Nurse and all the Priest have taught,°   30
Of airy Elves by Moonlight Shadows seen,
The silver Token, and the circled Green,°
Or Virgins visited by Angel-Pow'rs,
With Golden Crowns and Wreaths of heav'nly Flow'rs,
Hear and believe! thy own Importance know,   35
Nor bound thy narrow Views to Things below.
Some secret Truths from Learned Pride conceal'd,
To Maids alone and Children are reveal'd:
What tho' no Credit doubting Wits may give?
The Fair and Innocent shall still believe.   40
Know then, unnumber'd Spirits round thee fly,
The light *Militia* of the lower Sky;
These, tho' unseen, are ever on the Wing,
Hang o'er the *Box*, and hover round the *Ring*.°
Think what an Equipage° thou hast in Air,   45
And view with scorn *Two Pages* and a *Chair*.°
As now your own, our Beings were of old,
And once inclos'd in Woman's beauteous Mold;
Thence, by a soft Transition, we repair
From earthly Vehicles to these of Air.   50
Think not, when Woman's transient Breath is fled,
That all her Vanities at once are dead:
Succeeding Vanities she still regards,
And tho' she plays no more, o'erlooks the Cards.
Her Joy in gilded Chariots, when alive,   55

   23–26. *A Youth . . . in Whispers said, or seem'd to say:* In epic poetry, the gods occasionally appear to the hero in dreams.

   30. *Of all the Nurse and all the Priest have taught:* The fairy tales told in the nursery and the religious imagery and beliefs of Catholic priests seemed very dangerous for children to seventeenth- and eighteenth-century English philosophers and moralists.

   32. *The silver Token, and the circled Green:* Fairies were believed to dance circles in the grass and leave money behind.

   44. *Hang o'er the Box, and hover round the Ring:* The fashionable elite sat in the boxes at the theatre and paraded in their coaches around the Ring at Hyde Park.

   45. *Equipage:* A retinue; a private coach along with its horses, coachmen, footmen, and accessories.

   46. *Two Pages and a Chair:* A sedan chair was carried by two servants.

And Love of *Ombre*,° after Death survive.
For when the Fair in all their Pride expire,
To their first Elements° their Souls retire:
The Sprights of fiery Termagants in Flame
Mount up, and take a *Salamander*'s Name.   60
Soft yielding Minds to Water glide away,
And sip with *Nymphs,* their Elemental Tea.
The graver Prude sinks downward to a *Gnome,*
In search of Mischief still on Earth to roam.
The light Coquettes in *Sylphs* aloft repair,   65
And sport and flutter in the Fields of Air.
    Know farther yet; Whoever fair and chaste
Rejects Mankind, is by some *Sylph* embrac'd:
For Spirits, freed from mortal Laws, with ease
Assume what Sexes and what Shapes they please.   70
What guards the Purity of melting Maids,
In Courtly Balls, and Midnight Masquerades,°
Safe from the treach'rous Friend, the daring Spark,°
The Glance by Day, the Whisper in the Dark;
When kind Occasion prompts their warm Desires,   75
When Musick softens, and when Dancing fires?
'Tis but their *Sylph,* the wise Celestials know,
Tho' *Honour* is the Word with Men below.
    Some Nymphs there are, too conscious of their Face,
For Life predestin'd to the *Gnomes'* Embrace.   80
These swell their Prospects and exalt their Pride,
When Offers are disdain'd, and Love deny'd.
Then gay Ideas crowd the vacant Brain,
While Peers and Dukes, and all their sweeping Train,
And Garters, Stars, and Coronets appear,°   85
And in soft Sounds, *Your Grace* salutes their Ear.

---

    56. *Love of Ombre:* Ombre was a popular card game (see Part Two, Chapter 2).
    58. *To their first Elements:* Early psychology believed that human characters were
variously compounded of four basic elements: earth, air, fire, and water. Ariel is a
spirit (or spright) of air (a sylph), and Umbriel, in Canto IV, is a spirit of earth (a
gnome). Salamanders inhabited fire, and nymphs water.
    72. *Midnight Masquerades:* Masquerades were very popular in the early eighteenth
century; they allowed a degree of social freedom to women and offered a place to "try
on" different identities with different masks. (See Terry Castle, *Masquerade and Civi-
lization.*)
    73. *Spark:* A fashionable, lively young man; "contemptuous usage" [Johnson].
    85. *And Garters, Stars, and Coronets appear:* A garter signified the highest order
of English knighthood; stars were military decorations or part of the insignia of knight-
hood; coronets were small crowns worn by nobility.

'Tis these that early taint the Female Soul,
Instruct the Eyes of young *Coquettes* to roll,
Teach Infant-Cheeks a bidden Blush to know,
And little Hearts to flutter at a *Beau*.   90
      Oft when the World imagine Women stray,
The *Sylphs* thro' mystick Mazes guide their Way,
Thro' all the giddy Circle they pursue,
And old Impertinence° expel by new.
What tender Maid but must a Victim fall   95
To one Man's Treat, but for another's Ball?
When *Florio* speaks, what Virgin could withstand,
If gentle *Damon* did not squeeze her Hand?
With varying Vanities, from ev'ry Part,
They shift the moving Toyshop of their Heart;°   100
Where Wigs with Wigs, with Sword-knots Sword-
      knots strive,°
Beaus banish Beaus, and Coaches Coaches drive.
This erring Mortals Levity may call,
Oh blind to Truth! the *Sylphs* contrive it all.
      Of these am I, who thy Protection claim,   105
A watchful Sprite, and *Ariel* is my Name.
Late, as I rang'd the Crystal Wilds of Air,
In the clear Mirror° of thy ruling *Star*
I saw, alas! some dread Event impend,
Ere to the Main this Morning Sun descend.   110
But Heav'n reveals not what, or how, or where:
Warn'd by thy *Sylph*, oh Pious Maid beware!
This to disclose is all thy Guardian can.
Beware of all, but most beware of Man!
      He said; when *Shock*, who thought she slept too long,   115
Leapt up, and wak'd his Mistress with his Tongue.
'Twas then *Belinda*! if Report say true,

----

94. *Impertinence:* "Trifle: thing of no value" [Johnson].

100. *They shift the moving Toyshop of their Heart:* Toyshops sold trinkets, ornaments, fans, silks, purses, accessories, as well as toys; the common vanities of the social whirl, the poem claims, made women's hearts "unfix'd," daring after trifles.

101. *Where Wigs with Wigs, with Sword-knots Sword-knots strive:* This line echoes Pope's translation of the *Iliad:* "Now Shield with Shield, with Helmet Helmet clos'd,/To Armour Armour, Lance to Lance oppos'd" (IV.508ff); but here the weapons change from armor to ornament — fashionable men wore curled wigs and tied ribbons around their swords.

108. *In the clear Mirror:* "The Language of the Platonists, the writers of the intelligible world of Spirits, etc." [P].

Thy Eyes first open'd on a *Billet-doux;*°
Wounds, Charms, and *Ardors,* were no sooner read,
But all the Vision vanish'd from thy Head.   120
    And now, unveil'd, the *Toilet* stands display'd,°
Each Silver Vase in mystic Order laid.
First, rob'd in White, the Nymph intent adores
With Head uncover'd, the *Cosmetic* Pow'rs.
A heav'nly Image in the Glass appears,   125
To that she bends, to that her Eyes she rears;
Th'inferior Priestess,° at her Altar's side,
Trembling, begins the sacred Rites of Pride.
Unnumber'd Treasures ope at once, and here
The various Off'rings of the World appear;   130
From each she nicely culls with curious Toil,
And decks the Goddess with the glitt'ring Spoil.°
This Casket *India*'s glowing Gems unlocks,
And all *Arabia* breathes from yonder Box.
The Tortoise here and Elephant unite,   135
Transform'd to *Combs,* the speckled and the white.
Here Files of Pins extend their shining Rows,
Puffs, Powders, Patches,° Bibles, Billet-doux.
Now awful Beauty puts on all its Arms;°
The Fair each moment rises in her Charms,   140
Repairs her Smiles, awakens ev'ry Grace,
And calls forth all the Wonders of her Face;
Sees by Degrees a purer Blush arise,
And keener Lightnings quicken in her Eyes.
The busy *Sylphs* surround their darling Care;   145
These set the Head, and those divide the Hair,
Some fold the Sleeve, whilst others plait the Gown;
And *Betty's* prais'd for Labours not her own.°

---

118. *Billet-doux:* Love letters.
121. *Toilet:* Dressing table with mirror; the "altar" for the rites of beauty.
127. *Th'inferior Priestess:* Belinda's maid.
131. *Spoil:* Plunder taken from an enemy in war. Belinda's "spoil" includes jewels from India, or the "orient," perfume from the Middle East, and tortoiseshell and ivory combs.
138. *Patches:* Artificial beauty marks or moles.
139. *awful Beauty puts on all its Arms:* Belinda's beauty, enhanced by the full arsenal of cosmetic art, becomes awe-inspiring in its power.
147-48. *Some fold the Sleeve . . . And Betty's prais'd for Labours not her own:* The sylphs attend to the folds of Belinda's sleeves and skirts, while her maid, traditionally called "Betty," *seems* to be doing the work.

Canto 2.

Lud. Du Guernier inv.   c. Du Bosc sculp.

Plate for Canto II, showing the "painted Vessel" gliding up the Thames toward the East Front of Hampton Court; above the sails, the sylphs dissolve in air.

Canto II

Not with more Glories, in th' Etherial Plain,°
The Sun first rises o'er the purpled Main,°
Than issuing forth, the Rival of his Beams
Lanch'd on the Bosom of the Silver *Thames*.°
Fair Nymphs, and well-drest Youths around her shone,   5
But ev'ry Eye was fix'd on her alone.
On her white Breast a sparkling *Cross* she wore,
Which *Jews* might kiss, and Infidels adore.
Her lively Looks a sprightly Mind disclose,
Quick as her Eyes, and as unfix'd as those: 10
Favours to none, to all she Smiles extends,
Oft she rejects, but never once offends.
Bright as the Sun, her Eyes the Gazers strike,
And, like the Sun, they shine on all alike.
Yet graceful Ease, and Sweetness void of Pride,   15
Might hide her Faults, if *Belles* had Faults to hide:
If to her share some Female Errors fall,
Look on her Face, and you'll forget 'em all.
  This Nymph, to the Destruction of Mankind,
Nourish'd two Locks, which graceful hung behind   20
In equal Curls, and well conspir'd to deck
With shining Ringlets the smooth Iv'ry Neck.
Love in these Labyrinths his Slaves detains,
And mighty Hearts are held in slender Chains.
With hairy Sprindges° we the Birds betray,   25
Slight Lines of Hair surprize the Finny Prey,°
Fair Tresses Man's Imperial Race insnare,
And Beauty draws us with a single Hair.

---

1. *Etherial Plain:* The sky.
2. *the purpled Main:* The sea.
3–4. *Than issuing forth, . . . the Silver Thames:* After donning the armor of her beauty, Belinda resembles the epic hero equipped for battle; in her loveliness, Belinda is the rival of the sun as she steps into a pleasure boat on the river Thames, to sail upstream, presumably from Westminster (then a separate city from the more commercial London), to Hampton Court for the day. See the map of London in Part Two, Chapter 2 (pp. 392–93).
25. *Sprindges:* Traps.
26. *Finny Prey:* A deliberately exaggerated way of describing fish.

Th' Adventrous *Baron* the bright Locks admir'd,
He saw, he wish'd, and to the Prize aspir'd: 30
Resolv'd to win, he meditates the way,
By Force to ravish, or by Fraud betray;
For when Success a Lover's Toil attends,
Few ask, if Fraud or Force attain'd his Ends.
      For this, ere *Phœbus*° rose, he had implor'd   35
Propitious Heav'n, and ev'ry Pow'r ador'd,
But chiefly *Love* — to *Love* an Altar built,
Of twelve vast *French* Romances, neatly gilt.
There lay three Garters,° half a Pair of Gloves;
And all the Trophies of his former Loves.   40
With tender *Billet-doux* he lights the Pyre,
And breathes three am'rous Sighs to raise the Fire.
Then prostrate falls, and begs with ardent Eyes
Soon to obtain, and long possess the Prize:
The Pow'rs gave Ear, and granted half his Pray'r,   45
The rest, the Winds dispers'd in empty Air.
      But now secure the painted Vessel glides,
The Sun-beams trembling on the floating Tydes,
While melting Musick steals upon the Sky,
And soften'd Sounds along the Waters die.   50
Smooth flow the Waves, the Zephyrs° gently play,
Belinda smil'd, and all the World was gay.
All but the *Sylph* — With careful Thoughts opprest,
Th'impending Woe sate heavy on his Breast.
He summons strait his Denizens of Air;   55
The lucid Squadrons round the Sails repair:
Soft o'er the Shrouds° Aerial Whispers breathe,
That seem'd but *Zephyrs* to the Train beneath.
Some to the Sun their Insect-Wings unfold,
Waft on the Breeze, or sink in Clouds of Gold.   60
Transparent Forms, too fine for mortal Sight,
Their fluid Bodies half dissolv'd in Light.
Loose to the Wind their airy Garments flew,
Thin glitt'ring Textures of the filmy Dew;

35. *Phœbus:* Phoebus Apollo, god of the sun in Greek and Roman mythology.
39. *Garters:* In this case, the garters are not the badges of knighthood, as earlier, but ribbons to hold up stockings; the Baron has an impressive collection of such "Trophies" of women's clothing.
51. *Zephyrs:* Winds personified; the Zephyr was the warm wind from the west.
57. *Shrouds:* The ropes that support a ship's masts.

Dipt in the richest Tincture of the Skies,   65
Where Light disports in ever-mingling Dies,
While ev'ry Beam new transient Colours flings,
Colours that change whene'er they wave their Wings.
Amid the Circle, on the gilded Mast,
Superior by the Head, was *Ariel* plac'd;   70
His Purple Pinions° opening to the Sun,
He rais'd his Azure Wand, and thus begun.
    Ye *Sylphs* and *Sylphids,* to your Chief give Ear,
Fays, Fairies, Genii, Elves, and *Dæmons* hear!
Ye know the Spheres and various Tasks assign'd,   75
By Laws Eternal, to th' Aerial Kind.
Some in the Fields of purest *Æther*° play,
And bask and whiten in the Blaze of Day.
Some guide the Course of wandring Orbs on high,
Or roll the Planets thro' the boundless Sky.   80
Some less refin'd, beneath the Moon's pale Light
Pursue the Stars that shoot athwart the Night,
Or suck the Mists in grosser Air below,
Or dip their Pinions in the painted Bow,
Or brew fierce Tempests on the wintry Main,   85
Or o'er the Glebe° distill the kindly Rain.
Others on Earth o'er human Race preside,
Watch all their Ways, and all their Actions guide:
Of these the Chief the Care of Nations own,
And guard with Arms Divine the *British Throne.*   90
    Our humbler Province is to tend the Fair,
Not a less pleasing, tho' less glorious Care.
To save the Powder from too rude a Gale,
Nor let th' imprison'd Essences exhale,
To draw fresh Colours from the vernal Flow'rs,   95
To steal from Rainbows ere they drop in Show'rs
A brighter Wash; to curl their waving Hairs,
Assist their Blushes, and inspire their Airs;
Nay oft, in Dreams, Invention we bestow,
To change a *Flounce,* or add a *Furbelo.*°   100

71. *Pinions:* Wings.
77. *Æther:* The clear sky above the clouds.
86. *the Glebe:* The earth.
    100. *Furbelo:* "A piece of stuff plaited and puckered together, either below or above, on the petticoats or gowns of women" [Johnson].

This Day, black Omens threat the brightest Fair
That e'er deserv'd a watchful Spirit's Care;
Some dire Disaster, or by Force, or Slight,
But what, or where, the Fates have wrapt in Night.
Whether the Nymph shall break *Diana*'s Law,°   105
Or some frail *China* Jar receive a Flaw,
Or stain her Honour, or her new Brocade,
Forget her Pray'rs, or miss a Masquerade,
Or lose her Heart, or Necklace, at a Ball;
Or whether Heav'n has doom'd that *Shock* must fall.   110
Haste then ye Spirits! to your Charge repair;
The flutt'ring Fan be *Zephyretta's* Care;
The Drops° to thee, *Brillante,* we consign;
And, *Momentilla,* let the Watch be thine;
Do thou, *Crispissa,* tend her fav'rite Lock;   115
Ariel himself shall be the Guard of *Shock.*
    To Fifty chosen *Sylphs,* of special Note,
We trust th'important Charge, the *Petticoat:*
Oft have we known that sev'nfold Fence to fail,
Tho' stiff with Hoops, and arm'd with Ribs of Whale.   120
Form a strong Line about the Silver Bound,
And guard the wide Circumference around.°
    Whatever Spirit, careless of his Charge,
His Post neglects, or leaves the Fair at large,
Shall feel sharp Vengeance soon o'ertake his Sins,   125
Be stopt in *Vials,* or transfixt with *Pins;*
Or plung'd in Lakes of bitter *Washes*° lie,
Or wedg'd whole Ages in a *Bodkin's* Eye:°

---

105. *Diana's Law:* Diana was the Roman goddess of chastity, the moon, and the
hunt; a nymph or woman breaks Diana's law when she loses her virginity.
    113. *Drops:* "Diamond[s] hanging in the ear" [Johnson].
    117–22. *To Fifty chosen Sylphs, . . . guard the wide Circumference around:* Pope
again alludes to his *Iliad,* ironically comparing Belinda's petticoat to Achilles' "sev'n-
fold Shield" (VII.296), wrought by Vulcan, god of fire and metal: "Thus the broad
Shield complete the Artist crown'd / With his last Hand, and pour'd the Ocean round: /
In living Silver seem'd the Waves to roll, / And beat the Buckler's Verge, and bound the
whole" (*Iliad* XVIII.701–04). (See Pope's illustration of Achilles' shield, p. 352.) A
woman's petticoat was lined with hoops of whalebone to make it full and had several
layers. But even these formidable defenses, the poem suggests, are not enough to guard
virginity.
    127. *Washes:* Cosmetics for whitening the skin.
    128. *Bodkin's Eye:* The eye of a blunt needle; a bodkin can also be a hairpin or or-
nament (see Canto V).

Gums and *Pomatums*° shall his Flight restrain,
While clog'd he beats his silken Wings in vain;   130
Or Alom-*Stypticks*° with contracting Power
Shrink his thin Essence like a rivell'd Flower.
Or as *Ixion* fix'd, the Wretch shall feel
The giddy Motion of the whirling Mill,°
In Fumes of burning Chocolate shall glow,   135
And tremble at the Sea that froaths below!
   He spoke; the Spirits from the Sails descend;
Some, Orb in Orb, around the Nymph extend,
Some thrid the mazy Ringlets of her Hair,
Some hang upon the Pendants of her Ear;   140
With beating Hearts the dire Event they wait,
Anxious, and trembling for the Birth of Fate.

---

129. *Gums and Pomatums:* Scented ointments for skin and hair.
131. *Alom-Stypticks:* Astringents applied to small cuts to contract the tissue.
134. *Or as Ixion fix'd, . . . the whirling Mill:* Ixion was condemned to revolve upon a wheel forever in Hades; here, the guilty sylph would revolve forever on the wheel of a mill for grinding cocoa beans.

Canto 3.

Lud. Du Guernier inv. *C. Du Bofe sculp.*

Plate for Canto III, taking the climactic drawing room scene (complete with coffeepot) outside; while Belinda swoons, the Baron flourishes the ravished lock.

Canto III

Close by those Meads° for ever crown'd with Flow'rs,
Where *Thames* with Pride surveys his rising Tow'rs,
There stands a Structure of Majestick Frame,
Which from the neighb'ring *Hampton* takes its Name.°
Here *Britain*'s Statesmen oft the Fall foredoom   5
Of Foreign Tyrants, and of Nymphs at home;
Here Thou, Great *Anna*! whom three Realms obey,°
Dost sometimes Counsel take — and sometimes *Tea*.
    Hither the Heroes and the Nymphs resort,
To taste awhile the Pleasures of a Court;   10
In various Talk th' instructive hours they past,
Who gave the *Ball*, or paid the *Visit* last:
One speaks the Glory of the *British Queen*,
And one describes a charming *Indian Screen;*°
A third interprets Motions, Looks, and Eyes;   15
At ev'ry Word a Reputation dies.
Snuff,° or the *Fan*, supply each Pause of Chat,
With singing, laughing, ogling, and all that.
    Mean while declining from the Noon of Day,
The Sun obliquely shoots his burning Ray;   20
The hungry Judges soon the Sentence sign,
And Wretches hang that Jury-men may Dine;
The Merchant from th'*Exchange*° returns in Peace,

---

1. *Meads:* Meadows.

3–4. *a Structure of Majestick Frame, . . . Hampton takes its Name:* Hampton Court, several miles upstream from London, was one of the queen's residences; first built in the Tudor period, William III employed the great architect Christopher Wren to design additions. (See p. 383.)

7. *Great Anna! whom three Realms obey:* Queen Anne ruled from 1702 until her death in 1714. The three realms are probably England, Ireland, and Scotland, or if Pope considers England and Scotland as one Great Britain (formed 1707), then he could be alluding to the long English tradition of claiming sovereignty over France.

14. *Indian Screen:* A screen from India, Arabia, or Japan used to protect people from the heat of a fireplace.

17. *Snuff:* Taking snuff (that is, inhaling powdered tobacco by sniffing) was particularly popular during Anne's reign; Sir Plume is rendered nearly inarticulate by the practice (IV.125–30).

23. *The Merchant from th'Exchange:* The Royal Exchange, where merchants traded, was located in the commercial part of London. (See p. 397.)

And the long Labours of the *Toilette* cease —
Belinda now, whom Thirst of Fame invites,   25
Burns to encounter two adventrous Knights,
At *Ombre*° singly to decide their Doom;
And swells her Breast with Conquests yet to come.
Strait the three Bands prepare in Arms to join,
Each Band the number of the Sacred Nine.   30
Soon as she spreads her Hand, th' Aerial Guard
Descend, and sit on each important Card:
First *Ariel* perch'd upon a *Matadore,*
Then each, according to the Rank they bore;
For *Sylphs,* yet mindful of their ancient Race,   35
Are, as when Women, wondrous fond of Place.°
      Behold, four *Kings* in Majesty rever'd,°
With hoary Whiskers and a forky Beard;
And four fair *Queens* whose hands sustain a Flow'r,
Th' expressive Emblem of their softer Pow'r;   40
Four *Knaves* in Garbs succinct,° a trusty Band,
Caps on their heads, and Halberds° in their hand;
And Particolour'd Troops, a shining Train,
Draw forth to Combat on the Velvet Plain.°
      The skilful Nymph reviews her Force with Care;   45
Let Spades be Trumps! she said, and Trumps they were.
      Now move to War her Sable *Matadores,*
In Show like Leaders of the swarthy *Moors.*
Spadillio° first, unconquerable Lord!

27. *Ombre:* For a fuller discussion of the terms and rules of this card game, see Part Two, Chapter 2.

36. *wondrous fond of Place:* One's position in society, sometimes indicated by where one should be seated at a table.

37. *Behold, four Kings in Majesty rever'd:* This line begins an epic review of the forces assembled in the deck. See Pope's *Iliad,* III.175ff for a glimpse of "Each hardy *Greek* and valiant *Trojan* Knight" (175) resting on their spears or shields, and a list of the individual warriors.

41. *Four Knaves in Garbs succinct:* The four jacks wearing short tunics.

42. *Halberds:* Sixteenth-century weapons that combined a steel spear and a battle-axe blade.

44. *Velvet Plain:* The covered cardtable; the grassy battlefield.

49. *Spadillio:* The ace of spades.

Led off two captive Trumps, and swept the Board.   50
As many more *Manillio*° forc'd to yield,
And march'd a Victor from the verdant Field.
Him *Basto*° follow'd, but his Fate more hard
Gain'd but one Trump and one *Plebeian* Card.°
With his broad Sabre next, a Chief in Years,   55
The hoary Majesty of *Spades* appears;
Puts forth one manly Leg, to sight reveal'd;
The rest his many-colour'd Robe conceal'd.
The Rebel-*Knave*, who dares his Prince engage,
Proves the just Victim of his Royal Rage.   60
Ev'n mighty *Pam*° that Kings and Queens o'erthrew,
And mow'd down Armies in the Fights of *Lu*,°
Sad Chance of War! now, destitute of Aid,
Falls undistinguish'd by the Victor *Spade!*
    Thus far both Armies to *Belinda* yield;   65
Now to the *Baron* Fate inclines the Field.
His warlike *Amazon*° her Host invades,
Th' Imperial Consort of the Crown of *Spades*.
The *Club*'s black Tyrant first her Victim dy'd,
Spite of his haughty Mien, and barb'rous Pride: 70
What boots the Regal Circle on his Head,
His Giant Limbs in State unwieldy spread?
That long behind he trails his pompous Robe,
And of all Monarchs only grasps the Globe?
    The *Baron* now his *Diamonds* pours apace;   75
Th' embroider'd *King* who shows but half his Face,
And his refulgent *Queen,* with Pow'rs combin'd,
Of broken Troops an easie Conquest find.
Clubs, Diamonds, Hearts, in wild Disorder seen,

---

51. *Manillio:* The two of trumps.

53. *Basto:* The ace of clubs.

54. *one Plebeian Card:* Not royalty; a commoner; one of the plain numbers of the suit.

61. *Pam:* The jack of clubs; the card of highest value under certain circumstances in Loo.

62. *Lu:* Loo was another popular card game.

67. *Amazon:* A warrior woman; here, the queen of spades.

With Throngs promiscuous strow the level Green.   80
Thus when dispers'd a routed Army runs,
Of *Asia*'s Troops, and *Africk*'s Sable Sons,
With like Confusion different Nations fly,
Of various Habit and of various Dye,
The pierc'd Battalions dis-united fall,   85
In Heaps on Heaps; one Fate o'erwhelms them all.
   The *Knave* of *Diamonds* tries his wily Arts,
And wins (oh shameful Chance!) the *Queen of Hearts*.
At this, the Blood the Virgin's Cheek forsook,
A livid Paleness spreads o'er all her Look;   90
She sees, and trembles at th' approaching Ill,
Just in the Jaws of Ruin, and *Codille.*°
And now, (as oft in some distemper'd State)
On one nice *Trick* depends the gen'ral Fate.
An *Ace* of Hearts steps forth: The *King* unseen   95
Lurk'd in her Hand, and mourn'd his captive *Queen.*
He springs to Vengeance with an eager pace,
And falls like Thunder on the prostrate *Ace.*
The Nymph exulting fills with Shouts the Sky,
The Walls, the Woods, and long Canals reply.   100
   Oh thoughtless Mortals! ever blind to Fate,
Too soon dejected, and too soon elate!
Sudden these Honours shall be snatch'd away,
And curs'd for ever this Victorious Day.
   For lo! the Board with Cups and Spoons is crown'd,   105
The Berries crackle, and the Mill turns round.
On shining Altars of *Japan* they raise
The silver Lamp; the fiery Spirits blaze.
From silver Spouts the grateful Liquors glide,
While *China*'s Earth receives the smoking Tyde.°   110

---

92. *Codille:* The defeat of the challenger.
104–10. *The Berries crackle, . . . the smoking Tyde:* After the card game, the play-ers make coffee, roasting and grinding the coffee beans ("Berries"), then adding boiling water at the laquered table ("Altars of *Japan*") and pouring the coffee into china cups ("China's earth").

At once they gratify their Scent and Taste,
And frequent Cups prolong the rich Repast.
Strait hover round the Fair her Airy Band;
Some, as she sip'd, the fuming Liquor fann'd,
Some o'er her Lap their careful Plumes display'd,   115
Trembling, and conscious of the rich Brocade.
Coffee, (which makes the Politician wise,
And see thro' all things with his half-shut Eyes)
Sent up in Vapours to the *Baron*'s Brain
New Stratagems, the radiant Lock to gain.   120
Ah cease rash Youth! desist ere 'tis too late,
Fear the just Gods, and think of *Scylla*'s Fate!°
Chang'd to a Bird, and sent to flit in Air,
She dearly pays for *Nisus'* injur'd Hair!
But when to Mischief Mortals bend their Will,   125
How soon they find fit Instruments of Ill!
Just then, *Clarissa* drew with tempting Grace
A two-edg'd Weapon from her shining Case;
So Ladies in Romance assist their Knight,
Present the Spear, and arm him for the Fight.   130
He takes the Gift with rev'rence, and extends
The little Engine° on his Fingers' Ends,
This just behind *Belinda*'s Neck he spread,
As o'er the fragrant Steams she bends her Head:
Swift to the Lock a thousand Sprights repair,   135
A thousand Wings, by turns, blow back the Hair,
And thrice they twitch'd the Diamond in her Ear,
Thrice she look'd back, and thrice the Foe drew near.
Just in that instant, anxious *Ariel* sought
The close Recesses of the Virgin's Thought;   140
As on the Nosegay° in her Breast reclin'd,

122. *Scylla's Fate:* Scylla, daughter of King Nisus, was turned into a bird after she plucked a purple hair from her father's head (on which depended his and his kingdom's safety) to give to her beloved Minos, who nevertheless rejected her.
132. *Engine:* Mechanical instrument; here, a pair of scissors.
141. *Nosegay:* Small flower bouquet.

He watch'd th' Ideas rising in her Mind,
Sudden he view'd, in spite of all her Art,
An Earthly Lover lurking at her Heart.
Amaz'd, confus'd, he found his Pow'r expir'd,   145
Resign'd to Fate, and with a Sigh retir'd.
    The Peer now spreads the glitt'ring *Forfex* wide,
T'inclose the Lock; now joins it, to divide.
Ev'n then, before the fatal Engine clos'd,
A wretched *Sylph* too fondly interpos'd;   150
Fate urg'd the Sheers, and cut the *Sylph* in twain,
(But Airy Substance soon unites again)
The meeting Points the sacred Hair dissever
From the fair Head, for ever and for ever!
    Then flash'd the living Lightning from her Eyes,   155
And Screams of Horror rend th' affrighted Skies.
Not louder Shrieks to pitying Heav'n are cast,
When Husbands or when Lap-dogs breathe their last,
Or when rich *China* Vessels, fal'n from high,
In glittring Dust and painted Fragments lie!   160
    Let Wreaths of Triumph now my Temples twine,
(The Victor cry'd) the glorious Prize is mine!
While Fish in Streams, or Birds delight in Air,
Or in a Coach and Six the *British* Fair,
As long as *Atalantis* shall be read,°   165
Or the small Pillow grace a Lady's Bed,
While *Visits* shall be paid on solemn Days,
When numerous Wax-lights in bright Order blaze,
While Nymphs take Treats, or Assignations give,
So long my Honour, Name, and Praise shall live!   170
    What Time wou'd spare, from Steel receives its date,
And Monuments, like Men, submit to Fate!
Steel cou'd the Labour of the Gods destroy,

---

165. *As long as Atalantis shall be read*: *The New Atalantis* (1709), by Delarivier
Manley, part secret history, part amatory fiction, and all political scandal and sexual
intrigue, was enormously popular.

And strike to Dust th' Imperial Tow'rs of *Troy*;
Steel cou'd the Works of mortal Pride confound,   175
And hew Triumphal Arches to the Ground.
What Wonder then, fair Nymph! thy Hairs shou'd feel
The conqu'ring Force of unresisted Steel?

Canto 4.

Lud. Du Guernier inv.   C. Du Bofc sculp.

Plate for Canto IV, featuring miserable Belinda in the Cave of Spleen with the two handmaids Ill-nature and Affectation; later illustrators also personified "*Pain* at her side, and *Megrim* at her Head" (IV. 24).

Canto IV

But anxious Cares the pensive Nymph opprest,
And secret Passions labour'd in her Breast.
Not youthful Kings in Battel seiz'd alive,
Not scornful Virgins who their Charms survive,
Not ardent Lovers robb'd of all their Bliss,   5
Not ancient Ladies when refus'd a Kiss,
Not Tyrants fierce that unrepenting die,
Not *Cynthia* when her *Manteau*'s pinn'd awry,°
E'er felt such Rage, Resentment and Despair,
As Thou, sad Virgin! for thy ravish'd Hair.   10
    For, that sad moment, when the *Sylphs* withdrew,
And *Ariel* weeping from *Belinda* flew,
Umbriel, a dusky melancholy Spright,
As ever sully'd the fair face of Light,
Down to the Central Earth, his proper Scene,   15
Repair'd to search the gloomy Cave of *Spleen.*°
    Swift on his sooty Pinions flitts the *Gnome,*
And in a Vapour reach'd the dismal Dome.
No cheerful Breeze this sullen Region knows,
The dreadful *East* is all the Wind that blows.   20
Here, in a Grotto,° sheltred close from Air,
And screen'd in Shades from Day's detested Glare,
She sighs for ever on her pensive Bed,
Pain at her Side, and *Megrim*° at her Head.
    Two Handmaids wait the Throne: Alike in Place,   25
But diff'ring far in Figure and in Face.

---

8. *Cynthia when her Manteau's pinn'd awry:* Any lady furious when her loose upper garment is not put on correctly by her maid.

16. *Cave of Spleen:* The spleen was both a bodily organ and the name for many ills from headache to depression, known collectively as the "English Malady." The spleen was sometimes believed to cause delusions; so Belinda sees "Bodies chang'd to various Forms by *Spleen*" (IV.48).

21. *Grotto:* A picturesque, often artificial and ornamented, cave popular in the landscape of the eighteenth century. Pope would delight in the grotto at his Twickenham villa, working to enlarge and embellish it from the 1720s through the early 1740s.

24. *Megrim:* Another name for a migraine headache or spleen.

Here stood *Ill-nature* like an *ancient Maid*,
Her wrinkled Form in *Black* and *White* array'd;
With store of Pray'rs, for Mornings, Nights, and Noons,
Her Hand is fill'd; her Bosom with Lampoons.   30
   There *Affectation* with a sickly Mien
Shows in her Cheek the Roses of Eighteen,
Practis'd to Lisp, and hang the Head aside,
Faints into Airs, and languishes with Pride;
On the rich Quilt sinks with becoming Woe,   35
Wrapt in a Gown, for Sickness, and for Show.
The Fair-ones feel such Maladies as these,
When each new Night-Dress gives a new Disease.
   A constant *Vapour* o'er the Palace flies;
Strange Phantoms rising as the Mists arise;   40
Dreadful, as Hermit's Dreams in haunted Shades,
Or bright as Visions of expiring Maids.
Now glaring Fiends, and Snakes on rolling Spires,
Pale Spectres, gaping Tombs, and Purple Fires:
Now Lakes of liquid gold, *Elysian* Scenes,°   45
And Crystal Domes, and Angels in Machines.
   Unnumber'd Throngs on ev'ry side are seen
Of Bodies chang'd to various Forms by *Spleen*.
Here living *Teapots* stand, one Arm held out,
One bent; the Handle this, and that the Spout: 50
A Pipkin there like *Homer*'s *Tripod* walks;°
Here sighs a Jar, and there a Goose-pye° talks;
Men prove with Child, as pow'rful Fancy works,
And Maids turn'd Bottels, call aloud for Corks.

45. *Elysian Scenes:* In Greek mythology, Elysium was the place of the blessed after death.
   51. *A Pipkin . . . Homer's Tripod walks:* A pipkin was a small earthen jar. In the *Iliad*, Vulcan makes twenty tripods, or three-legged stands, that "plac'd on living Wheeles of massy Gold, / (Wond'rous to tell) instinct with Spirit roll'd / From Place to Place, around the blest Abodes, / Self-mov'd" (XVIII.441–43).
   52. *Goose-pye:* "Alludes to a real fact, a Lady of distinction imagin'd herself in this condition" [P].

Safe past the *Gnome* thro' this fantastick Band,   55
A Branch of healing *Spleenwort* in his hand.°
Then thus addrest the Pow'r — Hail wayward Queen!
Who rule the Sex to Fifty from Fifteen,
Parents of Vapors and of Female Wit,
Who give th' *Hysteric* or *Poetic* Fit,°   60
On various Tempers act by various ways,
Make some take Physick, others scribble Plays;
Who cause the Proud their Visits to delay,
And send the Godly in a Pett,° to pray.
A Nymph there is, that all thy Pow'r disdains,   65
And thousands more in equal Mirth maintains.
But oh! if e'er thy *Gnome* could spoil a Grace,
Or raise a Pimple on a beauteous Face,
Like Citron-Waters Matrons' Cheeks inflame,°
Or change Complexions at a losing Game;   70
If e'er with airy Horns I planted Heads,°
Or rumpled Petticoats, or tumbled Beds,
Or caus'd Suspicion when no Soul was rude,
Or discompos'd the Head-dress° of a Prude,
Or e'er to costive Lap-Dog gave Disease,   75
Which not the Tears of brightest Eyes could ease:
Hear me, and touch *Belinda* with Chagrin;
That single Act gives half the World the Spleen.
   The Goddess with a discontented Air
Seems to reject him, tho' she grants his Pray'r.   80
A wondrous Bag with both her Hands she binds,

---

56. *Spleenwort:* A kind of fern used to treat disorders of the spleen; the epic hero Aeneas carries a golden bough of the herb as his passport to the underworld.

60. *Hysteric or Poetic Fit:* Hysteria, or melancholy, was believed to contribute to creative genius as well as to bad temper.

64. *in a Pett:* In a fit of temper.

69. *Citron-Waters:* Brandy distilled with the rinds of citrons.

71. *If e'er with airy Horns I planted Heads:* Horns were the traditional sign of a cuckold (a husband with an adulterous wife), but in this case Umbriel loves to make husbands and wives *falsely* suspicious of each other — the horns are "airy," not real.

74. *Head-dress:* A cloth covering the hair; a custom introduced by the soberly dressed Puritans.

Like that where once *Ulysses* held the Winds;°
There she collects the Force of Female Lungs,
Sighs, Sobs, and Passions, and the War of Tongues.
A Vial next she fills with fainting Fears,   85
Soft Sorrows, melting Griefs, and flowing Tears.
The *Gnome* rejoicing bears her Gifts away,
Spreads his black Wings, and slowly mounts to Day.
    Sunk in *Thalestris*'° Arms the Nymph he found,
Her Eyes dejected and her Hair unbound.   90
Full o'er their Heads the swelling Bag he rent,
And all the Furies issued at the Vent.
Belinda burns with more than mortal Ire,
And fierce *Thalestris* fans the rising Fire.
O wretched Maid! she spread her Hands, and cry'd,   95
(While *Hampton*'s Ecchos, wretched Maid! reply'd)
Was it for this you took such constant Care
The *Bodkin, Comb,* and *Essence* to prepare;
For this your Locks in Paper-Durance bound,
For this with tort'ring Irons wreath'd around?   100
For this with Fillets strain'd your tender Head,
And bravely bore the double Loads of Lead?°
Gods! shall the Ravisher display your Hair,
While the Fops° envy, and the Ladies stare!
Honour forbid! at whose unrival'd Shrine   105
Ease, Pleasure, Virtue, All, our Sex resign.
Methinks already I your Tears survey,
Already hear the horrid things they say,
Already see you a degraded Toast,°
And all your Honour in a Whisper lost!   110
How shall I, then, your helpless Fame defend?

    82. *Ulysses held the Winds:* In the *Odyssey,* Ulysses is given a leather bag full of winds by Aeolus, warden of the gales.
    89. *Thalestris:* The queen of the Amazons.
    99–102. *For this your Locks ... Loads of Lead:* To create the perfect coiffure, Belinda endured the torture of curling irons, protective papers secured with hot lead, and the imprisonment of a thin crown, or "fillet," around her forehead.
    104. *Fops:* Overdressed and self-important men.
    109. *Toast:* "A celebrated woman whose health is often drunk" [Johnson].

'Twill then be Infamy to seem your Friend!
And shall this Prize, th' inestimable Prize,
Expos'd thro' Crystal to the gazing Eyes,
And heighten'd by the Diamond's circling Rays,   115
On that Rapacious Hand for ever blaze?°
Sooner shall Grass in *Hide*-Park *Circus* grow,
And Wits take Lodgings in the Sound of *Bow*;°
Sooner let Earth, Air, Sea, to *Chaos* fall,
Men, Monkies, Lap-Dogs, Parrots, perish all!   120
   She said; then raging to *Sir Plume* repairs,
And bids her *Beau* demand the precious Hairs:
(*Sir Plume*, of *Amber Snuff-box* justly vain,
And the nice Conduct of a *clouded Cane*)°
With earnest Eyes, and round unthinking Face,   125
He first the Snuff-box open'd, then the Case,
And thus broke out — "My Lord, why, what the Devil?
Z — ds! damn the Lock! 'fore Gad, you must be civil!
Plague on't! 'tis past a Jest — nay prithee, Pox!
Give her the Hair" — he spoke, and rapp'd his Box.°   130
   It grieves me much (reply'd the Peer again)
Who speaks so well shou'd ever speak in vain.
But by this Lock, this sacred Lock I swear,
(Which never more shall join its parted Hair,
Which never more its Honours shall renew,   135
Clipt from the lovely Head where late it grew)
That while my Nostrils draw the vital Air,

114–16. *Expos'd thro' Crystal . . . On that Rapacious Hand for ever blaze:* Hair
was often crafted into rings with a crystal face, set with diamonds.

117–18. *Hide-Park Circus . . . Sound of Bow:* It's as likely that grass will grow
over the well-traveled drive in Hyde Park and that fashionable young men ("Wits")
will condescend to live in the mercantile city, within the sound of the churchbells of St.
Mary-le-Bow, as it is that the Baron will get to keep the lock.

123–24. *Amber Snuff-box . . . clouded Cane:* Sir Plume is a fop, a beau, a spark,
proud of his clothes and accessories, full of mannerisms and little ceremonies; clouded,
or marbled, canes had a stylish popularity, especially for such as Plume.

126–30. *He first the Snuff-box open'd, . . . and rapp'd his Box:* Sir Plume (Sir
George Brown in real life) can only wage the war of words with an inarticulate jumble
of fashionable slang; "Z — ds!" is "Zounds!" an abbreviation of "God's wounds";
"Pox" refers to smallpox or venereal disease. Sir George was not pleased with this
portrait.

This Hand, which won it, shall for ever wear.
He spoke, and speaking, in proud Triumph spread
The long-contended Honours of her Head.   140
   But *Umbriel,* hateful *Gnome!* forbears not so;
He breaks the Vial whence the Sorrows flow.
Then see! the *Nymph* in beauteous Grief appears,
Her Eyes half-languishing, half-drown'd in Tears;
On her heav'd Bosom hung her drooping Head,   145
Which, with a Sigh, she rais'd; and thus she said.
   For ever curs'd be this detested Day,
Which snatch'd my best, my fav'rite Curl away!
Happy! ah ten times happy, had I been,
If *Hampton-Court* these Eyes had never seen!   150
Yet am not I the first mistaken Maid,
By Love of *Courts* to num'rous Ills betray'd.
Oh had I rather un-admir'd remain'd
In some lone Isle, or distant *Northern* Land;
Where the gilt *Chariot* never marks the Way,   155
Where none learn *Ombre,* none e'er taste *Bohea!*°
There kept my Charms conceal'd from mortal Eye,
Like Roses that in Desarts bloom and die.
What mov'd my Mind with youthful Lords to rome?
O had I stay'd, and said my Pray'rs at home!   160
'Twas this, the Morning *Omens* seem'd to tell;
Thrice from my trembling hand the *Patch-box* fell;
The tott'ring *China* shook without a Wind,
Nay, *Poll* sate mute, and *Shock* was most Unkind!
A *Sylph* too warn'd me of the Threats of Fate,   165
In mystic Visions, now believ'd too late!
See the poor Remnants of these slighted Hairs!
My hands shall rend what ev'n thy Rapine spares:
These, in two sable Ringlets taught to break,
Once gave new Beauties to the snowie Neck.   170
The Sister-Lock now sits uncouth, alone,

---

156. *Bohea:* "A species of tea, of higher colour, and more astringent taste, than green tea" [Johnson].

And in its Fellow's Fate foresees its own;
Uncurl'd it hangs, the fatal Sheers demands;
And tempts once more thy sacrilegious Hands.
Oh hadst thou, Cruel! been content to seize 175
Hairs less in sight, or any Hairs but these!

The Rape of the Lock

Canto 5.

Lud. Du Guernier inv.　　　*C. Du Bofc sculp.*

Plate for Canto V, depicting the feverish battle, while the lock, already a star, slips beyond mortal grasp.

Canto V

She said: the pitying Audience melt in Tears,
But *Fate* and *Jove*° had stopp'd the *Baron*'s Ears.
In vain *Thalestris* with Reproach assails,
For who can move when fair *Belinda* fails?
Not half so fixt the *Trojan* cou'd remain,   5
While *Anna* begg'd and *Dido* rag'd in vain.°
Then grave *Clarissa* graceful wav'd her Fan;°
Silence ensu'd, and thus the Nymph began.
    Say, why are Beauties prais'd and honour'd most,
The wise Man's Passion, and the vain Man's Toast?   10
Why deck'd with all that Land and Sea afford,
Why Angels call'd, and Angel-like ador'd?
Why round our Coaches crowd the white-glov'd Beaus,
Why bows the Side-box from its inmost Rows?°
How vain are all these Glories, all our Pains,   15
Unless good Sense preserve what Beauty gains:
That Men may say, when we the Front-box grace,
Behold the first in Virtue, as in Face!
Oh! if to dance all Night, and dress all Day,
Charm'd the Small-pox,° or chas'd old Age away;   20

---

2. *Jove:* The king of the gods; also Jupiter, Zeus.

5–6. *the Trojan . . . in vain:* The epic hero Aeneas left his raging lover Dido to found Rome; Dido sent her sister Anna to beg Aeneas to return, with no success.

7. *Clarissa:* "A new character introduced in the subsequent Editions, to open more clearly the MORAL of the Poem, in a parody of the speech of Sarpedon to Glaucus in Homer" [P]. See pp. 250–51 in Part Two for text of Sarpedon's speech urging Glaucus to join the attack on the Trojan ramparts. Clarissa is a new character in the sense that she has a spoken part, but she appears in the 1712 version at I.107 where, as in the 1714 version, III.127, she loans the Baron her scissors.

14. *Why bows the Side-box from its inmost Rows?:* Why do all the "best people" at the theatre, even those seated at the back of the boxes, rise and bow to us simply for our beauty?

20. *Small-pox:* Smallpox was a terrible threat in early-eighteenth-century England, and could cause blindness and disfigurement in those who survived it. The real-life Baron, Lord Petre, had died of it in 1713. Pope's friend (later enemy) Lady Mary Wortley Montagu, herself pitted from smallpox, would bring back an inoculation from Turkey in 1718.

Who would not scorn what Huswife's Cares produce,
Or who would learn one earthly Thing of Use?
To patch, nay ogle, might become a Saint,
Nor could it sure be such a Sin to paint.
But since, alas! frail Beauty must decay,   25
Curl'd or uncurl'd, since Locks will turn to grey,
Since painted, or not painted, all shall fade,
And she who scorns a Man, must die a Maid;
What then remains, but well our Pow'r to use,
And keep good Humour still whate'er we lose?   30
And trust me, Dear! good Humour can prevail,
When Airs, and Flights, and Screams, and Scolding fail.
Beauties in vain their pretty Eyes may roll;
Charms strike the Sight, but Merit wins the Soul.
 So spoke the Dame, but no Applause ensu'd;   35
Belinda frown'd, *Thalestris* call'd her Prude.
To Arms, to Arms! the fierce Virago° cries,
And swift as Lightning to the Combate flies.
All side in Parties, and begin th' Attack;
Fans clap, Silks russle, and tough Whalebones crack;   40
Heroes' and Heroins' Shouts confus'dly rise,
And base, and treble Voices strike the Skies.
No common Weapons in their Hands are found,
Like Gods they fight, nor dread a mortal Wound.
 So when bold *Homer* makes the Gods engage,°   45
And heav'nly Breasts with human Passions rage;
'Gainst *Pallas, Mars; Latona, Hermes* arms;
And all *Olympus* rings with loud Alarms.
Jove's Thunder roars, Heav'n trembles all around;
Blue *Neptune* storms, the bellowing Deeps resound;   50

---

37. *Virago:* "A female warriour, a woman with the qualities of a man" [Johnson].
 45. *the Gods engage:* The gods are named in the next several lines: Pallas Athena is the goddess of wisdom; Mars, the god of war; Latona, the mother of Apollo and Diana; Hermes, the gods' messenger; Olympus, the home of the gods; Neptune, the god of the sea.

Earth shakes her nodding Tow'rs, the Ground gives way;
And the pale Ghosts start at the Flash of Day!
    Triumphant *Umbriel* on a Sconce's° Height
Clapt his glad Wings, and sate to view the Fight:
Propt on their Bodkin Spears, the Sprights survey   55
The growing Combat, or assist the Fray.
    While thro' the Press enrag'd *Thalestris* flies,
And scatters Deaths around from both her Eyes,
A *Beau* and *Witling* perish'd in the Throng,
One dy'd in *Metaphor,* and one in *Song.*   60
O cruel Nymph! a living Death I bear,
Cry'd *Dapperwit,* and sunk beside his Chair.
A mournful Glance Sir *Fopling* upwards cast,°
Those Eyes are made so killing — was his last:
Thus on *Meander*'s° flow'ry Margin lies   65
Th' expiring Swan, and as he sings he dies.
    When bold Sir *Plume* had drawn *Clarissa* down,
Chloe stept in, and kill'd him with a Frown;
She smil'd to see the doughty° Hero slain,
But at her Smile, the Beau reviv'd again.   70
    Now *Jove* suspends his golden Scales in Air,°
Weighs the Men's Wits against the Lady's Hair;
The doubtful Beam° long nods from side to side;
At length the Wits mount up, the Hairs subside.
    See fierce *Belinda* on the *Baron* flies,   75
With more than usual Lightning in her Eyes;

53. *Sconce:* A wall bracket for candles.
62–63. *Cry'd Dapperwit, . . . Sir Fopling upwards cast:* Dapperwit, as his name suggests, is a fop in the popular Restoration comedy *Love in a Wood,* by Pope's early mentor, William Wycherley, and Sir Fopling comes from a contemporary play by George Etherege, *Man of Mode, or Sir Fopling Flutter.*
65. *Meander:* A river in Phrygia (modern-day Turkey).
69. *doughty:* Valiant, formidable (the sense here is sarcastic).
71. *his golden Scales:* The scales on which Jove weighs the fates of mortals; they are not exactly scales of justice, since, as in Dryden's translation of the *Aeneid,* life can be the "lucky Chance" that makes one side rise, and death what makes the other fall.
73. *The doubtful Beam:* The wavering crosspiece of the scales.

Nor fear'd the Chief th'unequal Fight to try,
Who sought no more than on his Foe to die.
But this bold Lord, with manly Strength indu'd,
She with one Finger and a Thumb subdu'd: 80
Just where the Breath of Life his Nostrils drew,
A Charge of *Snuff* the wily Virgin threw;
The *Gnomes* direct, to ev'ry Atome just,
The pungent Grains of titillating Dust.
Sudden, with starting Tears each Eye o'erflows,   85
And the high Dome re-ecchoes to his Nose.
   Now meet thy Fate, incens'd *Belinda* cry'd,
And drew a deadly *Bodkin*° from her Side.
(The same, his ancient Personage to deck,
Her great great Grandsire wore about his Neck   90
In three *Seal-Rings*;° which after, melted down,
Form'd a vast *Buckle* for his Widow's Gown:
Her infant Grandame's *Whistle* next it grew,
The *Bells* she gingled,° and the *Whistle* blew;
Then in a *Bodkin* grac'd her Mother's Hairs,   95
Which long she wore, and now *Belinda* wears.)
   Boast not my Fall (he cry'd) insulting Foe!
Thou by some other shalt be laid as low.
Nor think, to die dejects my lofty Mind;
All that I dread, is leaving you behind!   100
Rather than so, ah let me still survive,
And burn in *Cupid*'s° Flames, — but burn alive.
   Restore the Lock! she cries; and all around
Restore the Lock! the vaulted Roofs rebound.

---

   88. *Bodkin:* See the note for line 128, Canto II.
   91. *Seal-Rings:* Patterned rings to impress the wax sealing an envelope.
   93–94. *Her infant Grandame's Whistle . . . Bells she gingled:* Whistles sometimes had bells attached.
   102. *Cupid:* The god of love.

Not fierce *Othello*° in so loud a Strain   105
Roar'd for the Handkerchief that caus'd his Pain.
But see how oft Ambitious Aims are cross'd,
And Chiefs contend 'till all the Prize is lost!
The Lock, obtain'd with Guilt, and kept with Pain,
In ev'ry place is sought, but sought in vain: 110
With such a Prize no Mortal must be blest,
So Heav'n decrees! with Heav'n who can contest?
    Some thought it mounted to the Lunar Sphere,
Since all things lost on Earth, are treasur'd there.°
There Heroes' Wits are kept in pondrous Vases,   115
And Beaus' in *Snuff-boxes* and *Tweezer-Cases*.°
There broken Vows, and Death-bed Alms° are found,
And Lovers' Hearts with Ends of Riband bound;
The Courtier's Promises, and Sick Man's Pray'rs,
The Smiles of Harlots, and the Tears of Heirs,   120
Cages for Gnats, and Chains to Yoak a Flea;
Dry'd Butterflies, and Tomes of Casuistry.°
    But trust the Muse — she saw it upward rise,
Tho' mark'd by none but quick Poetic Eyes:
(So *Rome*'s great Founder to the Heav'ns withdrew,   125
To *Proculus* alone confess'd in view.)°
A sudden Star, it shot thro' liquid Air,
And drew behind a radiant *Trail of Hair.*

---

105. *Othello:* The Moorish king in Shakespeare's play of that name, who was falsely persuaded by the circumstantial evidence of a handkerchief, planted by his evil counselor Iago, that his wife Desdemona was unfaithful to him.

113–14. *Lunar Sphere . . . treasur'd there:* The moon apparently stores the detritus of human love affairs, as in Ariosto's poem *Orlando Furioso* (1532).

116. *Tweezer-Cases:* Like snuffboxes, tweezer-cases were accoutrements of the dandy.

117. *Death-bed Alms:* Charity given only from the panic of imminent death and the desire to be forgiven by God; not worth much.

121–22. *Cages for Gnats, . . . Tomes of Casuistry:* All the pointless experiments and tedious volumes of the pseudo-scientific and pseudo-moral enterprises of the day.

125–26. *(So Rome's great Founder . . . To Proculus alone confess'd in view.):* Romulus, legendary founder of Rome, is said to have appeared after his death in a vision to Proculus.

Not *Berenice*'s Locks° first rose so bright,
The Heav'ns bespangling with dishevel'd Light.   130
The *Sylphs* behold it kindling as it flies,
And pleas'd pursue its Progress thro' the Skies.
    This the *Beau-monde* shall from the *Mall* survey,°
And hail with Musick its propitious Ray.
This, the blest Lover shall for *Venus* take,   135
And send up Vows from *Rosamonda*'s Lake.°
This *Partridge* soon shall view in cloudless Skies,
When next he looks thro' *Galilæo*'s Eyes;
And hence th' Egregious Wizard shall foredoom
The Fate of *Louis,* and the Fall of *Rome.*°   140
    Then cease, bright Nymph! to mourn thy ravish'd Hair
Which adds new Glory to the shining Sphere!
Not all the Tresses that fair Head can boast
Shall draw such Envy as the Lock you lost.
For, after all the Murders of your Eye,   145
When, after Millions slain, your self shall die;
When those fair Suns shall sett, as sett they must,

129. *Berenice's Locks:* A legendary figure whose hair turned into stars. Underscoring Pope's concern in the *Rape* about fragments of things, only a fragment of the original poem about Berenice by Callimachus exists.

133. *This the Beau-monde shall from the Mall survey:* The members of the fashionable world will watch the lock-turned-star from the fashionable avenue Pall Mall, all offering their own interpretations of its identity and meaning.

135–36. *the blest Lover ... Rosamonda's Lake:* The lover, waiting at the rendezvous — Rosamond's Pond in St. James's Park — assumes the lock is Venus, the evening star (named for the goddess of love), and takes it as a good omen.

137–40. *This Partridge soon shall view ... the Fall of Rome:* "John Partridge was a ridiculous Star-gazer, who in his Almanacks every year, never fail'd to predict the downfall of the Pope, and the King of France, then at war with the English" [P]. Galileo improved the telescope in the early seventeenth century, and like the microscope, it was becoming more widely available to laypersons. The bogus astronomer Partridge, whom Swift had wickedly announced dead in 1708 (Partridge insisted he was still alive), regularly made outlandish predictions about world events — the fate of the French king Louis XIV and the fall of the Roman Catholic Church.

And all those Tresses shall be laid in Dust;
This Lock, the Muse shall consecrate to Fame,
And mid'st the Stars inscribe *Belinda*'s Name!   150

FINIS

Part Two

The Rape of the Lock
Cultural Contexts

Portrait of Alexander Pope. This particular portrait of Pope was painted by his drawing instructor, Charles Jervas (1675?–1739), in the autumn of 1714, a few months after the publication of the five-canto *Rape of the Lock*. The reception of the poem had been gratifying, and Lintot offered for sale an engraved version of the portrait. Pope presumably had something to say about Jervas's presentation: It is a flattering portrait, offering no hints of deformity or size, only an elegant head held high and a well-shaped hand. Painting, like poetry, can be useful in representing ways to see the world, and selecting ways to be seen.

1

The Poetic World

THE POET AND THE POEM

The opening materials on "The Poet and the Poem" offer some first- and second-hand historical perspectives on Pope's life and the creation of *The Rape of the Lock*. Samuel Johnson, perhaps the most influential critical voice of the eighteenth century, contributed in his *Lives of the Poets* (1781) to the shape of the English literary tradition and confirmed many of Pope's own judgments about himself. The excerpts from the *Life of Pope* included here recreate not just the trajectory of the writer but the character of the man. Johnson offers us his own version of "cultural contexts" by his literary decision to narrate the life and then, in separate sections, to position and explore the person and the works. We get a sense of Pope's "petty peculiarities," the sound of his voice in company, the sad indignity of his infirmities, the lasting loyalty of those who loved him.

Against the backdrop of this later-eighteenth-century biographical assessment of Pope, we see the poet's life as he himself fashions it, in his correspondence. In an early poem, the *Second Pastoral*, Pope played with traditional poetic genres as a way of placing himself — the shepherd Alexis — solidly in the English literary tradition: Alexis accepts a flute from Colin, the poem's figure for Edmund Spenser. Selections from Pope's letters (themselves carefully polished, fastidiously self-edited, and disingenuously open, artless, and sincere) that cluster around the writing and revisions of the *Rape* highlight Pope's delights, sorrows, ambitions, anxieties, self-confidence, and self-doubt, both as poet and as young man. In 1735 Pope wrote a retrospective of his life in his *Epistle to Dr. Arbuthnot* (not included here), a poem that differs pointedly and poignantly from the fresh, saucy, exuberant wit of the *Rape* in tone and content.

The next cluster of materials brings the source and story of the poem to life. Anecdotes from Pope's friend, the scholar Joseph Spence, combined with relevant correspondence to and from Pope, illuminate moments of publication and reception. The material on Arabella Fermor, poetically immortalized for her severed lock, attests to the sustained cultural power and appeal of the image and the poem, as Pope confidently predicted:

> Not all the Tresses that fair Head can boast
> Shall draw such Envy as the Lock you lost. . . .
> *This Lock*, the Muse shall consecrate to Fame,
> And mid'st the Stars inscribe *Belinda*'s Name! (V. 143–50)

But though *The Rape of the Lock* may seem a permanent literary fixture to us, appearing tirelessly in high school and college survey courses, the poem was not at first a complete critical success, and Pope found himself scrabbling energetically to define and keep his place in the English literary tradition. Several mixed reviews disclose the cynical hostility and contempt with which some readers greeted the *Rape*. There was, in fact, a time when Pope was new, young, relatively untried, a modern arrogant upstart, a threat to the existing literary establishment. Attacks, distortions, imitations abounded; Pope's apparent views of women, society, politics, and religion, all came under fire. Charles Gildon sneered at his "tolerable knack for Versification"; John Dennis, one of Pope's most vitriolic enemies, invoked the critical vocabulary of "toad" and "ape"; Giles Jacob in *The Rape of the Smock* pushed the sexual innuendos in Pope's *Rape* into virtual pornography; and Pope himself leaped wryly and pseudonymously into the fray with *A Key to the Lock*, a witty parody of the paranoiac anti-Catholic, political "close readings" of the day. The verbal hostility spilled into the visual, and this section includes a famous and representative example of Pope caricatured, his physical deformity reinscribed as moral deformity. But Pope *did* succeed in capturing the recognition of the literary world — and in the process managed to submerge most of these early critical opponents into historical "dunces" by 1729. In an early letter (1708) to Henry

Cromwell, Pope had prophesied: "Damnation follows Death in other Men, / But your damn'd Poet lives and writes agen"(*Correspondence* 2:49).

POETIC FORMS

Not much serious poetry these days is written in heroic couplets; in reading *The Rape of the Lock,* it helps to know that its poetic form was in some ways standard, almost *prescribed,* for the day, and that Pope was particularly adept at the form. The insistence of rhymed couplets in iambic pentameter can seem at first glance a poetic corset, a prison of limitation that oppresses variety and meaning into repetition and dullness. But as Samuel Johnson pronounced: "I suspect this objection to be the cant of those who judge by principles rather than perception" (*Life of Pope*). The couplet quickly emerges under Pope's hand as a flexible, tricksy, endlessly varied balancing of oppositions, paradoxes, and contradictions refusing closure. Employing rhetorical, linguistic, imaginative, psychological, social, and political devices that *appear* to capture and contain its subject, Pope develops its full and complicated cultural expression.

In his *Life of Pope* Samuel Johnson explores the intensity of Pope's commitment to his poetical products: "He examined lines and words with minute and punctilious observation, and retouched every part with indefatigable diligence, till he had left nothing to be forgiven." Pope himself said to Joseph Spence: "After writing a poem, one should correct it all over, with one single view at a time." Thus everything in the *Rape* is there for a reason, as part of a large and delicate design that depends on the intricate relationship between sound and sense, between linguistic patterns and poetic meanings. The heroic couplet *is* a rigorous form, and because of its fixed boundaries it demands much energy and ingenuity from the poet. In Pope's letter to William Walsh (October 22, 1706) and the selections from *An Essay on Criticism*, we see Pope outlining the rules for versification and then satirizing those who understand the rules too rigidly.

Two other important aspects of early-eighteenth-century poetry that provide a fuller contemporary context for reading the *Rape* are the assumptions about the sense of sight in relation to imagination and the close relationship of the "sister arts" of poetry and painting. In the excerpts from *The Spectator* included here, Addison claims that sight is the richest and most powerful of all the senses, through

which we are supplied with the raw material for all our mental im-
ages, but ultimately the *act* of imagination is even more powerful
than the *sense* of sight:

> [For] we have the Power of retaining, altering and compounding those
> Images, which we have once received, into all the varieties of Picture
> and Vision that are most agreeable to the Imagination; for by this Fac-
> ulty a Man in a Dungeon is capable of entertaining himself with Scenes
> and Landskips more beautiful than any that can be found in the whole
> Compass of Nature. (*Spectator* 411)

The reader, like the poet and the painter, actively assembles his or her
own images induced by visual experience or verbal description; in the
eighteenth century, such images were communal as well as personal.
As Jean Hagstrum has thoroughly shown, the relationship between
the "sister arts" of poetry and painting was virtually a commonplace;
pictorial poems were designed to recall painterly effects (Hagstrum
xxii). Pope himself was friend to two important artists, Charles Jer-
vas and Sir Godfrey Kneller, and he was an enthusiastic student of
the visual arts. In 1730 one of Pope's friends asked him, "'Which
gives you the most pleasure, sir, poetry or painting?' — 'I really can't
well say; both of them are extremely pleasing.' — P" (Spence 1:46).
Learning to draw and paint gave the poet added insight into the pow-
erful possibilities of light and color and shadow to render emotion,
and Pope would often draw the connections between poetry and
painting — "He best can paint 'em, who shall feel 'em most" (*Eloisa
to Abelard*, l. 366). This section includes a portrait of Lady Mary
Wortley Montagu by Jervas, along with Pope's poetic comments on
the subject.

Pope's knowledge of the history and conventions of painting is a
crucial context for understanding his art. He believed that images are
reflected from art to art, and for Pope and his contemporaries, paint-
ings of the Renaissance and its seventeenth-century "afterglow," as
Hagstrum calls it, provided many of the "images" that the imagina-
tion would "retain, alter, and compound." Hagstrum invokes Cor-
reggio as the most appropriate visual model for *The Rape of the
Lock*, noting that Daniel Webb made the same connection in 1760:

> In the description of the sylphs — "Some to the Sun their Insect-Wings
> unfold" [*Rape* II.59–62] — grace triumphs, and harsh, defining form
> tends, in this play of soft and blended color, to sink in clouds and dis-
> solve in light. . . . This rendition of delicate motion — of transient col-

ors and waving wings — is surely the closest that any poet has ever come to the *sfumato* [indistinct outlines] of Correggio. (Hagstrum 220)

In *Epistle to Jervis*, included here, Pope positions himself and Jervas paired in admiration of the Italian Renaissance artists, and invokes their particular strengths through the power of poetic distillation and arrangement:

> Each heav'nly piece unweary'd we compare,
> Match *Raphael*'s grace, with thy lov'd *Guido*'s air,
> *Caracci*'s strength, *Corregio*'s softer line,
> *Paolo*'s free stroke, and *Titian*'s warmth divine. (ll. 35–38)

The larger form of the *Rape* is that of mock-epic, and several documents help explain the contemporary fascination with both the epic and its satiric exploitation. Early eighteenth-century English literature is often called "Augustan" for its celebration and imitation of the politics and literature of classical Greece and Rome, especially from the time of Augustus Caesar. Augustan literature drew upon these classical models, but its versions were quite often satirical, mock forms of the genres employed. The power of the mock-epic depends on understanding the dimensions of the epic, and at the time of the *Rape* Pope was also beginning his translation of Homer's *Iliad*. In this section, *The Spectator* spells out the critical agenda for the epic, and examples from Pope's *Iliad* illustrate that agenda. Included here is Sarpedon's speech to Glaucus on the glory of risking everything in battle; this speech became the basis for Clarissa's speech in Canto V, added in 1717. Pope had Achilles's shield in mind when he described the "sev'nfold fence" of Belinda's petticoat, and he drew an image of the shield which was later engraved for the *Iliad*. Pope's "Receit to Make an Epic Poem" plays with the edges of form, satirizing the less skillful efforts of other modern translators of myth and legend.

The last two documents contextualize Pope's choice of "machinery," or "that Part which the Deities, Angels, or Daemons, are made to act in a Poem" (*Rape*, "To Mrs. Arabella Fermor"). Pope had added his impotent sylphs and tormenting gnomes in the 1714 edition. As the story goes, Addison counseled Pope against expanding the 1712 version of the poem, but Pope was too enchanted with his "machinery" of Rosicrucian mythology. Sylphs were in the air, so to speak — and most of their appearances elsewhere were equally unserious. The source to which Pope refers, *Le Comte de Gabalis* (translated into English in 1680 and republished after *The Rape of the Lock* appeared), seems satiric from the start. Pope notes in his preface to Arabella that "both in its Title and Size [*Le Comte*] is so like a *Novel,* that many of the Fair Sex have read it for one by Mistake," and the excerpts from the 1714 edition included here show that in its sustained narrative, its details, and its narrator's manifest skepticism of the Rosicrucian spokesperson, it indeed masquerades as fiction.

The Rape of the Lock was in part shaped by the poetic conventions of its day, but it remains perennially magical because of its ability to employ classical models, strict metrical forms, and the small events of a local world to produce *visions,* to paint images from sound and sense, and thus preserve a vivid vision of that local world.

The Poet and the Poem

SAMUEL JOHNSON

From *The Lives of the Poets*

Samuel Johnson (1709–1784) was one of the greatest literary critics and innovators of the eighteenth century. Like Pope, he struggled with early difficulties — poverty, failure, and disfigurement — to make his way in the literary market. He achieved success with his couplet satire *London, A Poem, in Imitation of the Third Satire of Juvenal,* published in the first monthly magazine, *Gentleman's,* in 1738. Johnson's biographer, James Boswell (1740–1791), wrote of Pope's first impression of Johnson from this poem:

> Pope, who then filled the poetical throne without a rival, it may reasonably be presumed, must have been particularly struck by the sudden appearance of such a poet; and, to his credit, let it be remembered, that his feelings and conduct on the occasion were candid and liberal. He requested ... [a friend] to find out who this new authour was.... [After being informed] only that his name was Johnson, and that he

was some obscure man, Pope said, "he will soon be *déterré* [unearthed]" (92).

Johnson's reputation climbed steadily until it nearly eclipsed and certainly affected the literary reputations of all around him, including those of past and future writers. Johnson wrote short, powerful, elegant essays on manners and morals and literature in his *Rambler* and *Idler* series. He presented his *Dictionary* in 1755 (without the help of patrons, as his preface sharply notes), which, with its illustrations of English usage from British literature would eventually become the model for the *Oxford English Dictionary*. The novelistic philosophical tale *Rasselas* (the favorite book of Helen Burns in Charlotte Brontë's *Jane Eyre*) was published in 1759, and his edition of Shakespeare with a critical preface appeared in 1765. *The Lives of the Poets*, which included biographies of Abraham Cowley, John Milton, Jonathan Swift, and Thomas Gray, among others, was issued in 1781. Johnson was a powerful force in shaping the directions of English language and literatures.

The Lives of the Poets, from which the *Life of Pope* is excerpted here, is a historical contribution to biographical art, emphasizing what Johnson considers the importance of "invisible circumstance" over "public occurrences" in understanding the biographical subject. Johnson believes that "more knowledge may be gained of a man's real character by a short conversation with one of his servants, than from a formal and studied narrative, begun with his pedigree, and ended with his funeral . . . by placing us, for a time, in the condition of him whose fortune we contemplate" (*Rambler* 60). The following selection comes at the end of the *Life of Pope*, in which Johnson presents a "Character" of the poet — a psychological portrait pieced together from letters, anecdotes, and memories from Pope and his circle. Most of this information describes an older Pope than the man who wrote *The Rape of the Lock*, but as it was commonly believed in the eighteenth century that "the boy is the man in miniature" (Boswell 35), the final portrait of the man integrates the younger version. This biographical portrait takes us through the sensuality as well as the pain and difficulty of what Pope called "this long Disease, my Life" (*Epistle to Arbuthnot*, l. 132); his love of artifice and his love of sincerity; his conversation and his temper; his physical dependence and his financial independence; his frugality and his materialism; his letters and his self-knowledge; his sensitivity to criticism and his self-importance; his "narrow view" of the world and his large-souled friendships; his religion and his levity; his good sense and his genius. Its crowning sentence sums up Pope's ultimate relationship to his own life: "To make verses was his first labour, and to mend them was his last."

The person of Pope is well known not to have been formed by the nicest model. He has, in his account of the "Little Club,"[1] compared himself to a spider, and by another is described as protuberant behind and before. He is said to have been beautiful in his infancy; but he was of a constitution originally feeble and weak, and as bodies of a tender frame are easily distorted his deformity was probably in part the effect of his application.[2] His stature was so low that, to bring him to a level with common tables, it was necessary to raise his seat. But his face was not displeasing, and his eyes were animated and vivid.

By natural deformity or accidental distortion his vital functions were so much disordered that his life was a "long disease."[3] His most frequent assailant was the headache, which he used to relieve by inhaling the steam of coffee, which he very frequently required.

Most of what can be told concerning his petty peculiarities was communicated by a female domestick of the Earl of Oxford,[4] who knew him perhaps after the middle of life. He was then so weak as to stand in perpetual need of female attendance; extremely sensible of cold, so that he wore a kind of fur doublet under a shirt of very coarse warm linen with fine sleeves. When he rose he was invested in boddice[5] made of stiff canvass, being scarce able to hold himself erect till they were laced, and he then put on a flannel waistcoat. One side was contracted. His legs were so slender that he enlarged their bulk with three pair of stockings, which were drawn on and off by the maid; for he was not able to dress or undress himself, and neither went to bed nor rose without help. His weakness made it very difficult for him to be clean.

---

[1] *his account of the 'Little Club'*: See *Guardian* 92: "The figure of the man is odd enough; he is a lively little creature with long arms and legs; a spider is no ill emblem of him; he has been taken at a distance for a small windmill."

[2] *the effect of his application*: Johnson suggests that Pope's disfigurement was in part the result of his working too hard.

[3] *his life was a "long disease"*: See Pope's *Epistle to Arbuthnot*, l. 132.

[4] *the Earl of Oxford*: Robert Harley, first Earl of Oxford (1661–1724), was a Tory statesman, a booklover, a friend of Pope and Swift, and a member of the Scriblerus Club.

[5] *boddice*: A vest.

His hair had fallen almost all away, and he used to dine sometimes with Lord Oxford, privately, in a velvet cap. His dress of ceremony was black, with a tye-wig and a little sword.

The indulgence and accommodation which his sickness required had taught him all the unpleasing and unsocial qualities of a valetudinary man. He expected that every thing should give way to his ease or humour, as a child whose parents will not hear her cry has an unresisted dominion in the nursery.

> C'est que l'enfant toujours est homme,
> C'est que l'homme est toujours enfant.[6]

When he wanted to sleep he "nodded in company";[7] and once slumbered at his own table while the Prince of Wales was talking of poetry.

The reputation which his friendship gave procured him many invitations; but he was a very troublesome inmate. He brought no servant, and had so many wants that a numerous attendance was scarcely able to supply them. Wherever he was he left no room for another, because he exacted the attention and employed the activity of the whole family. His errands were so frequent and frivolous that the footmen in time avoided and neglected him, and the Earl of Oxford discharged some of the servants for their resolute refusal of his messages. The maids, when they had neglected their business, alleged that they had been employed by Mr. Pope. One of his constant demands was of coffee in the night, and to the woman that waited on him in his chamber he was very burthensome; but he was careful to recompense her want of sleep, and Lord Oxford's servant declared that in a house where her business was to answer his call she would not ask for wages.

He had another fault, easily incident to those who suffering much pain think themselves entitled to whatever pleasures they can snatch. He was too indulgent to his appetite: he loved meat highly seasoned and of strong taste, and, at the intervals of the table, amused himself with biscuits and dry conserves. If he sat down to a variety of dishes he would oppress his stomach with repletion, and though he seemed angry when a dram[8] was offered him, did not forbear to drink it. His

---

[6] *'C'est que l'enfant . . . est toujours enfant'*: "The child is always a man, / The man is always a child."

[7] *he "nodded in company"*: See Pope's *Imitations of Horace, Satires* II.i.13: "I nod in company, I wake at night, / Fools rush into my head, and so I write."

[8] *dram*: A small draft of liquor.

friends, who knew the avenues to his heart, pampered him with presents of luxury, which he did not suffer to stand neglected. The death of great men is not always proportioned to the lustre of their lives. Hannibal, says Juvenal, did not perish by a javelin or a sword; the slaughters of Cannæ were revenged by a ring.[9] The death of Pope was imputed by some of his friends to a silver saucepan, in which it was his delight to heat potted lampreys.[10]

That he loved too well to eat is certain; but that his sensuality shortened his life will not be hastily concluded when it is remembered that a conformation so irregular lasted six and fifty years, notwithstanding such pertinacious diligence of study and meditation.

In all his intercourse with mankind he had great delight in artifice, and endeavoured to attain all his purposes by indirect and unsuspected methods. "He hardly drank tea without a stratagem."[11] If at the house of his friends he wanted any accommodation he was not willing to ask for it in plain terms, but would mention it remotely as something convenient; though, when it was procured, he soon made it appear for whose sake it had been recommended. Thus he teized Lord Orrery[12] till he obtained a screen. He practised his arts on such small occasions that Lady Bolingbroke used to say, in a French phrase, that "he plaid the politician about cabbages and turnips." His unjustifiable impression of *The Patriot King*, as it can be imputed to no particular motive, must have proceeded from his general habit of secrecy and cunning: he caught an opportunity of a sly trick, and pleased himself with the thought of outwitting Bolingbroke.[13]

In familiar or convivial conversation it does not appear that he excelled. He may be said to have resembled Dryden,[14] as being not one

[9] *Hannibal . . . revenged by a ring:* Hannibal's greatest victory over the Romans was at Cannae in 216 B.C.; in the end Hannibal committed suicide with poison hidden in a ring (Juvenal, *Satires* X.163–66).

[10] *potted lampreys:* Deviled, eel-like fish.

[11] *"He hardly drank tea without a stratagem":* Paraphrases a line in Edward Young's *Love of Fame, the Universal Fashion: Satire VI, On Women* (1728): "Nor take her tea without a stratagem" (l. 188).

[12] *Lord Orrery:* John Boyle, fifth Earl of Orrery (1707–1762), close friend of Pope, Swift, and Johnson; the demanded screen would protect Pope from the heat of the fire.

[13] *Bolingbroke:* Henry St. John, first Viscount Bolingbroke (1678–1751), was a powerful Tory statesman until Anne's death in 1713, after which he lived in exile in France until 1725. Pope's *Essay on Man* (1734) was inspired, at least in part, by Bolingbroke's classical republican/civic humanist philosophy of cultivating the public virtues of prudence, eloquence, liberty. Bolingbroke retired again to France in 1735 and wrote *The Idea of a Patriot King* in 1738, of which Pope published an unauthorized version.

[14] *Dryden:* John Dryden (1631–1700), poet, critic, and playwright; this one-time poet laureate was Pope's most immediate literary influence.

that was distinguished by vivacity in company. It is remarkable that, so near his time, so much should be known of what he has written, and so little of what he has said: traditional memory retains no sallies of raillery nor sentences of observation; nothing either pointed or solid, either wise or merry. One apophthegm only stands upon record. When an objection raised against his inscription for Shakespeare was defended by the authority of Patrick,[15] he replied — "horresco referens"[16] — that "he would allow the publisher of a Dictionary to know the meaning of a single word, but not of two words put together."

He was fretful and easily displeased, and allowed himself to be capriciously resentful. He would sometimes leave Lord Oxford silently, no one could tell why, and was to be courted back by more letters and messages than the footmen were willing to carry. The table was indeed infested by Lady Mary Wortley,[17] who was the friend of Lady Oxford, and who, knowing his peevishness, could by no intreaties be restrained from contradicting him, till their disputes were sharpened to such asperity that one or the other quitted the house.

He sometimes condescended to be jocular with servants or inferiors; but by no merriment, either of others or his own, was he ever seen excited to laughter.

Of his domestick character frugality was a part eminently remarkable. Having determined not to be dependent he determined not to be in want, and therefore wisely and magnanimously rejected all temptations to expence unsuitable to his fortune. This general care must be universally approved; but it sometimes appeared in petty artifices of parsimony, such as the practice of writing his compositions on the back of letters, as may be seen in the remaining copy of the *Iliad*, by which perhaps in five years five shillings were saved; or in a niggardly reception of his friends and scantiness of entertainment, as when he had two guests in his house he would set at supper a single pint upon the table, and having himself taken two small glasses would retire and say, "Gentlemen, I leave you to your wine." Yet he tells his

---

[15] *the authority of Patrick:* Samuel Patrick (1684–1748) was a classical scholar and lexicographer.

[16] *"horresco referens":* "I shudder in speaking of it" (*Aeneid* II.204). (Remember that Johnson was also a "dictionateur.")

[17] *Lady Mary Wortley:* Lady Mary Wortley Montagu (1689–1762), woman of letters and first friend, then enemy, of Pope; see the Introduction.

friends that "he has a heart for all, a house for all, and, whatever they may think, a fortune for all."[18]

He sometimes, however, made a splendid dinner, and is said to have wanted no part of the skill or elegance which such performances require. That this magnificence should be often displayed, that obstinate prudence with which he conducted his affairs would not permit; for his revenue, certain and casual, amounted only to about eight hundred pounds a year, of which, however, he declares himself able to assign one hundred to charity.

Of this fortune, which as it arose from publick approbation was very honourably obtained, his imagination seems to have been too full: it would be hard to find a man, so well entitled to notice by his wit, that ever delighted so much in talking of his money. In his Letters and in his Poems, his garden and his grotto, his quincunx[19] and his vines, or some hints of his opulence, are always to be found. The great topick of his ridicule is poverty: the crimes with which he reproaches his antagonists are their debts, their habitation in the Mint,[20] and their want of a dinner. He seems to be of an opinion, not very uncommon in the world, that to want money is to want every thing.

Next to the pleasure of contemplating his possessions seems to be that of enumerating the men of high rank with whom he was acquainted, and whose notice he loudly proclaims not to have been obtained by any practices of meanness or servility; a boast which was never denied to be true, and to which very few poets have ever aspired. Pope never set genius to sale: he never flattered those whom he did not love, or praised those whom he did not esteem. Savage,[21] however, remarked that he began a little to relax his dignity when he wrote a distich for "his Highness's dog."[22]

His admiration of the Great seems to have increased in the advance of life. He passed over peers and statesmen to inscribe his *Iliad*

[18] *"he has a heart . . . a fortune for all"*: Letter to Swift, March 23, 1737.

[19] *quincunx*: In a garden or landscape, the arrangement of five trees: one on each of the four corners and one in the center.

[20] *the Mint*: A district across the Thames from London, in Southwark, where debtors were protected from arrest.

[21] *Savage*: Richard Savage (1697?–1743), playwright and poet. Johnson published a *Life of Savage* and reprinted it in *Lives of the Poets*.

[22] *"his Highness's dog"*: "I am his Highness' dog at Kew; / Pray tell me, sir, whose dog are you?" Pope composed these lines for the collar of the dog of Frederick, Prince of Wales.

to Congreve,[23] with a magnanimity of which the praise had been compleat, had his friend's virtue been equal to his wit. Why he was chosen for so great an honour it is not now possible to know; there is no trace in literary history of any particular intimacy between them. The name of Congreve appears in the Letters among those of his other friends, but without any observable distinction or consequence.

To his latter works, however, he took care to annex names dignified with titles, but was not very happy in his choice; for, except Lord Bathurst,[24] none of his noble friends were such as that a good man would wish to have his intimacy with them known to posterity: he can derive little honour from the notice of Cobham, Burlington, or Bolingbroke.[25]

Of his social qualities, if an estimate be made from his Letters, an opinion too favourable cannot easily be formed; they exhibit a perpetual and unclouded effulgence of general benevolence and particular fondness. There is nothing but liberality, gratitude, constancy, and tenderness. It has been so long said as to be commonly believed that the true characters of men may be found in their letters, and that he who writes to his friend lays his heart open before him. But the truth is that such were simple friendships of the *Golden Age*, and are now the friendships only of children. Very few can boast of hearts which they dare lay open to themselves, and of which, by whatever accident exposed, they do not shun a distinct and continued view; and certainly what we hide from ourselves we do not shew to our friends. There is, indeed, no transaction which offers stronger temptations to fallacy and sophistication than epistolary intercourse. In the eagerness of conversation the first emotions of the mind often burst out before they are considered; in the tumult of business interest and passion have their genuine effect; but a friendly letter is a calm and

---

[23] *Congreve:* William Congreve (1670–1729), poet and playwright; see the Introduction.

[24] *Lord Bathurst:* Allen Bathurst (1685–1775), Tory politician, was made Baron Bathurst in 1712; he was a lifelong friend of Pope as well as of Congreve, Swift, and Prior, and an enthusiastic gardener. Pope's third *Moral Essay* is the *Epistle III. To Allen Lord Bathurst* (1733), "Of the Use of Riches."

[25] *Cobham, Burlington, or Bolingbroke:* Sir Richard Temple, Viscount Cobham (1675–1749), was a general whose estate, Stowe, was famous for its gardens. Richard Boyle, third Earl of Burlington and fourth Earl of Cork (1695–1753), was influential in promoting Palladian architecture; *Epistle IV* of the *Moral Essays* (the *Epistle to Burlington*, 1731), is also "Of the Use of Riches" in the areas of architecture and gardening. See note 13 for Bolingbroke. Johnson did not approve of the moral character or political beliefs of these three prominent friends of Pope's.

deliberate performance in the cool of leisure, in the stillness of soli-
tude, and surely no man sits down to depreciate by design his own
character.

Friendship has no tendency to secure veracity, for by whom can a
man so much wish to be thought better than he is as by him whose
kindness he desires to gain or keep? Even in writing to the world
there is less constraint: the author is not confronted with his reader,
and takes his chance of approbation among the different dispositions
of mankind; but a letter is addressed to a single mind of which the
prejudices and partialities are known, and must therefore please, if
not by favouring them, by forbearing to oppose them.

To charge those favourable representations, which men give of
their own minds, with the guilt of hypocritical falsehood, would shew
more severity than knowledge. The writer commonly believes him-
self. Almost every man's thoughts, while they are general, are right;
and most hearts are pure while temptation is away. It is easy to
awaken generous sentiments in privacy; to despise death when there
is no danger; to glow with benevolence when there is nothing to be
given. While such ideas are formed they are felt, and self-love does
not suspect the gleam of virtue to be the meteor of fancy.

If the Letters of Pope are considered merely as compositions they
seem to be premeditated and artificial. It is one thing to write because
there is something which the mind wishes to discharge, and another
to solicit the imagination because ceremony or vanity requires some-
thing to be written. Pope confesses his early letters to be vitiated with
"affectation and ambition":[26] to know whether he disentangled him-
self from these perverters of epistolary integrity his book and his life
must be set in comparison.

One of his favourite topicks is contempt of his own poetry. For
this, if it had been real, he would deserve no commendation, and in
this he certainly was not sincere; for his high value of himself was suf-
ficiently observed, and of what could he be proud but of his poetry?
He writes, he says, when "he has just nothing else to do":[27] yet Swift
complains that he was never at leisure for conversation because he
"had always some poetical scheme in his head."[28] It was punctually
required that his writing-box should be set upon his bed before he

---

[26] *"affectation and ambition"*: Pope's preface to his *Letters* (1737).

[27] *"he has just nothing else to do"*: Pope's preface to his *Works* (1717).

[28] *"had always some poetical scheme in his head"*: Swift to Mary Caesar, July 30,
1733.

rose; and Lord Oxford's domestick related that, in the dreadful winter of Forty,[29] she was called from her bed by him four times in one night to supply him with paper, lest he should lose a thought.

He pretends insensibility to censure and criticism, though it was observed by all who knew him that every pamphlet disturbed his quiet, and that his extreme irritability laid him open to perpetual vexation; but he wished to despise his cricks, and therefore hoped that he did despise them.

As he happened to live in two reigns when the Court paid little attention to poetry he nursed in his mind a foolish disesteem of Kings, and proclaims that 'he never sees Courts.'[30] Yet a little regard shewn him by the Prince of Wales melted his obduracy, and he had not much to say when he was asked by his Royal Highness "how he could love a Prince while he disliked Kings."[31]

He very frequently professes contempt of the world, and represents himself as looking on mankind, sometimes with gay indifference, as on emmets of a hillock[32] below his serious attention, and sometimes with gloomy indignation, as on monsters more worthy of hatred than of pity. These were dispositions apparently counterfeited. How could he despise those whom he lived by pleasing, and on whose approbation his esteem of himself was superstructed? Why should he hate those to whose favour he owed his honour and his ease? Of things that terminate in human life the world is the proper judge: to despise its sentence, if it were possible, is not just; and if it were just is not possible. Pope was far enough from this unreasonable temper; he was sufficiently "a fool to Fame,"[33] and his fault was that he pretended to neglect it. His levity and his sullenness were only in his letters; he passed through common life, sometimes vexed and sometimes pleased, with the natural emotions of common men.

His scorn of the Great is repeated too often to be real: no man thinks much of that which he despises; and as falsehood is always in danger of inconsistency he makes it his boast at another time that he lives among them.

---

[29] *the dreadful winter of Forty:* The winter of 1740 was so cold that the Thames froze.

[30] *"he never sees Courts":* Pope to Swift, January 1728.

[31] *"how he could love a Prince while he disliked Kings":* Owen Ruffhead, *The Life of Alexander Pope* (1769), 535.

[32] *emmets of a hillock:* Ants on a small hill.

[33] *"a fool to Fame":* Epistle to Arbuthnot, l. 127.

It is evident that his own importance swells often in his mind. He is afraid of writing lest the clerks of the Post-office should know his secrets; he has many enemies; he considers himself as surrounded by universal jealousy; "after many deaths, and many dispersions, two or three of us," says he, "may still be brought together, not to plot, but to divert ourselves, and the world too, if it pleases"; and they can live together, and "shew what friends wits may be, in spite of all the fools in the world."[34] All this while it was likely that the clerks did not know his hand: he certainly had no more enemies than a publick character like his inevitably excites, and with what degree of friendship the wits might live very few were so much fools as ever to enquire.

Some part of this pretended discontent he learned from Swift, and expresses it, I think, most frequently in his correspondence with him. Swift's resentment was unreasonable, but it was sincere; Pope's was the mere mimickry of his friend, a fictitious part which he began to play before it became him. When he was only twenty-five years old he related that "a glut of study and retirement had thrown him on the world," and that there was danger lest "a glut of the world should throw him back upon study and retirement."[35] To this Swift answered with great propriety that Pope had not yet either acted or suffered enough in the world to have become weary of it. And, indeed, it must be some very powerful reason that can drive back to solitude him who has once enjoyed the pleasures of society.

In the letters both of Swift and Pope there appears such narrowness of mind as makes them insensible of any excellence that has not some affinity with their own, and confines their esteem and approbation to so small a number, that whoever should form his opinion of the age from their representation would suppose them to have lived amidst ignorance and barbarity, unable to find among their contemporaries either virtue or intelligence, and persecuted by those that could not understand them.

When Pope murmurs at the world, when he professes contempt of fame, when he speaks of riches and poverty, of success and disappointment, with negligent indifference, he certainly does not express his habitual and settled sentiments, but either wilfully disguises his own character, or, what is more likely, invests himself with tempo-

---

[34] *"after many deaths, . . . fools in the world"*: Pope to Swift, September 14, 1725, and March 23, 1737.
[35] *"a glut of study . . . study and retirement"*: Pope to Swift, August 1723.

rary qualities, and sallies out in the colours of the present moment. His hopes and fears, his joys and sorrows, acted strongly upon his mind, and if he differed from others it was not by carelessness. He was irritable and resentful: his malignity to Philips, whom he had first made ridiculous, and then hated for being angry, continued too long. Of his vain desire to make Bentley contemptible, I never heard any adequate reason. He was sometimes wanton in his attacks, and before Chandos, Lady Wortley, and Hill, was mean in his retreat.[36]

The virtues which seem to have had most of his affection were liberality and fidelity of friendship, in which it does not appear that he was other than he describes himself. His fortune did not suffer his charity to be splendid and conspicuous, but he assisted Dodsley[37] with a hundred pounds that he might open a shop; and of the subscription of forty pounds a year that he raised for Savage twenty were paid by himself. He was accused of loving money, but his love was eagerness to gain, not solicitude to keep it.

In the duties of friendship he was zealous and constant: his early maturity of mind commonly united him with men older than himself, and therefore, without attaining any considerable length of life, he saw many companions of his youth sink into the grave; but it does not appear that he lost a single friend by coldness or by injury: those who loved him once continued their kindness. His ungrateful mention of Allen[38] in his will was the effect of his adherence to one whom he had known much longer, and whom he naturally loved with greater fondness. His violation of the trust reposed in him by Bolingbroke could have no motive inconsistent with the warmest affection;

[36] *He was irritable and resentful: . . . mean in his retreat:* Ambrose Philips (1675?–1749), pastoral poet, contemptuously called "Namby Pamby"; Richard Bentley (1662–1742), great classical scholar who apparently didn't fully appreciate Pope's *Iliad;* James Brydges, Duke of Chandos, whose estate, Cannons, was believed by some to be satirized as Timon's Villa in *Epistle to Burlington;* Lady Mary Wortley Montagu, see note 17; Aaron Hill (1685–1750), poet, playwright, and theater manager, satirized (along with all of the above) in the *Dunciad.*

[37] *Dodsley:* Robert Dodsley (1703–1764) wrote several poems while a footman; Pope helped him to set up as a bookseller in 1735; he is chiefly remembered as the publisher of works by Pope, Johnson, Edward Young, Oliver Goldsmith, and Thomas Gray.

[38] *Allen:* Ralph Allen (1694–1764), generally loved for his benevolence; the model for Squire Allworthy in Henry Fielding's *Tom Jones* (1749). In later visits to Allen with Martha Blount, Pope felt she was badly treated; "a clause in Pope's Will bequeathing Allen £150 — 'being to the best of my Calculation, the Account of what I have received from him; partly for my own, and partly for Charitable Uses' — may show that Pope's sense of the discourtesies suffered by Martha Blount had not quite been assuaged" (Mack 768).

he either thought the action so near to indifferent that he forgot it, or so laudable that he expected his friend to approve it.

It was reported, with such confidence as almost to enforce belief, that in the papers intrusted to his executors was found a defamatory *Life of Swift*, which he had prepared as an instrument of vengeance to be used, if any provocation should be ever given. About this I enquired of the Earl of Marchmont,[39] who assured me that no such piece was among his remains.

The religion in which he lived and died was that of the Church of Rome, to which in his correspondence with Racine[40] he professes himself a sincere adherent. That he was not scrupulously pious in some part of his life is known by many idle and indecent applications of sentences taken from the Scriptures; a mode of merriment which a good man dreads for its profaneness, and a witty man disdains for its easiness and vulgarity. But to whatever levities he has been betrayed, it does not appear that his principles were ever corrupted, or that he ever lost his belief of Revelation. The positions which he transmitted from Bolingbroke he seems not to have understood, and was pleased with an interpretation that made them orthodox.

A man of such exalted superiority and so little moderation would naturally have all his delinquences observed and aggravated: those who could not deny that he was excellent would rejoice to find that he was not perfect.

Perhaps it may be imputed to the unwillingness with which the same man is allowed to possess many advantages that his learning has been depreciated. He certainly was in his early life a man of great literary curiosity, and when he wrote his *Essay on Criticism* had for his age a very wide acquaintance with books. When he entered into the living world it seems to have happened to him as to many others that he was less attentive to dead masters: he studied in the academy of Paracelsus,[41] and made the universe his favourite volume. He gathered his notions fresh from reality, not from the copies of authors, but the originals of Nature. Yet there is no reason to believe that literature ever lost his esteem; he always professed to love reading, and Dobson, who spent some time at his house translating his *Essay on Man*, when I asked him what learning he found him to possess, answered, "More than I expected." His

---

[39] *Earl of Marchmont:* Hugh Hume, third Earl of Marchmont (1708–1774), one of Pope's closest friends and an executor of his estate.

[40] *Racine:* Pope to Louis Racine, September 1, 1742.

[41] *Paracelsus:* Theophrast Bombast Von Hohenheim (1493–1541), physician and alchemist.

frequent references to history, his allusions to various kinds of knowledge, and his images selected from art and nature, with his observations on the operations of the mind and the modes of life, shew an intelligence perpetually on the wing, excursive, vigorous, and diligent, eager to pursue knowledge, and attentive to retain it.

From this curiosity arose the desire of travelling, to which he alludes in his verses to Jervas,[42] and which, though he never found an opportunity to gratify it, did not leave him till his life declined.

Of his intellectual character the constituent and fundamental principle was Good Sense, a prompt and intuitive perception of consonance and propriety. He saw immediately, of his own conceptions, what was to be chosen, and what to be rejected; and, in the works of others, what was to be shunned, and what to be copied.

But good sense alone is a sedate and quiescent quality, which manages its possessions well, but does not increase them; it collects few materials for its own operations, and preserves safety, but never gains supremacy. Pope had likewise genius; a mind active, ambitious, and adventurous, always investigating, always aspiring; in its widest searches still longing to go forward, in its highest flights still wishing to be higher; always imagining something greater than it knows, always endeavouring more than it can do.

To assist these powers he is said to have had great strength and exactness of memory. That which he had heard or read was not easily lost; and he had before him not only what his own meditation suggested, but what he had found in other writers that might be accommodated to his present purpose.

These benefits of nature he improved by incessant and unwearied diligence; he had recourse to every source of intelligence, and lost no opportunity of information; he consulted the living as well as the dead; he read his compositions to his friends, and was never content with mediocrity when excellence could be attained. He considered poetry as the business of his life, and, however he might seem to lament his occupation, he followed it with constancy: to make verses was his first labour, and to mend them was his last.

[42] *Jervas:* Charles Jervas (1675?–1739), a pupil of Sir Godfrey Kneller (see the portrait of Lady Mary Wortley Montagu in "Poetic Forms") was for a time a prominent painter in London, whom Steele in *The Tatler* called, with exaggerated justice, "the last great painter Italy has sent us." In 1722 he became King's Painter to George I and then to George II. In March 1713 Pope "learned to draw of Jervas" (Spence 1:46), and continued his lessons for about twelve months. They became friends, and Pope stayed with Jervas on his frequent visits to London between 1713 and 1727.

ALEXANDER POPE

From *The Correspondence of Alexander Pope*

The following selections from Pope's *Correspondence* (1707–1717) showcase different aspects of a carefully self-edited portrait of a young man and a young poet. The March 25, 1705, letter to the elderly playwright William Wycherley humbly thanks this early mentor for his advice and encouragement. Wycherley would respond with a generous enthusiasm that justified Pope's pride in the recognition. A letter to his friend Henry Cromwell (not included here) — an older, lighthearted, dandified man-about-town, but also a critic — describes the early, pleasant pattern of his days, each of which has "the same Business, which is Poetry; and the same Pleasure, which is Idleness." In a January 25, 1711, letter to John Caryll, another older friend with whom he corresponded for over twenty years (and who entreated Pope to write the *Rape*), he reveals a bit more: He is increasingly aware of the widening gap between "the great Alexander Mr Caryll is so civil to" and "that little Alexander the women laugh at." The letter to Joseph Addison (December 14, 1713) is wonderfully vivid on the power of imagination; it is also, almost verbatim, a version of a letter he sent to Caryll the previous August, an example of Pope "revising" the history and shape of his original correspondence into a more impressive and coherent version for publication. The short, bawdy letter to Teresa Blount in 1716 about two lovers killed in a storm contrasts with the longer, romantic version of the same episode he sent to Lady Mary Wortley Montagu, in Turkey with her ambassador husband. This selection closes with her reply. Note the contrast between the way Pope would seem to open up his soul to Lady Mary, falling in love with her as if through the imaginative power of his own letters, and how crisply and unsentimentally she could answer back, refusing to play the game of epistolary gallantry.

Although Pope crafted his letters with publication in mind, and sometimes later altered their order or addressee, this should not obscure or undermine the often painful sincerity of these letters. His need to revise his letters corresponds to his urgent need to revise his world into something that could accommodate Pope the man as well as Pope the poet — into something as beautiful and powerful as *The Rape of the Lock*, in which the poet alone determines and records the final fates.

The text of the letters is taken from Volume I of *The Correspondence of Alexander Pope*, edited by George Sherburn (Oxford: Clarendon Press, 1956). We have reproduced the letters as Sherburn's scholarly care reconstructed them from Pope's various revisions for publication, omitting the brackets and half-brackets that indicate the various uncertainties or alterations. Also omitted are the locations of the manuscript letters. The student interested in the precise text of the letters at their different stages should consult Sherburn's edition. Notes taken from the *Correspondence* are cited [C].

Pope to Wycherley[1]

March 25, 1705.

When I write to you, I foresee a long Letter, and ought to beg your Patience beforehand; for if it proves the longest, it will be of course the worst I have troubled you with. Yet to express my Gratitude at large for your obliging Letter, is not more my Duty than my Interest; as some People will abundantly thank you for one Piece of Kindness, to put you in mind of bestowing another. The more favourable you are to me, the more distinctly I see my Faults; Spots and Blemishes you know, are never so plainly discover'd as in the brightest Sunshine. Thus, I am mortified by those Commendations which were design'd to encourage me: for Praise to a young Wit, is like Rain to a tender Flower; if it be moderately bestow'd, it chears and revives, but if too lavishly, overcharges and depresses him. Most Men in years, as they are generally discouragers of Youth, are like old Trees, that being past Bearing themselves, will suffer no young Plants to flourish beneath them: But as if it were not enough to have out-done all your Coævals in Wit, you will excel them in good Nature too. As for my green Essays,[2] if you find any pleasure in 'em, it must be such as a Man naturally takes in observing the first Shoots and Buddings of a Tree which he has rais'd himself: and 'tis impossible they should be esteem'd any otherwise, than as we value Fruits for being early, which nevertheless are the most insipid, and the worst of the Year. In a word, I must blame you for treating me with so much Compliment, which is at best but the Smoak of Friendship. I neither write, nor converse with you, to gain your Praise but your Affection. Be so much my Friend as to appear my Enemy, and tell me my Faults, if not as a young Man, at least as an unexperienc'd Writer.

I am, &c.

---

[1] *Wycherley:* William Wycherley (1641–1715), Restoration dramatist and leader of the literary circle at Will's coffee house. His two most popular plays (he only wrote four) were *The Country Wife* (1675) and *The Plain Dealer* (1676).

[2] *my green Essays:* Pope's *Pastorals*, which Wycherley praised and which Pope would publish in 1709.

Pope to Caryll

Jany. the 25. 1710/11.

Sir, — In a letter that abounds with so much wit as yours, nothing can be more pleasant than to hear you disclaiming all pretensions to it, like Ovid protesting in very good verse that he would never versify. But some people are so given to say witty things, that, like those who are given to swearing, they never know when they do it. And men that have a great deal of ready wit, like those that have a great deal of ready money, bestow it up and down in a careless manner, and never think they have given away much, because they find their heads and their pockets are full again the next morning. So true it is that 'tis with one that has wit always about him, as with one that constantly carries perfumes: he is not sensible himself of that which delights all besides.

To own the Truth, it was not without a design that I sent you the verses you are pleased to mention so kindly: I meant to give you an opportunity of returning good for evil, in favoring me with a sight of some of yours, for if I made any doubt that you write sometimes, I should hardly have troubled you with what I writ, as not much caring to reveal my poetical sins, but as other sinners commonly do theirs, to those who are equally guilty. As for my verses I may truly say they have never been the cause of any great vanity in me, excepting that they gave me in occasioning my first acquaintance and correspondence with you. Since when indeed I've been often in danger of being notably tainted with this vice, but never more than when I read your last letter. 'Tis certain the greatest magnifying glasses in the world are a mans own eyes, when they look upon his own person; yet even in those, I appear not the great Alexander Mr. Caryll is so civil to, but that little Alexander the women laugh at. But if I must be like Alexander, 'tis in being complimented into too good an opinion of my self: they made him think he was the son of Jupiter, and you persuade me I am a man of parts. Alas, Sir! is this all you can say in my honour? you said ten times as much before, when you called me your friend. After having made me believe I possess a share in your affection, to treat me with compliments and sweet sayings, is just like the proceeding with Sancho Pança;[3] first they put it into the poor fellow's head that he enjoyed a vast dominion, and then gave him nothing to

---

[3] *Sancho Pança:* Sancho Panza, the rustic squire who accompanies gentle, chivalric, delusionary Don Quixote in his travels in Cervantes's satirical romance *Don Quixote de la Mancha* (1605, 1615).

subsist upon but a few wafers and marmalade. I fear you observed with what greediness I swallowed whipt syllabubs[4] at your house a year ago? But I have something more to tell you out of Don Quixote. There was once a certain person in Seville who had a very dexterous knack at blowing up young puppies. He made use of your own instrument, a quill, which he clapt to their tails, and puffed 'em up as round as a bladder; then he would ask the standers-by, what think you, gentlemen? is it such an easy matter to blow up a puppy dog? Now to judge impartially betwixt the whelp and the poet, it is a much harder matter to puff up the cur than the creature, and therefore tho' your operation be very like this Spaniard's, you ought not to value yourself so much on the performance. But indeed tho' it be an easy thing enough to make a dull scribbler proud, yet to commend such an one well, is extremely hard, and in this (if you will needs be compared to a quack) you are like him that put into his bills — 'Let no man be discourag'd, for this doctor is one that delighteth much in matters of difficulty.' Yet, after all, a man is certainly obliged to any one who can make him vain of himself, since at the same time he makes him satisfied with himself; so nowadays the greatest obligation you can lay upon a wit, is to make a Fool of him. For as when madmen are found incurable, wise men give 'em their way, and please 'em as well as they can; so when those more incorrigible things, poets, are once irrecoverably be-mused, the best way both to quiet them, and to secure ourselves from the effects of their frenzy, is to feed their vanity, which indeed for the most part is all that's overfed in a poet.

But you have taken care I should not have this at least to complain of, by the kind present you sent me; without which, had I kept Lent here, I must have submitted to the common fate of my brethren, and have starved: yet I should (I think) have been the first poet that ever starved for the sake of religion. Now as your lady is pleased to say of my present, that St Luke himself never drew such a Madonna;[5] so I may say of yours, that the prince of the apostles himself, tho' he was a fisherman all his life, never eat so good oysters. And as she tells me that I did a thing I never thought of, and excelled a saint, I may tell you that you have done a thing you was not aware of, and reclaimed a sinner; for you'll be the cause that I shall obey a precept of the Church, and fast this Lent, which I have not done many years before.

---

[4] *syllabubs:* Desserts of sweetened curdled cream.
[5] *St Luke himself never drew such a Madonna:* "This remark shows that Pope was at this time making presents of his own pictures" [C].

Which (with my hearty thanks) is all I can say on this subject, for I
find upon scratching my head three times, that 'tis not so hard to get
pearls out of oysters, as wit.

I have been full an hour upon this foolish letter already, which was
only intended to bear off your compliments, and does not pretend to
return them. I do but parry your thrusts; I can't hope to hit you. Be-
sides I am unwilling to make tautologies after all the world, as I must,
if I should speak of Mr. Caryll. Sir, you may believe me, I could be
heartily glad all you say were as true applied to me, as it would be if
addressed to yourself: and you need not doubt but I wish I were every
way as good a man as you, for several weighty reasons; but for none
more than that I might have sense enough to honour you as much as
you deserve, whereas as it is, I can do it no more than is consistent
with the mean, tho' utmost capacity of

> Sir,
> Your most obliged and affectionate
> humble servant
> A: Pope

Pope to Addison[6]

Dec. 14, 1713.

I have been lying in wait for my own imagination, this week and
more, and watching what thoughts came up in the whirl of the fancy,
that were worth communicating to you in a letter. But I am at length
convinc'd that my rambling head can produce nothing of that sort; so
I must e'en be contented with telling you the old story, that I love you
heartily. I have often found by experience, that nature and truth, tho'
never so low or vulgar, are yet pleasing when openly and artlessly
represented; it would be diverting to me, to read the very letters of an
infant, could it write its innocent inconsistencies and tautologies just
as it thought 'em. This makes me hope a letter from me will not be
unwelcome to you, when I am conscious I write with more unre-
servedness than ever man wrote, or perhaps talk'd to another. I trust
your good nature with the whole range of my follies, and really love
you so well, that I would rather you should pardon me than esteem

---

[6] *Addison:* Joseph Addison (1672–1719), with Richard Steele, creator of the *Spec-
tator* and *Tatler* periodicals and center of the Whig literary establishment at Button's
coffee house. This letter is a very slightly altered version of one sent to John Caryll
dated August 14, 1713.

me, since one is an act of goodness and benevolence, the other a kind of constrain'd deference.

You can't wonder my thoughts are scarce consistent, when I tell you how they are distracted. Ev'ry hour of my life, my mind is strangely divided; this minute perhaps I am above the stars, with a thousand systems round about me, looking forward into a vast Abyss, and losing my whole comprehension in the boundless space of creation, in dialogues with W—— and the Astronomers; the next moment I am below all trifles, groveling with T—— in the very center of nonsense. Now I am recreated with the brisk sallies and quick turns of wit, which Mr. *Steele* in his liveliest and freest humours darts about him; and now levelling my application to the insignificant observations and quirks of *Grammar* of Mr. —— and D——.[7]

Good God! What an incongruous animal is Man? how unsettled in his best part, his Soul; and how changing and variable in his frame of Body? The constancy of the one shook by every Notion, the temperament of the other affected by every blast of wind! What is Man altogether, but one mighty Inconsistency! Sickness and Pain is the lot of one half of us; Doubt and Fear the portion of the other! What a bustle we make about passing our time, when all our space is but a point? What aims and ambitions are crowded into this little instant of our life, which (as *Shakespear* finely words it) is *Rounded with a Sleep*? Our whole extent of Being no more, in the eyes of him who gave it, than a scarce perceptible moment of duration. Those animals whose circle of living is limited to three or four hours, as the Naturalists assure us, are yet as long-lived and possess as wide a scene of action as man, if we consider him with an eye to all Space, and all Eternity. Who knows what plots, what atchievements a mite may perform in his kingdom of a grain of dust, within his life of some minutes? and of how much less consideration than even this, is the life of man in the sight of that God, who is from Ever, and for Ever!

Who that thinks in this train, but must see the world and its contemptible grandeurs lessen before him at every thought? 'Tis enough to make one remain stupify'd, in a poize of inaction, void of all desires, of all designs, of all friendships.

---

[7] *dialogues with W—— ... Mr. —— and D——*: See Sherburn's notes for the various possibilities for filling in the names; none is directly important for our purposes, although "D——" is the Dennis (in the letter to Caryll) who had quickly pounced on Pope after the publication of the *Rape* (see headnote to Dennis's "A True Character of Mr. Pope," p. 197).

But we must return (thro' our very condition of being) to our nar-
row selves, and those things that affect our selves: our passions, our
interests, flow in upon us, and unphilosophize us into meer mortals.
For my part I never return so much into my self, as when I think of
you, whose friendship is one of the best comforts I have for the in-
significancy of my self. I am

Your, &c.

Pope to Teresa Blount[8]

Madam. Since you prefer three hundred pound to two true Lovers,
I presume to send you the following Epitaph upon them, which seems
to be written by one of your Taste.

> Here lye two poor Lovers, who had the mishap
> Tho very chaste people, to die of a Clap.

I hope Miss Patty will not so much as smile at this: if she does, she
may know, she has less pity than I.

I hope you have had (with this) 4 letters from me. Don't I write
often enough?

Pope to Lady Mary Wortley Montagu[9]

August the 18th [1716]

Madam, — I can say little to recommend the Letters I am begin-
ning to write to you, but that they will be the most impartial Repre-
sentations of a free heart, and the truest Copies you ever saw, tho' of
a very mean Original. Not a feature will be soften'd, or any advanta-
geous Light employd to make the Ugly thing a little less hideous, but
you shall find it in all respects most Horribly Like. You will do me an
injustice if you look upon any thing I shall say from this instant as a
Compliment either to you or to myself: whatever I write will be the
real Thought of that hour, and I know you'll no more expect it of me
to persevere till Death in every Sentiment or notion I now sett down,

---

[8] *Teresa Blount:* One of the two sisters with whom Pope was very close — and
perhaps in love — in these early years. Teresa seems to have been the more flirtatious
of the two, Martha (Patty) the quieter; Pope's epistolary manner was accordingly dif-
ferent with each.

[9] *Lady Mary Wortley Montagu:* Lady Mary Wortley Montagu (1689–1762),
woman of letters and first friend, then enemy, of Pope; see the Introduction. At the
time of this letter, Lady Mary had departed for Turkey with her ambassador husband.

than you would imagine a man's Face should never change after his picture was once drawn.

The freedome I shall use in this manner of Thinking aloud (as somebody calls it) or Talking upon paper, may indeed prove me a fool, but it will prove me one of the best sort of fools, the honest ones. And since what Folly we have will infallibly Buoy up at one time or other, in spite of all our art to keep it down; tis almost foolish to take any pains to conceal it at all, and almost knavish to do it from those that are our friends. If Momus his project had taken of having Windows in our breasts,[10] I should be for carrying it further and making those windows Casements: that while a Man showd his Heart to all the world, he might do something more for his friends, e'en take it out, and trust it to their handling. I think I love you as well as King Herod could Herodias, (tho I never had so much as one Dance with you) and would as freely give you my heart in a Dish, as he did another's head.[11] But since Jupiter will not have it so, I must be content to show my taste in Life as I do my taste in Painting, by loving to have as little Drapery as possible. Not that I think every body naked, altogether so fine a sight as yourself and a few more would be: but because 'tis good to use people to what they must be acquainted with; and there will certainly come some Day of Judgment to uncover every Soul of us. We shall then see how the Prudes of this world owed all their fine Figure only to their being a little straiter-lac'd, and that they were naturally as arrant Squabs as those that went more loose, nay as those that never girded their loyns at all.

But a particular reason to engage you to write your thoughts the more freely to me is, that I am confident no one knows you better. For I find, when others express their Opinion of you, it falls very short of mine, and I am sure at the same time Theirs is such as You would think sufficiently in your favour.

You may easily imagine how desirous I must be of a Correspondence with a person, who had taught me long ago that it was as possible to Esteem at first sight, as to Love: and who has since ruin'd me for all the Conversation of one Sex, and almost all the Friendship of the other. I am but too sensible thro' your means that the Company of Men wants a certain Softness to recommend it, and that of Women

---

[10] *Momus his project . . . Windows in our breasts:* Momus was the Greek god of blame.

[11] *I love you as well as King Herod could Herodias:* A biblical allusion; Herodias (died after 39 A.D.), the wife of Herod, arranged the death of John the Baptist after Herod granted her daughter Salome's wish to have John's head on a platter.

wants every thing else. How often have I been quietly going to take possession of that Tranquility and indolence I had so long found in the Country, when one Evening of your Conversation has spoild me for a Solitaire too? Books have lost their effect upon me; and I was convinced since I saw you that there is something more powerful than Philosophy, and since I heard you that there is one alive wiser than all the Sages. A plague of female Wisdome! it makes a man ten times more uneasy than his own! What is very strange, Virtue herself, when you have the dressing her, is too amiable for one's Repose. What a world of Good might you have done in your time, if you had allowed half the fine Gentlemen who have seen you to have but conversd with you? They would have been strangely caught, while they thought only to fall in love with a fair Face, and You had bewitchd them with Reason and Virtue; two Beauties, that the very Fops pretend to no acquaintance with.

The unhappy Distance at which we correspond, removes a great many of those punctillious Restrictions and Decorums, that oftentimes in nearer Conversation prejudice Truth to save Good breeding. I may now hear of my faults, and you of your good qualities, without a Blush on either side. We converse upon such unfortunate generous Terms as exclude the regards of Fear, Shame or Design in either of us. And methinks it would be as ungenerous a part, to impose even in a single Thought upon each other, in this State of Separation, as for Spirits of a different Sphære who have so little Intercourse with us, to employ that little (as some would make us think they do) in putting Tricks and Delusions upon poor mortals.

Let me begin then, Madam, by asking you a question which may enable Me to judge better of my own Conduct than most Instances of my life. In what manner did I behave, the last hour I saw you? what degree of Concern did I discover when I felt a misfortune which I hope you never will feel, That of parting from what one most esteems? For if my Parting lookd but like that of your common Acquaintance, I am the greatest of all the Hypocrites that ever Decency made.

I never since pass by the House, but with the same Sort of Melancholy that we feel upon Seeing the Tomb of a Friend; which only serves to put us in mind of What we have lost. I reflect upon the Circumstances of your Departure, your Behavior in what I may call Your last Moments, and I indulge a gloomy kind of Satisfaction in thinking you gave some of those last moments to me. I would fain imagine this was not accidental, but proceeded from a Penetration

which I know you have in finding out the truth of people's Senti-
ments, and that you were not unwilling, the last man that would have
parted with you, should be the last that did. I really lookd upon you
then, as the friends of Curtius might have done upon that Hero in the
instant he was devoting himself to Glory, and running to be Lost out
of Generosity![12] I was oblig'd to admire your Resolution in as great a
degree as I deplor'd it; and could only wish, that Heaven would re-
ward so much Merit as was to be taken from us, with all the felicity it
could enjoy elsewhere. May that Person for whom you have left all
the world[13] be so just as to prefer you to all the world: I believe his
good understanding has engagd him to do so hitherto, and I think his
Gratitude must for the future. May you continue to think him worthy
of whatever you have done, may you ever look upon him with the
eyes of a first Lover, nay if possible with all the unreasonable happy
Fondness of an unexperienced one, surrounded with all the Enchant-
ments and Idæas of Romance and Poetry. In a word, may you receive
from him as many pleasures and gratifications as even I think you can
give. I wish this from my Heart, and while I examine what passes
there in regard to You, I cannot but glory in my own heart that it is
capable of so much Generosity. I am, with all unalterable esteem and
sincerity

> Madam
> Your most faithfull obedient
> humble Servant,
> A. Pope.

Pope to Lady Mary Wortley Montagu

[October 1716]

Madam, — After having dream'd of you severall nights, besides a
hundred Reveries by Day, I find it necessary to relieve myself by writ-
ing: tho this is the fourth letter I have sent, two by Mr Methuen, and
one by Lord James Hay, who was to be Your Convoy from Leg-
horne. In all I can say, I only make you a present in many words of
what can do you no manner of good, but only raises my own opinion

---

[12] *the friends of Curtius:* Refers to the myth of the young knight who, on the advice
of an oracle, leaped — mounted and armed — into the chasm of the Forum to save his
country.

[13] *that Person for whom you have left all the world:* Edward Wortley Montagu,
Lady Mary's husband, with whom she had eloped in 1712 and whom she accompa-
nied to Constantinople; the marriage proved to be unhappy.

of my self; All the good wishes and hearty dispositions I am capable of forming or feeling for a deserving object. But mine are indeed so warm, that I fear they can proceed from nothing but what I can't very decently own to you, much less to any other; yet what if a man has, he can't help it.

For God's sake Madam, let not my correspondence be like a Traffic with the Grave, from whence there is no Return. Unless you write to me, my wishes must be but like a poor Papists Devotions to seperate Spirits; who, for all they know or hear from them, either may or may not be sensible of their Addresses. None but your Guardian Angels can have you more constantly in mind, than I; and if they have, it is only because they can see you always. If ever you think of those fine young Beaus of Heaven, I beg you to reflect that you have just as much Consolation from them, as I at present have from you.

While all people here are exercising their speculations upon the Affairs of the Turks, I am only considering them as they may concern a particular person, and instead of forming prospects of the general Tranquility of Europe am hoping for some effect that may contribute to your greater Ease. Above all, I would fain indulge an imagination, that the nearer View of the unquiet Scene you are approaching to, may put a stop to your farther Progress. I can hardly yet relinquish a faint hope I have ever had, that Providence will take some uncommon care of one who so generously gives herself up to it, and I can't imagine God almighty so like some of his Vice-gerents, as absolutely to neglect those who surrender to his mercy.

May I thus tell you the truth of my heart; or must I put on a more unconcerned Person, and tell you gayly, that there is some difference between the Court of Vienna and the Camps in Hungary;[14] That scarce a Basha[15] living is so inoffensive a creature as Count Volkra; that the Wives of Ambassadours are as subject to human accidents, & as tender as their Shins, that it is not more natural for Glass to cutt, than for Turks and Tartars to plunder, (not to mention ravishing, against which I am told Beauty is no defence in those parts) That you are strangely in the wrong to forsake a Nation that but last year toasted Mrs Walpole,[16] for one that has no taste of Beauty after

---

[14] *the Court of Vienna and the Camps in Hungary:* Edward Wortley Montagu had been sent first to Vienna to mediate the war between Austria and Turkey; Hungary had been under Hapsburg rule since 1699, when the Austrians had pushed out the Turks.

[15] *Basha:* A Turkish officer of high rank, also called a pasha.

[16] *Mrs Walpole:* Wife (?) of Sir Robert Walpole, first Earl of Orford (1676–1745), principal minister of the crown from 1721–1742. Walpole married an heiress in 1700.

twenty, and where the finest Woman in England will be almost Superannuated. Would to God, Madam, all this might move either Mr Wortley or you; and that I may soon apply to you both, what I have read in one of Harlequin's Comedies:[17] He sees Constantinople in a Raree Show, vows it is the finest thing upon earth, and protests it is prodigiously Like. Ay Sir, says the Man of the Show, you have been at Constantinople I perceive — No indeed, (says Harlequin) I was never there myself, but I had a Brother I lov'd dearly, who had the greatest mind in the world to have gone thither.

This is what I really wish from my Soul, tho it would ruin the best project I ever lay'd, that of obtaining, thro' your means, my fair Circassian Slave.[18] She, whom my Imagination had drawn more amiable than Angels, as beautiful as the Lady who was to chuse her by a resemblance to so divine a face; she, whom my hopes had already transported over so many Seas and Lands, & whom my eager wishes had already lodg'd in my arms & heart; She, I say, upon this condition, may remain under the Cedars of Asia; and weave a garland of Palmes for the brows of a Turkish Tyrant, with those hands, which I had destined for the soft Offices of love, or at worst for transcribing Amorous Madrigals! Let that Breast, I say, be now joind to some Savage Heart, that never beat but with Lust or Rage; that Breast inhabited by far more truth, fidelity, and innocence, than those that heave with Pride and glitter with Diamonds; that Breast whose very Conscience would have been Love, where Duty and Rapture made but one thought, & Honour must have been the same with Pleasure!

I can't go on in this style: I am not able to think of you without the utmost Seriousness, and if I did not take a particular care to disguise it, my Letters would be the most melancholy things in the world. I believe you see my Concern thro' all this Affectation of gayety, which is but like a Fitt of Laughing in the deepest Spleen or Vapours. I am just alarmd with a piece of news, that Mr Wortley thinks of passing thro' Hungary notwithstanding the War there: If ever any man loved his Wife, or any Mother her Child, this offers you the strongest Reason imaginable for staying at Vienna, at least this winter. For God's sake, value Yourself a little more, and don't give us cause to imagine that such extravagant Virtue can exist any where else than in a Romance.

---

[17] *Harlequin's Comedies*: English pantomimes based on characters from Italian *commedia dell'arte*; Harlequin is a simple, childlike character.

[18] *Circassian Slave*: The Circassians inhabited a region in the northern Caucasus; they were renowned for their physical beauty and their young women were often sold into Turkish harems.

I tremble for you the more, because (whether you'll believe it or not) I am capable myself of following one I lov'd, not only to Constantinople, but to those parts of India, where they tell us the Women best like the Ugliest fellows, as the most admirable productions of nature, and look upon Deformities as the Signatures of divine Favour. But (so romantic as I am) I shoud scarce take these Rambles, without greater encouragement, than I fancy any one who has been long married can expect. You see what danger I shall be in, if ever I find a Fair one born under the same Planet with Astolfo's Wife?[19] If, instead of Hungary, you past thro' Italy, and I had any hopes That Lady's Climate might give a Turn to your inclinations, it is but your sending me the least notice, and I'll certainly meet you in Lombardy, the Scene of those celebrated Amours between the fair Princess and her Dwarf. From thence, how far you might Draw me, and I might run after you, I no more know than the Spouse in the Song of Solomon: This I know, that I could be so very glad of being with you in any pleasure, that I could be content to be with you in any danger. Since I am not to partake either, Adieu! But may God, by hearing my prayers, and Preserving you, make me a better Christian than any modern Poet is at present. I am

Madam, most faithfully Yours.
A. Pope.

Pope to Lady Mary Wortley Montagu

Sept. 1st [1718]

Madam, — I have been (what I never was till now) in debt to you for a letter some weeks. I was informd you were at Sea, & that 'twas to no purpose to write, till some news had been heard of your arriving somewhere or other. Besides, I have had a second dangerous Illness, from which I was more diligent to be recovered than from the first, having now some hopes of seeing you again. If you make any Tour in Italy, I shall not easily forgive you for not acquainting me soon enough to have mett you there: I am very certain I can never be Polite, unless I travel with you. And it is never to be repaird, the loss that Homer has sustained, for want of my translating him in Asia. You will come hither full of criticismes against a man, who wanted nothing to be in the right but to have kept you company. You have

---

[19] *Astolfo's Wife:* From Ariosto's *Orlando Furioso* (1532); Astolfo is the courteous English knight who, among other adventures, travels to the moon where he discovers all the things lost on earth (cf. *Rape* V.113–14).

no way of making me amends, but by continuing an Asiatic when you return, to me, whatever English Airs you may put on to other people. I prodigiously long for your Sonnets, your remarks, your oriental learning; but I long for nothing so much as your Oriental Self. You must of necessity be *advanced* so far *Back* into true nature & simplicity of manners, by these 3 years residence in the East, that I shall look upon you as so many years Younger than you was, so much nearer Innocence (that is, Truth) & Infancy (that is Openness.) I expect to see your Soul as much thinner dressd as your Body; and that you have left off, as unwieldy & cumbersome, a great many damn'd Europœan Habits. Without offence to your modesty be it spoken, I have a burning desire to see your Soul stark naked, for I am confident 'tis the prettiest kind of white Soul, in the universe — But I forget whom I am talking to, you may possibly by this time Believe according to the Prophet, that you have none. If so, show me That which comes next to a Soul; you may easily put it upon a poor ignorant Christian for a Soul, & please him as well with it: I mean your Heart: Mahomet[20] I think allows you Hearts: which (together with fine eyes & other agreeable equivalents) are worth all the Souls on this side the world. But if I must be content with seeing your body only, God send it to come quickly: I honor it more than the Diamond-Casket that held Homer's Iliads. For in the very twinkle of one eye of it, there is more Wit; and in the very dimple of one cheek of it, there is more Meaning, than in all the Souls that ever were casually put into Women since Men had the making them.

I have a mind to fill the rest of this paper with an accident that happen'd just under my eyes, and has made a great Impression upon me. I have past part of this Summer at an old romantic Seat of my Lord Harcourt's which he lent me; It overlooks a Common-field, where under the Shade of a Hay cock sate two Lovers, as constant as ever were found in Romance, beneath a spreading Beech.[21] The name of the one (let it sound as it will) was John Hewet, of the other Sarah Drew. John was a wellset man about five and twenty, Sarah a brown woman of about eighteen. John had for several months born the labour of the day in the same field with Sarah; When she milk'd, it was his morning & evening charge to bring the Cows to her pail:

---

[20] *Mahomet:* Founder of Islam.

[21] *two Lovers . . . beneath a spreading Beech:* Compare this telling of the story to Pope's ribald couplet version to Teresa Blount, p. 116, and to Lady Mary's cynical version, pp. 126–27.

Their Love was the Talk, but not the Scandal, of the whole neigh-
bourhood, for all they aimd at was the blameless possession of each
other in marriage. It was but this very morning that he had obtain'd
her Parents consent, and it was but till next week that they were to
wait to be happy. Perhaps, this very day in the intervals of their
work, they were talking of their wedding clothes, and John was now
matching several kinds of poppies and field-flowers to her Complex-
ion, to make her a Present of Knots for the day. While they were thus
employd (it was on the last of July) a terrible Storm of Thunder and
Lightning arose, that drove the Labourers to what Shelter the Trees
or hedges afforded. Sarah frighted, and out of breath, sunk down on
a Haycock, & John (who never seperated from her) sate by her side,
having rak'd two or three heaps together to secure her. Immediately
there was heard so loud a Crack as if Heaven had burst asunder: the
Labourers, all sollicitous for each other's safety, calld to one another:
those that were nearest our Lovers, hearing no answer, stept to the
place where they lay; they first saw a little Smoke, & after, this faith-
ful Pair. John with one arm about his Sarah's neck, and the other
held over her face as if to screen her from the Lightning. They were
struck dead, & already grown stiff and cold in this tender posture.
There was no mark or discolouring on their bodies, only that Sarah's
eyebrow was a little sindg'd, and a small Spot appeard between her
breasts. They were buried the next day in one grave, in the Parish of
Stanton-Harcourt in Oxfordshire; where my Lord Harcourt, at my
request, has erected a monument over them. Of the following Epi-
taphs which I made, the Criticks have chosen the godly one: I like
neither, but wish you had been in England to have done this office
better; I think 'twas what you could not have refused me on so mov-
ing an occasion.

> When Eastern Lovers feed the fun'ral fire,
> On the same Pile their faithful Fair expire;
> Here pitying Heav'n that virtue mutual found,
> And blasted both, that it might neither wound.
> Hearts so sincere, th' Almighty saw well-pleas'd,
> Sent his own Lightning, & the Victims seiz'd.

1.

> Think not, by rig'rous Judgment seiz'd,
> A Pair so faithful could expire;

Victims so pure Heav'n saw well-pleas'd,
And snatchd them in celestial fire.

2.

Live well, & fear no sudden fate:
    When God calls Virtue to the grave,
Alike 'tis Justice, soon, or late,
    Mercy alike, to kill, or save.
Virtue unmov'd, can hear the Call,
And face the Flash that melts the Ball.

Upon the whole, I can't think these people unhappy: The greatest happiness, next to living as they would have done, was to dye as they did. The greatest honour people of this low degree could have was to be remembered on a little monument; unless you will give them another, that of being honourd with a Tear from the finest eyes in the world. I know you have Tenderness; you must have it: It is the very Emanation of Good Sense & virtue: The finest minds like the finest metals, dissolve the easiest.

But when you are reflecting upon Objects of pity, pray do not forget one, who had no sooner found out an Object of the highest Esteem, than he was seperated from it: And who is so very unhappy as not to be susceptible of Consolation from others, by being so miserably in the right as to think other women what they really are. Such an one can't but be desperately fond of any creature that is quite different from these. If the Circassian be utterly void of such Honour as these have, and such virtue as these boast of, I am content. I have detested the Sound of *honest Woman, & loving Spouse* ever since I heard the pretty name of Odaliche.[22] Dear Madam I am for ever Yours, and your Slave's, Slave, & Servant.

My most humble Services to Mr Wortly.
Pray let me hear from you soon:
Tho' I shall very soon write again.
I am confident half our letters have been lost.

[22] *Odaliche:* "Odalisque: A female slave or concubine in an Eastern harem, especially in the seraglio of the Sultan of Turkey" [OED].

Lady Mary Wortley Montagu to Pope

Dover, Novr. 1, O.S. 1718.[23]

I have this minute received a letter of yours sent me from Paris. I believe and hope I shall very soon see both you and Mr. *Congreve*;[24] but as I am here in an inn, where we stay to regulate our march to London, bag and baggage, I shall employ some of my leisure time in answering that part of yours that seems to require an answer.

I must applaud your good nature in supposing that your pastoral lovers, (vulgarly called Haymakers) would have lived in everlasting joy and harmony, if the lightning had not interrupted their scheme of happiness. I see no reason to imagine that *John Hughes* and *Sarah Drew* were either wiser or more virtuous than their neighbours. That a well-set man of twenty-five should have a fancy to marry a brown woman of eighteen, is nothing marvellous; and I cannot help thinking that had they married, their lives would have passed in the common track with their fellow-parishioners. His endeavouring to shield her from a storm was a natural action, and what he would have certainly done for his horse, if he had been in the same situation. Neither am I of opinion that their sudden death was a reward of their mutual virtue. You know the Jews were reprov'd for thinking a village destroyed by fire, more wicked than those that had escaped the thunder. Time and chance happen to all men. Since you desire me to try my skill in an *epitaph*, I think the following lines perhaps more just, tho' not so poetical as yours.

> Here lies John Hughes and Sarah Drew;
> Perhaps you'll say, What's that to you?
> Believe me, friend, much may be said
> On that poor couple that are dead.
> On Sunday next they should have married;
> But see how oddly things are carried!
> On Thursday last it rain'd and lighten'd,
> These tender lovers sadly frighten'd,
> Shelter'd beneath the cocking hay
> In hopes to pass the time away.
> But the BOLD THUNDER found them out

---

[23] *Dover, Novr. 1, O.S. 1718:* Lady Mary dated this letter November, but Sherburn places it in September, as it answers Pope's letter of September 1 (*Correspondence* 1: 496n).

[24] *Mr. Congreve:* William Congreve (1670–1729), poet and playwright; see the Introduction.

(Commission'd for that end no doubt)
And seizing on their trembling breath,
Consign'd them to the shades of death.
Who knows if 'twas not kindly done?
For had they seen the next year's sun,
A beaten wife and cuckold swain
Had jointly curs'd the marriage chain;
Now they are happy in their doom,
FOR POPE HAS WROTE UPON THEIR TOMB.[25]

I confess these sentiments are not altogether so heroic as yours; but I hope you will forgive them in favour of the two last lines. You see how much I esteem the honour you have done them; tho' I am not very impatient to have the same, and had rather continue to be your stupid, *living*, humble servant, than be *celebrated* by all the pens in Europe.

I would write to Mr. C — ; but suppose you will read this to him if he enquires after me.

JOSEPH SPENCE

From *Observations, Anecdotes, and Characters of Books and Men, Collected from Conversation*

In 1726, Joseph Spence (1699–1768), a clergyman, scholar, and friend of Pope, began collecting anecdotes about and conversations with Pope and other authors. Although the accounts were not published until the early nineteenth century, they circulated widely in the eighteenth and provided an important source for Johnson's biography. In the *Anecdotes* we hear Pope's voice transcribed, recollecting both the events that produced the poem, and some that were produced by it. Poor Sir George Brown apparently took it rather ill that his character Sir Plume ("the very picture of the man") only sputtered nonsense.

---

[25] *FOR POPE HAS WROTE UPON THEIR TOMB:* Lady Mary gently satirizes one of Pope's most consistent rhetorical assumptions — that the poet transforms and eternalizes (and so in a sense eclipses) his subjects (cf. *Rape* V.123–50; *Eloisa to Abelard* 359–66).

Portrait of Arabella Fermor (artist and date unknown). Arabella Fermor
(1690?–1738) is, of course, the model for Belinda of *The Rape of the Lock* —
although, as Pope declares in his Epistle Dedicatory to the lady, "the charac-
ter of *Belinda,* as it is now manag'd, resembles you in nothing but in
Beauty." This particular portrait was clearly inspired by the poem, identify-
ing its subject as Pope's heroine and including the "sparkling Cross . . .
which Jews might kiss, and Infidels adore" (II. 7–8).

The text is taken from James M. Osborn's edition (Oxford: Clarendon Press, 1966), without the notes and without the editor's brackets indicating the collation of Spence's various manuscripts.

104. The stealing of Miss Belle Fermor's hair was taken too seriously, and caused an estrangement between the two families, though they had lived long in great friendship before. A common acquaintance and well-wisher to both desired me to write a poem to make a jest of it, and laugh them together again. It was in this view that I wrote my *Rape of the Lock*, which was well received and had its effect in the two families. Nobody but Sir George Browne was angry, and he was so a good deal and for a long time. He could not bear that Sir Plume should talk *nothing* but nonsense.

— POPE *June 1739*

105. Copies of it [the *Rape of the Lock*] got about, and 'twas like to be printed, on which I published the first draught of it (without the machinery), in a Miscellany of Tonson's.[1] The machinery was added afterwards to make it look a little more considerable; and the scheme of adding it was much liked and approved of by several of my friends, and particularly by Dr. Garth, who, as he was one of the best-natured men in the world, was very fond of it.

— POPE *June 1739*

106. I have been assured by a most intimate friend[2] of Mr. Pope's that the Peer in the *Rape of the Lock* was Lord Petre, the person who desired Mr. Pope to write it [was] old Mr. Caryll of Sussex, and that what is said of Sir George Browne in it was the very picture of the man.

— SPENCE *27 May 1749*

107. The things that I have written fastest have always pleased most. I wrote the *Essay on Criticism* fast, for I had digested all the matter in prose before I began upon it in verse. The *Rape of the Lock* was written fast. All the machinery, you know, was added afterwards, and the making that and what was published before hit so

---

[1] *Miscellany of Tonson's:* Actually Lintot's; see headnote to the 1712 edition of *The Rape of the Locke*, p. 130.
[2] *a most intimate friend:* Martha Blount (1690–1762), close friend of Pope (see the Introduction).

well together, is I think one of the greatest proofs of judgement of anything I ever did.

I wrote most of the *Iliad* fast — a great deal of it on journeys, from the little pocket Homer on that shelf there, and often forty or fifty verses on a morning in bed.

— POPE *February or March 1735*

ALEXANDER POPE

The Rape of the Locke, First Edition in Two Cantos

"Copies of it [*The Rape of the Lock*] got about, and 'twas like to be printed, on which I published the first draught of it (without the machinery), in a Miscellany of Tonson's," Pope told Joseph Spence in 1739 (Spence, 1: 44). The first version actually did *not* appear in Jacob Tonson the Elder's *Poetical Miscellanies, The Sixth Part,* which was published in 1709 and included Pope's *Pastorals,* but in *Miscellaneous Poems and Translations by several hands,* published in 1712 by printer and bookseller Bernard Lintot (1675–1736). Lintot and Pope would have a long and sometimes testy relationship: "Less manipulable than most of his colleagues in the trade, he resisted P[ope]'s plans and lost the poet's business" (Rogers 724). Pope spent a great deal of energy struggling to get free of the power that booksellers had over authors young and old. His own *Verses to be prefix'd before Bernard Lintot's New Miscellany* satirize Lintot's self-importance:

> [First are some lines about other booksellers, past and present]
> I, for my part, admire *Lintottus.* —
> His Character's beyond Compare,
> Like his own Person, large and fair.
> They print their Names in Letters small,
> But LINTOT stands in Capital:
> Author and he, with equal Grace,
> Appear, and stare you in the Face. . . .
> But *Lintot* is at vast Expence,
> And pays prodigious dear for — Sense.
> Their Books are useful but to few,
> A scholar, or a Wit or two:

Lintot's for gen'ral Use are fit;
For some Folks read, but all Folks sh — .

The lines gibe at Lintot for competing with authors for space on the title
page by capitalizing the letters of his own name (see facsimile title page
to the *Rape*: "Printed for BERNARD LINTOTT. 1712"), and the closing,
implicitly naughty rhyme suggests that what Lintot publishes for a popu-
lar audience can end up being universally useful — discarded books were
often recycled as toilet paper. That Lintot went ahead and published
these verses — not to mention the fact that Pope was willing to be impli-
cated in his own satire — suggests how well both men gauged their mar-
kets. Lintot published Pope's *Works* in 1717, and also made available
through his shop the engraving of the 1714 portrait of Pope by Charles
Jervas (see p. 88). But their relationship remained difficult, and Pope
wasn't finished gibing. In the *Dunciad Variorum* of 1729, Pope features
Lintot's well-known bulk (with Jacob Tonson for inspiration) in the
bookseller's race with the scurrilous Edmund Curll:

> As when a dab-chick waddles thro' the copse,
> On feet and wings, and flies, and wades, and hops;
> So lab'ring on, with shoulders, hands, and head,
> Wide as a windmill all his figure spread,
> With legs expanded Bernard urg'd the race,
> And seem'ed to emulate great Jacob's pace. . . .
> Here fortun'd Curl to slide; loud shout the band,
> And Bernard! Bernard! rings thro' all the Strand. (II.59–70)

MISCELLANEOUS

P O E M S

A N D

TRANSLATIONS.

MISCELLANEOUS

P O E M S

A N D

TRANSLATIONS.

B Y

SEVERAL HANDS.

—*Multa Poetarum veniet manus, auxilio quæ
Sit mihi*————.   Hor.

L O N D O N:

Printed for *Bernard Lintott* at the *Crofs-Keys* be-
tween the Two *Temple* Gates in *Fleetftreet.* 1712.

THE

CONTENTS.

The

The CONTENTS.

On

The CONTENTS.

The CONTENTS.

THE

THE

RAPE of the *LOCKE.*

AN

HEROI-COMICAL

P   O   E   M.

Nolueram, Belinda, *tuos violare capillos,*
Sed juvat hoc precibus me tribuiſſe tuis.
                        MART. Lib. 12. Ep. 86.

Printed for BERNARD LINTOTT. 1712.

THE

RAPE *of the* LOCKE.

CANTO I.

WHAT dire Offence from Am'rous Cau-
[fes fprings,
What mighty Quarrels rife from Trivial
[Things,
I fing—This Verfe to *C—l*, Mufe! is due;
This, ev'n *Belinda* may vouchfafe to view:
Slight is the Subject, but not fo the Praife,
If She infpire, and He approve my Lays,

Say what ftrange Motive, Goddefs! cou'd com-
[pel
A well-bred *Lord* t'affault a gentle *Belle?*
Oh fay what ftranger Caufe, yet unexplor'd,
Cou'd make a gentle *Belle* reject a *Lord?*
And dwells fuch Rage in *fofteft Bofoms* then?
And lodge fuch daring Souls in *Little Men?*

Sol thro' white Curtains did his Beams difplay,
And op'd thofe Eyes which brighter fhine than [they;
Shock juft had giv'n himfelf the rowzing Shake,
And Nymphs prepar'd their *Chocolate* to take;
Thrice the wrought Slipper knock'd againft the [Ground,
And ftriking Watches the tenth Hour refound.
Belinda rofe, and 'midft attending Dames
Launch'd on the Bofom of the filver *Thames*:
A Train of well-dreft Youths around her fhone,
And ev'ry Eye was fix'd on her alone;
On her white Breaft a fparkling *Crofs* fhe wore,
Which *Jews* might kifs, and Infidels adore.
Her lively Looks a fprightly Mind difclofe,
Quick as her Eyes, and as unfixt as thofe:
Favours to none, to all fhe Smiles extends;
Oft fhe rejects, but never once offends.
Bright as the Sun her Eyes the Gazers ftrike,
And, like the Sun, they fhine on all alike.
                                        Yet

The Rape of the Locke. 357

Yet graceful Eafe, and Sweetnefs void of Pride,
Might hide her Faults, if *Belles* had Faults to hide:
If to her fhare fome Female Errors fall,
Look on her Face, and you'll forgive 'em all.

This Nymph, to the Deftruction of Mankind,
Nourifh'd two Locks, which graceful hung behind
In equal Curls, and well confpir'd to deck
With fhining Ringlets her fmooth Iv'ry Neck.
Love in thefe Labyrinths his Slaves detains,
And mighty Hearts are held in flender Chains.
With hairy Sprindges we the Birds betray,
Slight Lines of Hair furprize the Finny Prey,
Fair Treffes Man's Imperial Race infnare,
And Beauty draws us with a *fingle Hair*.

Th'Adventrous *Baron* the bright Locks admir'd,
He faw, he wifh'd, and to the Prize afpir'd:

A a 3   Refolv'd

The Rape of the Locke.

Refolv'd to win, he meditates the way,
By Force to ravifh, or by Fraud betray;
For when Succefs a Lover's Toil attends,
Few ask, if Fraud or Force attain'd his Ends.

For this, e'er *Phœbus* rofe, he had implor'd
Propitious Heav'n, and ev'ry Pow'r ador'd,
But chiefly *Love*—to *Love* an Altar built,
Of twelve vaft *French* Romances, neatly gilt.
There lay the Sword-knot *Sylvia's* Hands had
                                                    [fown,
With *Flavia's* Busk that oft had rapp'd his own:
A Fan, a Garter, half a Pair of Gloves;
And all the Trophies of his former Loves.
With tender *Billet-doux* he lights the Pyre,
And breaths three am'rous Sighs to raife the Fire.
Then proftrate falls, and begs with ardent Eyes
Soon to obtain, and long poffefs the Prize:

The Rape of the Locke.   359

The Pow'rs gave Ear, and granted half his Pray'r,
The reft, the Winds difpers'd in empty Air.

Clofe by thofe Meads for ever crown'd with
                                      [Flow'rs,
Where*Thames* withPride furveys his rifingTow'rs,
There ftands a Structure of Majeftick Frame,
Which from the neighb'ring *Hampton* takes its
                                      [Name.
Here *Britain's* Statefmen oft the Fall foredoom
Of Foreign Tyrants, and of Nymphs at home;
HereThou,great *Anna!* whom threeRealms obey,
Doft fometimesCounfel take---and fometimes*Tea.*

Hither our Nymphs and Heroes did refort,
To tafte awhile the Pleafures of a Court;
In various Talk the chearful hours they paft,
Of, who was *Bitt,* or who *Capotted* laft:
This fpeaks the Glory of the *Britifh Queen,*
And that defcribes a charming *Indian Screen;*

A third interprets Motions, Looks, and Eyes;
At ev'ry Word a Reputation dies.
Snuff, or the *Fan*, supply each Pause of Chatt,
With singing, laughing, ogling, and all that.

Now, when declining from the Noon of Day,
The Sun obliquely shoots his burning Ray;
When hungry Judges soon the Sentence sign,
And Wretches hang that Jury-men may Dine;
When Merchants from th' *Exchange* return in
                                    [Peace,
And the long Labours of the *Toilette* cease——
The Board's with Cups and Spoons, alternate,
                              [crown'd;
The Berries crackle, and the Mill turns round;
On shining Altars of *Japan* they raise
The silver *Lamp*, and fiery Spirits blaze;
From silver Spouts the grateful Liquors glide,
And *China*'s Earth receives the smoking Tyde:

                                        At

The Rape of the Locke. 361

At once they gratifie their Smell and Tafte,

While frequent Cups prolong the rich Repaft.

Coffee, (which makes the Politician wife,

And fee thro' all things with his half fhut Eyes)

Sent up in Vapours to the *Baron*'s Brain

New Stratagems, the radiant Locke to gain.

Ah ceafe rafh Youth! defift e'er 'tis too late,

Fear the juft Gods, and think of * *Scylla*'s Fate!

Chang'd to a Bird, and fent to flitt in Air,

She dearly pays for *Nifus*' injur'd Hair!

But when to Mifchief Mortals bend their Mind,

How foon fit Inftruments of Ill they find?

Juft then, *Clariffa* drew with tempting Grace

A two-edg'd Weapon from her fhining Cafe;

So Ladies in Romance affift their Knight,

Prefent the Spear, and arm him for the Fight.

* *Vide* Ovid. Metam. 8.

He

362   *The Rape of the Locke.*

He takes the Gift with rev'rence, and extends
The little Engine on his Finger's Ends,
This juft behind *Belinda*'s Neck he fpread,
As o'er the fragrant Steams fhe bends her Head:
He firft expands the glitt'ring *Forfex* wide
T'inclofe the Lock; then joins it, to divide;
One fatal ftroke the facred Hair does fever
From the fair Head, for ever, and for ever!

The living Fires come flafhing from her Eyes,
And Screams of Horror rend th'affrighted Skies.
Not louder Shrieks by Dames to Heav'n are caft,
When Husbands die, or *Lap-dogs* breath their laft;
Or when rich *China* Veffels fal'n from high,
In glittring Duft and painted Fragments lie!

Let Wreaths of triumph now my Temples twine,
(The Victor cry'd) the glorious Prize is mine!

                                        While

The Rape of the Locke   363

While Fish in Streams, or Birds delight in Air,
Or in a Coach and Six the *British* Fair,
As long as *Atalantis* shall be read,
Or the small Pillow grace a Lady's Bed,
While *Visits* shall be paid on solemn Days,
When num'rous Wax-lights in bright Order blaze,
While Nymphs take Treats, or Assignations give,
So long my Honour, Name, and Praise shall live!

What Time wou'd spare, from Steel receives its
                                      [date,
And Monuments, like Men, submit to Fate!
Steel did the Labour of the Gods destroy,
And strike to Dust th' aspiring Tow'rs of *Troy*;
Steel cou'd the Works of mortal Pride confound,
And hew Triumphal Arches to the ground.
What Wonder then, fair Nymph! thy Hairs shou'd
                                      [feel
The conqu'ring Force of unresisted Steel?

T H E

THE

RAPE *of the* LOCKE.

CANTO II.

BUT anxious Cares the pensive Nymph op- [prest,
And secret Passions labour'd in her Breast.
Not youthful Kings in Battel seiz'd alive,
Not scornful Virgins who their Charms survive,
Not ardent Lover robb'd of all his Blifs,
Not ancient Lady when refus'd a Kifs,
Not Tyrants fierce that unrepenting die,
Not *Cynthia* when her *Manteau*'s pinn'd awry,
E'er felt such Rage, Resentment, and Despair,
As Thou, sad Virgin! for thy ravish'd Hair.

                                    While

The Rape of the Locke. 365

While her rackt Soul Repose and Peace requires,

The fierce *Thaleſtris* fans the riſing Fires.

O wretched Maid (ſhe ſpread her hands, and cry'd,

And *Hampton*'s Ecchoes, wretched Maid! reply'd)

Was it for this you took ſuch conſtant Care,

Combs, Bodkins, Leads, Pomatums, to prepare?

For this your Locks in Paper Durance bound,

For this with tort'ring Irons wreath'd around?

Oh had the Youth but been content to ſeize

Hairs leſs in ſight ——— or any Hairs but theſe!

Gods! ſhall the Raviſher diſplay this Hair,

While the Fops envy, and the Ladies ſtare!

Honour forbid! at whoſe unrival'd Shrine

Eaſe, Pleaſure, Virtue, All, our Sex reſign.

Methinks already I your Tears ſurvey,

Already hear the horrid things they ſay,

Already ſee you a degraded Toaſt,

And all your Honour in a Whiſper loſt!

How

366   *The Rape of the Locke.*

How fhall I, then, your helplefs Fame defend?
'Twill then be Infamy to feem your Friend!
And fhall this Prize, th'ineftimable Prize,
Expos'd thro' *Cryftal* to the gazing Eyes,
And heighten'd by the *Diamond*'s circling Rays,
On that Rapacious Hand for ever blaze?
Sooner fhall Grafs in *Hide-*Park *Circus* grow,
And Wits take Lodgings in the Sound of *Bow*;
Sooner let Earth, Air, Sea, to *Chaos* fall,
Men, Monkies, Lap-dogs, Parrots, perifh all!

She faid ; then raging to *Sir Plume* repairs,
And bids her *Beau* demand the precious Hairs:
(*Sir Plume*, of *Amber Snuff-box* juftly vain,
And the nice Conduct of a *clouded Cane*)
With earneft Eyes, and round unthinking Face,
He firft the Snuff-box open'd, then the Cafe,

And

The Rape of the Locke.   367

And thus broke out—"My Lord, why, what the
[Devil ?
" Z---ds! damn the Lock! 'fore Gad, you muft be
[civil!
" Plague on't! 'tis paft a Jeft—nay prithee, Pox!
" Give her the Hair—he fpoke, and rapp'd his Box.

It grieves me much (reply'd the Peer again)
Who fpeaks fo well fhou'd ever fpeak in vain.
But * by this Locke, this facred Locke I fwear,
(Which never more fhall join its parted Hair,
Which never more its Honours fhall renew,
Clipt from the lovely Head where once it grew)
That while my Noftrils draw the vital Air,
This Hand, which won it, fhall for ever wear.
He fpoke, and fpeaking in proud Triumph fpread
The long-contended Honours of her Head.

But fee! the *Nymph* in Sorrow's Pomp appears,
Her Eyes half languifhing, half drown'd in Tears;

* *In allufion to* Achilles's *Oath in* Homer. *Il.* 1.

368   *The Rape of the Locke.*

Now livid pale her Cheeks, now glowing red;
'On her heav'd Bosom hung her drooping Head,
Which, with a Sigh, she rais'd; and thus she said.

For ever curs'd be this detested Day,
Which snatch'd my best, my fav'rite Curl away!
Happy! ah ten times happy, had I been,
If *Hampton-Court* these Eyes had never seen!
Yet am not I the first mistaken Maid,
By Love of Courts to num'rous Ills betray'd.
Oh had I rather un-admir'd remain'd
In some lone *Isle,* or distant *Northern* Land;
Where the gilt *Chariot* never mark'd the way,
Where none learn *Ombre,* none e'er taste *Bohea!*
There kept my Charms conceal'd from mortal Eye,
Like Roses that in Desarts bloom and die.
What mov'd my Mind with youthful Lords to rome?
O had I stay'd, and said my Pray'rs at home!

                                    'Twas

The Rape of the Locke.   369

'Twas this, the Morning *Omens* did foretel;
Thrice from my trembling hand the *Patch-box* fell;
The tott'ring *China* shook without a Wind,
Nay, *Poll* sate mute, and *Shock* was *most Unkind!*
See the poor Remnants of this slighted Hair!
My hands shall rend what ev'n thy own did spare.
This, in two sable Ringlets taught to break,
Once gave new Beauties to the snowie Neck.
The Sister-Locke now sits uncouth, alone,
And in its Fellow's Fate foresees its own;
Uncurl'd it hangs! the fatal Sheers demands;
And tempts once more thy sacrilegious Hands.

She said: the pitying Audience melt in Tears,
But *Fate* and *Jove* had stopp'd the *Baron's* Ears.
In vain *Thalestris* with Reproach assails,
For who can move when fair *Belinda* fails?

B b   Not

370   *The Rape of the Locke.*

Not half fo fixt the *Trojan* cou'd remain,
While *Anna* begg'd and *Dido* rag'd in vain.
To Arms, to Arms! the bold *Thaleftris* cries,
And fwift as Lightning to the Combate flies.
All fide in Parties, and begin th' Attack;
Fans clap, Silks rufsle, and tough Whalebones crack;
Heroes and Heroins Shouts confus'dly rife,
And bafe, and treble Voices ftrike the Skies.
No common Weapons in their Hands are found,
Like Gods they fight, nor dread a mortal Wound.

  * So when bold *Homer* makes the Gods engage,
And heav'nly Breafts with human Paffions rage;
'Gainft *Pallas*, *Mars*; *Latona*, *Hermes* Arms;
And all *Olympus* rings with loud Alarms.
Jove's Thunder roars, Heav'n trembles all around;
Blue *Neptune* ftorms, the bellowing Deeps refound;

      * Homer. *Il.* 20.

                                          Earth

The Rape of the Locke.   371

Earth fhakes her nodding Tow'rs, the Ground
[gives way,
And the pale Ghofts ftart at the Flafh of Day!

While thro' the Prefs enrag'd *Thaleftris* flies,
And fcatters Deaths around from both her Eyes,
A *Beau* and *Witling* perifh'd in the Throng,
One dy'd in *Metaphor,* and one in *Song.*
O cruel Nymph! a living Death I bear,
Cry'd *Dapperwit,* and funk befide his Chair.
A mournful Glance Sir *Fopling* upwards caft,
Thofe Eyes are made fo killing——was his laft:
Thus on *Meander*'s flow'ry Margin lies
Th'expiring Swan, and as he fings he dies.

As bold Sir *Plume* had drawn *Clariffa* down,
Chloë ftept in, and kill'd him with a Frown;
She fmil'd to fee the doughty Hero flain,
But at her Smile, the Beau reviv'd again.

B b 2   Now

372 *The Rape of the Locke.*

* Now *Jove* ſuſpends his golden Scales in Air;
Weighs the Mens Wits againſt the Lady's Hair;
The doubtful Beam long nods from ſide to ſide;
At length the Wits mount up, the Hairs ſubſide.

See fierce *Belinda* on the *Baron* flies,
With more than uſual Lightning in her Eyes;
Nor fear'd the Chief th'unequal Fight to try,
Who ſought no more than on his Foe to die.
But this bold Lord, with manly Strength indu'd,
She with one Finger and a Thumb ſubdu'd:
Juſt where the Breath of Life his Noſtrils drew,
A Charge of *Snuff* the wily Virgin threw;
Sudden, with ſtarting Tears each Eye o'erflows,
And the high Dome re-ecchoes to his Noſe.

Now meet thy Fate, th'incens'd *Virago* cry'd,
And drew a deadly *Bodkin* from her Side.

* *Vid.* Homer Iliad. 22. & Virg. Æn. 12.

Boaſt

The Rape of the Locke.   373

Boaſt not my Fall (he ſaid) inſulting Foe!
Thou by ſome other ſhalt be laid as low.
Nor think, to dye dejects my lofty Mind;
All that I dread, is leaving you behind!
Rather than ſo, ah let me ſtill ſurvive,
And ſtill burn on, in *Cupid*'s Flames, *Alive.*

Reſtore the Locke! ſhe cries; and all around
Reſtore the Locke! the vaulted Roofs rebound.
Not fierce *Othello* in ſo loud a Strain
Roar'd for the Handkerchief that caus'd his Pain.
But ſee! how oft Ambitious Aims are croſs'd,
And Chiefs contend 'till all the Prize is loſt!
The Locke, obtain'd with Guilt, and kept with Pain,
In ev'ry place is ſought, but ſought in vain.
With ſuch a Prize no Mortal muſt be bleſt,
So Heav'n decrees! with Heav'n who can conteſt?

374   *The Rape of the Locke.*

Some thought, it mounted to the Lunar Sphere,
* Since all that Man e'er loft, is treafur'd there.
Their Heroe's Wits are kept in pondrous Vafes,
And Beau's in *Snuff-boxes* and *Tweezer-Cafes.*
There broken Vows, and Death-bed Alms are
                                    [found,
And Lovers Hearts with Ends of Riband bound;
The Courtiers Promifes, and Sick Man's Pray'rs,
The Smiles of Harlots, and the Tears of Heirs,
Cages for Gnats, and Chains to Yoak a Flea;
Dry'd Butterflies, and Tomes of Cafuiftry.

But truft the Mufe—fhe faw it upward rife,
Tho' mark'd by none but quick Poetic Eyes:
(Thus *Rome*'s great Founder to the Heav'ns with-
                                    [drew,
To *Proculus* alone confefs'd in view.)
A fudden Star, it fhot thro' liquid Air,
And drew behind a radiant *Trail of Hair*.

* *Vid.* Ariofto. Canto 34.

                                    Not

The Rape of the Locke.   375

Not *Berenice's* Locks first rose so bright,

The Skies befpangling with difhevel'd Light.

This, the *Beau-monde* fhall from the *Mall* furvey,

As thro' the Moon-light fhade they nightly ftray,

And hail with Mufick its propitious Ray.

This *Partridge* foon fhall view in cloudlefs Skies,

When next he looks thro' *Galilæo's* Eyes;

And hence th' Egregious Wizard fhall foredoom

The Fate of *Louis*, and the Fall of *Rome*.

[Hair
Then ceafe, bright Nymph! to mourn the ravifh'd

Which adds new Glory to the fhining Sphere!

Not all the Treffes that fair Head can boaft

Shall draw fuch Envy as the Locke you loft.

For, after all the Murders of your Eye,

When, after Millions flain, your felf fhall die;

B b 4   When

376   *The Rape of the Locke.*

When thofe fair Suns fhall fett, as fett they muft,

And all thofe Treffes fhall be laid in Duft;

This Locke, the Mufe fhall confecrate to Fame,

And mid'ft the Stars infcribe *Belinda*'s Name!

F I N I S.

BOOKS

ALEXANDER POPE

From *The Correspondence of Alexander Pope*

Letters to and from Pope between 1711 and 1715 supply more imme-
diate details about the revisions and reception of *The Rape of the Lock*,
as well as about the choice of prefaces. A few days after the publication
of the two-canto version, one of Pope's closest friends asks eagerly about
the poem's release ("Where hangs the *Lock* now?"). Pope has an ac-
quaintance distribute advance copies to the key players, yet, as he tells
John Caryll, Jr. (November 8, 1712), the reception is not universally en-
thusiastic among the principals: "Sir Plume blusters, I hear; nay, the cele-
brated lady herself is offended, and, which is stranger, not at herself, but
me." In December 1713 Pope considers "dedicating that poem to Mrs
Fermor by name, as a piece of justice in return to the wrong interpreta-
tions she has suffered under on the score of that piece" (not included
here). A month later, however (January 1713), Pope believes he has ac-
complished his diplomatic mission — "the young lady approves of it." In
February 1714 he has finished the five-canto edition of the poem. Once
again he sends around advance copies; in a letter to Mrs. or Miss Mar-
riot (February 28 [1713/14]), he describes his "whimsical piece of work"
as a "sort of writing very like tickling." In the final letter Pope congratu-
lates Arabella Fermor on her marriage to Francis Perkins — "how much
the tenderness of one man of merit is to be prefer'd to the addresses of a
thousand." Pope remains always the poet, and always ready to point that
out: "It may be expected, perhaps, that one who has the title of Poet,
should say something more polite on this occasion." Here, instead of cel-
ebrating her beauty, he commemorates her happiness, and closes: "I beg
you will think it but just, that a man who will certainly be spoken of as
your admirer, after he is dead, may have the happiness to be esteem'd
while he is living, Your, &c." Thus the letter that concludes the social
story of *The Rape of the Lock* manages, like the poem itself, to combine
the real and the circumstantial with the glimpse of immortality.

The text of the letters is taken from *The Correspondence of Alexan-
der Pope*, edited by George Sherburn (Oxford: Clarendon Press, 1956).
The text of the letters omits Sherburn's scholarly apparatus of brackets
and half-brackets that indicate various uncertainties or alterations. The
student interested in the precise text of the letters at their different stages
should consult Sherburn's edition. In general the letters are printed in
full, to give the varying sense of proportion that Pope assigned to his dis-
cussions of the fate of his poem, but occasionally long discussions of

other matters are omitted. Only the key characters and presumably unfamiliar literary references are glossed. Notes taken from the *Correspondence* are cited [C].

Edward Bedingfield[1] to Pope

Graysin May the 16th, 1712.

Sir, — Last Night I had the favour of yours of the eleventh Instant and according to the directions therein I have enclosed the Copys for Lord Petre and that for Mrs Belle Fermor[2] — she is out of Towne and therefore all I can do is to leave her pacquet at her lodgeing — the Gout has seised 2 fingers of my right hand which as it putts me on the necessety of concludeing abrutly will oblige you to pardon it in

Sir

Your very Humble Servant

Edw. Bedingfeld

Caryll to Pope

May 23, 1712.

I am very glad for the sake of the Widow and for the credit of the deceas'd, that *Betterton*'s remains[3] are fallen into such hands as may render 'em reputable to the one and beneficial to the other. Besides the publick acquaintance I long had with that poor man, I also had a slender knowledge of his parts and capacity by private conversation, and ever thought it pity, he was necessitated by the straitness of his fortune, to act (and especially to his latest hours) an imaginary and fictitious part, who was capable of exhibiting a real one, with credit to himself and advantage to his neighbour.

I hope your health permitted you to execute your design of giving us an imitation of *Pollio*,[4] I am satisfy'd 'twill be doubly *Divine* and I

---

[1] *Edward Bedingfield:* A relative of John Caryll.

[2] *for Mrs Belle Fermor:* "*The Rape of the Lock* was on sale the 20th. Advance copies were evidently sent to the parties most concerned. Caryll had not received his on May 23. See his letter of that date [above]" [C].

[3] Betterton's *remains:* Thomas Betterton (1635–1710), famous Restoration actor, was survived by his wife Mary. His "remains" include "Chaucer's *Characters, or the Introduction to the* Canterbury *Tales,*" printed in Lintot's *Miscellany* along with *The Rape of the Locke.* (See table of contents in the 1712 facsimile, p. 137.)

[4] *an imitation of* Pollio: "The imitation of Pollio, Pope's *Messiah*, had already appeared in *Spectator*, No. 378 for 14 May 1712" [C].

shall long to see it. I ever thought church-musick the most ravishing of all harmonious compositions, and must also believe sacred subjects, well handled, the most inspiring of all Poetry.

But where hangs the *Lock* now? (tho' I know that rather than draw any just reflection upon your self, of the least shadow of ill-nature, you would freely have suprest one of the best of Poems.) I hear no more of it — will it come out in *Lintot*'s Miscellany or not? I wrote to Lord *Petre* upon the subject of the Lock, some time since, but have as yet had no answer, nor indeed do I know when he'll be in *London*. I have since I saw you corresponded with Mrs. *W.* I hope she is now with her Aunt, and that her journey thither was something facilitated by my writing to that Lady as pressingly as possible, not to let any thing whatsoever obstruct it. I sent her obliging answer to the party it most concern'd; and when I hear Mrs. *W.* is certainly there, I will write again to my Lady, to urge as much as possible the effecting the only thing that in my opinion can make her Niece easy. I have run out my extent of paper, and am

Your, &c.

Pope to Martha Blount

May the 25. 1712.

Madam, — At last I do myself the honour to send you the Rape of the Locke; which has been so long coming out, that the Ladies Charms might have been half decay'd, while the Poet was celebrating them, and the Printer publishing them. But yourself and your fair Sister must needs have been surfeited already with this Triffle; and therfore you have no hopes of Entertainment but from the rest of this Booke, wherein (they tell me) are some things that may be dangerous to be lookd upon; however I think You may venture, tho' you shou'd Blush for it, since Blushing becomes you the best of any Lady in England, and then the most dangerous thing to be lookd upon is Yourself — Indeed Madam, not to flatter you, our Virtue will be sooner overthrown by one Glance of yours, than by all the wicked Poets can write in an Age, as has been too dearly experienc'd by the wickedest of 'em all, that is to say, by

Madam
Your most obedient
humble Servant,
A: Pope:

Pope to Caryll

May 28. 1712.

. . . I am afraid to insinuate to you how much I esteem you. Flatterers have taken up the style which was once peculiar to friends only, and an honest man has now no way left to express himself by, besides the common one of knaves, so that true friends nowadays differ in their address from flatterers, much as right mastiffs do from spaniels, and show themselves by a dumb, surly, sort of fidelity, rather than by the complaisant and open manner of kindness. This last, however, is what you use to me, and which I account for the best way, tho' I should suspect it in most others. Will you never leave commending my poetry? In fair truth, sir, I like it but too well myself already. Expose me no more, I beg you, to the great danger of vanity, (the rock of all men, but most of young men) and be kindly content for the future when you would please me thoroughly, to say only, you like what I write. The eclogue on the Messiah in imitation of Pollio, I had transcribed a week since with design to send it to you; but finding it printed in the *Spectator* of the fourteenth (which paper I know is constantly sent down to you) I gave it to Mr Englefield. I hope Lewis[5] has conveyed you by this time the *Rape of the Lock,* with what other things of mine are in Lintot's collection; the whole book I will put into your hands when I have the satisfaction to meet you at Reading, which unfeignedly I passionately long for. What hitherto reprieved you from my company was my long illness, which was no sooner over, but Mr Englefield told me you was upon the point of going in Warwickshire, from whence I hope you will bring home all you express; that is, all that man desires. I shall partake so much of the young gentleman's joy, that I fear the nice casuists may account it a sort of enjoying my neighbor's wife, in spirit. But seriously, no friend you have can be more nearly concerned in any thing that regards your happiness and family's than I am. I only hope (as I told Mr Bedingfield the other day, who has done me the favor to send some books of the Rape, to my Lord Petre, and Mrs Fermor) that extreme happiness, which usually causes people to forget old acquaintance, will not make young Mr Caryll entirely forget me in the number of his humble servants. If I might presume to offer any advice in this important change of his life, it should be comprehended in this

---

[5] *Lewis:* "W. Lewis, a Catholic bookseller and a friend of Pope's and Caryll's" [C].

short sentence, Let him fear the Lord, love his lady, and read the Tatler.[6]

To conclude, as no happiness comes without some allay, so it seems the young gentleman must carry me down with his fair lady: and I shall supply the place of the Egyptian skeleton[7] at the entertainments on your return. But I'll be satisfied to make an odd figure in your triumphs, for the pleasure I shall take in attending 'em. The *Imperatrix Triumphans*[8] shall not be without a slave in her chariot, to hold a wreath over the conqueress. I am, dear sir, with the sincerest respect and affection

> your most faithfull friend and
> humble servant
> A:P:

I beg your lady and the whole family may be assured of my most humble service.

Pope to John Caryll, Jr.

Nov. 8, 1712.

There is a passage in your last letter which, I may reasonably say, makes it the kindest I ever received; but as people are never more apt to take little exceptions than when they love most, so there are two things in yours which I will blame no farther than in barely mentioning them, — that compliment you pass upon my wit, as if I writ rather to soothe my own vanity than to prove my affection, and the excuse you seem to make for not writing sooner, as if I pretended to so ridiculous a dominion over your time, or expected you to be very punctual where you are not in debt. One might as well be displeased at the sun for not shining out every day we would wish him to do so, though he be always serviceable to us when most he seems retired, as at a friend, who is ever in a kind disposition towards us, for not manifesting it every day by writing. But if the inclination of a

---

[6] *the Tatler:* Periodical founded by Richard Steele in collaboration with Joseph Addison; it appeared three times a week from April 12, 1709, to January 2, 1711, and was succeeded by *The Spectator*.

[7] *the Egyptian skeleton:* "A reminder of serious or saddening things in the midst of enjoyment; a source of gloom or depression. An allusion to the practice of the ancient Egyptians, as recorded by Plutarch in his *Moralia*" [OED].

[8] *The* Imperatrix Triumphans: The triumphant female general.

friend towards us, and his bare good will and benevolence be ever to be acknowledged, how much more that convincing rhetoric of action and protection, which you so gallantly slur over with the gay term of *wrestling for a friend*. But consider, sir, your person and limbs are not absolutely your own; there is a lady has her part in them, who would lament much more if but a nerve of yours were sprained, than all the friends I have would ever do though my brains were beat out; for, to tell you the plain truth, this is the opinion I entertain of almost all those who are generally styled such in the world — our nominal, unperforming friends. As for my own part, whom have I been ever able to oblige? whom have I ever served to that degree? by what right or merit can I pretend to expect a signal service from any man? I am seriously far from imagining that because people have twice or thrice been civil to me, they are bound always to serve me; the prior obligation was mine, not theirs. Or, if they like my poetry, that because they *laugh with me*, they will *cry for me*. But I must be content to take my fortune, with all my own sins upon my own head. Sir Plume[9] blusters, I hear; nay, the celebrated lady herself is offended, and, which is stranger, not at herself, but me. Mr. Weston,[10] they say, is gloomy upon the matter, — the tyrant meditates revenge; nay, the distressed dame herself has been taught to suspect I served her but by halves, and without prudence. Is not this enough to make a man for the future neither presume to blame injustice or pity innocence? as in Mr. Weston's case; to make a writer never be tender of another's character or fame? as in Belinda's; to act with more reserve and write with less?

I have another storm, too, rising from the bigot, the most violent of animals, on the score of not having altered some true lines in the second edition of the Essay on Criticism. Yet, as to the two first quarrels, I can be satisfied in my conscience of having acted with honour; and as to the last, I dare stand to posterity in the character of an unbigoted Roman Catholic and impartial critic. I dare trust future times, and lie down contented under the impotence of my present censurers, which, like other impotence, would naturally vex and tease one more the less it can do. As to my writings, I pray God they may never have other enemies than those they have met with — which

---

[9] *Sir Plume:* Sir George Brown.
[10] *Mr. Weston:* Sherburn suggests that Mr. Weston doesn't actually have anything to do with the poem and that this sentence begins a separate matter (see *Correspondence* 1: 151n).

are, first, priests; secondly, women, who are the fools of priests; and thirdly, beaus and fops, who are the fools of women.

You see I write in some heat, but I would not do so if I had not a great idea of the friendship of him to whom I write. This frankness, the less discreet it is, is the more an act of trust in me to you. My temper is really a little soured by all this, and yet more by a piece of scurvy news Mr. Southcote yesterday sent me, that the rascally scribbler, the Flying Post, has maliciously reflected upon Mr. Caryll, on account of his crossing the seas at this time. Whether he is yet returned I know not; but if he be, I beg you to offer him my utmost service, if he can think me capable of any, with the only weapon I have, my pen, in reply to, or raillery upon, that scoundrel, and in whatever method he thinks most proper. I am on fire to snatch the first opportunity I ever had of doing something, or at least endeavouring to do something, for your father and my friend. I hope he is not now to be told with what ardour I love, and with what esteem I honour him, any more than you how sincerely and affectionately I shall ever be, dear sir, your most faithful and obedient and obliged humble servant.

The verses you inquire about were never written upon you anywhere else than in the letter I sent you. It was a mere piece of raillery as you will see, if you have not yet done justice upon them, being only Mrs. Nelson's verses on your lady altered in a whimsical way, and applied to yourself. My most humble service attends the whole family. I have given order to Lewis to send two of my Essays to Ladyholt.

Pope to Caryll

London. Jan 9. 1713. [January 9, 1713/14]

Tho' I believe I am one of the last who has congratulated yourself and Mr Caryll upon the birth of his first born, yet this I dare assure you both — that no man is more rejoiced at that blessing, except the father (unless you will require me to speak more correctly, and say, except the grandfather too). I ought also to felicitate you in particular, that you are so early arrived to the dignity of a patriarch, and that you can bear that venerable name without the stooping in the shoulders and that length of beard, which I have observed to denote one of those sires in all the representations of 'em hitherto. I cannot flatter your son so far as to say any thing fine upon the beauty of the babe, or the near resemblance it has to his own lineaments; not having yet had the pleasure of conversing with the nurse upon that agreeable subject. But I am told here, that few statues of Phidias or Praxiteles[11] themselves made so good a figure the first month of their appearing. And what very much adds to the perfection and reputation of this piece of work of his, is, that one may affirm of it, as they do of the fine statue in the Place de Victoire, that it was done, all at a *Jette*.[12]

I am thoroughly sensible of your most righteous endeavours to serve me in my new capacity of a Greek translator, and I hope, by the assistance of such solicitours as Mr Caryll, to make Homer's works of more value and benefit to me than ever they were to himself. What I have in particular to desire further is, that you will send me the subscriptions by the first sitting of the parliament[13] at which time it will be necessary for me to know exactly what number we have secure, — there being then to be printed a list of those who already have subscribed or shall to that time: upon the Credit and figure of which persons a great part of the success with the town will inevitably depend.

I now think it pretty certain, that I shall be warmly supported on all sides in this undertaking.

As to the *Rape of the Lock*, I believe I have managed the dedication so nicely that it can neither hurt the lady, nor the author. I writ it very lately, and upon great deliberation; the young lady approves of it; and the best advice in the kingdom, of the men of sense has been made use of in it, even to the Treasurer's.[14] A preface which salved the lady's honour, without affixing her name, as also prepared, but by herself superseded in favour of the dedication. Not but that, after all, fools will talk, and fools will hear 'em.

. . . Believe me, dear sir, under all circumstances whatever, and in all respects whatever, with the last sincerity and deference

Your most obliged and most faithful
Freind and servant
A: P:

My most humble service attends all the good family even from the grandsire to the grandson. I shall be in London all the winter.

---

[11] *Phidias or Praxiteles:* Phidias (born c. 490 B.C.) and Praxiteles (c. 364 B.C.) were Athenian sculptors.
[12] *all at a* Jette: All at one throw.
[13] *the first sitting of the parliament:* February 18.
[14] *the Treasurer's:* Robert Harley was Lord Treasurer.

Pope to Mrs. or Miss Marriot

February, the last Day, 1713. [February 28, 1713/14]
I have of late been so much a man of business[15] that I have almost
forgot to write (as I used to do) long letters about nothing. Indeed, I
see people every day so very busy about nothing, that I fancy I am no
improper historian to write their actions. It would be but filling the
paper as they do their lives, no manner with what. I do not do this
when I write to you who are much too good to have such tricks put
upon you. Nor ought I to endeavour to make you pass one quarter of
an hour of all your life ill in reading such impertinence, as is but too
natural for me to write. What excuse then, can I offer for the poem
that attends this letter,[16] where 'tis a chance but you are diverted
from some very good action or useful reflection for more hours than
one. I know it is no sin to laugh, but I had rather your laughter
should be at the vain ones of your own sex than at me, and therefore
would rather have you read my poem than my letter. This whimsical
piece of work, as I have now brought it up to my first design, is at
once the most a satire, and the most inoffensive, of anything of mine.
People who would rather it were let alone laugh at it, and seem
heartily merry, at the same time that they are uneasy. 'Tis a sort of
writing very like tickling. I am so vain as to fancy a pretty complete
picture of the life of our modern ladies in this idle town from which
you are so happily, so prudently, and so philosophically retired. My
friend, Mr. Rowe, in his new play[17] has a description that puts me ex-
ceedingly in mind of Sturston: —

> Far from the crowd and the tumultuous city
> There stands a lonely but a healthful dwelling
> Built for convenience, and the use of Life.
> Around it, fallows, meads, and pastures fair,
> A little garden, and a limpid brook,
> By Nature's own contrivance, seem dispos'd;
> No neighbours but a few poor simple clowns,
> Honest and true; with a well-meaning priest.

[15] *a man of business:* "As a result of the subscription for the translation of the
Iliad" [C].

[16] *the poem that attends this letter:* "Evidently an advance copy of *The Rape of the
Lock* (1714)" [C].

[17] *Mr. Rowe, in his new play:* Nicholas Rowe (1674–1718) was a popular play-
wright acquainted with Pope and Addison. His new play, *Jane Shore,* was published by
Lintot; see the advertisements in the *Daily Courant,* p. 177.

By this well-meaning priest, I mean Mr. Brome, who, Mr. Marriot tells me, is to minister unto you.

Pope to Mrs. Arabella Fermor

[1714–15]

You are by this time satisfy'd how much the tenderness of one man of merit is to be prefer'd to the addresses of a thousand. And by this time, the Gentleman you have made choice of is sensible, how great is the joy of having all those charms and good qualities which have pleas'd so many, now apply'd to please one only. It was but just, that the same Virtues which gave you reputation, should give you happiness; and I can wish you no greater, than that you may receive it in as high a degree your self, as so much good humour must infallibly give it to your husband.

It may be expected perhaps, that one who has the title of Poet, should say something more polite on this occasion: But I am really more a well-wisher to your felicity, than a celebrater of your beauty. Besides, you are now a married woman, and in a way to be a great many better things than a fine Lady; such as an excellent wife, a faithful friend, a tender parent, and at last as the consequence of them all, a saint in heaven. You ought now to hear nothing but that, which was all you ever desired to hear (whatever others may have spoken to you) I mean *Truth*: And it is with the utmost that I assure you, no friend you have can more rejoice in any good that befalls you, is more sincerely delighted with the prospect of your future happiness, or more unfeignedly desires a long continuance of it. I beg you will think it but just, that a man who will certainly be spoken of as your admirer, after he is dead, may have the happiness to be esteem'd while he is living

Your, &c.

ALEXANDER POPE

"To Belinda on the Rape of the Lock"

Pope offered Arabella Fermor a choice of dedications, prose or poem, to the 1714 expanded version of the *Rape* (he wrote both in 1713). She chose the prose letter that has traditionally prefaced the poem; the rejected poetic dedication (as the story goes) first appeared anonymously in 1717 in a miscellany edited by Pope.

Pleas'd in these lines, *Belinda*, you may view
How things are priz'd, which once belong'd to you:
If on some meaner head this Lock had grown,
The nymph despis'd, the Rape had been unknown.
But what concerns the valiant and the fair,   5
The Muse asserts as her peculiar care.
Thus *Helens* Rape and *Menelaus'* wrong
Became the Subject of great *Homer*'s song;
And, lost in ancient times, the golden fleece
Was rais'd to fame by all the wits of *Greece*.   10
      Had fate decreed, propitious to your pray'rs,
To give their utmost date to all your hairs;
This Lock, of which late ages now shall tell,
Had dropt like fruit, neglected, when it fell.
      Nature to your undoing arms mankind   15
With strength of body, artifice of mind;
But gives your feeble sex, made up of fears,
No guard but virtue, no redress but tears.
Yet custom (seldom to your favour gain'd)
Absolves the virgin when by force constrain'd.   20
Thus *Lucrece* lives unblemish'd in her fame,
A bright example of young *Tarquin*'s shame.
Such praise is yours — and such shall you possess,
Your virtue equal, tho' your loss be less.
Then smile Belinda at reproachful tongues,   25
Still warm our hearts, and still inspire our songs.
But would your charms to distant times extend,
Let *Jervas* paint them, and let *Pope* commend.
Who censure most, more precious hairs would lose,
To have the *Rape* recorded by his Muse.   30

ANONYMOUS

From "The Celebrated Beauties. A Poem, Occasioned upon Being Suspected of Writing The British Court"

Along with Pope's *Pastorals*, Jacob Tonson the Elder's *Poetical Miscellanies, The Sixth Part* (1709) included a poem by an anonymous author that celebrated the "toasts" or reigning beauties of the day — "Ye Female Glories, which exalt our Isle." Excerpted here is the tribute to Arabella Fermor, the seventeenth stanza in the middle of a twenty-page encomium on a select few of the "Charmers in Millions [who] grace this happy Sphere." Following standard eighteenth-century practice, the poem discreetly drops the vowels of the women's names. In satire, the ploy was used to sidestep libel charges; here it protects the "modesty" of the ladies thus publicly exposed. This excerpt provides another local voice on Arabella Fermor's position in her world, the epitome of "feminine virtues" that balance oppositions — not too much this, not too much that — described in a pattern that recalls the much-admired lines on the Thames in Sir John Denham's *Cooper's Hill* (1655): "Though deep, yet clear, though gentle, yet not dull, / Strong without rage, without o'er-flowing full" (ll. 191–92). (Pope himself made use of the pattern in the *Dunciad*: "Flow Welsted, flow! like thine inspirer, Beer, / Tho' stale, not ripe; tho' thin, yet never clear; / So sweetly mawkish, and so smoothly dull; / Heady, not strong; o'erflowing, tho' not full" [III. 169–72].)

> *F–rm–r*'s a Pattern for the Beauteous Kind,
> Compos'd to please, and ev'ry way refin'd;
> Obliging with Reserve, and Humbly Great,
> Tho' Gay, yet Modest, tho' Sublime, yet Sweet;
> Fair without Art, and graceful without Pride,
> By Merit and Descent to deathless Fame ally'd.

HESTER LYNCH THRALE PIOZZI

From *Observations and Reflections Made in the Course of a Journey Through France, Italy, and Germany*

Hester Thrale Piozzi (1741–1821) was a close friend of Samuel Johnson, known for her acerbic wit and respected for her patronage of literary society. Piozzi's anecdotal account from Arabella Fermor's niece gives a sharp little picture of the effect of the poem on its principal character and a disillusioned memory of the poet himself.

The excerpt is taken from Vol. I (London: Printed for A. Strahan and T. Cadell, 1789), 20–21.

... Mrs. Fermor, the Prioress,[1] niece to Belinda in the Rape of the Lock, taking occasion to tell me, comically enough, "That she believed there was but little comfort to be found in a house that harboured *poets;* for that she remembered Mr. Pope's praise made her aunt very troublesome and conceited, while his numberless caprices would have employed ten servants to wait on him; and he gave one" (said she) "no amends by his talk neither, for he only sate dozing all day, when the sweet wine was out, and made his verses chiefly in the night; during which season he kept himself awake by drinking coffee, which it was one of the maids business to make for him, and they took it by turns."

THE DAILY COURANT

Advertisements for *The Rape of the Lock*

It seems fitting that *The Rape of the Lock*, a poem very much about contemporary life, was advertised in London's first daily newspaper. (The poem's publisher, Bernard Lintot, also advertised in the *Post Boy*, a weekly journal that started in 1695.) The *Daily Courant* had made its own debut on March 11, 1702. Before this, papers had been published irregularly three or four times a week, but news of the wars with France

---

[1] *the Prioress:* Hester Piozzi was visiting "my old acquaintance the English Austin [Augustinian] Nuns at the Fossée" (Notre Dame de Sion, in the Rue des Fossés St. Victor in Paris); "Mrs.," or "mistress," was a term of respect for ladies, married or not.

and Holland, combined with the increasing cultural "fixation on contemporaneity, part of [a] larger interest in discovery, enlightenment, and novelty" (Hunter 167; see also Handover 127), made the idea of the daily transmission of news appealing (and profitable). The *Daily Courant* was printed on a single sheet, usually 12½ by 7½ inches. Advertisements — for books, cures, cosmetics, services, items lost, and items found — increasingly competed with news for space on the page. The following three announcements of the publication of the *Rape* describe the editions, quote the price, and tell readers where they can buy the books. Note that in two of the advertisements Pope's poem is wedged behind the works of more popular, established writers even though its earlier version had done well enough to now earn itself two reincarnations, an affordable and a deluxe edition. By April 10, 1714, *The Count de Gabalis* is included in the advertisement as "Necessary for the Readers of the Rape of the Lock."

Friday, January 29, 1714
No. 3827

In a few Days will be published,

The Tragedy of Jane Shore; written in Imitation of the Style of Shakespear, by Mr. Rowe.[1] A small Number will be printed on a large fine Paper, Price 2 s. or gilt 2 s. 6 d.[2] There will likewise be published, The Rape of the Lock; an Heroi-comical Poem, now first Printed compleat in 5 Canto's; to which are added, 6 Copper-Plates finely engrav'd by Mr. Du Bosse.[3] A small Number will be printed on a fine Royal Paper, Price 2 s. Those who are willing to have these are desired to send in their Names to Bernard Lintott between the two Temple-Gates. N. B. The Subscribers will have their Books ready to be delivered two Days before the Day of general Publication.[4]

---

[1] *The Tragedy of Jane Shore; . . . by Mr. Rowe:* Nicholas Rowe (1674–1718) was a popular playwright and acquaintance of Pope and Addison. He edited Shakespeare's plays, dividing them into acts and scenes, and made use of Shakespearean tragic conventions in plays like *Jane Shore* (1714).

[2] *Price 2 s, or gilt 2 s. 6 d.:* Two shillings for the plainer version, two shillings sixpence for the deluxe gilt-edge edition.

[3] *Mr. Du Bosse:* Claude Du Bosc (fl. 1714), who engraved onto copper plates the illustrations designed by Louis Du Guernier (?1687–1716). See "Notes on the Text and Engravings" p. 46.

[4] *Subscribers:* Those who want to pay in advance for the finer copy and receive it "two Days before the Day of general Publication." Pope published his *Iliad* by subscription, the money up front funding the work in progress; as a reward, subscribers' names were listed in the book.

Wednesday, March 10, 1714
No. 3861

This Day is Published,

The Rape of the Lock: An Heroic-comical Poem, by Mr. Pope. Now first published compleat, with the Addition of 3 new Canto's, adorn'd with 6 Copper Plates. N.B. A small Number are printed on fine Royal Paper. Most of Mr. Pope's Writings are collected together in a Volume of Miscellanies, by Several Hands.[5] Price 5 s. Printed for Bernard Lintott between the 2 Temple-Gates in Fleetstreet.

Saturday, April 10, 1714
No. 3888

This Day is Published,

The Third Edition of the Works of Mr. George Farquhar: Containing all his Letters, Poems, Essays, and Comedies, publish'd in his Life-Time.[6] Illustrated with Cutts.[7] Printed on a finer Paper than the former Editions. Price 6 s. The ad Edition of the Rape of the Lock, an Heroi-Comical Poem, in 5 Canto's, with Cutts. By Mr. Pope, Price 1 s. The Count de Gabalis; Necessary for the Readers of the Rape of the Lock. Pr. 1 s. 6 d. The Tragedy of Jane Shore, written in Imitation of Shakespear's Style. Pr 1 s. 6 d. All printed for B Lintott between the 2 Temple Gates.

ALEXANDER POPE

From *A Key to the Lock or, a Treatise Proving,* beyond All Contradiction, the Dangerous Tendency of a Late Poem, Entitled, The Rape of the Lock to Government and Religion

Pope first published this "key" to his own work anonymously in 1715. It's a multiple satire: first, it parodies the popular genre of authorized and unauthorized keys to satirical work published usually by the booksellers; second, it anticipates and caricatures all the hostile critical

---

[5] *Miscellanies:* See the headnote to the facsimile of *The Rape of the Locke*, p. 130.

[6] *Farquhar:* George Farquhar (1678–1707), a popular Restoration playwright.

[7] *Cutts:* Copperplate engravings (illustrations).

interpretations of the *Rape*; and third, it satirizes the religious and political paranoia of the day. The pseudonymous "Esdras Barnivelt," a self-satisfied Dutch Protestant apothecary (something between a pharmacist and a general practitioner), claims to decode the nefarious papist subtext (or secret plot) of the poem to smuggle into the minds of innocent readers wicked Catholic ideas about overthrowing the government and the state religion (Church of England, or the Anglican Church). But as Thomas Burnet (1694–1753), a lawyer, judge, pamphleteer, and critic of Pope, irritatedly notices in *The Grumbler* 14 (May 6, 1715), the author of *A Key* also manages "modestly [to take] an opportunity to commend the Smoothness of his own Verses, and to publish a Sale of Six Thousand of his Books." *A Key* is Pope at his cleverest, at once teaching us how *not* to read (how *not* to force an interpretation onto a text, twisting everything to fit a preconceived meaning), and enticing us to read on.

The text is taken from the third edition, published in 1718. I have excerpted the Epistle Dedicatory to Mr. Pope, the introduction, and the anti-Catholic reading of the *Rape*, cutting other prefatory letters and poems and the political satire.

The Epistle Dedicatory to Mr. POPE.

Though it may seem foreign to my Profession, which is that of making up and dispensing salutary Medicines to his Majesty's Subjects, I might say my Fellow-Subjects, since I have had the Advantage of being naturalized) yet cannot I think it unbecoming me to furnish an Antidote against the Poyson which hath been so artfully distilled through your Quill, and conveyed to the World through the pleasing Vehicles of your Numbers. Nor is my Profession as an Apothecary, so abhorrent from yours as a Poet, since the Ancients have thought fit to make the same God the Patron of Both. I have, not without some Pleasure, observ'd the mystical Arms of our Company; wherein is represented *Apollo* killing the fell Monster *Python*; this in some measure admonishes me of my Duty, to trample upon and destroy, as much as in me lies, that Dragon, or baneful Serpent, *Popery*.

I must take leave to make you my Patient, whether you will or no; though out of the Respect I have for you, I should rather chuse to apply Lenitive than Corrosive Medicines; happy, if they may prove an Emetic sufficient to make you cast up those Errors, which you have imbibed in your Education, and which, I hope, I shall never live to see this Nation digest.

Sir, I cannot but lament, that a Gentleman of your acute Wit, rectified Understanding, and sublimated Imagination, should misapply those Talents to raise ill Humours in the Constitution of the Body Politick, of which your self are a Member, and upon the Health whereof your own Preservation depends. Give me leave to say, such Principles as yours would again reduce us to the fatal Necessity of the Phlebotomy of War, or the Causticks of Persecution.[1]

In order to inform you of this, I have sought your Acquaintance and Conversation with the utmost Diligence, for I hoped in Person to persuade you to a publick Confession of your Fault, and a Recantation of these dangerous Tenets. But finding all my Endeavours ineffectual, and being satisfied with the Conscience of having done all that became a Man of an honest Heart and honourable Intention; I could no longer omit my Duty in opening the Eyes of the World by the Publication of this Discourse. It was indeed written some Months since, but seems not the less proper at this Juncture, when I find so universal Encouragement given by both Parties to the Author of a libellous Work that is designed equally to prejudice them both. The uncommon Sale of this Book (for above 6000 of 'em have been already vended) was also a farther Reason that call'd aloud upon me to put a stop to its further Progress, and to preserve His Majesty's Subjects, by exposing the whole Artifice of your Poem in Publick.

Sir, to address my self to so florid a Writer as you, without collecting all the Flowers of Rhetorick, would be an unpardonable *Indecorum*; but when I speak to the World, as I do in the following Treatise, I must use a simple Stile, since it would be absurd to prescribe an universal Medicine, or *Catholicon*,[2] in a Language not universally understood.

As I have always professed to have a particular Esteem for Men of Learning, and more especially for your self, nothing but the Love of Truth should have engaged me in a Design of this Nature. *Amicus Plato, Amicus Socrates, sed magis Amica Veritas.*[3]

> I am,
> Your most Sincere Friend,
> and Humble Servant,
> *E. Barnivelt*

---

[1] *the Phlebotomy of War, or the Causticks of Persecution:* Refers to common eighteenth-century medical remedies: Phlebotomy was the practice of opening a vein to let blood; caustics were substances used to burn living tissue.

[2] Catholicon: "A universal remedy or prophylactic" [OED].

[3] Amicus Plato, Amicus Socrates, sed magis Amica Veritas: Latin for "Plato is a friend, Socrates is a friend, but Truth is a greater friend."

. . . Since this unhappy Division of our Nation into Parties, it is not to be imagined how many Artifices have been made use of by Writers to obscure the Truth, and cover Designs, which may be detrimental to the Publick; in particular, it has been their Custom of late to vent their Political Spleen in Allegory and Fable. If an honest believing Nation is to be made a Jest of, we have a Story of *John Bull* and his Wife;[4] if a Treasurer is to be glanced at, an *Ant* with a *white Straw* is introduced;[5] if a Treaty of Commerce is to be ridiculed, 'tis immediately metamorphosed into a Tale of Count *Tariff*.

But if any of these Malevolents have never so small a Talent in Rhime, they principally delight to convey their Malice in that pleasing way; as it were, gilding the Pill, and concealing the Poison under the Sweetness of Numbers. Who could imagine that an *Original Canto* of *Spencer* should contain a Satyr upon one Administration;[6] or that *Yarhel's Kitchen*, or the *Dogs of Egypt*, should be a Sarcasm upon another.[7]

It is the Duty of every well-designing Subject to prevent, as far as in him lies, the ill Consequences of such pernicious Treatises; and I hold it mine to warn the Publick of the late Poem, entitled, the *RAPE of the LOCK*; which I shall demonstrate to be of this nature. Many of these sort of Books have been bought by honest and well-meaning People purely for their Diversion, who have in the end found themselves insensibly led into the Violence of Party Spirit, and many domestick Quarrels have been occasioned by the different Application of these Books. The Wife of an eminent Citizen grew very noisy upon reading *Bob Hush*; *John Bull*, upon *Change*,[8] was thought not only to concern the State, but to affront the City; and the Poem we are now treating of, has not only dissolved an agreeable Assembly of Beaux and Belles, but (as I am told) has set Relations at as great a distance, as if they were married together.

It is a common and just Observation, that when the Meaning of any thing is dubious, one can no way better judge of the true Intent

---

[4] John Bull *and his Wife*: "A personification of the English nation; Englishmen collectively, or the typical Englishman [and his wife]" [OED].

[5] *an* Ant *with a* white Straw: An image of Harley holding the white staff — the symbol of the office of Lord Treasurer.

[6] *an* original Canto of Spencer . . . *a* Satyr *upon one* Administration: In 1714 "Nestor Ironside" (Samuel Croxall) published *An Original Canto of Spencer*, an attack on the Earl of Oxford (Hammond 308).

[7] Yarhel's Kitchen, *or the* Dog's *of Egypt . . . a* Sarcasm *upon another*: Yarhell's-Kitchen: Or, The Dogs of Egypt. An Heroic Poem (1713), in praise of Oxford — Yarhell is an anagram of Harley (Hammond, 308).

[8] Change: The Royal Exchange in the City.

of it, than by considering who is the Author, what is his Character in general, and his Disposition in particular.

Now that the Author of this Poem is professedly a *Papist*, is well known; and that a Genius so capable of doing Service to that Cause, may have been corrupted in the Course of his Education by *Jesuits* or others, is justly very much to be suspected; notwithstanding that seeming *Coldness* and *Moderation*, which he has been (perhaps artfully) reproached with, by those of his own Profession. They are sensible that this Nation is secured with good and wholesome Laws, to prevent all evil Practices of the Church of *Rome*; particularly the Publication of Books, that may in any sort propagate that Doctrine: Their Authors are therefore oblig'd to couch their Designs the deeper; and tho' I cannot aver that the Intention of this Gentleman was directly to spread Popish Doctrines, yet it comes to the same Point if he touch the Government: For the Court of *Rome* knows very well, that the Church at this time is so firmly founded on the State, that the only way to shake the one is by attacking the other.

What confirms me in this Opinion, is an accidental Discovery I made of a very artful Piece of Management among his Popish Friends and Abettors, to hide this whole Design upon the Government, by taking all the Characters upon themselves.

Upon the Day that this Poem was published, it was my Fortune to step into the *Cocoa Tree*,[9] where a certain Gentleman was railing very liberally at the Author, with a Passion extremely well counterfeited, for having (as he said) reflected upon him in the Character of Sir *Plume*. Upon his going out, I enquired who he was, and they told me, *a Roman Catholick Knight*.

I was the same Evening at *Will*'s, and saw a Circle round another Gentleman, who was railing in like manner, and shewing his Snuffbox and Cane, to prove he was satyrized in the same Character. I asked this Gentleman's Name, and was told, he was *a Roman Catholick Lord*.

A Day or two after I was sent for, upon a slight Indisposition, to the young Lady's to whom the Poem is dedicated. She also took up the Character of *Belinda* with much Frankness and good Humour, tho' the Author has given us a Key in his Dedication,[10] that he meant something further. This Lady is also a *Roman Catholick*. At the same

---

[9] *Cocoa Tree:* A coffee house.

[10] *Dedication:* "The Character of Belinda *(as it is here manag'd) resembles you in nothing but in Beauty*. Dedication to the *Rape of the Lock*" [P].

time others of the Characters were claim'd by some Persons in the Room; and all of them *Roman Catholicks*.

But to proceed to the Work it self.

In all things which are intricate, as Allegories in their own Nature are, and especially those that are industriously made so, it is not to be expected we should find the Clue at first sight; but when once we have laid hold on that, we shall trace this our Author through all the Labyrinths, Doublings and Turnings of this intricate Composition.

. . .

We have now considered this Poem in its Political View, wherein we have shewn that it hath two different Walks of Satyr, the one in the Story it self, which is a Ridicule on the late Transactions in general; the other in the Machinary, which is a Satyr on the Ministers of State in particular. I shall now show that the same Poem, taken in another Light, has a Tendency to Popery, which is secretly insinuated through the whole.

In the first place, he has conveyed to us the Doctrine of Guardian Angels and Patron Saints in the Machinary of his *Sylphs*, which being a Piece of Popish Superstition that hath been endeavoured to be exploded ever since the Reformation, he would here revive under this Disguise. Here are all the Particulars which they believe of those Beings, which I shall sum up in a few Heads.

1*st*. The Spirits are made to concern themselves with all human Actions in general.

2*dly*. A distinct Guardian Spirit or Patron is assigned to each Person in particular.

> Of these am I, who they Protection claim,
> A watchful Sprite———

3*dly*. They are made directly to inspire Dreams, Visions, and Revelations.

> Her Guardian Sylph prolong'd her balmy Rest,
> 'Twas he had summon'd to her silent Bed
> The Morning Dream———

4*thly*. They are made to be subordinate, in different Degrees, some presiding over others. So *Ariel* hath his several Under-Officers at Command.

> Superior by the Head was *Ariel* plac'd.

5thly. They are employed in various Offices, and each hath his Office assigned him.

> Some in the Fields of purest Æther play,
> And bask and whiten in the Blaze of Day.
> Some guide the Course, *&c.*

6thly. He hath given his Spirits the Charge of the several Parts of Dress; intimating thereby, that the Saints preside over the several Parts of Human Bodies. They have one Saint to cure the Tooth-ach, another cures the Gripes, another the Gout, and so of all the rest.

> The flutt'ring Fan be *Zephyretta*'s Care,
> The Drops to thee, *Brillante*, we consign, *&c.*

7thly. They are represented to know the Thoughts of Men.

> As on the Nosegay in her Breast reclin'd,
> He watch'd th' Ideas rising in her Mind.

8thly. They are made Protectors even to Animal and Irrational Beings.

> *Ariel* himself shall be the Guard of *Shock.*

So St. *Anthony* presides over Hogs, *&c.*

9thly. Others are made Patrons of whole Kingdoms and Provinces.

> Of these the Chief the Care of Nations own.

So St. *George* is imagined by the *Papists* to defend *England*; St. *Patrick*, *Ireland*; St. *James*, *Spain*, &c. Now what is the Consequence of all this? By granting that they have this Power, we must be brought back again to pray to them.

The *Toilette* is an artful Recommendation of the *Mass*, and pompous Ceremonies of the *Church of Rome*. The *unveiling* of the *Altar*, the *Silver Vases* upon it, being *rob'd* in *White*, as the Priests are upon the chief Festivals, and the *Head uncover'd*, are manifest Marks of this.

> A Heav'nly Image in the Glass appears,
> To that she bends————

Plainly denotes *Image Worship.*

The *Goddess*, who is deck'd with *Treasures*, *Jewels*, and the *various Offerings of the World*, manifestly alludes to the Lady of *Loretto*. You have Perfumes breathing from the *Incense Pot* in the following Line,

> And all *Arabia* breathes from yonder Box.

The Character of *Belinda*, as we take it in this third View, represents the Popish Religion, or the Whore of *Babylon*; who is described in the State this malevolent Author wishes for, coming forth in all her Glory upon the *Thames*, and overspreading the Nation with Ceremonies.

> Not with more Glories in th' æthereal Plain,
> The Sun first rises o'er the Purple Main,
> Than issuing forth the Rival of his Beams,
> Launch'd on the Bosom of the Silver *Thames*.

She is dressed with a Cross on her Breast, the Ensign of Popery, the Adoration of which is plainly recommended in the following Lines:

> On her white Breast a sparkling *Cross* she wore,
> Which Jews might *kiss*, and Infidels *adore*.

Next he represents her as the *Universal Church*, according to the Boasts of the Papists:

> And like the Sun she shines on all alike.

After which he tells us,

> If to her Share some Female Errors fall,
> Look on her Face, and you'll forget them all.

Tho' it should be granted some Errors fall to her Share, look on the pompous Figure she makes throughout the World, and they are not worth regarding. In the Sacrifice following soon after, you have these Two Lines:

> For this, e'er Phoebus rose, he had implor'd,
> Propitious Heav'n, and ev'ry Pow'r ador'd.

In the first of them, he plainly hints at their *Matins*; in the second, by adoring ev'ry Power, the *Invocation of Saints*.

Belinda's Visits are described with numerous *Wax lights*, which are always used in the Ceremonial Parts of the *Romish* Worship.

——Visits shall be paid on solemn Days,
When num'rous Wax-lights in bright Order blaze.

The *Lunar Sphere* he mentions, opens to us their Purgatory, which is seen in the following Line,

Since all Things lost on Earth are treasur'd there.

It is a Popish Doctrine, that scarce any Person quits this World, but he must touch at Purgatory in his Way to Heaven; and it is here also represented as the *Treasury* of the *Romish Church*. Nor is it much to be wonder'd at, that the *Moon* should be *Purgatory*, when a Learned Divine hath in a late Treatise proved *Hell* to be in the *Sun*.[11]

I shall now before I conclude, desire the Reader to compare this Key with those upon any other Pieces, which are supposed to be secret Satyrs upon the State, either Ancient or Modern; as with those upon *Petronius Arbiter*, *Lucian*'s true History, *Barclay*'s *Argenis*, or *Rablais*'s *Garagantua*; and I doubt not he will do me the Justice to acknowledge, that the Explanations here laid down, are deduced as naturally, and with as little Force, both from the general Scope and Bent of the Work, and from the several Particulars, and are every Way as consistent and undeniable as any of those; and ev'ry way as candid as any modern Interpretations of either Party, on the mysterious State Treatises of our Times.

To sum up my whole Charge against this Author in a few Words: He has ridiculed both the present Mi——ry and the last; abused great Statesmen and great Generals; nay, the Treaties of whole Nations have not escaped him, nor has the Royal Dignity it self been omitted in the Progress of his Satyr; and all this he has done just at the Meeting of a new Parliament. I hope a proper Authority may be made use of to bring him to condign Punishment: In the mean while I doubt not, if the Persons most concern'd would but order Mr. *Bernard Lintott*, the Printer and Publisher of this dangerous Piece to be taken into Custody, and examin'd; many farther Discoveries might be made, both of this Poet's and his Abettor's secret Designs, which are doubtless of the utmost Importance to the Government.

F I N I S.

---

[11] *proved Hell to be in the* Sun: "The Reverend Dr. Swinden" [P]. Refers to Tobias Swinden (1659–1719), *An Enquiry into the Nature and Place of Hell,* 1714.

CHARLES GILDON

From *A New Rehearsal, or, Bays the Younger*

Charles Gildon (1665–1724) was a poet, dramatist, critic, biographer, and writer of miscellaneous works. Pat Rogers labels him "among the most able of the dunces" (721); Pope calls him "a writer of criticism and libels of the last age. . . . He signalized himself as a Critic, having written some very bad plays; abused Mr. *P.* very scandalously in an anonymous Pamphlet of the Life of Mr. *Wycherly* printed by *Curl,* in another called the New Rehearsal printed in 1714, in a third entitled the compleat Art of English Poetry" (*Dunciad Variorum,* I.250n). Gildon was indeed a persistent critic of Pope, and *A New Rehearsal* — the title alluding to George Villiers's *The Rehearsal* (1671), a satire on Dryden — ushers in a number of what would become standard criticisms of contemporary literary standards and practices in general, and of Pope and *The Rape of the Lock* in particular. I have included here only the direct attacks on Pope from Act I, Scene 1, and Act II, Scene 2. The characters Mr. Freeman and Mr. Truewit critique the poet as a modern upstart (in the same category with Defoe), in an age in which "a tolerable knack at Versification sets any Man up for an Author," as long as he substitutes novelty for wit: "then you must chuse some odd out of the way Subject, some Trifle or other that wou'd surprize the Common Reader that any thing cou'd be written upon it, as a *Fan,* a *Lock of Hair,* or the like." The character Sawny Dapper brazenly announces he is translating Homer without knowing Greek (a snipe at Pope's lack of formal classical education). The upstart poet makes up his own rules, invents his own genre of the "*Heroic-Comical* . . . that no Man ever thought of before." And his poetry exploits lasciviousness: "you must make the Ladies speak Bawdy . . . [and] prefer the Locks of her Poll, to her Locks of another more sacred and secret Part."

The text is taken from the first edition in the British Library.

THE PERSONS NAMES.

MR. FREEMAN.	*A Gentleman of a good Taste and Learning.*
MR. TRUEWIT.	*A Man of Wit and good Taste.*
SIR INDOLENT EASIE.	*A Man of Wit, but one who is, or seems to be pleas'd with every Thing and every Writer.*

188

SAWNY DAPPER. $\left\{ \begin{array}{l} \textit{A young Poet of the Modern} \\ \textit{stamp, an easy Versifyer, Con-} \\ \textit{ceited and a Contemner secretly} \\ \textit{of all others.} \end{array} \right.$

MR. BAYS. $\left\{ \begin{array}{l} \textit{A Pedantic, Reciting Poet, ad-} \\ \textit{mir'd by the Mob and himself,} \\ \textit{but justly contemn'd by Men of} \\ \textit{Sense and Learning, and a de-} \\ \textit{spiser of Rules and Art.} \end{array} \right.$

SCENE: *the* Rose Tavern *Covent-Garden.*[1]

ACT I. SCENE I.

A Room in the Rose Tavern. *Covent-Garden.*

Freeman *and* True-Wit.

FREE. Well, *Dick*, Here's your welcome to Town. [Drinks.]

TRUE. *Joseph* I thank thee, there is nothing can make the Town more agreeable to me, after so long an Absence, than an Evenings Converse with thee now and then, disengag'd from all the Impertinence, which generally renders Conversation here so intolerable.

FREE. Our Town Impertinence is at least so much the more tolerable, than that of the Country, as it has more of Variety and Pertness.

TRUE. I shou'd as soon believe Pain were to be render'd so by being of various kinds. 'Tis true your Coxcombs are more pert, than ours in the Country; but that renders them the more troublesom and talkative; whereas a Country Fool may pass, by his Silence, on us for a Man of Thought.

FREE. Oh! Sir, if your grave Sot be to your Goust,[2] you may be furnish'd with a Dish or two every Night within the Precincts of *Covent-Garden.* There is no Resort of the Wits but are replenish'd with your solemn Listners, who with their Nods keep Time to the Talkers, and seem to Approve and Understand all that is said.

TRUE. Just as it was I find when I us'd *Will*'s; but pray Sir does that Ancient Rendezvous of the *Beaux Esprits* hold its Ground? And

---

[1] Covent-Garden: The theatre district, located in the "Town," between the old City of London and Westminster.

[2] *Goust:* Taste.

do Men now, as formerly, become WITS by sipping Coffee and Tea with *Wycherly* and the reigning Poets?

FREE.　No, no, there has been great Revolutions in this State of Affairs since you left us; *Buttons*[3] is now the Establish'd *Wits* Coffeehouse, and all the Young Scriblers of the Times pay their Attendance Nightly there, to keep up their Pretensions to Sense and Understanding.

TRUE.　And who and who honest *Jo*, are the Dispensers of Fame now? What bright Spirits entertain the Town with their Pens?

FREE.　Ah *Dick*! such a Race of Poets, as never were seen or heard of before. A tolerable knack at Versification sets any Man up for an Author; but as for force of Genius, Art, Imagery, and true Sense, they are still thought very needless Qualifications in a Poet. Nay they are so very averse to them, that whoever presumes to advance any thing in their favour, is sure to have all the Votes of the House against him; for they think Ignorance is the Mother of *Wit*, and Poetry, as the Papists believe it the Mother of Devotion.

TRUE.　By this I find the Town is not yet much chang'd in their detestable Taste; and I must confess, I always thought that there was hardly any where to be found a more insipid Race of Mortals, than those whom we Moderns are pleased to Complement with the Name of Poets, meerly for having attain'd the Chiming Faculty of a Language, with an Injudicious random use of *Wit* and *Fancy*.

. . .

ACT. II.

SCENE the same Room.

Sir Indolent Easy, Joseph Freeman, Dick True-Wit,
and Sawny Dapper.

DAP.　Well, I protest, I think 'tis a Glass of excellent Wine. Well, and how and how, and what were you upon my dear Knight? on *Wit, Politics*, or *Religion*?

SIR IND.　Oh! for *Politics* and *Religion*, I leave them to the Statesmen and the Clergy; for they thrive so ill in their Hands, that I am afraid they wou'd be quite lost in ours.

---

[3] Will's . . . Buttons: London coffee houses patronized by the literary establishment; see the Introduction.

DAP.   I protest Pithy and Satiric enough Sir *Indolent*; well, then I find you have been upon *Wit*, as indeed what cou'd you have been on within the Air of *Covent-Garden*, besides *Wit*?

FREE.   But Mr. *Dapper* we were upon *Poetry*.

DAP.   Better still, I love *Poetry* with all my Heart. Why, Sir, I am a small Dabbler in *Helicon*[4] my self. [To True-wit.]

TRUE.   Doubtless, Sir, a great Proficient in the Art.

DAP.   Why faith I think so; yet I believe I may say, thanks to my own Industry, and my good Friends Applause, that I am got into the Front part of the Sons of *Parnassus*,[5] and therefore I am sorry I mist your Discouse of *Poetry*.

FREE.   But dear *Sawny*, it was Criticizing upon *Poetry*, which you, Gentlemen, that now entertain the Town in that way, are mortal Enemies to.

DAP.   I must needs say that, if I had not written on *Criticism* my self[6] I shou'd not say much in its Praise; but I thought to do in my Progress to Poetry, as Mr. *Bays* the Elder did with his Prologues. I appear'd first in the Character of a *Critic in Terrorem*[7] to the Reigning Wits of the Time, that they shou'd the more easily admit me into their Number: But then for their Encouragement, I writ in Rhime, and faith, to say Truth, as to Matter, not so far above them, as to make them fear that I shou'd not fall down to their Level.

TRUE.   I find, Sir, then, that there is a great deal of Art, as well as good Fortune, in attaining to the Honour of a *Wit,* or Poetic Author.

DAP.   Oh! Sir, the greatest Art in the World; for, Sir, if you trust to mere Merit, you'll never be taken Notice of by the Town.

TRUE.   I find then, Sir, that Merit is no more the way to Preferment in the Present State of *Parnassus*, than at Court; Interest with the Powerful, in both, supplies all manner of Defects.

DAP.   True, Sir, pray to confirm this, give me leave to tell you how I came to this Authority which I now profess.

---

[4] Helicon: A mountain, and source of two fountains, sacred to the Muses; "Helicon" was used to refer to both the mountain and its fountains as a source of poetic inspiration.

[5] Parnassus: The mountain sacred to Apollo and the Muses; the highest literary home.

[6] *If I had not written on* Criticism *my self:* Reference to Pope's *Essay on Criticism* (1711).

[7] Critic in Terrorem: A critic in terror of the reigning wits (that is, one who ingratiates himself to Wycherley).

TRUE.   Strangely Ridiculous [Aside]—By all means, Sir, pray pro-
ceed, you will infinitely oblige me, and I believe, *Freeman*, and Sir
Indolent; I am a Country Gentleman, and it will be all Novelty
to me.

DAP.   Novelty, Sir; why then, Sir, it is *Wit*, and therefore must please
every polite Person. *Novelty*, Sir, is *Wit*; for *Wit* at best without
Novelty, will signify nothing in this Town.

SIR IND.   Prithee *Sawny* how does *Ned Doggrel* and Dr. *Scandal* do?
'Foregad they are very Facetious, Pretty Fellows; nay, the Doctor is
a good *Scholar*. Prithee *Sawny* bring them to dine with me some
day.

DAP.   *Ned Doggrel* and Dr. *Scandal*! Why Sir *Indolent*, I wou'd have
you to know I keep no such Company; the mere *Canaille*[8] of Writ-
ers, who never were at *Button*'s or *Will*'s, or kept Company with a
Gentleman of the *Covent-Garden* Air.

FREE.   [Aside to True-wit.] Sir *Indolent* has ingeniously diverted the
Fool from exposing himself, and he is not sensible of the Design.

SIR IND.   'Foregad *Sawny*, I think they write very pretty Verses, as
good as any of our present Authors, I mean in their way *Sawny*.

DAP.   Ay, they may write, and write their Eyes out, before they ar-
rive to my Reputation or my Conversation; they have not the Ad-
dress of raising themselves by Art.

FREE.   Faith *Sawny*, I wou'd have thee set up to teach the Art of rais-
ing a Name by Poetry, without any.

DAP.   As much a Jest as you mean that now *Jo*, it is in Fact, and
I know not but it might be a good Project, and what I wou'd un-
dertake, did not the Greek Poets lie on my hands now for a
Translation.[9]

SIR IND.   'Foregad *Sawny*, I did not know that you understood
Greek; nay, I must needs say, thou art a pretty Industrious Young
Fellow.

DAP.   Why, Sir *Indolent*, if I did not understand *Greek*, what of that;
I hope a Man may Translate a *Greek* Author without understand-
ing *Greek*; What d'ye think of *Josephus*, *Polybius*, and many

---

[8] Canaille: Rabble, mob.
[9] *the Greek Poets lie on my hands now for a Translation*: Reference to Pope's
translation in progress of the *Iliad*; Pope was frequently criticized for allegedly not
knowing Greek because as a Catholic he had been barred from attending university.

more, whose Translators never cou'd read *Greek*?[10] Ah! Sir *Indo-
lent*, you don't know half the Arts of getting a Reputation in this
Town for *Learning* and *Poetry*.

FREE.   I find you are an Experienc'd Man this way Mr. *Dapper*, pray
proceed in your Account, it must be surprizing.

DAP.   Why, Sir, you must know for getting a Reputation for *Poetry*,
there are some Qualifications absolutely necessary, as a happy
knack at Rhime, and a flowing Versification; but that is so com-
mon now that very few do want it; then you must chuse some odd
out of the way Subject, some Trifle or other that wou'd surprize
the Common Reader that any thing cou'd be written upon it, as a
Fan,[11] a *Lock of Hair*, or the like.

TRUE.   As the *Lutrin* of *Boileau*, or the *Dispensary* of Dr. *Garth* I
suppose.[12]

DAP.   Ah, Sir, that won't do; *Boileau* and *Garth* have treated of little
things with Magnificence of Verse, as *Homer* did of the Frogs; but
that is now Old, we must have something New; Heroic Doggrel is
but lately found out, where the Verse and the Subject agree, as,

> ——My Lord, why what the Devil?
> Zounds, Damn the Lock, 'foregad you must be Civil;
> Plague on't 'tis past a Jest; nay prithee, Pox
> Give her the Hair ——

If a Man wou'd distinguish himself, it must be by something
New and Particular. *Boileau* and *Garth* had arriv'd to so much
Fame and Reputation in the former way, that there was no coming
after them in the same Track; we therefore found out the *Heroic-
Comical* way of Writing, that no Man ever thought of before.

TRUE.   That I dare swear. True, we have heard of *Tragi-Comical*, a
very preposterous and unnatural Mixture, and now I think pretty

---

[10] Josephus, Polybius, *and many more, whose Translators never cou'd read* Greek:
Sometimes sixteenth- and seventeenth-century translations of Greek authors were
based on previous Latin translations rather than on the Greek originals. Flavius Jose-
phus (c. A.D. 37–100) was a Jewish historian and soldier, author of *The History of the
Jewish Wars*; Polybius (203?–c.120 B.C.), a Greek historian, wrote a forty-volume his-
tory of Roman conquests.

[11] Fan: John Gay had published his mock-heroic *The Fan* in 1713.

[12] *the* Lutrin *of* Boileau, *or the* Dispensary *of* Dr. Garth: Nicholas Despreaux
Boileau (1636–1711), French critic and poet, published *Le Lutrin*, a mock-heroic satire
on priests squabbling over a lectern, in 1674; Sir Samuel Garth (1661–1719) published
his popular satire on a medical dispute, *The Dispensary*, in 1699. Pope greatly admired
both poets.

well exploded; but for this *Heroic-Comical*, I confess it is new and
more odd than the other.

DAP.   Ay, Sir, and that makes it do. But, Sir, that is not enough, be-
sides the newness of the Verse, you must have a new manner
of Address; you must make the Ladies speak Bawdy, no matter
whether they are Women of Honour or not; and then you must
dedicate your Poem to the Ladies themselves. Thus a Friend of
mine has lately, with admirable Address, made *Arabella F — m — r*
prefer the Locks of her Poll, to her Locks of another more sacred
and secret Part.

> Oh! hadst thou Cruel! been content to seize
> Hairs less in Sight—*or any Hairs* but these.

But this is likewise a Complement to those Parts of the Lady, to let
the World know that the Lady had *Hairs* elsewhere, which she valu'd
less.

> Nor fear'd the chief th' unequal Fight to try,
> Who sought no more than on his Foe to Die.

Admirable Good again, you know what Dying is on a fair Lady Sir
Indolent, prettily express'd, I vow, *than on his Foe to Die*. But then,
Sir, the *Machinary* of this Poem is admirably contriv'd to convey a
luscious Hint to the Ladies, by letting them know, that their Noctur-
nal Pollutions are a Reward of their Chastity, and that when they
Dream of the Raptures of Love, they are immortalizing a *Silph* as that
Ingenious and Facetious Author sweetly intimates in his Epistle Dedi-
catory, as the Book of the *Count de Gabalis* recommended ex-
plains it.

TRUE.   I have seen that most Ingenious Piece, in which I find some-
what extraordinary in the Contrivance of the Author. He Pub-
lish'd his Poem first without his *Machinary*, and afterwards with
it, this is an extraordinary Method indeed. Now the Poets of An-
tiquity, founded their Poems on their Machinary; but I find it is the
new way of Writing to invent the Machinary, after the Poem is not
only Written but Publish'd.

DAP.   Alack a day Sir, I find you are a perfect Country Gentleman
indeed, to think that we new Authors care one Farthing for what
the old Authors did; no, no, Sir, we know better things, we know
how to purchase Fame cheaper.

FREE.   Why prithee *Dick*, every Age improves, why else does the
World grow Older?

DAP.   Improve, ay marry does it, nor ever were the Arts of getting a
Name arriv'd to greater Perfection; why, Sir, I was fain to write a
Copy of Verses in my own Praise, for none knew my Merit better
than my self; then I put the Name of a Celebrated Old Author to
it, but the Devil of it was, tho' that Author was of an Establish'd
Reputation for *Wit*, yet he was remarkable for an ill Versification,
so that my Stile discover'd me; and indeed, when I heard them
prais'd, I cou'd not help owning to my Friends, that I writ them
my self.

TRUE.   Why, faith Mr. *Dapper*, that's a new way indeed, and not
very difficult; a Man might soon get Fame, if writing a Copy of
Verses in his own Praise wou'd do it.

DAP.   Phoo, Sir, that was but one step in my Advancement. You
must know that there are two Parties of WITS, and two or three
Men at the Head of them. Now I first fixt my self on the good Na-
ture and easy Temper (by my Application) of the Men of real
Merit; they cry'd me up, recommended me to the Town, and the
Town took their Words, and so I set up for my self; for you must
know, they can't so easily destroy a Man's Reputation, as make it;
then I gave my Approbation of the Works of the Heads of the
other Party; that is of those who have Vogue and no Merit; by this
means I gain'd all their Friends, and bring those I approve, to a
sort of Dependance upon me.

TRUE.   I protest, Sir, you are a great Politician, I know not but you
may make a Minister of State in time, if ever the Pretender[13]
shou'd come, by your Candour and Penetration.

DAP.   Whoo! Pox you don't know me yet. Why t'other day I was de-
sir'd to read over *Jane Shore*,[14] and what do you think I writ upon
it when I had done?

TRUE.   Faith I can't tell —— unless that it was the most Stupid Piece
that ever was Written.

DAP.   Oh! gad, Sir, directly the contrary —— I writ down on the
Copy, *This is the best Play that has been Written since* Euripides.

FREE.   Did you believe what you writ?

---

[13] *Pretender:* James Francis Edward Stuart, the Old Pretender, son of the late exiled
and excluded James II. The Old Pretender's son, Charles Edward Stuart, was known
either as the Young Pretender or as Bonnie Prince Charlie, leader of the failed 1745 Ja-
cobite Rebellion (the last attempt to restore the Stuarts).
[14] Jane Shore: The play by Nicholas Rowe, advertised with the *Rape*; see the *Daily
Courant* advertisements and notes, p. 177–79.

DAP.   Egad, I can't say that in strict Truth I did, tho' *Consideratis Considerandis*,[15] I don't know but there might be something in it; but be that as it will I had my end in it, I complemented the Author, and his Vanity receiv'd it as Sterling Praise, without the least Allay of Flattery; besides, if it had been exactly true, I had not done it, for then it had been my Business to have cry'd it down; but the less real Merit it had, the more service I did him, and so the better maintain'd my Authority in the Disposal of Fame.

TRUE.   Is this one of our Modern Methods too?

DAP.   Oh yes, Sir, ever while you live, the less Merit an Author has that applies for our Commendation, the more we think our selves oblig'd to cry him up; for that multiplies the Votes against the *Critics*, who wou'd tear us all to Pieces if they cou'd. But telling Noses[16] is now the Standard of Wit, and the most Voices carry it, as in the Members of Parliament. Not but that we have sometimes our Committees of Election too, that can make Three a greater number than Thirteen; that is when our Occasions require it.

TRUE.   But *Sawny*, thou cou'dst never have pick'd out such another Poet as *Euripides*, to mention with the Author of *Jane Shore*; the first is a Master of the Fable, Manners, Sentiments and Diction; we see Nature and Art go Hand in Hand thro' all he Writes; neither of which were ever the least known to the latter.

DAP.   Whoo! a mere Baggatelle with us, Sir. But Sir *Indolent* is fast asleep —— Sir *Indolent*, Sir *Indolent*, come, here's a Health to the Lock least in sight.

SIR IND. 'Foregad *Sawny* thou hast talk'd me asleep —— But come the 'foresaid Health, and the bright Poets that sung it.

---

[15] Consideratis Considerandis: Latin for "The things to be considered having been considered."

[16] *Noses:* "To count, or tell, noses, denoting the counting of persons, especially those on one side or party" [OED].

JOHN DENNIS

From *Selected Writings*

John Dennis (1657–1734) was Pope's bitterest and most virulent antagonist. He was a poet, playwright, and a rather gifted literary critic, but as Maynard Mack describes him, he was "vain to the point of paranoia, [and] he could not easily tolerate the opinions of others when they differed from his own, or their success if it were greater than what he had himself met with" (Mack 179). He was exceedingly jealous of the rising young star Pope, whose witty rebuttals to Dennis's criticisms only made matters worse. Dennis launched his first major attack when Pope's *Essay on Criticism* appeared in 1711, skewering contemporary critics: "Some have at first for *Wits*, then *Poets* past, / Turn'd *Criticks* next, and prov'd plain *Fools* at last." Dennis responded in print, calling Pope "as stupid and as venemous [*sic*] as a hunchbacked Toad." Pope's *Dunciad Variorum* gives its own devastating little biography of Dennis in return: "Mr. *John Dennis* was the Son of a Sadler in *London*, born in 1657. He paid court to Mr. *Dryden*; and having obtained some correspondence with Mr. *Wycherly* and Mr. *Congreve*, he immediately obliged the publick with their Letters. He made himself known to the Government by many admirable Schemes and Projects; which the Ministry, for reasons best known to themselves, constantly kept private. For his character as a writer, it is given us as follows. 'Mr. *Dennis* is *excellent* at pindarick writings, *perfectly regular* in all his performances, and a person of *sound Learning*. That he is master of a great deal of *Penetration* and *Judgment*, his criticisms . . . do sufficiently demonstrate.' From the same account it also appears, that he writ Plays 'more to get *Reputation* than *Money*.' DENNIS *of himself*. See *Jacob*'s Lives of Dram. Poets" (*Dunciad Variorum* I.104n; the closing reference is to Giles Jacob's *Poetical Register: or, The Lives and Characters of all the English Poets* [1723], a collection of biographies). (Jacob often solicited material from his subjects themselves.) But later in his life Dennis fell on hard times, and Pope seems to have quietly contributed money to him, and wrote a not unkind prologue for a benefit performance in 1733.

The first excerpt, from "A True Character of Mr. Pope," published in 1716, draws the connection between Pope's physical deformities and their alleged psychological parallels, reading the twisted body as the index of a twisted mind. The excerpts from *Remarks on Mr. Pope's Rape of the Lock* attack that poem from every direction: for its machinery, its sexual suggestiveness, its tampering with genres, its representation of women.

From "A True Character of Mr. Pope, and His Writings. In a Letter to a Friend."

A Lump Deform'd and Shapeless was he Born,
Begot in Love's Despight, and Nature's Scorn.

Aw'd by no Shame, by no Respect controul'd
In Scandal busie, in Reproaches bold:
Spleen to Mankind his envious Heart possest,
And much he hated All, but most the Best.

From "Remarks on Mr. Pope's Rape of the Lock. In Several Letters to a Friend."

... The impartial Reader, who knows the *Rape of the Lock*, and who will read the following *Remarks*, will be able to determine whether *A. P — E* has shewn one Dram of Judgment, either in the Choice of this trifling *Subject*, or of his more senseless *Machinery*, or in the *Manners* and *Behaviour* of his fine Lady, who is so very rampant, and so very a Termagant, that a Lady in the Hundreds of *Drury*,[1] would be severely chastis'd, if she had the Impudence in

---

[1] *a Lady in the Hundreds of* Drury: An actress; actresses were thought to be loose in language and morals.

Opposite: "The PHIZ and CHARACTER of [an *Alexandrine*] Hyper-critick & Comentator" (1729). The artist and engraver of this famous caricature of Pope's "phiz" (physiognomy, or facial features believed to reveal character) are unknown. It appeared as the frontispiece to *Pope Alexander's Supremacy and Infallibility Examined* (printed in the *Monthly Chronicle* in 1729). Perched on a pedestal, Pope is represented as a malignant, hunchbacked, rat-like ape leaning against a stack of his own works and wearing a papal crown (his signature "A. Pope" was easily distorted into A-P-E).

The **PHIZ** and **CHARACTER** of ———————— the Hyper-critick & Comentator.

Nature her self shrunk back when thou wert born, 　*And half o'ercome with Beast, stood doubting long,*
And cry'd the Works not mine ———　*Whose right in thee were more :*
The Midwife stood agast ; and when she saw 　——*thou art all one Error ; Soul and Body ;*
Thy Mountain back, and thy distorted legs, 　*The first young tryal of some unskill'd Power ;*
Thy face half minted with the stamp of Man, 　*Rude in the making Art an Ape of* **Jove.** *&c.*

There is no fear of God before his Eyes. He flattereth himself in his own eyes, until his iniquity be found to be hateful. The words of his Mouth are iniquity and deceit ; he hath left off to be wise, and to do good. He deviseth Mischief upon his Bed ; he setteth himself in a way that is not good ; he abhorreth not evil. Psalm 36.

Sold by the Print-sellers of London and Westminster. *price* 6.ᵈ

some Company to imitate her in some of her Actions. The impartial Reader is to determine whether the *Sentiments* are not often exceeding poor, and mean, and sometimes ridiculous, and whether the *Diction* is not often impure and ungrammatical. . . .

'Tis a sure Sign that we live in a poor, undiscerning, degenerate World, when one who has writ and acted as this little Gentleman has done, has been able to delude it for so long. . . .

Letter I.

May 1. 1714.

SIR, I shall now, according to my Promise, send you some *Observations* upon the *Rape of the Lock*, which is one of the last Imitations of the little mimicking Bard, and one of the most impertinent; to so high a Degree impertinent, that I am afraid of being accus'd of writing a *Satire* upon *Nothing*, as my Lord *Rochester* wrote a *Panegyrick*.[2]

The Faults of this ridiculous Poem begin at the Title-Page. I will not insist upon the fantastical Composition of the word *Heroi-Comical*; but I desire Leave to dwell a little upon the Thing. What can this Author mean by creating in his Readers an Expectation of Pleasantry, when there is not so much as one Jest in his book? Of all Blockheads he is the most emphatically Dull, who, to an insipid tedious Tale, prefixes this impertinent Prelude; *Now, Gentlemen, expect a very good Jest! Now, my Masters, prepare to laugh!* Instead of *Heroi-Comical*, it should have been *Heroi-Tragical*, since it seems there was a Necessity for a fantastical Word: For there is a great deal of *Tragedy* in this Poem, but not one Jot of *Comedy*. But at the same Time there is nothing so *Tragical* in it, as what the Author *designs* for *Comedy*; For whenever he aims at a *Jest*, 'tis such sad deplorable Stuff, that he never fails to move *Compassion* by it. . . .

. . . [W]hat he calls his *Machinery* has no Manner of Influence upon what he calls his *Poem*, not in the least promoting or preventing, or retarding the Action of it. . . . He has taken his *Machines*, he tells us, from the *Rosycrucians*, and 'tis with them, he tells his fair Patroness, that he must bring her acquainted. And how bring her ac-

---

[2] *my Lord* Rochester *wrote a* Panegyrick: John Wilmot, second Earl of Rochester (1647–1680), was a lyric poet and sexually explicit satirist; he wrote a grim but witty poem "Upon Nothing."

quainted? Why, he must tell her what the Count *de Gabalis* says of them, who has given, it seems, the best Account he knows of them.

. . . I would direct him to a better Account of them, which is to be found in a Writer of our own, who is infinitely a better Judge both of Persons and Things, than the fantastick Count *de Gabalis*: and That is the most ingenious and most judicious Author of *Hudibras*,[3] who has given this short Account of the *Rosycrucians* in his Comment upon two Lines which are to be found in the Character of *Ralpho*, the facetious Squire of *Hudibras, Canto I, Part I.* and which two I have chosen for the Motto to these *Letters*.

> *In* Rosycrucian *Lore as learned*
> *As he that* vere Adeptus *earned.*

The short Comment upon which is this:

> *The Fraternity of the* Rosycrucians *is very like the Sect of the antient* Gnostici; *who called themselves so from the excellent Learning they pretended to, although they were really the most ridiculous Sots of all Mankind.*

. . . And now tell me in good Earnest, Sir, is not the *Fair Lady* infi-nitely oblig'd to him for her new Acquaintance? an Acquaintance very *unbecoming Her*, tho' very *becoming of Him*. . . .

Letter III.

. . . But there is no such Thing as a *Character* in the *Rape of the Lock*.

Belinda, who appears in most of it, is a Chimera, and not a Char-acter. She is represented by the Author perfectly *beautiful* and *well-bred*, *modest* and *virtuous*. . . . And yet in the latter End of this very Canto [I] he makes her owe the greater Part of her Beauty to her Toi-lette. . . . Nay, the very *favourite Lock*, which is made the Subject for so many Verses, is not shewn so desirable for its native Beauty, as for the constant Artifice employ'd about it. . . .

But *Belinda* is not only shewn *beautiful* and *well-bred*, she is repre-sented *virtuous* too:

> *Favours to none, to all she Smiles extends.*

---

[3] *Author of* Hudibras: Samuel Butler (1613–1680), English poet and satirist.

"The only portrait that was ever drawn of Mr. POPE at full Length," by William Hoare. As Helen Deutsch notes, not all unauthorized portraits of Pope were hostile: "The motivation in these rare cases — ... informal sketches made in private company — seems to have been less the desire to inflict pain than an urge, like that of the critic who points beyond the page toward the poet's uniquely distorted figure, to fix the poet's 'true character'" (Deutsch, "Pope and Deformity" 20). The following account of the line drawing by William Hoare, a fashionable portrait painter, appeared with its publication in 1797 in Joseph Warton's edition of *The Works of Alexander Pope*:

> This is the only Portrait that was ever drawn of Mr. POPE at full length. — It was done without his knowledge, as he was deeply engaged in conversation with Mr. ALLEN in the Gallery at Prior park, by Mr. HOARE, who sat at the other end of the Gallery [c. 1741]. — Pope would never have forgiven the Painter had he known it — He was too sensible of the Deformity of his Person to allow the whole of it to be represented. — This Drawing is therefore exceedingly valuable, as it is an Unique of this celebrated Poet.

And yet in the latter End of the fourth *Canto* she talks like an errant *Suburbian*:[4]

> *Oh hadst thou, Cruel, been content to seize*
> *Hairs less in sight, or any Hairs but these.*

Thus, Sir, has this Author given his fine Lady *Beauty* and good *Breeding*, *Modesty* and *Virtue* in Words, but has in Reality and in Fact made her an *artificial dawbing Jilt*; a *Tomrig*, a *Virago*, and a *Lady of the Lake.*[5]

GILES JACOB

The Rape of the Smock.
An Heroi-Comical Poem. In Two Books

Giles Jacob (1686–1744), trained as an attorney and author of a law dictionary, also produced a collection of literary biographies in 1720 (*The Poetical Register*) in which was included a brief life of Pope, corrected (certainly favorably) by Pope himself, but not, as his enemies claimed, written by him. *The Rape of the Smock* first appeared in 1715; as its preface notes, it attacks both the sexual implications of the *Lock* and what it perceives as the general immodesty of the age. Written in two cantos, like the first version of *The Rape of the Lock*, the poem employs many of the patterns and symbols used by Pope, including the opening ("I sing!"), the emphasis on aggression and vanity (both male and female), the detailing of clothes and cosmetics, the love of lapdogs (Shock again), and most important, the hypocritical distinction between virtue and the *reputation* of virtue. As Charles Gildon had pointed out in *A New Rehearsal* (see headnote, p. 188), many critics felt that Belinda was far too willing to sacrifice "Hairs less in sight, or any Hairs but these," (IV.176) — to give up the reality of chastity to preserve its appearance.

---

[4] *an errant* Suburbian: "Belonging to or characteristic of the suburbs (of London) as a place of inferior, debased, and especially licentious habits of life" [*OED*].

[5] *an* artificial dawbing Jilt; *a* Tomrig, *a* Virago, *and a* Lady of the Lake: Dawbing: painted, made-up; Jilt: "A woman who gives her lover hopes, and deceives him" [Johnson], but also one who has lost her chastity, a harlot; Tomrig: a version of tomboy, "a wanton girl or woman" [*OED*]; Virago: "A bold, impudent (and/or wicked) woman; a termagant; a scold" [*OED*]; Lady of the Lake: A kept mistress (John Farmer, *Slang and Its Analogues*, Kraus Reprint 1965).

Jacob simply makes the relatively delicate sexual innuendoes of the *Lock* more overtly bawdy, more insistently violent (although he elaborately denies this in the preface): The fetish is no longer a lock of hair but a woman's undergarment; the gaze of male admiration becomes peephole voyeurism; swordknots turn into swords; and the final terms for restoring the smock require the real, not just the metaphorical, loss of virginity.

The Preface

I *Hope my* FAIR READERS *will not be prejudiced against this* POEM, *upon the Account of the* Title *which the* Author *gives it; nor infer, that he must needs be an Impudent Fellow, from his daring to commit a* Rape *upon a Part of their Furniture, that ought to be Sacred, before they see how he handles the Subject.*

He will assure them before-hand, That every thing is wrapt up in Clean Linen: *and that, setting aside the bare Mention of a* SMOCK,[1] *which perhaps may give* Offence *to the Scrupulous, there is nothing but what the Chastest Eye may peruse, or the Chastest Ear give Attention to. Indeed, in such an Age of Immodesty, one can hardly think how a* Poet *can treat such a Subject, without giving Scandal, and the* Muses *being long since become errant Prostitutes; the modest Part of the Sex have as little Quarter to expect at their Hands, as they themselves must expect at the Hands of the* Criticks.

But now I think on't, why should a poor Author *be at the Trouble of making an Apology for Writing upon a* SMOCK, *when the* BEAUTIES *of this Age look upon it as a Want of Good Breeding, to Blush at a harmless* Double Entendre;[2] *and I have seen, a* Front-Box[2] *sit so Unconcern'd at the* smuttiest COMEDY, *that a* Stranger *would have been apt to question, whether there were One* Natural Complexion *among them All; and one would imagin, that some* Procurers *of Renown (like* Potentates, *when they are put to't very hard for* Men*) had Listed all the* Sex, *from* Sixteen *to* Sixty.

I doubt not, however, but the Modest Part of the Sex will easily excuse me for the Deficiency in this Poem of obscene Allusions of any Kind, however relative they may be to the Subject: And I hope, at least, if they will not permit the Smock *to be the Foundation of the* Bays,[3] *that I shall obtain a Pardon from the Generous Fair.*

---

[1] *Smock:* A woman's undergarment, a shift or chemise, worn closest to the skin.

[2] *Front-box:* Upper-class seating at the theater.

[3] *if they will not permit the* Smock *to be the Foundation of the* Bays: That is, if this poem isn't *quite* good enough to earn its author the poet laureateship.

I conclude with requesting the Publick, *to excuse the first Attempt of this Kind the* Author *ever made; and since a* Rape *is* Felony *by the* Law, *all the Favour I beg, is, That whosoever sits as my* Judge, *will only vouchsafe not to try me by a* Jury *of* Criticks.

VALE.[4]

Book I.

A Virgin's SMOCK, I sing! the direful Cause
Of horrid Bloodshed, and of Breach of Laws;
That Linen Veil, which pendent Ruffles grace,
Of *Indian* Muslin, or of *Flanders* Lace;
Wide stretch'd and falling down in many a Plait,   5
From the fair Bosom, to the snowy Feet;
White as the Lilly, or the Skin it hides,
Where charming Nature shines, and Love resides.
Let OZELL sing the *Bucket*,° Pope the *Lock*,
My daring Muse prefers the *Rape of Smock*.   10
But CÆLIA, CÆLIA, here I ought to ask
A gracious Pardon for this impious Task:
My beauteous CÆLIA, be not too severe,
Thy Charms I worship, and thy sense revere;
Forgive this Tale, since Modesty in vain,   15
Would curb the Poet's Flight, and Song restrain.

It was the Time, when Transports crown the Night,
And Charms unseen the eager Swains delight;
When Lovers by the silent Minutes blest,
Fatigu'd with Pleasure, lay them down to Rest: 20
'Twas then bright CÆLIA, (never yet enjoy'd)
On her PHILEMON all her Thoughts employ'd;
The gay PHILEMON, full of Life and Air,
Who Pains unequal'd took to gain the Fair.
Dire Cogitations seiz'd her troubled Breast,   25
Distracted Looks confirm her want of Rest;
She sighs and moans, and strives the Flame to hide,
To curb her Passion, and her Fondness chide;
Now by her self, she thus at lengths confest,
With Grief unfelt, but in a Lover's Breast.   30

---

[4] *Vale:* Good-bye, farewell (Latin).
    9. *Let OZELL sing the* Bucket: John Ozell (d. 1743) wrote *The Rape of the Bucket*; he appears in Jacob's *Poetical Register*.

Should I then fix my Happiness and Love
On dear PHILEMON, and He faithless prove,
What Pain to me, alas! might thence arise?
Perhaps the Youth my Charms might then despise:
'Tis possible; but yet I can't refrain,°   ⎫   35
There's something so engaging in the Swain, ⎬
Him I must Love, and venture his Disdain.   ⎭

These Thoughts revolv'd she takes another View
Of rich AMBROSIO, her Lover too:
AMBROSIO, who to Inns of Courts° belongs,   40
Where *Coxcombs* and where *Knaves* resort in Throngs;
He on the Nymph had cast an Eye before,
And much depended on his shining Store.
CÆLIA has various Conflicts in her Mind,
To either Spark alternately inclin'd: 45
And now a Contest great did soon commence
Between the Charms of one, and t'other's Pence.
But soon PHILEMON turn'd the doubtful Scale,
And did o'er all his Rival's Wealth prevail,
Thus she broke forth; PHILEMON, Thou art He,   50
He only, who shall my Possessor be:
Henceforth, AMBROSIO, from my Presence fly,
My dear PHILEMON, 'tis for Thee I dye!

This said, fair CÆLIA bared her lovely Breast,
Approach'd her *Toilet*, and her self undrest: 55
First, the Gold Watch and Lockets are laid by,
Those great Allurements to a Lover's Eye;
The decent Necklace is pull'd off with Care,
And Orient Pearls that grace the pretty Ear;
Her taper Fingers now from Prison freed,   60
The glitt'ring Diamond no longer need.

35–37. *'Tis possible . . . Disdain:* Triplets, as opposed to standard couplets, were
signaled by brackets. Pope and Swift despised the use of triplets as an easy way out.

40. *Inns of Courts:* "The four sets of buildings in London (the Inner Temple, the
Middle Temple, Lincoln's Inn, and Gray's Inn) belonging to the four legal societies
which have the exclusive right of admitting persons to practise at the bar, and hold a
course of examination and instruction for that purpose; hence, these four societies
themselves" [OED].

That done, the Pinners° are laid by with Care,
Which to the Sight expose her Auborn Hair;
Down to her Waist in careless curls it plays,
And negligently flows a thousand Ways;   65
Part forward falls, her Iv'ry Front to shade,
And Part hangs careless, on her Back display'd;
Some Locks disorder'd, her white Breasts conceal,
But here, and there, a pleasing Glance you steal.
The *Night-Dress* covers now her lovely Head,   70
And *Mobs*,° which Ladies chuse to wear in Bed:
She takes the Glass, and does her Form survey,
Nor thinks her Graces fewer than by Day.
She then proceeds, takes off her *Tissue-Gown;*
And lets the spacious Petticoat fall down.   75
The *Stays* that compass round her slender Waist, ⎫
Which Kings themselves might wish to have embrac'd, ⎬
Now leave her unconfin'd, and there unlac'd. ⎭
Then CÆLIA bending to pull off her Shoe,
Exposes all the tempting Prize to view.   80

    Almost undrest, her *Smock* pull'd off the last,
Thinking no Lover near an Eye to cast;
But, ah! PHILEMON, in a luckless Hour,
By Stealth came up, and peep'd in thro' the Door;
That Door, thro' which his Eyes a Passage found,   85
And ev'ry thing he saw increas'd his Wound.
Thro' Crevice small, with Joy his Bliss reviews,
In Extasie the pleasing Sight pursues;
Her beauteous Face now unobserv'd, alas!
His Eye he fixes on another Place: 90
He view'd her Breast; but lower, what was there!
Too much to view, and not enjoy the Fair:
PHILEMON out of Patience grown at last,
To see the Charm, and not the Pleasure taste,
Assails the Door, and by his youthful Might,   95
An Entrance made to try his Fate that Night.

---

62. *Pinners:* "A coif with two long flaps, one on each side, pinned on and hanging down, and sometimes fastened at the breast; worn by women, esp. of rank, in the 17th and 18th centuries" [OED].
71. *Mobs:* A mob dress was a sort of negligee; a mob cap was a lace or cloth hair covering.

CÆLIA, alarm'd at this untimely Noise,
Slips on her *Night-Shift*, and exalts her Voice;
Her *Wrapping-Gown* she hudled on in haste,
And negligently threw it round her Waist.   100
Now young PHILEMON boldly ventures in,
Fearless of Danger, and of Female Din,
Made his Advances to the beauteous Maid,
And many fine and pleasing Things he said.
CÆLIA, confus'd, lays by the Dress of Day,   105
By chance the *Smock* expos'd and careless lay;
Which bold PHILEMON seiz'd, and kiss'd the Veil,
Which stoln from CÆLIA, made the *Nymph* grow pale.
His Blood's on fire, and Love his Heart invades;
Joy fills his Bosom, Anger fills the Maid's.   110

Whilst CÆLIA in Confusion senseless lay,
Of Speech depriv'd, at *Smock* thus forc'd away.
But e'er 'twas long, with Anger and Surprize,
Her Visage chang'd, she darts her flaming Eyes;
Her Wrath no longer able to conceal,   115
She thus upbraided his officious Zeal.

Dar'st thou, vile Traytor! take this wicked Course,
T' attempt thy Mistress, and her Room to force?
On me thus boldly venture to intrude,
At this unseemly Time, on Purpose Lewd?   120
Be gone at my Command, avoid thy Fate!
Obey, or be the Object of my Hate!
The *Smock* deliver, or you soon shall know,
I am no Mistress, but a deadly Foe.

Then gay PHILEMON with submissive Air,   125
In Accents soft, address'd the charming Fair;
His sly Apology he thus begun:
Why does my Dear her truest Lover shun?
Have you forgot so soon? and can you see
My ardent Love, and not be touch'd like me?   130
By all our Kisses, by our softer Nights,
And melting Sweets of Innocent Delights;
By all that's Sacred, by my Love, 'tis true,
'Tis Love alone has made me Rude to you.
Forgive my Rashness, Dearest, I implore,   135
And you shall find your PHIL. transgress no more.

   The Lady strait reply'd, Too forward Swain!
Is this the Way, thy CÆLIA's Heart to gain?
Think'st thou, that I, who like a Fortress stand,
With, Virtue's Guard, and Honour's sacred Band,   140
Can fall a Victim to thy treach'rous Hand?
Ah! hope not thus my Virtue to assay,
Nor vainly think that I shall fall thy Prey:
Restore the *Smock*, then shall PHILEMON find,
His Love Rewarded, and his Mistress Kind.   145

   These Words pronounc'd with a true Female Art,
Made some Impression on PHILEMON's Heart:
A while he paus'd, as seeming to comply;
But then survey'd it with a greedy Eye;
And whilst he tender'd back, held fast the Prize;   150
Like one that half consents, and half denies:
Surveying fondly, with a Lover's Air,
The Nymph, divided betwixt Hope and Fear:
Then starting sudden, out he rush'd at last,
And left her to reflect on what had past.   155

Book II.

Now had the Morn unbarr'd the Gates of Light,
And the sad Nymph in Sorrow spent the Night;
In vain as down she lay, the drowsie God
Touch'd her soft Temples with his Leaden Rod;
Restless she roll'd, and sometimes dropt a Tear;   5
No Muse is able to express her Care.
She rung the Bell, and up her NANCY came,
NANCY, the nearest Fav'rite to the Dame:
Haste, haste, she cry'd, and to AMBROSIO run,
Bid him speed hither with the Rising Sun;   10
Away the Damsel posts, and hardly stood
To take her *Pattens*° or her *Riding-Hood*.
In *Lincoln's-Inn*, she finds the Youth in Bed,
Fast snoring, and oppress'd with Fumes of *Red*.°

---

   12. Pattens: Wooden shoes or clogs worn to protect good shoes from the filth of the
streets.
   14. *Fumes of* Red: Wine.

She wak'd AMBROSIO without more Delay,   15
Un-us'd to be disturb'd by Break of Day;
Told him her Errand: Up with speed rose he,
Drest, and went out, (O strange!) without his *Tea*.
To CÆLIA now the happy Youth approach'd:
Some say, he walk'd on Foot, some say, was Coach'd.   20
But Oh! what Joy was his, by NANCY led,
When he (unhop'd-for Bliss!) drew near the Bed.
Thus spoke the Nymph — Canst thou, too faithful Swain,
Forgive unhappy CÆLIA's past Disdain?
And wilt thou, wilt thou, maugre° all my Pride,   25
Revenge my Cause, and lay thy Scorn aside?
Wrong'd by PHILEMON, to thy Arms I fly;
O do not, do not then, thy Help deny.
Retrieve the *Smock*, which he has basely stole,   30
And win, for ever win, my Virgin Soul.
O doubt not, beauteous Nymph, the Swain reply'd,
My Sword's Success, and Valour often try'd:
For if there's Faith in Man, thou may'st believe,
I'll lose my Life, or else thy *Smock* retrieve.   35

   Then eager with his Lips her Hand he prest,
And of his Rival fiercely goes in quest.
PHILEMON starts, to see AMBROSIO near,
Wonders; but still a Stranger is to Fear.
AMBROSIO's Eyes with Rage and Anger glow,   40
He meets his Rival like a deadly Foe.
Or pay me down thy forfeit Life, he cries,
Or give me back, rash Youth, the Linen Prize:
I mean, fair CÆLIA's *Smock*, full well thou know'st;
Of such a Triumph make not now thy Boast.   45
Hence to *Hyde-Park*,° and we will soon decide,
Which best deserves fair CÆLIA for his Bride,
PHILEMON answer'd, (not at all dismay'd)
Art thou turn'd Bully for the peerless Maid?
Then do thy worst; the *Smock* I'll not return;   50
I give it back! no, it shall sooner burn.

   Now on the Green the Combatants engage,
Inspir'd alike, and fill'd with equal Rage:

25. *maugre:* In spite of.
46. *Hyde-Park:* The traditional place for duels.

Their Swords were of a Length, their Pushes just,
And as one Parry'd, t'other made a Thrust: 55
With Crimson Blood the Field was dy'd around,
And each receiv'd, and gave, full many a Wound.
Long was the Struggle, and each show'd his skill,
No Rivals ever fought with better Will.
At last PHILEMON made a furious Pass,   60
And stretch'd AMBROSIO bleeding on the Grass:
Sore hurt and vanquish'd, on the Ground he lay,
PHILEMON sheath'd his Sword, and ran away,
Lord of the *Smock*, and of his Conquest proud,
Stole off, whilst t'other calls for Help aloud.   65

    Now *Fame*, which daily Travels round the Ball,
In CÆLIA's Ear proclaim'd AMBROSIO's Fall.
The Nymph unable to express her Grief,
Straight from her faithful NANCY sought Relief:
Ah! I'm undone, my dearest Wench, she said;   70
Perhaps AMBROSIO's kill'd, PHILEMON fled!
I was to blame to hazard either's Life:
Was then a *Smock* fit Argument for Strife?
Go, find out PHIL. if PHIL. can yet be found,
(For much I tremble for my Champion's Wound)   75
Coax, flatter, lye; thy utmost Art employ,.
To Articles to bring th' ill-natur'd Boy:
For since it is in vain to think of Force
To gain my *Shift*, I'll take another Course.
Nor must that Trophy, which he owes to Theft,   80
Whate'er it costs, in impious Hands be left.
Some wicked Lye he may perhaps invent,
And boast he had the *Smock* with my Consent:
Of farther Favours none will make a Doubt;
And, ah! what Fables may not Folks give out!   85
Then spare no Labour to retrieve the Veil;
For CÆLIA's ruin'd, should her NANCY fail.

    Swifter than Lightning flew the nimble Maid,
And to PHILEMON strait a Visit paid.
(PHILEMON of his Conquest grown so proud,   90
He could not help proclaiming it aloud.)
Fair NANCY, quoth the Youth, what brings thee here?
Why on thy Face does such Concern appear?

Has CÆLIA sent thee? — For the *Smock*, I ween!
And is she for a Trifle so Chagrin?   95
Why does she envy me so small a Prize,
And persecute a Swain, who for her Dyes?
'Twas but this Moment she my Rival sent,
Who may his Errand now perhaps repent:
Yonder I left him, bleeding on the Plain,   100
Henceforth he draws no Sword in haste again.

So spake the Youth, and NANCY thus reply'd:
My Mistress must not, must not be deny'd,
Without Delay do you the *Smock* restore,
Or be condemn'd to see her Face no more.   105
A Veil so sacred, thus to snatch away,
Was in a Lover sure the foulest Play.
Nor would it be by half so great a Sin,
Had you in Streets a publick Felon been.
Weigh but the Justice of my Lady's Cause: 110
Besides, to steal a *Smock*; 'tis Breach of Laws,
And if with Vigour she pursues the Thing,
At the next *Sessions* you perhaps may swing:
Then carry on your Jest, if wise you be,
No farther now, but send the *Smock* by me.   115

PHILEMON paus'd at this, and mus'd a while,
Whether he should restore, or keep the Spoil:
Plague on these Women, to himself said he,
What if indeed she should in Earnest be!
How far *Revenge* may push her on, who knows?   120
For anger'd Females are the worst of Foes,
PHILEMON is undone, beyond all doubt,
If injur'd CÆLIA takes a Warrant out:
'Tis better far, to make up the Dispute,
Than lie in *Newgate*, or than stand a Suit.°   125

Well, NANCY, then he cry'd, let's all be Friends,
This very Night the fatal Quarrel ends:
In the mean while, bid CÆLIA be at rest,
I'll bring the *Smock*, and terminate the Jest.

---

125. *Than lie in* Newgate, *or than stand a Suit*: To go to prison or be sued at court.

Pleas'd with the News, the Damsel posts away   130
To CÆLIA, who in Bed impatient lay:
Rise, Madam, rise! she cry'd, your Point is gain'd!
The ravish'd *Smock* will be no more detain'd!
PHILEMON, at my Threats, in Mortal Fright,
Will without fail, the Trophy bring at Night.   135
Then, Madam, haste to Dress; dispel your Cares,
And to revenge you, put on all your Airs.

Up got the lovely Virgin in a trice,
Revolving to appear exactly Nice;
At her *Toilet* she puts on ev'ry Toy,   140
That Ladies use, when eager to destroy.
Three Hours by the Clock, (and some say Four) ⎫
She sate in polishing her Form all o'er,   ⎬
And culling Arrows from her fatal Store.   ⎭

But ah! when thoroughly drest from Top to Toe,   145
How Charming did she look, how Lovely show!
At Play, or Birth-Night Ball, was never seen
A Beauty so compleat, so gay, so clean.
Of crimson Sattin was her costly *Gown*;
Her *Petticoat* was all embroider'd down;   150
The *Watch* was TOMPION's° with a Golden Chain,
And her *Pearl-Necklace* of the finest Grain:
Her Brilliant *Ear-rings*, which did Stars out-shine,
Came not from *Bristol*,° but from th' *Indian* Mine:
Her *Shoes* were Velvet, and her *Stockins* Silk;   155
Her *Lace* true *Flanders*, and as white as Milk.
So rigg'd at last along the Room she mov'd,
And in her *Looking-Glass* each Charm improv'd:
Scarce HEBE° look'd so Blooming, Young, or Fair,
Or VENUS had when Dress'd, a nobler Air: 160
For now on Mischief she was fully bent,
And had against her PHIL. a dire Intent;
To make him grieve for putting her to Pain,
And punish the rash Youth with just Disdain.

---

151. *The* Watch *was* TOMPION's: Thomas Tompion was an important watchmaker
during Queen Anne's reign.
154. *Came not from* Bristol: A "Bristol diamond" was rock crystal; Caelia's gems
are genuine.
159. *HEBE:* The goddess of youth and spring.

The Sun below th' Horizon was declin'd,   165
And beauteous CÆLIA now had lately Din'd;
When in comes PHIL. to his Appointment true;
At whose Approach, the Servants straight withdrew.
CÆLIA awhile stood mute, then Silence broke;
Looking demure, and blushing as she spoke.   170

   Thou base Usurper of a Maiden's *Shift*,
O tell me what could be thy impious Drift?
So lewd an Action can admit no Plea;
I little could expect all this from Thee!
Had you my *Snuff-box*, or my *Fan* purloin'd,   175
Or on my *Gloves*, or *Mask*, your Theft design'd;
Or stole away, what's worse, my Darling *Shock*;
Or any Moveable, besides my *Smock*;
I could forgive, and with the Crime dispense:
But who can pardon such a rude Offence?   180

   Fair Maid, he answer'd, finish the Dispute:
As for what's past, I'll be for ever mute;
And in no *Coffee-House* will make my Boast,
That of her *Smock* I once depriv'd a Toast.
But since your Lover with your Suit complies,   185
You must be Kind, if he restores the Prize:
Be mine Anon, the whole, the live-long Night,
And bless thy Lover's Arms with vast Delight.
But less than that, no Motive can prevail,
To make me tender back the Mystick Veil.   190

   CÆLIA confus'd, scarce knew what to reply,
Look'd much surpriz'd, and downward cast her Eye;
And will no Terms but these suffice, said she?
And must I for a *Shift*, your *Victim* be?
Conditions much too hard, and too unjust!   195
Is then PHILEMON's Love all turn'd to Lust?
Yet, tho' till now, my Heart was like a Rock,
I'll sooner yield, than you shall keep the *Smock*.

   In Raptures now, the happy Youth survey'd,
And in his Arms embrac'd, the beauteous Maid: 200
With decent Action, he the *Smock* resigns,
And ardently round CÆLIA's Waist he twines.
Soft Pleasure now succeeds an Age of Pain,
And the glad Youth enjoys, what long he sought in vain.

Poetic Forms

SAMUEL JOHNSON

From *The Life of Pope*

"From his attention to poetry he was never diverted." This selection from Johnson's *Life* illustrates Pope's dedication to poetry, his working methods, the circumstances of life and temper that shaped what he wrote and how. Johnson also does some contextualizing of his own here, positioning Pope in relation to Dryden, the poet to whom he was most overtly indebted. Throughout the eighteenth century Pope was constantly compared to Dryden, as the successor who made couplet poetry *dance*: "Dryden is read with frequent astonishment, and Pope with perpetual delight."

See the earlier headnote to Johnson's *Lives of the Poets*, pp. 96–98, for information about Johnson and his biography of Pope.

From his attention to poetry he was never diverted. If conversation offered anything that could be improved he committed it to paper; if a thought, or perhaps an expression more happy than was common, rose to his mind, he was careful to write it; an independent distich was preserved for an opportunity of insertion, and some little fragments have been found containing lines, or parts of lines, to be wrought upon at some other time.

He was one of those few whose labour is their pleasure; he was never elevated to negligence, nor wearied to impatience; he never passed a fault unamended by indifference, nor quitted it by despair. He laboured his works first to gain reputation, and afterwards to keep it.

Of composition there are different methods. Some employ at once memory and invention, and, with little intermediate use of the pen, form and polish large masses by continued meditation, and write their productions only when, in their own opinion, they have completed them. It is related of Virgil that his custom was to pour out a great number of verses in the morning, and pass the day in retrenching exuberances and correcting inaccuracies. The method of Pope, as may be collected from his translation, was to write his first thoughts in his first words, and gradually to amplify, decorate, rectify, and re-fine them.

With such faculties and such dispositions he excelled every other writer in *poetical prudence;* he wrote in such a manner as might expose him to few hazards. He used almost always the same fabrick of verse; and, indeed, by those few essays which he made of any other, he did not enlarge his reputation.[1] Of this uniformity the certain consequence was readiness and dexterity. By perpetual practice language had in his mind a systematical arrangement; having always the same use for words, he had words so selected and combined as to be ready at his call. This increase of facility he confessed himself to have perceived in the progress of his translation.

But what was yet of more importance, his effusions were always voluntary, and his subjects chosen by himself. His independence secured him from drudging at a task, and labouring upon a barren topick: he never exchanged praise for money, nor opened a shop of condolence or congratulation. His poems, therefore, were scarce ever temporary.[2] He suffered coronations and royal marriages to pass without a song, and derived no opportunities from recent events, nor any popularity from the accidental disposition of his readers. He was never reduced to the necessity of soliciting the sun to shine upon a birth-day, of calling the Graces and Virtues to a wedding, or of saying what multitudes have said before him. When he could produce nothing new, he was at liberty to be silent.

His publications were for the same reason never hasty. He is said to have sent nothing to the press till it had lain two years under his inspection: it is at least certain that he ventured nothing without nice examination. He suffered the tumult of imagination to subside, and the novelties of invention to grow familiar. He knew that the mind is always enamoured of its own productions, and did not trust his first fondness. He consulted his friends, and listened with great willingness to criticism; and, what was of more importance, he consulted himself, and let nothing pass against his own judgment.

---

[1] *same fabrick of verse; . . . he did not enlarge his reputation:* Pope wrote almost entirely in heroic couplets; only in a relatively few works, such as his *Ode for Musick, on St. Cecilia's Day* (written c. 1708, published 1713), *The Universal Prayer* (c. 1715; published 1738), and some minor poems and translations, did he experiment with other rhyme schemes and metrical patterns.

[2] *temporary:* Contemporary; dealing with local or current events. Poets who depended for a living on aristocratic patrons were typically expected to produce poems celebrating the character of their patrons or events in their lives.

He professed to have learned his poetry from Dryden,[3] whom, whenever an opportunity was presented, he praised through his whole life with unvaried liberality; and perhaps his character may receive some illustration if he be compared with his master.

Integrity of understanding and nicety of discernment were not allotted in a less proportion to Dryden than to Pope. The rectitude of Dryden's mind was sufficiently shewn by the dismission of his poetical prejudices, and the rejection of unnatural thoughts and rugged numbers.[4] But Dryden never desired to apply all the judgement that he had. He wrote, and professed to write, merely for the people; and when he pleased others, he contented himself. He spent no time in struggles to rouse latent powers; he never attempted to make that better which was already good, nor often to mend what he must have known to be faulty. He wrote, as he tells us, with very little consideration; when occasion or necessity called upon him, he poured out what the present moment happened to supply, and, when once it had passed the press, ejected it from his mind; for when he had no pecuniary interest, he had no further solicitude.

Pope was not content to satisfy; he desired to excel, and therefore always endeavoured to do his best: he did not court the candour, but dared the judgment of his reader, and, expecting no indulgence from others, he shewed none to himself. He examined lines and words with minute and punctilious observation, and retouched every part with indefatigable diligence, till he had left nothing to be forgiven.

For this reason he kept his pieces very long in his hands, while he considered and reconsidered them. The only poems which can be supposed to have been written with such regard to the times as might hasten their publication, were the two satires of *Thirty-eight*;[5] of which Dodsley[6] told me that they were brought to him by the author, that they might be fairly copied. 'Almost every line,' he said, 'was then written twice over; I gave him a clean transcript, which he sent

---

[3] *Dryden:* John Dryden (1631–1700), poet and playwright.

[4] *rugged numbers:* Uneven or irregular metrical patterns.

[5] *satires of* Thirty-eight: *One Thousand Seven Hundred and Thirty-Eight* (or *Epilogues to the Satires*), two poems in dialogue form published in 1738 in response to attacks from Walpole's government press; in them, Pope defends the political as well as the aesthetic power of poetry.

[6] *Dodsley:* Robert Dodsley (1703–1764) wrote several poems while a footman; Pope helped set him up as a bookseller in 1735; he is chiefly remembered as the publisher of works by Pope, Johnson, Edward Young, Oliver Goldsmith, and Thomas Gray.

some time afterwards to me for the press, with almost every line writ-
ten twice over a second time.'

His declaration that his care for his works ceased at their publica-
tion was not strictly true.[7] His parental attention never abandoned
them; what he found amiss in the first edition, he silently corrected in
those that followed. He appears to have revised the *Iliad*, and freed it
from some of its imperfections; and the *Essay on Criticism* received
many improvements after its first appearance. It will seldom be found
that he altered without adding clearness, elegance, or vigour. Pope
had perhaps the judgment of Dryden; but Dryden certainly wanted[8]
the diligence of Pope.

In acquired knowledge the superiority must be allowed to Dryden,
whose education was more scholastick, and who before he became an
author had been allowed more time for study, with better means of
information. His mind has a larger range, and he collects his images
and illustrations from a more extensive circumference of science.
Dryden knew more of man in his general nature, and Pope in his
local manners. The notions of Dryden were formed by comprehensive
speculation, and those of Pope by minute attention. There is more
dignity in the knowledge of Dryden, and more certainty in that of
Pope.

Poetry was not the sole praise of either, for both excelled likewise
in prose; but Pope did not borrow his prose from his predecessor.
The style of Dryden is capricious and varied, that of Pope is cautious
and uniform; Dryden obeys the motions of his own mind, Pope con-
strains his mind to his own rules of composition. Dryden is some-
times vehement and rapid; Pope is always smooth, uniform, and
gentle. Dryden's page is a natural field, rising into inequalities, and
diversified by the varied exuberance of abundant vegetation; Pope's is
a velvet lawn, shaven by the scythe, and levelled by the roller.

Of genius, that power which constitutes a poet; that quality with-
out which judgement is cold and knowledge is inert; that energy
which collects, combines, amplifies, and animates — the superiority
must, with some hesitation, be allowed to Dryden. It is not to be in-
ferred that of this poetical vigour Pope had only a little, because Dry-
den had more, for every other writer since Milton must give place to

---

[7] *His declaration . . . not strictly true:* This refutes a remark in *Guardian* 40: "He
takes the greatest care of his works before they are published, and has the least concern
for them afterwards."

[8] *wanted:* Lacked.

Pope; and even of Dryden it must be said that if he has brighter paragraphs, he has not better poems. Dryden's performances were always hasty, either excited by some external occasion, or extorted by domestick necessity; he composed without consideration, and published without correction. What his mind could supply at call, or gather in one excursion, was all that he sought, and all that he gave. The dilatory caution of Pope enabled him to condense his sentiments, to multiply his images, and to accumulate all that study might produce, or chance might supply. If the flights of Dryden therefore are higher, Pope continues longer on the wing. If of Dryden's fire the blaze is brighter, of Pope's the heat is more regular and constant. Dryden often surpasses expectation, and Pope never falls below it. Dryden is read with frequent astonishment, and Pope with perpetual delight.

JOSEPH SPENCE

From *Anecdotes*

Spence draws from conversations with Pope and others about the sources and progress of Pope's poetry. His early education was intense and independent; he claims to have taught himself Greek and Latin, primarily, it seems, as a way of finding his own voice: "I did not follow the grammar; but rather hunted in the authors, for a syntax of my own." His father taught him to revise his rhymes, and he taught himself the art of versification "wholly from Dryden's works," striving on the advice of William Walsh to be a "correct" (that is, true, accurate, consistent) poet. Although Pope constantly revised his poetry, he wrote his first drafts easily and indeed claims the most success for those poems "written fastest" — including *The Rape of the Lock.* He also gives his opinions about language, tone, rhyme, imitation, style, sound and sense, and the status of "middling poets."

A remark Pope makes of the *Dunciad* certainly applies to *The Rape of the Lock* as well: "A poem on a slight subject requires the greater care to make it considerable enough to be read." Though on the slightest of subjects, the *Rape* is a rich, clean, finished, complex, dazzling little satire. Pope's great care is clear.

See the headnote to the earlier selection from the *Anecdotes* in "The Poet and the Poem," p. 127, for more information about Joseph Spence and this work.

11. Mr. Pope's father who was an honest merchant and dealt in Hollands[1] wholesale was no poet, but he used to set him to make English verses when very young. He was pretty difficult in being pleased and used often to send him back to new turn them. "These are not good rhymes" he would say, for that was my husband's word for verses.

— MRS. POPE *1728?*

21. My next period was in Windsor Forest, where I set down with an earnest desire of reading, and applied as constantly as I possibly could to it for some years. I was between twelve and thirteen when I first went thither, and continued in this close pursuit of pleasure and languages till nineteen or twenty.

Considering how very little I had when I came from school, I think I may be said to have taught myself Latin as well as French or Greek, and in all three my chief way of getting them was by translations.

— POPE *January 1743*

22. I did not follow the grammar, but rather hunted in the authors for a syntax of my own, and then began translating any parts that pleased me particularly in the best Greek and Latin poets. By that means I formed my taste, which I think verily at about sixteen was very near as good as it is now.

— POPE *18–21 January 1743*

23. I had learned very early to read and delighted extremely in it. I taught myself to write very early, too, by copying from printed books with which I used to divert myself, as other children do with scrawling out pictures.

— POPE *March 1743*

32. I began writing verses of my own invention farther back than I can remember.

— POPE *March? 1743*

55. I learned versification wholly from Dryden's works, who had improved it much beyond any of our former poets, and would proba-

---

[1] *Hollands:* Linen imported from Flanders.

bly have brought it to its perfection, had not he been unhappily obliged to write so often in haste.

— POPE *March 1743*

56. Dryden always uses proper language: lively, natural, and fitted to the subject. 'Tis scarce ever too high or too low — never perhaps, except in his plays.

— POPE *March 1743*

73. When about fifteen, I got acquainted with Mr. Walsh.[2] He encouraged me much, and used to tell me that there was one way left of excelling, for though we had had several great poets, we never had any one great poet that was correct — and he desired me to make that my study and aim.

— POPE *March 1743*

This I suppose first led Mr. Pope to turn his lines over and over again so often, which he continued to the last, and did it with a surprising facility.

— SPENCE

107. The things that I have written fastest have always pleased most. I wrote the *Essay on Criticism* fast, for I had digested all the matter in prose before I began upon it in verse. The *Rape of the Lock* was written fast. All the machinery, you know, was added afterwards, and the making that and what was published before hit so well together, is I think one of the greatest proofs of judgement of anything I ever did.

I wrote most of the *Iliad* fast — a great deal of it on journeys, from the little pocket Homer on that shelf there, and often forty or fifty verses on a morning in bed.

— POPE *February or March 1735*

381. The great matter to write well is "to know thoroughly what one writes about," and "not to be affected" (or as he expressed the same thing afterwards in other words, "to write naturally and from one's knowledge").

— POPE *December 1743*

---

[2] *Walsh:* William Walsh (1663–1708), poet and critic.

382. A writer is not to be blamed if he hits his aim.

"Unless he has made a bad choice of an end?" suggested Spence. Aye, that's true.

— POPE *1–7 May 1730*

383. A poem on a slight subject requires the greater care to make it considerable enough to be read. (Just after speaking of his *Dunciad*.)

— POPE *1728?*

384. 'Tis a great fault in descriptive poetry to describe everything that is one fault in Thomson's *Seasons*.[3] The good ancients (but when I named them I meant Virgil) have no long descriptions, commonly not above ten lines, and scarce ever thirty. One of the longest in Virgil is when Aeneas is with Evander, and that is frequently broken by what Evander says.[4]

— POPE *February or March 1735*

391. After writing a poem one should correct it all over with one single view at a time. Thus for language, if an elegy: "these lines are very good, but are not they of too heroical a strain?", and so vice versa. It appears very plainly from comparing parallel passages touched both in the *Iliad* and *Odyssey* that Homer did this, and 'tis yet plainer that Virgil did so, from the distinct styles he uses in his three sorts of poems. It always answers in him, and so constant an effect could not be the effect of chance.

— POPE *1–7 May 1730*

392. There is nothing more foolish than to pretend to be sure of knowing a great writer by his style.

— POPE *1735*

Mr. Pope seemed fond of this opinion. I have heard him mention it several times, and he has printed it as well as said it. But, I suppose, in both he must speak of writers when they use a borrowed style, and not when they write in their own. He himself had the greatest compass in

---

[3] *Thomson's* Seasons: James Thomson (1700–1748), poet. He was acquainted with Pope, Swift, and Gay. His topographical poem *The Seasons*, published in 1726–30, was extremely popular, frequently reprinted and illustrated, and very different from the urbane style and urban topics of Pope.

[4] *what Evander says: Aeneid* VIII.314–61.

imitating styles that I ever knew in any man, and he had it partly from his method of instructing himself after he was out of the hands of his bad masters, which was at first almost wholly by imitation. Mr. Addison did not discover Mr. Pope's style in the letter on pastorals, which he published in the *Guardian*, but then that was a disguised style. Mr. Pope had certainly a style of his own which was very distinguishable. Mr. Browne,[5] in his imitation of styles of several different sorts of poets, has pointed it out strongly, and Mr. Pope himself used to speak of those likenesses as very just and very well taken. 'Tis much the same in writing as in painting: a painter who has a good manner of his own and a good talent for copying may quite drop his own manner in his copies, and yet be very easy to be distinguished in his originals.

— SPENCE

395. I have nothing to say for rhyme, but that I doubt whether a poem can support itself without it in our language, unless it be stiffened with such strange words as are like to destroy our language itself.

The high style that is affected so much in blank verse would not have been borne even in Milton, had not his subject turned so much on such strange out-of-the-world things as it does.

— POPE *June 1739*

396. I have followed that (the significance of the numbers and the adapting them to the sense) much more even than Dryden, and much oftener than anyone minds it: particularly in the translations of Homer, where 'twas most necessary to do so, and in the *Dunciad* often, and indeed in all my poems.

— POPE *1–4 May 1744*

397. The great rule of verse is to be musical. This, however, is only a secondary consideration and should not jar too much with the former. I remember two lines I wrote when I was a boy, that were very faulty this way. 'Twas on something that I was to describe as passing away as quick as thought what could not be measured by time; he could not even lift up his wing while 'twas doing:

> So swift, this moment here, the next 'tis gone,
> So imperceptible the motion.

— POPE *1–4 May 1744*

---

[5] *Mr. Browne*: Isaac Hawkins Browne (1705–1760), who parodied the style of contemporary poets; see "An Imitation of Mr. Pope's Style" in *Four Poems in Praise of Tobacco*, Chapter 2, p. 364.

403. In versification there's a sensible difference between softness and sweetness that I could distinguish from a boy. Thus, on the same points, Dryden will be found to be softer and Waller sweeter. 'Tis the same with Ovid and Virgil, and Virgil's Eclogues in particular are the sweetest poems in the world.

— POPE *1–7 May 1730*

To Mr. Blacklock, the *sweetness* of verses seemed to depend upon a proper management of the pauses, *softness* on a proper intermixture of the vowels and consonants.

— SPENCE

407. Middling poets are no poets at all. There is always a great number of such in each age that are almost totally forgotten in the next. A few curious inquirers may know that there were such men and that they wrote such and such things, but to the world they are as if they had never been.

— POPE *June 1739*

ALEXANDER POPE

Letter to William Walsh "On the Subject of *English* Versification"

In this very early letter to his mentor-poet William Walsh (1663–1708), Pope outlines his principles of versification. Even though a series of heroic couplets seems to dance effortlessly along (as if chiming in with Pope's claim about his childhood in *Epistle to Arbuthnot*: "I lisp'd in Numbers, and the Numbers came"), Pope in fact takes great care with the patterns and structures of meter and rhyme to achieve in poetry what the gardener designs in a landscape—to *hide* under the appearance of ease the very effort taken:

> He gains all points, who pleasingly confounds,
> Surprizes, varies, and conceals the Bounds.
> (*Epistle to Burlington*, ll. 55–56)

Pope to Walsh

Oct. 22, 1706

After the Thoughts I have already sent you on the subject of *English* Versification, you desire my opinion as to some farther particulars. There are indeed certain Niceties, which tho' not much observed even by correct Versifiers, I cannot but think deserve to be better regarded.

1. It is not enough that nothing offends the Ear, but a good Poet will adapt the very Sounds, as well as Words, to the things he treats of. So that there is (if one may express it so) a Style of Sounds. As in describing a gliding Stream, the Numbers shou'd run easy and flowing; in describing a rough Torrent or Deluge, sonorous and swelling, and so of the rest. This is evident every where in *Homer* and *Virgil*, and no where else that I know of to any observable degree. . . .

This, I think, is what very few observe in practice, and is undoubtedly of wonderful force in imprinting the Image on the reader: We have one excellent Example of it in our Language, Mr. *Dryden*'s Ode on St. *Cæcilia*'s Day, entitled, *Alexander's Feast.*

2. Every nice Ear, must (I believe) have observ'd, that in any smooth *English* Verse of ten syllables, there is naturally a *Pause* at the fourth, fifth, or sixth syllable. It is upon these the Ear rests, and upon the judicious Change and Management of which depends the Variety of Versification. For example,

> At the fifth. *Where-e'er thy Navy* || *spreads her canvass Wings,*
> At the fourth. *Homage to thee* || *and Peace to all she brings.*
> At the sixth. *Like Tracts of Leverets* || *in Morning Snow.*[1]

Now I fancy, that to preserve an exact Harmony and Variety, the Pauses of the 4th or 6th shou'd not be continu'd above three lines together, without the Interposition of another; else it will be apt to weary the Ear with one continu'd Tone, as least it does mine: That at the 5th runs quicker, and carries not quite so dead a weight, so tires not so much tho' it be continued longer.

3. Another nicety is in relation to *Expletives*, whether Words or Syllables, which are made use of purely to supply a vacancy: *Do* before Verbs plural is absolutely such; and it is not improbable but

---

[1] Where-e'er thy Navy . . . in Morning Snow: These lines are from Edmund Waller (1606–1687).

future Refiners may explode *did* and *does* in the same manner, which are almost always used for the sake of Rhime. The same Cause has occasioned the promiscuous use of *You* and *Thou* to the same Person, which can never sound so graceful as either one or the other.

4. I would also object to the Irruption of *Alexandrine* Verses[2] of twelve syllables, which I think should never be allow'd but when some remarkable Beauty or Propriety in them attones for the Liberty: Mr. *Dryden* has been too free of these, especially in his latter Works. I am of the same opinion as to *Triple Rhimes*.[3]

5. I could equally object to the *Repetition* of the same Rhimes within four or six lines of each other, as tiresome to the Ear thro' their Monotony.

6. *Monosyllable-Lines*, unless very artfully managed, are stiff, or languishing: but may be beautiful to express Melancholy, Slowness, or Labour.

7. To come to the *Hiatus*, or Gap between two words which is caus'd by two Vowels opening on each other (upon which you desire me to be particular) I think the rule in this case is either to use the *Cæsura*,[4] or admit the *Hiatus*, just as the Ear is least shock'd by either: For the *Cæsura* sometimes offends the Ear more than the *Hiatus* itself, and our language is naturally overcharg'd with Consonants: As for example; If in this Verse,

> *The Old have Int'rest ever in their Eye,*

we should say, to avoid the *Hiatus*,

> *But th' Old have Int'rest——*

The *Hiatus* which has the worst effect, is when one word ends with the same Vowel that begins the following; and next to this, those Vowels whose sounds come nearest to each other are most to be avoided. O, A, or U, will bear a more full and graceful Sound than E, I, or Y. I know some people will think these Observations trivial, and therefore I am glad to corroborate them by some great Authorities, which I have met with in *Tully* and *Quintilian*. . . . To conclude, I believe the *Hiatus* should be avoided with more care in Poetry than

---

[2] Alexandrine *Verses:* Lines with an extra foot relative to the five-foot (ten-syllable) pentameter line.

[3] Triple Rhimes: Sets of three rhyming lines, as opposed to the usual couplet, or pair of rhymed lines.

[4] Caesura: A pause or break in phrasing in a line.

in Oratory; and I would constantly try to prevent it, unless where the cutting it off is more prejudicial to the Sound than the *Hiatus* itself. I am, &c.

ALEXANDER POPE

From *An Essay on Criticism*

In some ways, the following excerpts from *An Essay on Criticism* demonstrate as well as recapitulate the principles of versification Pope articulated in his letter to Walsh (p. 224). He argues first that the poet must "follow NATURE." "Nature," in the eighteenth century, implied a number of things at once: the observable world fashioned by God, the invisible, underlying principles of life and value, and the innate harmony linking both. The poet also advises the critic *not* to look for perfection, or for something perfectly "correct" that follows all the rules of poetry religiously—instead, look at the whole and see how the parts relate; look at the end and see how the means contribute. The selection includes one of the most famous passages in which the lines *act out* precisely what they condemn:

> While Expletives their feeble Aid *do* join,
> And ten low Words oft creep in one dull Line,
> While they ring round the same *unvary'd Chimes*,
> With sure *Returns* of still *expected Rhymes*.

(Note as well the alexandrine and the triple rhyme Pope castigates in his letter to Walsh.) Finally, Pope proffers the best advice to all scholars, all critics, all poets, all of us: "*Good-Nature* and *Good-Sense* must ever join; / To Err is *Humane*; to Forgive, *Divine*."

'Tis hard to say, if greater Want of Skill
Appear in *Writing* or in *Judging* ill;
But, of the two, less dang'rous is th' Offence,
To tire our *Patience*, than mis-lead our *Sense*:
Some few in *that*, but Numbers err in *this*,   5
Ten Censure wrong for one who Writes amiss;
A *Fool* might once *himself* alone expose,
Now *One* in *Verse* makes many more in *Prose*.
    'Tis with our *Judgments* as our *Watches*, none

Go just *alike*, yet each believes his own.   10
In *Poets* as true *Genius* is but rare,
True *Taste* as seldom is the *Critick*'s Share;
Both must alike from Heav'n derive their Light,
These *born* to Judge, as well as those to Write.
Let such teach others who themselves excell,   15
And *censure freely* who have *written well.*
Authors are partial to their *Wit*, 'tis true,
But are not *Criticks* to their *Judgment* too?
    Yet if we look more closely, we shall find
Most have the *Seeds* of Judgment in their Mind;   20
Nature affords at least a *glimm'ring Light*;
The *Lines*, tho' touch'd but faintly, are drawn right.
But as the slightest Sketch, if justly trac'd,   ⎫
Is by ill *Colouring* but the more disgrac'd,   ⎬
So by *false Learning* is *good Sense* defac'd;   ⎭   25
Some are bewilder'd in the Maze of Schools,
And some made *Coxcombs*° Nature meant but *Fools.*
In search of *Wit* these lose their *common Sense*,
And then turn Criticks in their own Defence.
Each burns alike, who can, or cannot write,   30
Or with a *Rival*'s or an *Eunuch*'s spite.
All *Fools* have still an Itching to deride,
And fain *wou'd* be upon the *Laughing Side*:
If *Mævius*° Scribble in *Apollo*'s spight,
There are, who *judge* still *worse* than he can *write.*   35
    Some have at first for *Wits*, then *Poets* past,°
Turn'd *Criticks* next, and prov'd plain *Fools* at last;
Some neither can for *Wits* nor *Criticks* pass,
As heavy Mules are neither *Horse* nor *Ass.*
Those half-learn'd Witlings, num'rous in our Isle,   40
As half-form'd Insects on the Banks of *Nile*;
Unfinish'd Things, one knows not what to call,
Their Generation's so *equivocal*:°

27. Coxcombs: Fops, beaus, conceited asses.
34. Mævius: A particularly spiteful poet of the Augustan age.
36. *Some have at first for* Wits, *then* Poets *past:* This stanza might be an attack on
John Dennis; he certainly took it that way. See Dennis's early responses to Pope in
"The Poet and the Poem," pp. 197–203.
43. *Their Generation's so* equivocal: "The (supposed) production of plants and an-
imals without parents; spontaneous generation" [T].

To tell 'em, wou'd a *hundred Tongues* require,
Or *one vain Wit's*, that might a hundred tire.   45
   But *you* who seek to *give* and *merit* Fame,
And justly bear a Critick's noble Name,
Be sure *your self* and your own *Reach* to know,
How far your *Genius*, *Taste*, and *Learning* go;
Launch not beyond your Depth, but be discreet,   50
And mark *that Point* where Sense and Dulness *meet*.
   Nature to all things fix'd the Limits fit,
And wisely curb'd proud Man's pretending Wit:
As on the *Land* while *here* the *Ocean* gains,
In *other Parts* it leaves wide sandy Plains;   55
Thus in the *Soul* while *Memory* prevails,
The solid Pow'r of *Understanding* fails;
Where Beams of warm *Imagination* play,
The *Memory*'s soft Figures melt away.
One *Science* only will one *Genius* fit;   60
So *vast* is Art, so *narrow* Human Wit;
Not only bounded to *peculiar Arts*,
But oft in *those*, confin'd to *single Parts*.
Like Kings we lose the Conquests gain'd before,
By vain Ambition still to make them more: 65
Each might his *sev'ral Province* well command,
Wou'd all but *stoop* to what they *understand*.
   First follow NATURE, and your Judgment frame
By her just Standard, which is still the same:
Unerring Nature, still divinely bright,   70
One *clear*, *unchang'd*, and *Universal* Light,
Life, Force, and Beauty, must to all impart,
At once the *Source*, and *End*, and *Test* of Art.
Art from that Fund each *just Supply* provides,
Works *without Show*, and *without Pomp* presides: 75
In some fair Body thus th' informing Soul
With Spirits feeds, with Vigour fills the whole,
Each Motion guides, and ev'ry Nerve sustains;
It self unseen, but in th' *Effects*, remains.
Some, to whom Heav'n in Wit has been profuse,   80
Want as much more, to turn it to its use;
For *Wit* and *Judgment* often are at strife,
Tho' meant each other's Aid, like *Man* and *Wife*.
'Tis more to *guide* than *spur* the Muse's Steed;

Restrain his Fury, than provoke his Speed;   85
The winged Courser, like a gen'rous Horse,
Shows most true Mettle when you *check* his Course.
    Those RULES of old *discover'd*, not *devis'd*,
Are *Nature* still, but *Nature Methodiz'd*;
Nature, like *Liberty*, is but restrain'd   90
By the same Laws which first *herself* ordain'd.

. . .

    A perfect Judge will *read* each Work of Wit
With the same Spirit that its Author *writ*,
Survey the *Whole*, nor seek slight Faults to find,   235
Where *Nature moves*, and *Rapture warms* the Mind;
Nor lose, for that malignant dull Delight,
The *gen'rous Pleasure* to be charm'd with Wit.
But in such Lays as neither *ebb*, nor *flow*,
Correctly cold, and *regularly low*,   240
That shunning Faults, one quiet *Tenour* keep;
We cannot *blame* indeed — but we may *sleep*.
In Wit, as Nature, what affects our Hearts
Is not th' Exactness of peculiar Parts;
'Tis not a *Lip*, or *Eye*, we Beauty call,   245
But the joint Force and full *Result* of *all*.
Thus when we view some well-proportion'd Dome,
(The *World*'s just Wonder, and ev'n *thine* O *Rome*!)
No single Parts unequally surprize;
All comes *united* to th' admiring Eyes;   250
No monstrous Height, or Breadth, or Length appear;
The *Whole* at once is *Bold*, and *Regular*.
    Whoever thinks a faultless Piece to see,
Thinks what ne'er was, nor is, nor e'er shall be.
In ev'ry Work regard the *Writer's End*,   255
Since none can compass more than they *Intend*;
And if the *Means* be just, the *Conduct* true,
Applause, in spite of trivial Faults, is due.
As Men of Breeding, sometimes of Men of Wit,
T' avoid *great Errors*, must the *less* commit,   260
Neglect the Rules each *Verbal Critick* lays,
For *not* to know some Trifles, is a Praise.
Most Criticks, fond of some subservient Art,
Still make the *Whole* depend upon a *Part*,

They talk of *Principles*, but Notions prize,   265
And All to one lov'd Folly Sacrifice.

           . . .

  But most by *Numbers* judge a Poet's Song,
And *smooth* or *rough*, with them, is *right* or *wrong*;
In the bright *Muse* tho' thousand *Charms* conspire,
Her *Voice* is all these tuneful Fools admire,   340
Who haunt *Parnassus* but to please their Ear,
Not mend their Minds; as some to *Church* repair,
Not for the *Doctrine*, but the *Musick* there.
These *Equal Syllables* alone require,
Tho' oft the Ear the *open Vowels* tire,   345
While *Expletives* their feeble Aid *do* join,
And ten low Words oft creep in one dull Line,
While they ring round the same *unvary'd Chimes*,
With sure *Returns* of still *expected Rhymes*.
Where-e'er you find *the cooling Western Breeze*,   350
In the next Line, it *whispers thro' the Trees*;
If *Chrystal Streams with pleasing Murmurs creep*,
The Reader's threaten'd (not in vain) with *Sleep*.
Then, at the *last*, and *only* Couplet fraught
With some *unmeaning* Thing they call a *Thought*,   355
A *needless Alexandrine* ends the Song,
That like a wounded Snake, drags its slow length along.
Leave such to tune their own dull Rhimes, and know
What's *roundly smooth*, or *languishingly slow*;
And praise the *Easie Vigor* of a Line,   360
Where *Denham*'s Strength, and *Waller*'s Sweetness° join.
True Ease in Writing comes from Art, not Chance,
As those move easiest who have learn'd to dance.
'Tis not enough no Harshness gives Offence,
The *Sound* must seem an *Eccho* to the *Sense*.   365
Soft is the Strain when *Zephyr* gently blows,
And the *smooth Stream* in *smoother Numbers* flows;

---

361. Denham's *Strength, and* Waller's *Sweetness:* Sir John Denham (1615–1669),
chiefly known for *Cooper's Hill;* Edmund Waller (1606–1687), a poet whom Pope
compared to Dryden, calling Waller's works sweeter and Dryden's softer (see Spence's
Anecdotes, particularly 1:403, p. 224).

But when loud Surges lash the sounding Shore,
The *hoarse, rough Verse* shou'd like the *Torrent* roar.
When *Ajax*° strives, some Rocks' vast Weight to throw,   370
The Line too *labours*, and the Words move *slow*;
Not so, when swift *Camilla*° scours the Plain,
Flies o'er th'unbending Corn, and skims along the Main.
Hear how *Timotheus'*° vary'd Lays surprize,
And bid Alternate Passions fall and rise!   375
While, at each Change, the Son of *Lybian Jove*°
Now *burns* with Glory, and then *melts* with Love;
Now his *fierce Eyes* with *sparkling Fury* glow;
Now *Sighs* steal out, and *Tears begin to flow*:
Persians and *Greeks* like *Turns of Nature* found,   380
And the *World's Victor* stood subdu'd by *Sound*!
The Pow'rs of Musick all our Hearts allow;
And what *Timotheus* was, is *Dryden* now.

    Avoid *Extreams*; and shun the Fault of such,
Who still are pleas'd *too little*, or *too much*.   385
At ev'ry Trifle scorn to take Offence,
That always shows *Great Pride*, or *Little Sense*;
Those *Heads* as *Stomachs* are not sure the best
Which nauseate all, and nothing can digest.
Yet let not each gay *Turn* thy Rapture move,   390
For Fools *Admire*, but Men of Sense *Approve*;
As things seem *large* which we thro' *Mists* descry,
Dulness is ever apt to *Magnify*.

. . .

    Be thou the *first* true Merit to befriend;
His Praise is lost, who stays till *All* commend;   475
Short is the Date, alas, of *Modern Rhymes*;
And 'tis but just to let 'em live *betimes*.
No longer now that Golden Age appears,
When *Patriarch-Wits* surviv'd a *thousand Years*;
Now Length of *Fame* (our *second* Life) is lost,   480

---

370. Ajax: In Homer's *Iliad*, Ajax is admired and feared for his strength.
372. Camilla: A maiden warrior in Virgil's *Aeneid*.
374. Timotheus: A musician (c. 450–360 B.C.) of Miletus who influenced the work of Euripides and figures in Dryden's *Alexander's Feast* (1697).
376. *Son of* Lybian Jove: In 331 B.C. Alexander the Great visited the oracle of Ammon in the Libyan desert and was proclaimed the son of the king of gods.

And bare Threescore is all ev'n That can boast:
Our Sons their Fathers' *failing Language* see,
And such as *Chaucer* is, shall *Dryden* be.
So when the faithful *Pencil* has design'd
Some *bright Idea* of the Master's Mind, 485
Where a *new* World leaps out at his command,
And ready Nature waits upon his Hand;
When the ripe Colours *soften* and *unite*,
And sweetly *melt* into just Shade and Light,
When mellowing Years their full Perfection give, 490
And each Bold Figure just begins to *Live*;
The *treach'rous Colours* the fair Art betray,
And all the bright Creation fades away!
　　Unhappy *Wit*, like most mistaken Things,
Attones not for that *Envy* which it brings. 495
In *Youth* alone its empty Praise we boast,
But soon the Short-liv'd Vanity is lost!
Like some fair *Flow'r* the early *Spring* supplies,
That gaily Blooms, but ev'n in blooming *Dies*.
What is this *Wit* which must our Cares employ? 500
The *Owner's Wife*, that *other Men* enjoy,
Then most our *Trouble* still when most *admir'd*,
And still the more we *give*, the more *requir'd*;
Whose Fame with *Pains* we guard, but lose with *Ease*,
Sure *some* to *vex*, but never *all* to *please*; 505
'Tis what the *Vicious fear*, the *Virtuous shun*;
By *Fools* 'tis *hated*, and by *Knaves undone*!
　　If *Wit* so much from *Ign'rance* undergo,
Ah let not *Learning* too commence its Foe!
Of old, those met *Rewards* who cou'd *excel*, 510
And such were *Prais'd* who but *endeavour'd well*:
Tho' *Triumphs* were to *Gen'rals* only due,
Crowns were reserv'd to grace the *Soldiers* too,
Now, they who reached *Parnassus'* lofty Crown,
Employ their Pains to spurn some others down; 515
And while Self-Love each jealous Writer rules,
Contending Wits becomes the *Sport of Fools*:
But still the *Worst* with most Regret commend,
For each *Ill Author* is as bad a *Friend*.
To what base Ends, and by what abject Ways, 520
Are Mortals urg'd thro' *Sacred Lust of Praise*!

Ah ne'er so *dire* a *Thirst of Glory* boast,
Nor in the *Critick* let the *Man* be lost!
Good-Nature and *Good-Sense* must ever join;
To Err is *Humane*; to Forgive, *Divine*.

JOSEPH ADDISON

From *The Spectator*, No. 253
[On *An Essay on Criticism*]

This *Spectator* essay is actually an early (1711) literary review of *An Essay on Criticism*, reading it in the context of early-eighteenth-century aesthetic principles and practices. In it Addison, who had not yet met Pope, praises the poem for its ability to make the familiar seem radiantly new ("what oft was *Thought*, but ne'er so well *Exprest*" being one of Pope's own aspirations and criteria in that very poem) and spotlights parts of the poem that perform the faults they critique. Addison, however, regrets Pope's vindictiveness. Within a poem that criticizes poets who "to secure their Reign / Must have their Brothers, Sons, and Kindred Slain," Addison is "sorry to find that an Author [Pope], who is very justly esteemed among the best Judges, has admitted some Stroaks of this Nature into [this] very fine Poem."

The text is from the standard edition of *The Spectator*, edited by Donald F. Bond, vol. II (Oxford: Clarendon Press, 1965), 481–86. Notes used from this edition are marked [B].

No. 253

Thursday, December 20, 1711

Indignor quicquam reprehendi, non quia crassè
Compositum, illepidève putetur, sed quia nuper.[1]
— Hor.

There is nothing which more denotes a great Mind, than the abhorrence of Envy and Detraction. This Passion reigns more among Bad Poets, than among any other Set of Men.

---

[1] Indignor ... nuper: The motto is from Horace (*Epistles* 2.1.76–77) and was translated by Thomas Creech (1658–1700): "I hate a Fop should scorn a *faultless* Page, / Because 'tis *New*, nor yet approv'd by Age."

As there are none more ambitious of Fame, than those who are conversant in Poetry, it is very natural for such as have not succeeded in it to depreciate the Works of those who have. For since they cannot raise themselves to the Reputation of their Fellow-Writers, they must endeavour to sink it to their own Pitch, if they would still keep themselves upon a Level with them.

The greatest Wits that ever were produced in one Age, lived together in so good an Understanding, and celebrated one another with so much Generosity, that each of them receives an additional Lustre from his Contemporaries, and is more famous for having lived with Men of so extraordinary a Genius, than if he had himself been the sole Wonder of the Age. I need not tell my Reader, that I here point at the Reign of *Augustus*, and I believe he will be of my Opinion, that neither *Virgil* nor *Horace* would have gained so great a Reputation in the World, had they not been the Friends and Admirers of each other. Indeed all the great Writers of that Age, for whom singly we have so great an Esteem, stand up together as Vouchers for one another's Reputation. But at the same time that *Virgil* was celebrated by *Gallus, Propertius, Horace, Varius, Tucca* and *Ovid*, we know that *Bavius* and *Mævius* were his declared Foes and Calumniators.[2]

In our own Country a Man seldom sets up for a Poet, without attacking the Reputation of all his Brothers in the Art. The Ignorance of the Moderns, the Scriblers of the Age, the Decay of Poetry are the Topicks of Detraction, with which he makes his Entrance into the World: But how much more noble is the Fame that is built on Candour[3] and Ingenuity, according to those Beautiful Lines of Sir *John Denham*, in his Poem on *Fletcher*'s Works.

> But whither am I straid? I need not raise
> Trophies to thee from other Mens Dispraise;
> Nor is thy Fame on lesser Ruins built,
> Nor needs thy juster Title the foul Guilt

---

[2] Gallus . . . Maevius: "Gaius Cornelius Gallus was a friend of Virgil. The poems in which he may have praised Virgil are not extant, but Virgil refers to him in *Eclogues* 6 and 10. Lucius Varius Rufus and Plotius Tucca were friends to whom Virgil bequeathed his unfinished writings and who afterwards published the *Aeneid*. For the praise of Propertius, see *Elegies*, 2.34.61 ff. (line 65 is used by Addison as the motto of No. 267). Horace praises the work of Virgil in various places; Ovid praises the *Aeneid* in *Ars amatoria*, 3.337–8. Bavius and Maevius, minor poets, are pilloried by Virgil in a famous passage (*Eclogue*, 3. 90)" [B].

[3] Candour: The eighteenth-century connotations of this word included "kindness" as well as "fairness, impartiality."

Of Eastern Kings, who to secure their Reign
Must have their Brothers, Sons, and Kindred Slain.[4]

I am sorry to find that an Author, who is very justly esteemed
among the best Judges, has admitted some Stroaks of this Nature into
a very fine Poem, I mean *The Art of Criticism*, which was published
some Months since, and is a Master-piece in its kind. The Observa-
tions follow one another like those in *Horace*'s *Art of Poetry*, with-
out that Methodical Regularity which would have been requisite in a
Prose Author. They are some of them uncommon, but such as the
Reader must assent to, when he sees them explained with that Ele-
gance and Perspicuity in which they are delivered. As for those which
are the most known, and the most received, they are placed in so
beautiful a Light, and illustrated with such apt Allusions, that they
have in them all the Graces of Novelty, and make the Reader, who
was before acquainted with them, still more convinced of their Truth
and Solidity. And here give me leave to mention what Monsieur
Boileau[5] has so very well enlarged upon in the Preface to his Works,
that Wit and fine Writing doth not consist so much in advancing
things that are new, as in giving things that are known an agreeable
Turn. It is impossible, for us who live in the later Ages of the World,
to make observations in Criticism, Morality, or in any Art or Science,
which have not been touched upon by others. We have little else left
us, but to represent the common Sense of Mankind in more strong,
more beautiful, or more uncommon Lights. If a Reader examines
Horace's Art of Poetry, he will find but very few Precepts in it, which
he may not meet with in *Aristotle*, and which were not commonly
known by all the Poets of the Augustan Age. His way of Expressing
and Applying them, not his Invention of them, is what we are chiefly
to admire.

For this reason I think there is nothing in the World so tiresom as
the Works of those Criticks, who write in a positive Dogmatick Way,
without either Language, Genius or Imagination. If the Reader would
see how the best of the *Latin* Criticks writ, he may find their manner
very beautifully described in the Characters of *Horace*, *Petronius*,
Quintilian and *Longinus*, as they are drawn in the Essay of which I
am now speaking.

---

[4] *his Poem in* Fletcher's *Works*: Sir John Denham (1615–1669), *On Mr. John
Fletcher's Works*.
[5] Boileau: Nicholas Despreaux Boileau (1636–1711), French critic and poet.

Since I have mentioned *Longinus*,[6] who in his Reflections has given us the same kind of Sublime, which he observes in the several Passages that occasioned them; I cannot but take notice, that our *English* Author has after the same manner exemplified several of his Precepts in the very Precepts themselves. I shall produce two or three Instances of this kind. Speaking of the insipid Smoothness which some Readers are so much in love with, he has the following Verses.

> These *Equal Syllables* alone require,
> Tho' oft the Ear the *open Vowels* tire,
> While *Expletives* their feeble Aid *do* join,
> And ten low Words oft creep in one dull Line.

The gaping of the Vowels in the second line, the Expletive *do* in the third, and the ten Monosyllables in the fourth, give such a Beauty to this Passage, as would have been very much admired in an Ancient Poet. The Reader may observe the following Lines in the same View.

> A *needless Alexandrine* ends the Song,
> That like a wounded Snake, drags its slow Length along.

And afterwards,

> 'Tis not enough no Harshness gives Offence,
> The *Sound* must seem an *Eccho* to the *Sense.*
> *Soft* is the Strain when *Zephir* gently blows,
> And the *smooth Stream* in *smoother Numbers* flows
> But when loud Surges lash the sounding Shore,
> The *hoarse, rough Verse* shou'd like the *Torrent* roar.
> When *Ajax* strives, some Rock's vast Weight to throw,
> The Line too *labours*, and the Words move *slow;*
> Not so, when swift *Camilla* scours the *Plain,*
> Flies o'er th'unbending Corn, and skims along the Main.

The beautiful Distich upon *Ajax* in the foregoing Lines, puts me in mind of a Description in *Homer*'s Odyssey,[7] which none of the Criticks have taken notice of. It is where *Sisiphus* is represented lifting his Stone up the Hill, which is no sooner carried to the Top of it, but it immediately tumbles to the Bottom. This double Motion of the Stone is admirably described in the Numbers of these Verses. As in the four first it is heaved up by several *Spondees*, intermixed with proper

---

[6] Longinus: The author of the critical treatise *On the Sublime*, written about the first century A.D., translated by Boileau in 1674.

[7] Homer's *Odyssey*: *Odyssey* II.593–98. Addison quotes from the Greek.

Breathing-places, and at last trundles down in a continued Line of *Dactyls*.[8] . . .

It would be endless to quote Verses out of *Virgil* which have this particular kind of Beauty in the Numbers; but I may take an Occasion in a future Paper to shew several of them which have escaped the Observation of others.

I cannot conclude this Paper without taking notice that we have three Poems in our Tongue, which are of the same Nature, and each of them a Master-piece in its kind; the Essay on Translated Verse, the Essay on the Art of Poetry, and the Essay upon Criticism.[9]

JOSEPH ADDISON

From *The Spectator*, No. 411
[On Imagination]

This *Spectator* essay (June 21, 1712) discusses sight as the primary human sense and explains how it contributes to the imagination. Understanding the importance of the visual to readers of eighteenth-century poetry helps *us* read *The Rape of the Lock* and catch its visual, even painterly, allusions and creations. Poetry appeals to "those Secondary Pleasures of the Imagination which flow from the *Ideas* of visible Objects, when the Objects are not actually before the Eye, but are called up into our Memories, or form'd into agreeable Visions of Things that are either Absent or Fictitious." We are meant to *see* the images in *The Rape of the Lock* — the key imaginative words are designed to call up a rich host of visions, as with the sylphs: "Some to the sun their insect-wings unfold, / Waft on the breeze, or sink in clouds of gold."

---

[8] Spondees . . . Dactyls: A spondee is a metrical foot of two equally stressed syllables; a dactyl is a metrical foot of three syllables—one accented followed by two unaccented (as in "critical").

[9] *three Poems in our Tongue . . . Criticism*: "*The Essay on Translated Verse*, by Wentworth Dillon, Earl of Roscommon, appeared in 1684. The 'Essay on the Art of Poetry' is the *Essay on Poetry* by John Sheffield, Earl of Mulgrave (Duke of Buckinghamshire), published in 1682" [B].

No. 411
Saturday, June 21, 1712

Avia Pieridum peragro loca, nullius ante
Trita solo; juvat integros accedere fonteis;
Atque haurire: . . .[1]

— Lucr.

Our Sight is the most perfect and most delightful of all our Senses. It fills the Mind with the largest Variety of Ideas converses with its Objects at the greatest Distance, and continues the longest in Action without being tired or satiated with its proper Enjoyments. The Sense of Feeling can indeed give us a Notion of Extention, Shape, and all other Ideas that enter at the Eye, except Colours; but at the same time it is very much streightned and confined in its Operations, to the number, bulk, and distance of its particular Objects. Our Sight seems designed to supply all these Defects, and may be considered as a more delicate and diffusive kind of Touch, that spreads it self over an infinite Multitude of Bodies, comprehends the largest Figures, and brings into our reach some of the most remote Parts of the Universe.

It is this Sense which furnishes the Imagination with its Ideas; so that by the Pleasures of the Imagination or Fancy (which I shall use promiscuously) I here mean such as arise from visible Objects, either when we have them actually in our view, or when we call up their Ideas into our Minds by Paintings, Statues, Descriptions, or any the like Occasion. We cannot indeed have a single Image in the Fancy that did not make its first Entrance through the Sight; but we have the Power of retaining, altering and compounding those Images, which we have once received, into all the varieties of Picture and Vision that are most agreeable to the Imagination; for by this Faculty a Man in a Dungeon is capable of entertaining himself with Scenes and Landskips more beautiful than any that can be found in the whole Compass of Nature.

There are few Words in the *English* Language which are employed in a more loose and uncircumscribed Sense than those of the *Fancy* and the *Imagination*. I therefore thought it necessary to fix and determine the Notion of these two Words, as I intend to make use of them

---

[1] Avia . . . haurire: The motto is from Lucretius (*De Rerum Natura* I.926–28): The Muses close Retreat I wander o'er, / Their unacquainted Solitudes explore, / At the Spring-head it charms me to be first, / And in th' untainted Stream to quench my Thirst.

in the Thread of my following Speculations, that the Reader may conceive rightly what is the Subject which I proceed upon. I must therefore desire him to remember, that by the Pleasures of the Imagination, I mean only such Pleasures as arise originally from Sight, and that I divide these Pleasures into two kinds: My Design being first of all to Discourse of those Primary Pleasures of the Imagination, which entirely proceed from such Objects as are before our Eyes; and in the next place to speak of those Secondary Pleasures of the Imagination which flow from the Ideas of visible Objects, when the Objects are not actually before the Eye, but are called up into our Memories, or form'd into agreeable Visions of Things that are either Absent or Fictitious.

The Pleasures of the Imagination, taken in their full Extent, are not so gross as those of Sense, not so refined as those of the Understanding. The last are, indeed, more preferable, because they are founded on some new Knowledge or improvement in the Mind of Man; yet it must be confest, that those of the Imagination are as great and as transporting as the other. A beautiful Prospect delights the Soul, as much as a Demonstration; and a Description in *Homer* has charmed more Readers than a Chapter in *Aristotle*. Besides, the Pleasures of the Imagination have this Advantage, above those of the Understanding, that they are more obvious, and more easie to be acquired. It is but opening the Eye, and the Scene enters. The Colours paint themselves on the Fancy, with very little Attention of Thought or Application of Mind in the Beholder. We are struck, we know not how, with the Symmetry of any thing we see, and immediately assent to the Beauty of an Object, without enquiring into the particular Causes and Occasions of it.

A Man of a Polite Imagination, is let into a great many Pleasures that the Vulgar are not capable of receiving. He can converse with a Picture, and find an agreeable Companion in a Statue. He meets with a secret Refreshment in a Description, and often feels a greater Satisfaction in the Prospect of Fields and Meadows, than another does in the Possession. It gives him, indeed, a kind of Property in every thing he sees, and makes the most rude uncultivated Parts of Nature administer to his Pleasures: So that he looks upon the World, as it were, in another Light, and discovers in it a Multitude of Charms, that conceal themselves from the generality of Mankind.

There are, indeed, but very few who know how to be idle and innocent, or have a Relish of any Pleasures that are not Criminal; every Diversion they take is at the Expence of some one Virtue or another, and their very first Step out of Business is into Vice or Folly. A Man should endeavour, therefore, to make the Sphere of his innocent Pleasures as wide as possible, that he may retire into them with Safety, and find in them such a Satisfaction as a wise Man would not blush to take. Of this Nature are those of the Imagination, which do not require such a Bent of Thought as is necessary to our more serious Employments, nor, at the same time, suffer the Mind to sink into that Negligence and Remissness, which are apt to accompany our more sensual Delights, but, like a gentle Exercise to the Faculties, awaken them from Sloth and Idleness, without putting them upon any Labour or Difficulty.

We might here add, that the Pleasures of the Fancy are more conducive to Health, than those of the Understanding, which are worked out by Dint of Thinking, and attended with too violent a Labour of the Brain. Delightful Scenes, whether in Nature, Painting, or Poetry, have a kindly Influence on the Body, as well as the Mind, and not only serve to clear and brighten the Imagination, but are able to disperse Grief and Melancholly, and to set the Animal Spirits in pleasing and agreeable motions. For this reason Sir *Francis Bacon*,[2] in his Essay upon Health, has not thought it improper to prescribe to his Reader a Poem or a Prospect,[3] where he particularly dissuades him from knotty and subtile Disquisitions, and advises him to pursue Studies, that fill the Mind with splendid and illustrious Objects, as Histories, Fables, and Contemplations of Nature.

I have in this Paper, by way of Introduction, settled the Notion of those Pleasures of the Imagination, which are the Subject of my present Undertaking, and endeavoured, by several Considerations, to recommend to my Reader the Pursuit of those Pleasures. I shall, in my next Paper, examine the several Sources from whence these Pleasures are derived.

---

[2] *Sir* Francis Bacon: Sir Francis Bacon (1561–1626), first Baron Verulam and Viscount St. Albans; philosopher, essayist, and empirical scientist. Addison refers here to Bacon's essay "Of Regiment of Health."

[3] *Prospect:* A plan or description.

ALEXANDER POPE

"Epistle to Mr. Jervas"

In 1695 the poet John Dryden translated *De arte graphica* (1668), or *The Art of Painting*, by the painter and poet Charles Alphonse Dufresnoy (1611–1665). In this poem, Pope suggests a similar union of the "sister arts" of poetry and painting in his friendship with the painter Charles Jervas (see "Portrait of Pope by Charles Jervas," p. 88). "Each from each contract new strength and light"; the poet and the painter, working together under "summer suns," learn to see differently — to see *more* — from each other's art. And both engage in the art of immortalizing, polishing, and preserving the image of beauty in the Countess of Bridgewater, the image of dear friends in Martha and Teresa Blount (see "The Characters of Men and Women," pp. 293–94), the image of a poem's inspiration in Arabella Fermor. Yet the poem closes with a qualification relatively rare for the young Pope, a recognition of the *limits* as well as the *power* of the kindred arts, even in combination: "Alas! how little from the grave we claim? / Thou but preserv'st a Face and I a Name."

This verse be thine, my friend, nor thou refuse
This, from no venal or ungrateful Muse.
Whether thy hand strike out some free design,
Where life awakes, and dawns at ev'ry line;
Or blend in beauteous tints the colour'd mass,   5
And from the canvas call the mimic face:
Read these instructive leaves, in which conspire
Fresnoy's close art, and *Dryden*'s native fire:°
And reading wish, like theirs, our fate and fame,
So mix'd our studies, and so join'd our name,   10
Like them to shine thro' long succeeding age,
So just thy skill, so regular my rage.
   Smit with the love of Sister-arts° we came,
And met congenial, mingling flame with flame;
Like friendly colours found them both unite,   15
And each from each contract new strength and light.

8. Fresnoy's *close art, and* Dryden's *native fire:* Refers to Dryden's 1695 translation of Charles Alphonse Dufresnoy's (1611–1665) *De arte graphica*.

13. *Sister-arts:* Poetry and painting were frequently called "sister arts" or "kindred arts" because of the ways each borrowed from the other in order to render an image — visual or verbal — more vivid.

How oft' in pleasing tasks we wear the day,
While summer suns roll unperceiv'd away?
How oft' our slowly-growing works impart,
While images reflect from art to art?   20
How oft' review; each finding like a friend
Something to blame, and something to commend?
What flatt'ring scenes our wand'ring fancy wrought,
Rome's pompous glories rising to our thought!
Together o'er the *Alps* methinks we fly,   25
Fir'd with ideas of fair *Italy*.
With thee, on *Raphael*'s Monument° I mourn,
Or wait inspiring dreams at *Maro*'s Urn:°
With thee repose, where *Tully*° once was laid,
Or seek some ruin's formidable shade;   30
While fancy brings the vanish'd piles to view,
And builds imaginary *Rome* a-new.
Here thy well-study'd Marbles fix our eye;
A fading Fresco here demands a sigh:
Each heav'nly piece unweary'd we compare,   35
Match *Raphael*'s grace, with thy lov'd *Guido*'s air,
Caracci's strength, *Correggio*'s softer line,
Paulo's free stroke, and *Titian*'s warmth divine.°
    How finish'd with illustrious toil appears
This small, well-polish'd gem, the work of years!   40
Yet still how faint by precept is exprest
The living image in the Painter's breast?
Thence endless streams of fair ideas flow,
Strike in the sketch, or in the picture glow;
Thence beauty, waking all her forms, supplies   45
An Angel's sweetness, or *Bridgewater*'s eyes.°

27. *Raphael's Monument*: Raphael Sanzio (1483–1520), Italian artist of the high Renaissance style best known for his madonnas; he became chief Vatican architect in 1514.

28. *Maro's Urn*: Publius Vergilius Maro (70–19 B.C.), Virgil or Vergil, greatest of Latin poets, author of the *Aeneid* among many other works.

29. Tully: Marcus Tullius Cicero (106–43 B.C.), Roman orator, statesman, philosopher.

38. *Guido's air . . .* Titian's *warmth divine*: All influential Italian Renaissance painters. Guido da Siena (fl. 1200s); the brothers Ludovico, Agostino, and Annibale Carracci (late 1500s to early 1600s); Antonio Allegri Corregio (c. 1489–1534); Paolo Caliari Veronese (c. 1528–1588); Tiziano Vecello, or Titian (c. 1487–1576).

46. Bridgewater's eyes: "Elizabeth, Countess of Bridgewater, was the third of the four beautiful daughters of the Duke of Marlborough, who are alluded to in l. 59" [T].

Muse! at that name thy sacred sorrows shed,
Those tears eternal, that embalm the dead:
Call round her tomb each object of desire,
Each purer frame inform'd with purer fire: 50
Bid her be all that chears or softens life,
The tender sister, daughter, friend and wife;
Bid her be all that makes mankind adore;
Then view this marble, and be vain no more!
 Yet still her charms in breathing paint engage;   55
Her modest cheek shall warm a future age.
Beauty, frail flow'r that ev'ry season fears,
Blooms in thy colours for a thousand years.
Thus *Churchill*'s race shall other hearts surprize,
And other Beauties envy *Worsley*'s eyes,   60
Each pleasing *Blount* shall endless smiles bestow,
And soft *Belinda*'s blush for ever glow.°
 Oh lasting as those colours may they shine,
Free as thy stroke, yet faultless as thy line!
New graces yearly, like thy works, display;   65
Soft without weakness, without glaring gay;
Led by some rule, that guides, but not constrains;
And finish'd more thro' happiness than pains!
The kindred arts shall in their praise conspire,
One dip the pencil, and one string the lyre.   70
Yet should the Graces all thy figures place,
And breathe an air divine on ev'ry face;
Yet should the Muses bid my numbers roll,
Strong as their charms, and gentle as their soul;
With *Zeuxis*' *Helen* thy *Bridgewater* vie,   75
And these be sung 'till *Granville*'s *Myra* die;°
Alas! how little from the grave we claim?
Thou but preserv'st a Face and I a Name.

59–62. *Thus* Churchill's *race . . . for ever glow:* Churchill is the family name of
Marlborough; the wife of Sir Robert Worsley replaced "Wortley" (Lady Mary Wortley
Montagu) in this line after Pope's quarrel with the latter; "Blount" of course refers to
Martha and Teresa, and "Belinda" to Arabella Fermor.
 76. Granville's Myra: "George Granville Lord Lansdowne (1667–1735), who in his
poems frequently celebrated the Countess of Newburgh under the name of Myra" [T].

Portrait of Lady Mary Wortley Montagu, by Charles Jervas (1710). Portraits, like poetic character sketches, are attempts not just to represent but to understand a human subject — "to render the soul of Man visible," as Pope wrote to his friend, painter Charles Jervas (*Correspondence* 2:23). This portrait of Lady Mary was painted in 1710, when she was not yet married. Jervas called the portrait one of his "shepherdesses." It reflects her taste for relatively simple dress. Lady Mary, however, apparently didn't think much of Jervas's abilities to depict either soul or body; when she was in Turkey she wrote to a friend describing her experiences in a bagnio: "To tell you the truth, I had wickedness enough to wish secretly that Mr. Gervase [Jervas] could have been there invisible. I fancy it would have very much improv'd his art to see so many fine Women naked in different postures, some in conversation, some working, others drinking Coffee or sherbet" (*Correspondence of Lady Mary Wortley Montagu* 1:314).

JOSEPH ADDISON

From *The Spectator,* No. 267 [On Epic Poems]

Addison draws from three of the great epics familiar to contemporary readers — Homer's *Iliad*, Virgil's *Aeneid*, and Milton's *Paradise Lost* — to clarify some of the formal principles of the epic poem as outlined by Aristotle, particularly in regard to the unity, completeness, and greatness of the "action," or series of represented events. Glossing *all* of the many details of the epics Addison mentions is beyond the scope of this volume; the excerpt provides the general flavor of literary criticism that Pope well understood and respected. These archetypes, and their lofty qualifications, supplied him with the structures for mock-epic in *The Rape of the Lock* and for parody in "Receit to Make an Epick Poem" (p. 251).

The text is taken from *The Spectator*, ed. Donald F. Bond, vol. II (Oxford: Clarendon Press, 1965), 537–44.

No. 267

Saturday, January 5, 1712

Cedite Romani Scriptores, cedite Graii.[1]
— Propert.

There is nothing in Nature more irksom than general Discourses, especially when they turn chiefly upon Words. For this Reason I shall wave the Discussion of that Point which was started some Years since, Whether *Milton*'s *Paradise Lost* may be called an *Heroick Poem*? Those who will not give it that Title, may call it (if they please) a *Divine Poem*. It will be sufficient to its Perfection, if it has in it all the Beauties of the highest kind of Poetry; and as for those who alledge it is not an Heroick Poem, they advance no more to the Diminution of it, than if they should say *Adam* is not *Æneas*, nor *Eve Helen*.[2]

---

[1] Cedite . . . Graii: The motto is from Propertius (*Elegies* 2.34.65): "Give place, ye bards of Rome and Grecian wits!"

[2] Adam *is not* Æneas, *nor* Eve Helen: Adam and Eve are the central figures of Milton's *Paradise Lost* (1667); Æneas is the hero of Virgil's *Æneid* and Helen of Troy the heroine of Homer's *Iliad*. Addison is saying that the critics who argue that *Paradise Lost* is not a heroic poem (or epic) are simply prejudiced because Milton's poem is the product of modern rather than ancient times. He will measure the poem against Aristotle's criteria to show that epic poetry is not the sole property of the classical past.

I shall therefore examine it by the Rules of Epic Poetry, and see whether it falls short of the *Iliad* or *Æneid* in the Beauties which are essential to that kind of Writing. The first thing to be considered in an Epic Poem, is the Fable, which is perfect or imperfect, according as the Action which it relates is more or less so. This Action should have three Qualifications in it. First, It should be but one Action. Secondly, It should be an entire Action; and Thirdly, It should be a great Action. To consider the Action of the *Iliad*, *Æneid*, and *Paradise Lost* in these three several Lights. *Homer* to preserve the Unity of his Action hastens into the midst of things, as *Horace* has observed: Had he gone up to *Leda*'s Egg, or begun much later, even at the Rape of *Helen*, or the Investing of *Troy*, it is manifest that the Story of the Poem would have been a Series of several Actions.[3] He therefore opens his Poem with the Discord of his Princes, and artfully interweaves in the several succeeding parts of it, an account of every thing material which relates to them, and had passed before this fatal Dissension. After the same manner *Æneas* makes his first appearance in the *Tyrrhene* Seas, and within sight of *Italy*, because the Action proposed to be celebrated was that of his Settling himself in *Latium*. But because it was necessary for the Reader to know what had happened to him in the taking of *Troy*, and in the preceding parts of his Voyage, *Virgil* makes his Hero relate it by way of Episode in the second and third Books of the *Æneid*. The Contents of both which Books come before those of the first Book in the Thread of the Story, tho' for preserving of this Unity of Action, they follow it in the Disposition of the Poem. *Milton*, in Imitation of these two great Poets, opens his *Paradise Lost* with an Infernal Council plotting the Fall of Man, which is the Action he proposed to celebrate; and as for those great Actions, the Battel of the Angels, and the Creation of the World, (which preceded in point of time, and which, in my Opinion, would have entirely destroyed the Unity of his Principal Action, had he related them in the same Order that they happened) he cast them into the fifth, sixth and seventh Books, by way of Episode to this noble Poem.

[3] Leda's Egg . . . *the Rape of* Helen . . . *the Investing of* Troy: Refers to events before the opening scene of the *Iliad* (a violent quarrel between Agamemnon and Achilles, two commanders in the expedition against Troy, over some women captured in a recent raid). Leda, pursued and ravished by Zeus in the form of a swan, laid an egg from which hatched Helen, later wife of Menelaus, who was abducted ("raped") by Paris, son of King Priam of Troy. The Achaean princes, led by Agamemnon and Achilles, then attacked ("invested") Troy to recover Helen.

Aristotle himself allows, that *Homer* has nothing to boast of as to the Unity of his Fable, tho' at the same time that great Critick and Philosopher endeavours to palliate this Imperfection in the *Greek* Poet, by imputing it in some Measure to the very Nature of an Epic Poem. Some have been of Opinion, that the *Æneid* also labours in this particular, and has Episodes which may be looked upon as Excrescencies rather than as Parts of the Action. On the contrary, the Poem which we have now under our Consideration, hath no other Episodes than such as naturally arise from the Subject, and yet is filled with such a multitude of astonishing Incidents, that it gives us at the same time a Pleasure of the greatest Variety, and of the greatest Simplicity; uniform in its Nature, tho' diversified in the Execution.

I must observe also, that as *Virgil* in the Poem which was designed to celebrate the Original of the *Roman* Empire, has described the Birth of its great Rival, the *Carthaginian* Commonwealth: *Milton* with the like Art in his Poem on the Fall of Man, has related the Fall of those Angels who are his professed Enemies. Besides the many other Beauties in such an Episode, it's running Parallel with the great Action of the Poem, hinders it from breaking the Unity so much as another Episode would have done, that had not so great an Affinity with the principal Subject. In short, this is the same kind of Beauty which the Criticks admire in the *Spanish Fryar*, or the *Double Discovery*,[4] where the two different Plots look like Counterparts and Copies of one another.

The second Qualification required in the Action of an Epic Poem is, that it should be an *entire* Action: An Action is entire when it is compleat in all its Parts; or as *Aristotle* describes it, when it consists of a Beginning, a Middle, and an End. Nothing should go before it, be intermix'd with it, or follow after it, that is not related to it. As on the contrary, no single Step should be omitted in that just and regular Progress which it must be supposed to take from its Original to its Consummation. Thus we see the Anger of *Achilles* in its Birth, its Continuance and Effects; and *Æneas*'s Settlement in *Italy*, carried on through all the Oppositions in his way to it both by Sea and Land. The Action in *Milton* excels (I think) both the former in this particular; we see it contrived in Hell, executed upon Earth, and punished by Heaven. The parts of it are told in the most distinct manner, and grow out of one another in the most natural Order.

---

[4] *the* Spanish Fryar, *or the* Double Discovery: A tragi-comedy by John Dryden (*The Double Discovery* is a subtitle), produced and published in 1681.

The third Qualification of an Epic Poem is its *Greatness*. The Anger of *Achilles* was of such Consequence, that it embroiled the Kings of *Greece*, destroy'd the Heroes of *Asia*, and engaged all the Gods in Factions. *Æneas's* Settlement in *Italy* produced the *Cæsars*, and gave Birth to the *Roman* Empire. *Milton's* Subject was still greater than either of the former; it does not determine the Fate of single Persons or Nations, but of a whole Species. The united Powers of Hell are joyned together for the Destruction of Mankind, which they effected in part, and would have completed, had not Omnipotence it self interposed. The principal Actors are Man in his greatest Perfection, and Woman in her highest Beauty. Their Enemies are the fallen Angels: The Messiah their Friend, and the Almighty their Protector. In short, every thing that is great in the whole Circle of Being, whether within the Verge of Nature, or out of it, has a proper Part assigned it in this admirable Poem.

In Poetry, as in architecture, not only the whole, but the principal Members, and every part of them, should be Great. I will not presume to say, that the Book of Games in the *Æneid*,[5] or that in the *Iliad*, are not of this nature, nor to reprehend *Virgil's* Simile of the Top,[6] and many other of the same Kind in the *Iliad*, as liable to any Censure in this Particular; but I think we may say, without derogating from those wonderful Performances, that there is an Indisputable and Unquestioned Magnificence in every Part of *Paradise Lost*, and indeed a much greater than could have been formed upon any Pagan System.

But *Aristotle*, by the Greatness of the Action, does not only mean that it should be great in its Nature, but also in its Duration, or in other Words, that it should have a due length in it, as well as what we properly call Greatness. The just Measure of this kind of Magnitude, he explains by the following Similitude. An Animal, no bigger than a Mite, cannot appear perfect to the Eye, because the Sight takes it in at once, and has only a confused Idea of the whole, and not a distinct Idea of all its Parts; If on the contrary you should suppose an Animal of ten thousand Furlongs in length, the Eye would be so filled

---

[5] *the Book of Games in the* Æneid: Book V of the *Æneid*, when Æneas holds funeral games on the anniversary of the death of his father Anchises.

[6] Virgil's *Simile of the Top*: Æneid 7.378–84. Juno, who disapproves of Æeneas marrying Lavinia, sends a fury to drive Lavinia's mother mad; the text compares her to a spinning toy. Along with the epic games, this is not one of the poem's grandest moments, according to Addison.

with a single Part of it, that it could not give the Mind an Idea of the whole. What these Animals are to the Eye, a very short or a very long Action would be to the Memory. The first would be, as it were, lost and swallowed up by it, and the other difficult to be contained in it. *Homer* and *Virgil* have shewn their principal Art in this Particular; the Action of the *Iliad*, and that of the *Æneid*, were in themselves exceeding short, but are so beautifully extended and diversified by the Invention of *Episodes*, and the Machinery of Gods, with the like Poetical Ornaments, that they make up an agreeable Story sufficient to employ the Memory without overcharging it. *Milton*'s Action is enriched with such a variety of Circumstances, that I have taken as much Pleasure in reading the Contents of his Books, as in the best invented Story I ever met with. It is possible, that the Traditions on which the *Iliad* and *Æneid* were built, had more Circumstances in them than the History of *the Fall of Man*, as it is related in Scripture. Besides it was easier for *Homer* and *Virgil* to dash the Truth with Fiction, as they were in no danger of offending the Religion of their Country by it. But as for *Milton*, he had not only a very few Circumstances upon which to raise his Poem, but was also obliged to proceed with the greatest Caution in every thing that he added out of his own Invention. And, indeed, notwithstanding all the Restraints he was under, he has filled his Story with so many surprising Incidents, which bear so close Analogy with what is delivered in Holy Writ, that it is capable of pleasing the most delicate Reader, without giving Offence to the most scrupulous.

The Modern Criticks have collected from several Hints in the *Iliad* and *Æneid* the Space of Time, which is taken up by the Action of each of those Poems; but as a great Part of *Milton*'s Story was transacted in Regions that lie out of the reach of the Sun and the Sphere of Day, it is impossible to gratifie the Reader with such a Calculation, which indeed would be more curious than instructive; none of the Criticks, either Ancient or Modern, having laid down Rules to circumscribe the Action of an Epic Poem with any determined number of Years, Days or Hours.

But of this more particularly hereafter.

ALEXANDER POPE

Sarpedon's Speech from the *Iliad*

Clarissa as a character enters the fray in later editions (1717 and after), with a speech (as Pope himself explains) to "*open more clearly the* MORAL *of the Poem.*" That moral urges young women to concentrate less on their beauty, which is by nature fragile and temporary, and more on the social power of good humor. But Clarissa, of course, is the same character who gives the Baron the scissors in the first place (III.127–30), arming the "Knight" for the battle. Clarissa's speech, as Pope's note elaborately highlights, is a parody — a mock version of the speech in which Sarpedon urges his nephew Glaucus to glory by leading the Trojan attack on the Greek ramparts, pointing out epic versions of Clarissa's concerns: the certainty of mortality, the disgrace of ignominy, the immortality of honor. But where the pause after Sarpedon's speech is followed by the roar of enthusiastic warriors *responding* to the ardor of the speech, Clarissa's words meet with peevish silence, and the battle breaks out *in spite of* her counsel. Is this a comment on Clarissa, on women, or on the beau monde?

Pope's translation of Sarpedon's speech would have been familiar to readers of Pope's works in 1717 since he published a version in *Episode of Sarpedon; Translated from the Twelfth and Sixteenth Books of Homer's Iliads* in the 1709 *Miscellany*. Pope also praises Sir John Denham's translation in *Miscellany Poems: The First Part* (3rd ed., 1702). The clashes between epic and mock-epic style, content, phrasing, and meaning would have resonated roundly for a contemporary reader; pairing epic allusion and mock-epic content within the poetic form of heroic couplets both emphasizes and elides their differences — they should live far apart, yet in *The Rape of the Lock* they nestle comfortably together.

> Why boast we, *Glaucus*! our extended Reign,
> Where *Xanthus*' Streams enrich the *Lycian* Plain,
> Our num'rous Herds that range the fruitful Field,
> And Hills where Vines their purple Harvest yield,
> Our foaming Bowls with purer Nectar crown'd   375
> Our Feasts enhanc'd with Music's sprightly Sound?
> Why on those Shores are we with Joy survey'd,
> Admir'd as Heroes, and as Gods obey'd?
> Unless great Acts superior Merit prove,
> And vindicate the bount'ous Pow'rs above.   380

'Tis ours, the Dignity they give, to grace;
The first in Valour, as the first in Place.
That when with wond'ring Eyes our martial Bands
Behold our Deeds transcending our Commands,
Such, they may cry, deserve the sov'reign State,   385
Whom those that envy, dare not imitate!
Could all our Care elude the gloomy Grave,
Which claims no less the fearful than the brave,
For Lust of Fame I should not vainly dare
In fighting Fields, nor urge thy Soul to War.   390
But since, alas! Ignoble Age must come,
Disease, and Death's inexorable Doom;
The Life which others pay, let us bestow,
And give to Fame what we to Nature owe;
Brave tho' we fall, and honour'd if we live,   395
Or let us Glory gain, or Glory give!
   He said; his Words the list'ning Chief inspire
With equal Warmth, and rouze the Warrior's Fire;
The Troops pursue their Leaders with Delight,
Rush to the Foe, and claim the promis'd Fight.   400

ALEXANDER POPE

"A Receit to Make an Epick Poem,"
The Guardian, No. 78

Pope published this parody of epic theory in *The Guardian* 78 (June 10, 1713), and published a different version of it later as *Peri Bathous or the Art of Sinking in Poetry* in 1728, to correspond with the *Dunciad*. This parody, like *The Rape of the Lock* itself, simultaneously targets the great and the small, the past and the present. On the one hand it satirizes modern minor poets and critics who scrabble to impose and follow rules; but in its parody of Longinus it also sabotages the authority of the great treatises on the epic. (The "recipe" also pokes a finger at the criticisms Pope himself suffered over his lack of classical training.) Note that the *Rape* sometimes bends the parodic prescriptions laid down here: It does not antiquate its language, but in the sputterings of Sir Plume, modernizes it.

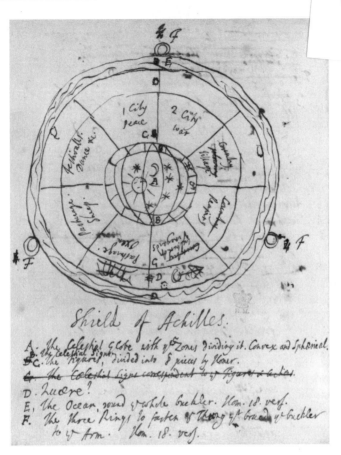

Rough sketch for the shield of Achilles by Alexander Pope. Although Pope's translation of the *Iliad* first appeared after *The Rape of the Lock*, he was constantly making connections between the two: "perhaps as a compensation for Greekless readers who had to wait a few years to appreciate fully the role of the *Iliad* in Belinda's adventures, he appears to have translated several passages so as to provide specific epic contexts for certain passages of his already existent mock-epic, thus achieving a kind of 'parody in reverse time'" (Kinsley 30). In the *Rape*, Pope conjures up various epic shields in his description of Belinda's petticoat, "that sev'nfold Fence" (II.119), particularly the shields of Ajax (which had "sev'n thick Folds o'ercast, / Of tough Bullhides; of solid Brass the last" [*Iliad* VII.267–68]) and Achilles (which Vulcan bound "in living Silver" [XVIII.701–704]). The petticoat, like the shield, is ornament as well as protection; but like the shield, is not always invincible to attack.

Wednesday, June 10, 1713

Docebo Unde parentur opes, quid alat, formetque Poetam.
— Hor.[1]

It is no small pleasure to me, who am zealous in the Interests of Learning, to think I may have the Honour of leading the Town into a very new and uncommon Road of Criticism. As that kind of Literature is at present carried on, it consists only in a Knowledge of Mechanick Rules, which contribute to the Structure of different sorts of Poetry, as the Receits of good Houswives do to the making Puddings of Flower, Oranges, Plumbs, or any other Ingredients. It would, methinks, make these my instructions more easily intelligible to ordinary Readers, if I discoursed of these Matters in the Stile in which Ladies Learned in Œconomicks dictate to their Pupils for the Improvement of the Kitchin and Larder.

I shall begin with Epick Poetry, because the Criticks agree it is the greatest Work Human Nature is capable of. I know the *French* have already laid down many Mechanical Rules for Compositions of this Sort, but at the same time they cut off almost all Undertakers from the Possibility of ever performing them; for the first Qualification they unanimously require in a Poet, is a *Genius*. I shall here endeavour (for the Benefit of my Countrymen) to make it manifest, that Epick Poems may be made *without a Genius*, nay without Learning or much Reading. This must necessarily be of great Use to all those Poets who confess they never Read, and of whom the World is convinced they never Learn. What *Moliere*[2] observes of making a Dinner, that any Man can do it *with Mony*, and if a profest Cook cannot *without*, he has his Art for nothing; the same may be said of making a Poem, 'tis easily brought about by him that *has* a Genius, but the Skill lies in doing it without one. In pursuance of this End, I shall present the Reader with a plain and certain *Recipe*, by which even Sonneteers and Ladies may be qualified for this grand Performance.

I know it will be objected, that one of the chief Qualifications of an Epick Poet, is to be knowing in all Arts and Sciences. But this ought not to discourage those that have no Learning, as long as Indexes and Dictionaries may be had, which are the Compendium of all

---

[1] Docebo . . . Poetam: "I will teach the poet's office and duty; whence he draws his stories; what nurtures and fashions him" (Horace, *Ars Poetica*).

[2] Moliere: Molière, pseudonym of Jean-Baptiste Poquelin (1622–1673), French comic playwright and actor.

Knowledge. Besides, since it is an established Rule, that none of the Terms of those Arts and Sciences are to be made use of, one may venture to affirm, our Poet cannot impertinently offend in this Point. The Learning which will be more particularly necessary to him, is the ancient Geography of Towns, Mountains, and Rivers: For this let him take *Cluverius*, Value Four-pence.[3]

Another Quality required is a compleat Skill in Languges. To this I answer, that it is notorious Persons of no Genius have been oftentimes great Linguists. To instance in the *Greek*, of which there are two Sorts; the Original *Greek*, and that from which our Modern Authors translate. I should be unwilling to promise Impossibilities, but modestly speaking, this may be learned in about an Hour's time with Ease. I have known one, who became a sudden Professor of *Greek*, immediately upon Application of the Left-hand Page of the *Cambridge Homer* to his Eye. It is, in these Days, with Authors as with other Men, the well bred are familiarly acquainted with them at first Sight, and as it is sufficient for a good General to have *survey'd* the Ground he is to conquer, so it is enough for a good Poet to have *seen* the Author he is to be Master of. But to proceed to the Purpose of this Paper.

A RECEIT TO MAKE AN *EPICK* POEM.

For the *Fable.*

Take out of any old Poem, History books, Romance, or Legend (for instance Geffry of Monmouth *or* Don Belianis of Greece:[4] *those Parts of Story which afford most Scope for long Descriptions; Put these Pieces together, and throw all the Adventures you fancy into one Tale. Then take a Hero, whom you may chuse for the Sound of his Name, and put him into the midst of these Adventures; There let him* work, *for twelve Books; at the end of which you may take him out, ready prepared to conquer or to marry; it being necessary that the Conclusion of an Epick Poem be fortunate.*

[3] Cluverius, *Value Four-pence:* Philipp Clouver (1580–1622), geographer; the price refers to one of his books, perhaps the *Atlas Geographus,* translated 1711.

[4] Geffry of Monmouth *or* Don Belianis of Greece: Geoffrey of Monmouth wrote the first account of the Arthurian legend, c. 1135; the romance *The History of Don Belianis* first appeared in English in 1598, followed by translations and editions by Francis Kirkman in 1672 and John Shirley in 1683.

To make an Episode.

Take any remaining Adventure of your former Collection, in which you could no way involve your Hero; or any unfortunate Accident that was too good to be thrown away; and it will be of Use, applyed to any other Person; who may be lost and evaporate in the Course of the Work, without the least Damage to the Composition.

For the Moral and Allegory.

These you may Extract out of the Fable afterwards at your Leisure: Be sure you strain them sufficiently.

For the *Manners*.

For those of the Hero, take all the best Qualities you can find in all the best celebrated Heroes of Antiquity; if they will not be reduced to a Consistency, lay 'em all on a heap upon him. But be sure they are Qualities which your Patron *would be thought to have; and to prevent any Mistake which the World may be subject to, select from the Alphabet those Capital Letters that compose his Name, and set them at the Head of a Dedication before your Poem. However, do not absolutely observe the exact Quantity of these Virtues, it not being determined whether or no it be necessary for the Hero of a Poem to be an honest Man — For the* Under-Characters *gather them from* Homer *and* Virgil, *and change the Names as Occasion serves.*

For the *Machines*.

Take of Deities, Male and Female, as many as you can use. Separate them into two equal parts, and keep Jupiter *in the middle. Let* Juno *put him in a Ferment, and* Venus *mollifie him. Remember on all Occasions to make use of Volatile* Mercury. *If you have need of Devils, draw them out of* Milton's Paradise, *and extract your Spirits from* Tasso,[5] *The Use of these Machines is evident; for since no Epick Poem can possibly subsist without them, the wisest way is to reserve them for your greatest Necessities. When you cannot extricate your Hero by any Human Means, or your self by your own Wit, seek Relief from Heaven, and the Gods will do your Business very readily. This is according to the direct Prescription of* Horace *in his Art of Poetry.*

[5] Tasso: Torquato Tasso (1544–1595), poet of the Italian Renaissance.

Nec Deus intersit, nisi dignus vindice Nodus *Inciderit*——

That is to say, a Poet should never call upon the Gods for their Assistance, but when he is in great Perplexity.

For the *Descriptions.*

For a *Tempest.*

Take Eurus, Zephyr, Auster *and* Boreas, *and cast them together in one Verse.*[6] *Add to these of Rain, Lightning, and of Thunder (the loudest you can)* quantum sufficit. *Mix your Clouds and Billows well together till they foam, and thicken your description here and there with a Quicksand. Brew your Tempest well in your Head, before you set it a blowing.*

For a *Battel.*

Pick a large quantity of Images and Descriptions from Homer's *Iliads, with a Spice or two of* Virgil, *and if there remain any Overplus, you may lay them by for a* Skirmish. *Season it well with* Similes, *and it will make an* Excellent Battel.

For a *Burning Town.*

If such a Description be necessary, because it is certain there is one in Virgil, *Old* Troy *is ready burnt to your Hands. But if you fear That would be thought* Borrowed, *a Chapter or two of the Theory of the* Conflagration, *well circumstanced, and done into Verse, will be a good* Succedaneum.[7]

As for Similes *and* Metaphors, *they may be found all over the Creation, the most ignorant may gather them, but the danger is in applying them. For this, advise with your Bookseller.*

For the *Language.*

(I mean the Diction*). Here it will do well to be an Imitator of* Milton, *for you'll find it easier to imitate him in this than any thing else.* Hebraisms *and* Grecisms *are to be found in him, without the trouble*

---

[6] Eurus, Zephyr, Auster, *and* Boreas: Personifications of the east, west, south, and north winds.

[7] Succedaneum: "A drug, frequently of inferior efficacy, substituted for another" [OED].

of Learning the Languages. I knew a Painter, who (like our Poet) had no Genius, *make his Dawbings be thought* Originals *by setting them in the* Smoak: *You may in the same manner give the venerable Air of Antiquity to your Piece, by darkening it up and down with* Old English. *With this you may be easily furnished upon any Occasion, by the Dictionary commonly Printed at the end of* Chaucer.

I must not conclude, without cautioning all Writers without Genius in one material Point; which is, never to be afraid of having *too much Fire* in their Works. I should advise rather to take their warmest Thoughts, and spread them abroad upon Paper; for they are observed to cool before they are read.

ABBÉ DE MONTFAUCON DE VILLARS

From *The Count of Gabalis*

A proper epic relies on established mythological machinery; for his mock-epic purposes Pope employed the Rosicrucian mythology that had first appeared in Germany in the early seventeenth century and had been published in a series of five discourses by the Abbé de Montfaucon de Villars in 1670. Two English translations appeared in 1680, by Philip Ayres and A. Lovell; this excerpt is from a third translation, by John Ozell, inspired by *The Rape of the Lock* and following closely on the heels of its publication. Pope mentions it in a postscript of a letter to Caryll: "The book of Count Gabalais [*sic*] is genuine; who translated it I know not. I supose [*sic*] at the instigation of none but the bookseller who paid for it" (*Correspondence* 1:268). (See the advertisement in *The Daily Courant*, p. 179.)

The selection includes "Some Account of the Rosicrucians," a more or less factual history of the religious sect. But the "history" quickly turns into adventure, shedding light on Pope's charge that some readers took the text for a novel. The history is followed by five "Discourses upon the Occult Sciences" between the narrator and the mysterious, learned Count, who seems fond of showing up unexpectedly and speaking in odd and ponderous phrases. The narrator, a skeptic who pretends to be a cult admirer, addresses the Count through letters and dialogue on the various philosophical and physical aspects of this doctrine. In Discourse II, reproduced here, the Count explains that the Rosicrucian sages are required to be sexually chaste, to give up all intercourse with (human) women. As it turns out, their "reward" is unlimited "commerce" with the far more beautiful females of the spirit world — the sylphs, salamanders, gnomids, and nymphs, who in their turn acquire immortality "when [each] is so happy as to marry a Sage." Thus the same erotic hypocrisy governs the "real" Rosicrucian doctrine as in Belinda's poetic version; the "original machinery" is as inclined toward satire as its mock-epic vehicle *The Rape of the Lock*.

The Translator's Preface.

The following Piece is an Account of the Rosicrucian *Doctrine of* Spirits.

Monsieur Bayle[1] *informs us, that it was publish'd at* Paris *by the celebrated Abbot* de Villars, *in the Year 1670; and adds, that some have been of Opinion, that* Le Comte de Gabalis, *was originally founded upon two* Italian *Chymical Letters written by* Borri, *others affirm, that* Borri *took the chief Hints in his Letters from this Work; but the Discussion of this Point, Monsieur* Bayle *leaves to those who are more critically curious.*

The present Revival of it, was occasion'd by The Rape of the Lock; *in the Dedication of which Poem Mr.* Pope *has given us his Opinion,* That the best Account he knew of the *Rosicrucian* System, is in this Tract: *Which we doubt not will be a sufficient Recommendation of it to the Publick.*

The following, is a new Translation from the Paris *Edition,[2] which is now very difficult to be met with; and there are some Notes interspers'd, the better to illustrate several passages and Authors referr'd to.*

Some Account of the *Rosicrucians*.

This Sect is of *German* Extraction, and were originally stil'd *Rose-Croix*, or *Rosicrucians*, call'd also the *Inlightened, Immortal*, and *Invisible*. This Name was given to a certain Fraternity, or Cabal, which appear'd in *Germany* in the Beginning of the XVIIth Age. Those that

---

[1] Monsieur *Bayle:* Pierre Bayle (1647–1706), French Protestant philosopher and author of *Dictionnaire historique et critique* (1695–97), a collection of biographical entries on historical, modern, classical, and biblical figures.

[2] a new Translation from the *Paris* edition: De Villars's 1670 edition was reprinted in 1700.

are admitted thereunto, called *the Brethren*, or *Rosicrucians*, swear
Fidelity, promise Secrecy, write Enigmatically, or in Characters, and
oblige themselves to observe the Laws of that Society, which hath for
its End the re-establishing of all Disciplines and Sciences, and espe-
cially Physick, which, according to their Notion, is not understood,
and but ill practised: They boast they have excellent Secrets, whereof
the Philosopher's Stone is the least; and they hold, that the ancient
Philosophers of *Egypt*, the *Chaldeans*, *Magi* of *Persia*, and *Gym-
nosophists* of the *Indies*,[3] have taught nothing but what they them-
selves teach. They affirm, That in 1378, a Gentleman of *Germany*,
whose Name is not known, but by these two Letters *A. C.* being put
into a Monastery, had learned the *Greek* and *Latin* Tongue; and that
some Time after going into *Palastine*, he fell sick at *Damascus*, where
having heard speak of the Sages of *Arabia*, he consulted them at
Damus, where they had an University. It's added, That these wise
Arabians saluted him by his Name, taught him their Secrets and that
the *German*, after he had travelled a long Time, return'd into his own
Country; where associating with some Companions, he made them
Heirs of his Knowledge, and died in 1484.

These Brothers had their Successors till 1604, when one of the
Cabal found the Tomb of the first of them, with divers Devices, Char-
acters, and Inscriptions thereon; the principal of which contained
these four Letters in Gold, A. C. R. E. and a Parchment-Book written
in Golden Letters, with the Encomium of that pretended Founder.

"A certain Person, having Occasion to dig somewhat deep in the
Ground where this Philosopher lay interr'd, met with a small Door,
having a Wall on each Side of it. His Curiosity, and the Hopes of find-
ing some hidden Treasure, soon prompted him to force open the Door.
He was immediately surpriz'd by a sudden Blaze of Light, and discov-
er'd a very fair Vault: At the upper End of it was a Statue of a Man in
Armour, sitting by a Table, and leaning on his Left Arm. He held a
Truncheon in his Right Hand, and had a Lamp burning before him.
The Man had no sooner set one Foot within the Vault, than the Statue,
erecting it self from its leaning Posture, stood bolt upright; and upon
the Fellow's advancing another Step, lifted up the Truncheon in his
Right Hand. The Man still ventur'd a third Step, when the Statue, with

[3] Chaldeans, Magi *of* Persia, *and* Gymnosophists *of the* Indies: The Chaldeans
were skilled in occult sciences and astrology; the Magi were of the ancient Persian
priest caste, skilled in magic and astrology (hence magician or sorcerer); Gym-
nosophists were a sect of ancient Hindu philosophers of ascetic habits.

a furious Blow, broke the Lamp into a thousand Pieces, and left his Guest in a sudden Darkness. Upon the Report of this Adventure, the Country-People soon came with Lights to the Sepulchre, and discover'd that the Statue, which was made of Brass, was nothing more than a Piece of Clockwork; that the Floor of the Vault was all loose, and underlaid with several Springs, which, upon any Man's entering, naturally produced that which happened. ROSICRUCIUS, say his Disciples, made Use of this Method, to show the World, that he had re-invented the ever-burning Lamps of the Ancients, tho' he was resolv'd no one should reap any Advantage from the Discovery."

Afterwards, that Society, which in Reality, is but a Sect of Mountebanks, began to multiply, but durst not appear publickly, and for that Reason was sir-nam'd the *Invisible.* The *Inlightned,* or *Illuminati,* of *Spain,* proceeded from them; both the one and the other have been condemn'd for Fanaticks and Deceivers: We must add, That *John Bringeret* Printed, in 1615, a Book in *Germany,* which comprehends two Treatises, Entituled, *The Manifesto and Confession of Faith of the Fraternity of the* Rosicrucians *in Germany*: It was dedicated to Monarchs, States, and the Learned. These Persons boasted themselves to be the *Library* of *Ptolemy Philadelphus,* the *Academy* of *Plato,* the *Lycæum,* &c. and bragg'd of extraordinary Qualifications, whereof the least was, That they could speak all Languages; and after, in 1622, they gave this Advertisement to the Curious: *We, deputed by our College, the Principal of the Brethren of the* ROSICRUSIANS, *to make our visible and invisible Abode in this City, thro' the Grace of the Most High, towards whom are turned the Hearts of the Just: We teach without Books or Notes, and speak the Languages of the Countries wherever we are, to draw Men, like our selves, from the Error of Death.* This Bill was Matter of Merriment; in the mean Time, the Brethren of the *Rosicrucians* have disappear'd, tho' it be not the Sentiment of that *German* Chymist, the Author of a Book, entitled, *De Volucri Arbored;* and of another, who hath compos'd a Treatise stil'd, *De Philosophiâ Purâ.*

. . .

Discourse II.

The Count was pleas'd to allow me the whole Night, to be spent in Prayer; and the next Morning, by Break of Day, he gave me to understand, by a Billet, that he would wait on me about Eight of the Clock;

and that, if I approv'd of it, we would go take a Turn together
Abroad. I waited for him: He came; and, Compliments pass'd, Let's
go (says he) to some Place where we may be free, and our Conversa-
tion uninterrupted. I told him, I thought *Ruel* an agreable Place, and
solitary enough. Come along then, cry'd he. We went into his Coach;
and all the Way I made Observations upon my new Master. I never,
in my Life, met with any Person who had so great a Self-Satisfaction,
as he seem'd to have, in all he said and did. His Mind was more
serene and free, I thought, than 'twas possible for that of a Wizard to
be. His Air had nothing in it of a Man whose Conscience was not
perfectly clear; and I had a marvellous Impatience to hear him begin;
not being able to conceive a Person, who seem'd to be so judicious
and accomplish'd in every Thing else, should have spoil'd his Brain
with such Crotchets as I perceiv'd in him the Day before. He dis-
cours'd divinely of Politics, and was overjoy'd to find that I had read
Plato upon that Subject. You will one Day, (said he to me) have more
Occasion for those Notices than you now think for: And if we concur
in Sentiments to Day 'tis not impossible but, in Time, you may put in
Practise those sage Maxims. We were now entering *Ruel*; we went to
the Garden: the Count superciliously neglected the Beauties of it, and
made directly to the Labyrinth.

Being now as retir'd as he could wish; Blessed, (cries he, lifting up
his Hands and Eyes to Heaven) Blessed be the eternal Wisdom, for in-
spiring me to reveal to you his ineffable Truths! How happy will you
be, my Son, if He is pleased to put into your Soul the dispositions
which those high Mysteries require! You are going to learn how to
command over Nature's Self: You'll have God alone to your Teacher,
and the Sages alone to your Equals: The supreme Intelligences will be
proud to obey you; the *Dæmons* will not dare to be present where
you are; your Voice will make them tremble in the Well-Hole of the
bottomless Pit, and all the invisible Nations, who inhabit the four
Elements, will esteem themselves happy in being the Ministers of
your Pleasure. I adore Thee, Thou great God! that thou hast crown'd
Mankind with so much Glory, and establish'd him the Sovereign
Monarch over all the Works of thine Hand! Do you feel, my Son,
(added he, turning to me) do you feel in yourself that Heroick Ambi-
tion, which is the assured Character of the Children of Wisdom?
Have you the Courage to desire to serve God alone, and to rule over
whatever is not God? Are you appriz'd what it is to be a Man? And
does it not go against you to be a Slave, since you were born to be a
Sovereign? And if you have these noble Thoughts, as the Figure of

your Nativity permits me not to doubt that you have, consider maturely, whether you shall have the Courage and the Strength to renounce all those things that may obstruct your arriving to that elevated State for which you were born? Here he stopp'd, and look'd wistfully upon me, as if he expected my Answer, or was trying to read it in my Heart.

As much as the Beginning of his Speech had made me hope that we should soon come to the Point, so much did these last Words make me despair of it. The Word *renounce* startled me; and I concluded he was going to propose to me the renouncing Baptism or Paradise. So, not knowing how to get over this ticklish Step; Renounce! (said I to him) Is there any Thing to be renounc'd? Indeed there is, (replies he) and so necessarily to be renounc'd, that you must begin with it. I can't tell whether you can prevail with yourself so far. But sure I am, that Wisdom dwells not in a Body subject to Sin, as it enters not into a Soul taken up by Error or Malice. The Sages will never admit you into their Society, if you do not this Moment renounce a Thing which cannot stand with Sageness. *You must,* (added he, whispering in my Ear) *you must renounce all carnal Commerce with Women.*

I broke into a loud Laugh at this odd Proposal. You have acquitted me very cheaply, Sir, cry'd I. I thought you were going to propose some prodigious Renunciation; but since 'tis only Women you allude to, 'tis done and all over long ago. I am chaste enough, God wot. However, Sir, since *Solomon* was a wiser Man than perhaps I shall ever be; and since all his Wisdom could not hinder him from sliding, pray tell me what Expedient you Gentlemen have to live without that Sex? and what Inconvenience there would be, if, in the Paradise of Philosophers, every *Adam* had his *Eve?*

You ask me mighty Things, (reply'd he, consulting with himself whether or no he should answer my Question.) However, since I see you will wean your self from Women without Difficulty, I will impart to you one of the Reasons which have oblig'd the Sages to exact that Condition from their Disciples, and you will thereby perceive in what Ignorance all those live, who are not of our Number.

When you are enroll'd among the Sons of the Philosophers, and your Eyes strengthen'd by the Application of the thrice-sacred Collyrium,[4] you will instantly discover, that the Elements are tenanted by most perfect Creatures; with whom, thro' the Sin of unhappy *Adam,*

---

[4] *Collyrium:* "A topical remedy for disorders of the eyes; an eye-salve or eye-wash" [OED].

his most unhappy Posterity have no Commerce nor Acquaintance. That immense Space, which is between Earth and Heaven, has far nobler Inhabitants, than Birds and Flies, those vast Seas have quite other Inmates, than Dolphins and Whales; the Bowels of the Earth, is not for Moles alone, and the Element of Fire, more noble than the other three, was not design'd to remain useless and empty.

The Air is full of countless Multitudes of Nations of a human Figure, somewhat haughty in appearance, but tractable in Reality: Great Lovers of the Sciences, subtil, officious about the Sages, and Enemies to Sots and Blockheads. Their Wives and Daughters are masculine Beauties, such as the *Amazons* are describ'd to be. How, Sir! (cry'd I) are those Elves marry'd, say you?

Don't make a Noise about nothing, reply'd he. Depend upon't, all I speak to you, is solid and true. These are but the Elements of the ancient Cabala; and 'twill be your Fault, and no Body's else, if you don't experience it with your own Eyes. Mean while receive with an humble Mind the Light sent you from God by me. Unlearn all that you learn'd upon this Head in the Schools of the Ignorant, or you'll have the Mortification (when you're convinc'd by Experience) of being oblig'd to own, that you was absolutely in the Wrong.

Listen then to the End, and know, that the Seas and Rivers are inhabited, as well as the Air; the Sages have call'd this Kind Undines, or Nymphs. There are few Males, but Females in great abundance; their Beauty is exquisite, and incomparably beyond that of the Daughters of Men.

The Earth, almost to the Center, is fill'd with *Gnomes*; a People of a small Size, Guardians of Treasures, Minerals, and precious Stones. These are Ingenious, Friends to Man, and easy to be govern'd. They supply the Sons of the Sages with what Money they have Occasion for, and desire nothing for their Pains but the Glory of serving them. The *Gnomids* (their Wives) are low of Stature, but very agreeable, and their Dress very curious.

As for the *Salamanders*, the inflam'd Guests of the Region of Fire, they serve the Philosophers: But they are not importunately fond of their Company, and their Daughters and Wives very rarely shew themselves. They do well, (interrupted I, for I had rather have their Room than their Company. Why so! (said the Count) Why so! (reply'd I) Who would care to converse with so hideous a Beast as a Salamander, Male or Female? You mistake, (reply'd he) that's the Idea which ignorant Painters and Sculptors have of them; the *Salamanders* Wives are beautiful, nay, more beautiful than any of the others, as they are of a more pure Element. I give you but a hasty Description of these Nations, because you will see them at Leisure, and with Ease, if you have that Curiosity. You will see their Habits, their Meats, their Manners, their Polity, their admirable Laws. You'll be charm'd with their intellectual beauty, even more than with their corporeal; but then you'll melt with Pity, when you hear them tell you, that their Soul is mortal, and that they have no Hope of everlastingly enjoying the Supream Essence, whom they know, and religiously adore. They'll tell you, that, being compos'd of the purest Parts of the Element they inhabit, and having in them no contrary Qualities, since they are made but of one Quality, they do not dye 'till after many Ages: But what is time in comparison to Eternity? They must re-enter for ever and for ever into Nothing. This Thought afflicts them mightily, and we have a hard Task of it to console them.

Our Fathers, the Philosophers, speaking to God Face to Face, lamented these Peoples Misfortunes: And God, whose Mercy is boundless, reveal'd to them, that 'twas not impossible to find a Remedy to that Evil. He suggested to them, that in like Manner as Man, by Means of the Alliance, which he has contracted with God, is made Partaker of his Divinity: So the *Sylphs*, the *Gnomes*, the *Nymphs*, and the *Salamanders*, by an Alliance which they may contract with Man, may be made Partakers of Immortality. Thus a *Nymph*, or a *Sylphid*, become immortal, and capable of the Beatitude to which we aspire, when she is so happy as to marry a Sage: And a *Gnome*, or a *Sylph*, ceases to be mortal the Moment he espouses one of our Daughters. . . .

Ah! our Sages had more Wit, than to impute to the Love of Women, the Fall of the first Angels, any more than to debase Man beneath the Power of the Devil, in ascribing to him the many Adventures of the *Nymphs* and *Sylphs*, which our Historians are fill'd with. There never was any Thing like a Crime in all that. 'Twas the *Sylphs* who had a Desire to be immortal. Their innocent Pursuits, far from scandalizing the Philosophers, appear'd in our Eyes so just, that we all, with one Accord, resolv'd never, in the least, to have to do with Women; but to make it our sole Business to immortalize the *Nymphs* and *Sylphids*.

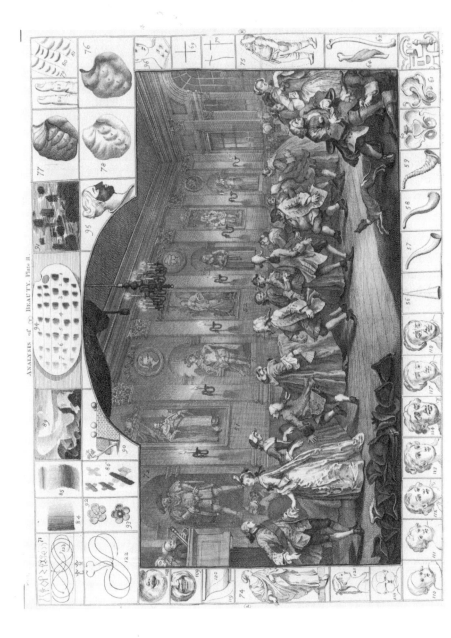

2

The Social World

THE "CHARACTERS" OF MEN AND WOMEN

> Say what strange Motive, Goddess! cou'd compel
> A well-bred *Lord* t'assault a gentle *Belle*?
> Oh say what stranger Cause, yet unexplor'd,
> Cou'd make a gentle *Belle* reject a *Lord*?
> In Tasks so bold, can Little Men engage,
> And in soft Bosoms dwells such mighty Rage?
> — *The Rape of the Lock* I.6–10

These lines from the *Rape* ask large mock-serious questions not only about Belinda and the Baron, but also about the general dispositions of men and women, and in the asking employ certain assumptions about human nature. Understanding the power and implications

Opposite: "The Happy Marriage," by William Hogarth (1753). This engraving illustrates a treatise on aesthetics published by Hogarth in 1753, *The Analysis of Beauty*. The engraving presents a gallery of eighteenth-century figures, from the elegant to the graceless. Notice the similarity in the silhouettes of men's and women's clothing and the elaborately arranged and ornamented hair (or rather, wigs) of the prancing gentlemen. Like Pope, Hogarth (1697–1764) was endlessly amused at the ridiculous postures of the people around him (and, like Pope, was generally aware of his own).

of Pope's couplet structures, explored in Part Two, chapter 1, helps explain these philosophical assumptions. Pope views human nature in some ways as occupying fixed categories or "characters," but in others as sliding endlessly and uneasily between terms, never quite contained or defined but hanging between, "in doubt to act, or rest, / In doubt to deem himself a God, or Beast; / In doubt his Mind or Body to prefer, / Born but to die, and reas'ning but to err; / . . . Created half to rise, and half to fall; / . . . The glory, jest, and riddle of the world!" (*Essay on Man* II.7–17). In *The Rape of the Lock*, women behave like women and men behave like men — but they also slip out of their characters and categories and behave like each other, at moments blurring the boundaries of gender in ways that invite very different angles of interpretation.

The documents in the first part of this chapter present a variety of contemporary perspectives on human nature in general and the nature of gender in particular. First is Pope's own serious (nonsatirical) exploration in *An Essay on Man*, which outlines an orderly, well-directed universe in which, if we could only see and understand clearly enough, "whatever IS, is RIGHT." The early-seventeenth-century poet Katherine Philips presents a version of human nature in "The Soul" (1667) that also underscores the paradox of human achievement and presumption, and the perverse difficulties of self-knowledge. The poem contrasts the tension between an eternally stable soul and its murky, earthly idiosyncrasies but — like Pope's *Essay on Man* and to some extent *The Rape of the Lock* — it also insists on the existence and power of the higher measure.

Other writers suggest a much darker vision of human nature than Pope or Philips. Lady Mary Wortley Montagu had a few things to say about Pope's *Essay on Man* in *An Epistle from Pope to Lord Bolingbroke* (1733). The poem satirizes Pope as a moral philosopher ("All I can do is flatter, lie, and cheat") and the *Essay* for its complacent justification of the status quo ("We know that all is right, in all we do"). *Gulliver's Travels* (1726) furiously exaggerates this conflicting vision; seven months after publication of his memoirs, Gulliver is dismayed to discover *no* discernible improvement in politics, laws, education, literature, morals, or general human misbehavior. The world is still a revolting place, and Gulliver prefers the company of his horses.

John Gay's fable "The Council of Horses" (1726) offers a mediating image between Gulliver's pessimism about the human race and Pope's vexed optimism in *An Essay on Man*. "The Council of Horses" wryly balances idealism and experience, fitting passion and self-love, courage and cooperation, within a smoothly seamed world — to which "the colt submitted, / And, like his ancestors, was bitted."

Sometimes included in and sometimes excluded from the category "man" are the images of woman and women's roles in the metaphysical, social, and literary spheres. The next group of documents airs some not particularly harmonious voices, emphasizing cultural ambivalences over women's variously defined identities and roles. Pope's own voice gets more overtly critical toward women over the years, but the figures of Martha and Teresa Blount — whose portrait is reprinted here — remain relatively stable, unidealized, yet differentiated models. The *Epistle to Miss Blount, with the Works of Voiture* (1712) suggests the complicated spectrum of Pope's views on women. The poem to some degree acknowledges a woman's cultural entrapment alluded to in Clarissa's speech ("what then remains?") — a painfully limited social and sexual position that simultaneously demands energy and resignation.

Gay's fable "The Lady and the Wasp" (1726) watches Doris — like Belinda — at her dressing table, plagued (if deservedly) by a pesky wasp, the diminished beau that her vain habits inevitably attract: "Nor were they banish'd, 'till she found / That wasps have stings, and felt the wound." Swift too attends a lady's toilette in "The Progress of Beauty" (1719/20) but brutally dismembers what Belinda had so carefully prepared, suggesting a dark end to that bright beginning. The lead in the lady's make-up destroys the complexion it was intended to improve, and the general artificiality of cosmetic enhancement degenerates into grotesque horrors, with nothing of the original woman left: "Two Balls of Glass may serve for Eyes, / White Lead can plaister up a Cleft, / But these alas, are poor Supplyes / If neither Cheeks, nor Lips be left."

The women of Pope's world, not surprisingly, had rather different perspectives on their status. In *An Essay in Defense of the Female Sex* (1696), Judith Drake argues for the value of women's conversation and explains the cultural customs that produced the disabling stereotypes. Anne Finch, Countess of Winchilsea and one-time friend of Pope, acknowledges in the poems selected here the tradition of women's weaknesses, but insists on redefining possibilities for women's rights and women's place in this socially constricting and disabling world.

Men endure their own punishment at Pope's hands in the *Rape*, where

Heroes' Wits are kept in pondrous Vases,
And Beaus' in *Snuff-boxes* and *Tweezer-Cases*. (V.112–13)

The fetishism of objects, the attention to dress, the love of mirrors, the inconstancy of mind and habit, infect men as well as women. Pope's *Epistle to Cobham* (1734) anatomizes the ruling passions and follies of men *qua* men. The judgments of Judith Drake and Anne Finch on masculine self-aggrandizement and self-deception resonate within Gay's fable "The Monkey who had seen the World," which encapsulates the dominant male flaws: "He drinks, games, dresses, whores and swears, / O'erlooks with scorn all virtuous arts, / For vice is fitted to his parts." Vanity and superficiality seem as much a product of the age as of gender. Difficult as Pope's world might have been for women, it is important to understand that despite male textual and political dominance, very few writers — male or female — constructed monolithic images of men as consistently superior, or of women as utterly different and always subordinate.

THEIR APPEARANCES

Wigs with Wigs, with Sword-knots Sword-knots strive,
Beaus banish beaus, and Coaches Coaches drive.
— *The Rape of the Lock* (I. 101–02)

The appearance and dress of eighteenth-century men and women further complicate the contemporary cultural perceptions of gender differences and roles. The rather striking similarities in silhouettes alert us to the implicit tensions, the similarities threatening difference, the unpoised balance of social and cultural oppositions, already exposed in the art of the couplet and assumptions of sexuality and gender. Hogarth's engraving of the country dance in "The Happy Marriage" (see page 266) illustrates the suggestive similarities in masculine and feminine silhouettes within their larger social satire. His early engraving of a scene in Canto IV of the *Rape* (see page 72) features his own image of Sir Plume and the Baron in a rather bare room ornamented by not much else beyond a coffee table, but the fact that he engraved it for a snuffbox adds the context of fashionable luxury. In his "Five Orders of Periwigs" (see page 325), men's hair luxuriantly outcurls women's. *The Spectator* essays included here worry that the blurred distinctions between men's and women's clothes might signify a dangerous blurring of gender difference itself. *Tatler* 113 itemizes the accessories of a deceased fashionable gentleman, a virtual model for Sir Plume, complete with amber cane and snuffbox; that same *Tatler* also advertises a cosmetic wash to smooth and whiten the faces of "both Sexes." Women dressing and behaving like men, men dressing and behaving like women — the anxieties that these documents record about gender difference and its apparent decline surface in *The Rape of the Lock* in the sylphs who "assume what Sexes and what Shapes they please" (I.70), challenging but not (perhaps) threatening sexual boundaries. For example, that gender-bending sylph Ariel proves ultimately impotent — or femininely trapped and resigned — in the face of Belinda's secret desires: "Amaz'd, confus'd, he found his Pow'r expir'd, / Resign'd to Fate, and with a Sigh retir'd" (III.145–46). But the sylphs are not the only captives of style; the men too are indicted for their sartorial fetishism: It's as much Wigs with Wigs in that "moving Toyshop" of hearts. Pope's trademarks — ambiguity and ambivalence — surface here strongly and delicately in a perhaps unsortable intertwining of visual image, verbal construction, and cultural implication.

THEIR PLEASURES

> For lo! the Board with Cups and Spoons is crown'd,
> The Berries crackle, and the Mill turns round.
> — *The Rape of the Lock* (III.105–06)

Drinking coffee and tea, attending the theater, playing card games, dancing, and flirting are still pleasures in the Western world, hardly in need of contextual explanations. But it's important not simply to translate an earlier work into contemporary terms; we also need to understand it on its own, and in the case of these particular pleasures, we should try to recover their powerful *novelty* for the fashionable world of the early eighteenth century.

Clarinda's journal in *The Spectator* satirizes the life of ease and idleness: Masquerades, balls, the theatre, are all standard ways of filling up time and space. John Macky's description of the English theatre in 1722 grants us a glimpse of its unfamiliarly lighted spaces, where audience is as much a spectacle as what's on stage — witness Belinda (or Arabella Fermor) performing her published drama. And just as Pope's poem also reminds us of the pains as well as pleasures

of this lovely idle world lurking in the Cave of Spleen, so Anne
Finch's poem *The Spleen* (which Pope greatly admired) discovers the
concomitant ulcers of high society in the early-eighteenth century —
the so-called English Malady.

Coffee and tea are themselves performers in this social drama (as
well as in the economic and political world, as we will see in the next
section). Both coffee and tea were introduced to London in the mid-
seventeenth century from the wider nets of English trade, and both
were immediately advertised, celebrated, prescribed, and proscribed
in poems, broadsides, engravings, and essays. The Royal Society pub-
lished various descriptive essays on the properties of both drinks (as,
indeed, they published descriptive essays on just about every aspect of
the natural world). The widespread passion for coffee produced the
institution of coffee houses, those places where one could go to read
the papers, argue the politics, and drink the beverage — where, as
some historians have argued, social classes mixed and conversed
more freely, and where, as John Macky's description shows, social
boundaries were further mingled, confused, crossed, and redefined.

Tobacco makes an appearance here in snuffboxes and snuffling
rhetoric ("'Z — ds! damn the Lock! 'fore Gad, you must be civil! /
Plague on't! 'tis past a Jest — nay prithee, Pox! / Give her the
Hair' — he spoke, and rapp'd his Box" [*Rape* IV.128–30]). *The Rape
of the Lock* was imitated and parodied in any number of ways — one
of which is Isaac Hawkins Browne's poem in praise of tobacco: "An
Imitation of Mr. Pope's Style." And the card game ombre, which oc-
cupies such a prominent role in the *Rape*, occupied a correspondingly
prominent role in its social world; excerpts from Richard Seymour's
The Court Gamester offer a sense of the history, vocabulary, and
popularity of the game.

THEIR PLACES

> This the *Beau-monde* shall from the *Mall* survey,
> And hail with Musick its propitious Ray.
> This, the blest Lover shall for *Venus* take,
> And send up Vows from *Rosamonda*'s Lake.
> — *The Rape of the Lock* V.133–36

The world of Pope's *Rape* is very particularly situated in place as
well as in time. London in the early 1700s was highly conscious of it-

self as a center of world trade, as a revived, flourishing city unlike any other in Europe, and as the center and source of fashion. Although the poem takes place primarily outside the city, in Hampton Court, Belinda and the Baron are products of this urban space as much as of this political and social clime, as the poem itself insistently underscores. Belinda's drama is enacted within a world in which the merchants of the Exchange and the judges in the courts indirectly shape much of daily life.

The documents included in this final section of Chapter 2 show London as variously perceived by its inhabitants. Gay's *Trivia* blends fascination and fear in a simultaneously exultant and anxious description of London's physical and economic explosion. One of Swift's city poems, "A Description of the Morning," offers a contemporary countervision to Pope's glittering and Gay's careful surfaces that is nasty, brutal, and unequivocally rank. Pope celebrates leaving London in a farewell poem to his friends as he returns to Binfield in 1720 to resume his translation of Homer. London in the early eighteenth century became an increasingly potent cultural signifier for all that was exciting, compelling, corrupting, and dangerous, as well as for much that was boring, monotonous, and narrow.

But the country had its limitations as well, as we see in Pope's "Epistle to Miss Blount," in which he wickedly exaggerates the horrors of a slow, silent, solitary country life after the exhilarations of a London season. Pope himself enjoyed both worlds, but particularly the life of pastoral retirement which the success of his *Iliad* made possible. Pope built himself a suburban paradise up the river from London at Twickenham.[1] Here he indulged himself with gardens and landscape theory, a grotto and grotto theory. Pope's works often resonate with his interest in the relationship between place and person, habitation and habit. Hampton Court, redesigned by Christopher Wren at the end of the seventeenth century, is the focal point of place in Canto III of the *Rape*, an important symbol of the social and political world. The palace occupies a strategic position between town and country, a place of national cultural identity, standing at the end of Belinda's boat ride up the Thames as the symbolic place where Queen Anne "dost sometimes Counsel take — and sometimes Tea" (*Rape* III.8).

---

[1] Part of the significance of Twickenham as a *place* for Pope lies in the fact that the anti-Catholic laws did not allow him to live within ten miles of London.

The "Characters" of Men and Women

ALEXANDER POPE

From *An Essay on Man*

Pope published this poem at intervals in 1733 and 1734 as a series of four "ethic epistles." He did not attach his name and he used a new publisher, successfully distancing himself from the poem so that it could be judged critically on its own, rather than as a work of the now-famous, much admired, and much hated satirist. Pope meant the *Essay* to be a serious philosophical work exploring "*Man* in the abstract, his *Nature* and his *State*" in order to prove moral duty, enforce moral precepts, and examine the perfections and imperfections of human nature ("The Design" of *An Essay on Man*). "This I might have done in prose," he admits, "but I chose verse, and even rhyme, for two reasons. The one will appear obvious; that principles, maxims, or precepts so written, both strike the reader more strongly at first, and are more easily retained by him afterwards: The other may seem odd, but is true, I found I could express them more *shortly* this way than in prose itself; and nothing is more certain, than that much of the *force* as well as *grace* of arguments or instructions, depends on their *conciseness*" ("The Design").

The poem was enormously successful, even among some of Pope's "dunces" who rushed into praise of it (and were very discomfited later when they discovered its author). The excerpts here give us a glimpse first of an ordered, hierarchical universe, where all things are "parts of one stupendous Whole" (I.x.267) in a world which, to a limited perspective and self-interested view, often seems incomprehensible if not unbearable, but which, if fully understood (with perfect faith), is one in which "Whatever IS, is RIGHT." But Pope always plays at least one more hand — here, that utterly vexed and apparently permanent experience of the world ("Plac'd on this isthmus of a middle state, / A being darkly wise, and rudely great" [II.i.3–4]).

Within this world, all human beings are governed by two principles — self-love and reason — which, like the terms of a couplet, exist in constant tension but are capable of resolution. Or so the poem asserts. The poem ends,

> That REASON, PASSION, answer one great aim;
> That true SELF-LOVE and SOCIAL are the same;

That VIRTUE only makes our Bliss below;
And all our Knowledge is, OURSELVES TO KNOW. (IV.vii.395–98)

We might ask if all the aggressively capitalized nouns are powerful enough to close the open vowels of the final couplet, to shut our gaping mouths, so to speak, given the "fixed" definition of ourselves in the beginning: "reas'ning but to err, / Alike in ignorance, [our] reason such, / Whether [we think] too little, or too much: / . . . Still by [ourselves] abus'd, or disabus'd" (II.i.10–14). The tension between self-love and reason emphasized in *An Essay on Man* mirrors that in the *Rape*: Both Belinda and the Baron may be said to think too little and too much, to mislead themselves in their dreams and desires, to fall far short of self-knowledge.

Text is from the Reduced Twickenham edition.

I.x.

Cease then, nor ORDER Imperfection name:
Our proper bliss depends on what we blame.
Know thy own point: This kind, this due degree
Of blindness, weakness, Heav'n bestows on thee.
Submit — In this, or any other sphere,   285
Secure to be as blest as thou canst bear:
Safe in the hand of one disposing Pow'r,
Or in the natal, or the mortal hour.
All Nature is but Art, unknown to thee;
All Chance, Direction, which thou canst not see;   290
All Discord, Harmony, not understood;
All partial Evil, universal Good:
And, spite of Pride, in erring Reason's spite,
One truth is clear, 'Whatever IS, is RIGHT.'

II.i.

Know then thyself, presume not God to scan;
The proper study of Mankind is Man.
Plac'd on this isthmus of a middle state,
A being darkly wise, and rudely great:
With too much knowledge for the Sceptic side,   5

With too much weakness for the Stoic's pride,°
He hangs between; in doubt to act, or rest,
In doubt to deem himself a God, or Beast;
In doubt his Mind or Body to prefer,
Born but to die, and reas'ning but to err;   10
Alike in ignorance, his reason such,
Whether he thinks too little, or too much:
Chaos of Thought and Passion, all confus'd;
Still by himself abus'd, or disabus'd;
Created half to rise, and half to fall;   15
Great lord of all things, yet a prey to all;
Sole judge of Truth, in endless Error hurl'd:
The glory, jest, and riddle of the world!

II.ii

   Self-love, the spring of motion, acts° the soul;
Reason's comparing balance rules the whole.   60
Man, but for that, no action could attend,
And, but for this, were active to no end;
Fix'd like a plant on his peculiar spot,
To draw nutrition, propagate, and rot;
Or, meteor-like, flame lawless thro' the void,   65
Destroying others, by himself destroy'd.
   Most strength the moving principle requires;
Active its task, it prompts, impels, inspires.
Sedate and quiet the comparing lies,
Form'd but to check, delib'rate, and advise.   70
Self-love still stronger, as its objects nigh;
Reason's at distance, and in prospect lie:
That sees immediate good by present sense;
Reason, the future and the consequence.
Thicker than arguments, temptations throng,   75
At best more watchful this, but that more strong.
The action of the stronger to suspend
Reason still use, to Reason still attend:

---

6. *the Stoic's pride:* Stoicism was a school of Greek philosophy founded by Zeno about 300 B.C. that believed in the virtue of cultivating indifference to pleasure and pain.
   59. *acts:* Activates.

Attention, habit and experience gains,
Each strengthens Reason, and Self-love restrains.   80

IV.vii

    Come then, my Friend, my Genius,° come along,
Oh master of the poet, and the song!
And while the Muse now stoops, or now ascends,   375
To Man's low passions, or their glorious ends,
Teach me, like thee, in various nature wise,
To fall with dignity, with temper rise;
Form'd by the converse, happily to steer
From grave to gay, from lively to severe;   380
Correct with spirit, eloquent with ease,
Intent to reason, or polite to please.
Oh! while along the stream of Time thy name
Expanded flies, and gathers all its fame,
Say, shall my little bark attendant sail,   385
Pursue the triumph, and partake the gale?
When statesmen, heroes, kings, in dust repose,
Whose sons shall blush their fathers were thy foes,
Shall then this verse to future age pretend°
Thou wert my guide, philosopher, and friend?   390
That urg'd by thee, I turn'd the tuneful art
From sounds to things, from fancy to the heart;
For Wit's false mirror held up Nature's light;
Shew'd erring Pride, WHATEVER IS, IS RIGHT;
The REASON, PASSION, answer one great aim;   395
That true SELF-LOVE and SOCIAL are the same;
That VIRTUE only makes our Bliss below;
And all our Knowledge is, OURSELVES TO KNOW.

---

373. *come then, my Friend, my Genius:* The poem is dedicated to Pope's friend
and intellectual mentor Henry St. John, Viscount Bolingbroke (1678–1751), politician
and philosopher. "Genius" here means inspirer.
    389. *pretend:* Proclaim.

KATHERINE PHILIPS

"The Soul"

Katherine Philips (1631–1664), a poet and playwright, was admiringly known throughout the seventeenth and eighteenth centuries as the "Matchless Orinda." Although she initially refused to publish her poems, subscribing to contemporary beliefs that discouraged a woman from entering the public eye, a pirated edition of her poems in 1664 prompted her into authorizing a correct version, which was published posthumously in 1667. Her supporters included John Dryden and Abraham Cowley, and she had a patron in the Earl of Orrery. Philips died from smallpox in the midst of her success.

This poem, like Pope's *Essay on Man*, traces the almost impossible imperative of self-knowledge — like Belinda, we are so many of us "ignorant at home." We constantly get in our own way: Our desires get in the way of our interests, our interests get in the way of our good intentions. To be sure, the soul has the power to distinguish concepts like honesty and honor, and the power to act according to those concepts. Yet that power is so difficult to attain that "He that Commands himself, is more a Prince, / Then he who Nations keeps in Awe" (ll. 77–78).

The text is taken from the corrected 1667 edition.

1.

How vain a thing is Man, whose noblest part,
   That soul which through the World doth rome,
Traverses Heav'n, finds out the depth of Art,
   Yet is so ignorant at home?

2.

In every Brook or Mirrour we can find   5
   Reflections of our face to be;
But a true Optick° to present our Mind
   We hardly get, and darkly see.

3.

Yet in the search after our selves we run,
   Actions and Causes we survey;   10

7. *Optick:* A lens.

And when the weary Chase is almost done,
   Then from our Quest we slip away.

4.

'Tis strange and sad, that since we do believe
   We have a Soul must never die,
There are so few that can a Reason give   15
   How it obtains that Life, or why.

5.

I wonder not to find those that know most,
   Profess so much their Ignorance;
Since in their own Souls greatest Wits are lost,
   And of themselves have scarce a glance.   20

6.

But somewhat sure doth here obscurely lie,
   That above Dross° would fain advance,
And pants and catches at Eternity,
   As 'twere its own Inheritance.

7.

A Soul self-mov'd which can dilate, contract,   25
   Pierces and judges things unseen:
But this gross heap of Matter cannot act,
   Unless impulsed from within.

8.

Distance and Quantity, to Bodies due,
   The state of Souls cannot admit;   30
And all the Contraries which Nature knew
   Meet there, nor hurt themselves, nor it.

9.

God never Body made so bright and clean,
   Which Good and Evil could discern:

22. *Dross:* Impure matter; here, the body.

What these words Honesty and Honour mean,   35
    The Soul alone knows how to learn.

10.

And though 'tis true she is imprison'd here,
    Yet hath she Notions of her own,
Which Sense doth only jog, awake, and clear,
    But cannot at the first make known.   40

11.

The Soul her own felicity hath laid,
    And independent on the Sense,
Sees the weak terrours which the World invade
    With pity or with negligence.

12.

So unconcern'd she lives, so much above   45
    The Rubbish of a sordid Jail,
That nothing doth her Energy improve
    So much as when those structures fail.

13.

She's then a substance subtile, strong and pure,
    So immaterial and refin'd,   50
As speaks her from the Body's fate secure,
    And wholly of a diff'rent kind.

14.

Religion for reward in vain would look,
    Vertue were doom'd to misery,
All actions were like bubbles in a brook,   55
Were 't not for Immortality.

15.

But as that Conquerour who Millions spent
    Thought it too mean to give a Mite;

So the World's Judge can never be content
    To bestow less then Infinite.   60

16.

Treason against Eternal Majesty
    Must have eternal Justice too;
And since unbounded Love did satisfie,
He will unbounded Mercy shew.

17.

It is our narrow thoughts shorten these things,   65
    By their companion Flesh inclin'd;
Which feeling its own weakness gladly brings
    The same opinion to the Mind.

18.

We stifle our own Sun, and live in Shade;
    But where its beams do once appear,   70
They make that person of himself afraid,
    And to his own acts most severe.

19.

For ways, to sin close, and our breasts disguise
    From outward search, we soon may find:
But who can his own Soul bribe or surprise,   75
    Or sin without a sting behind?

20.

He that commands himself is more a Prince
    Then he who Nations keeps in awe;
Who yield to all that does their Souls convince,
    Shall never need another Law.   80

LADY MARY WORTLEY MONTAGU

"An Epistle from Pope to Lord Bolingbroke"

Lady Mary Wortley Montagu (1689–1762) was an earl's daughter who taught herself Latin, wrote essays and poems, and as a young woman mingled actively in the literary and social world of Pope and his friends. At the time of *The Rape of the Lock,* Lady Mary liked and admired Pope perhaps almost as much as he her. Their correspondence during her years in Turkey (1716–18) with her ambassador husband Edward Wortley Montagu records the exchange of intellectual ideas as well as of social gallantries; he sent her volumes of the *Iliad* and she sent him her translations of Turkish poetry. But sometime in the 1720s their friendship soured (one prevalent but unsubstantiated story is that she laughed when he proposed love), and Pope began to savage her in his satires. She responded in 1733 with *Verses Addressed to the Imitator of . . . Horace* and the following satire (not published until 1803) on the *Essay on Man.* The poem attacks both the concepts and the tone of Pope's *Essay,* figuring Pope as a toadying disciple of a corrupt philosopher and politician. Pope's philosophy, she scoffs, is not a universal exploration of human nature, but something historically local and self-justifying: "We know that all is right, in all we do."

The text is taken from *The Works of The Right Honourable Lady Mary Wortley Montagu, Including her Correspondence, Poems, and Essays* (1st ed.), 5 vols., ed. James Dallaway (London: R. Phillips, 1803). Notes taken from the 1803 edition are in quotation marks and cited [*Works*].

CONFESS, dear Lælius!° pious, just, and wise,
Some self-content does in that bosom rise,
When you reflect, as sure you sometimes must,
What talents Heaven does to thy virtue trust,
While with contempt you view poor human-kind,   5
Weak, wilful, sensual, passionate, and blind.

---

1. *Lælius!:* "Pope first addressed his Essay on Man to Lord Bolingbroke, as Lælius" [*Works*]. Much of this poem has to do with Bolingbroke's policies and conduct during the War of the Spanish Succession, which ended with the Peace of Utrecht. Prominent under Anne, he lost favor in the Hanoverian succession, when the Whigs began impeaching as traitors the Tories who had arranged the peace, and fled to France (to the "deserted court" of the Pretender, son of James II). Bolingbroke was granted a limited pardon in 1723, upon which he returned to England to lead a movement against Robert Walpole; it failed, and he retired from public view in 1735.

Amid these errors thou art faultless found,
(The moon takes lustre from the darkness round)
Permit me too, a small attendant star,
To twinkle, tho' in a more distant sphere;   10
Small things with great, we Poets oft compare.
With admiration all your steps I view,
And almost envy what I can't pursue.
The world must grant, and ('tis no common fame)
My courage and my probity the same;   15
But you, great Lord, to nobler scenes were born;
Your early youth did Anna's court° adorn.
Let Oxford° own, let Catalonia° tell,
What various victims to your wisdom fell;
Let vows or benefits the vulgar bind,   20
Such ties can never chain th' intrepid mind.
Recorded be that memorable hour,
When, to elude exasperated pow'r,
With blushless front, you durst your friend betray,
Advise the whole confederacy to stay,   25
While with sly courage you run brisk away.
By a deserted court with joy receiv'd
Your projects all admir'd, your oaths believ'd;
Some trust obtain'd, of which good use you made,
To gain a pardon where you first betray'd.   30
But what is pardon to th' aspiring breast?
You shou'd have been First Minister at least:
Failing of that, forsaking and depress'd,
Sure any soul but your's had sought for rest;
And mourn'd in shades, far from the public eye,   35
Successless fraud, and useless infamy.
And here, my Lord! let all mankind admire
The bold efforts of unexhausted fire;
You stand the champion of the people's cause,
And bid the mob reform defective laws.   40
Oh! was your pow'r, like your intention, good!
Your native land wou'd stream with civic blood.

17. *Anna's court:* The court of Queen Anne (ruled 1702–1714).
18. *Oxford:* Robert Harley, first Earl of Oxford (1661–1724), led the Tory ministry from 1710–1714. He was impeached and sent to the Tower after the Whigs took power, but was released. *Catalonia:* Perhaps a reference to what Spain lost in the Peace of Utrecht?

I own these glorious schemes I view with pain;
My little mischiefs to myself seem mean.
Such ills are humble tho' my heart is great,   45
All I can do is flatter, lie, and cheat;
Yet I may say 'tis plain that you preside   ⎫
O'er all my morals, and 'tis much my pride   ⎬
To tread with steps unequal where you guide.   ⎭
My first subscribers,° I have first defam'd,   50
And when detected, never was asham'd;
Rais'd all the storms I could in private life,
Whisper'd the husband to reform the wife;
Outwitted Lintot in his very trade,
And charity with obloquy repaid.   55
Yet while you preach'd in prose, I scold in rhymes,
Against the injustice of flagitious times.
You, learned Doctor of the public stage,
Give gilded poison to corrupt the age;
Your poor toad-eater I, around me scatter   60
My scurril jests, and gaping crowds bespatter.
This may seem envy to the formal fools,
Who talk of virtue's bounds and honour's rules;
We, who with piercing eyes look nature through,
We know that all is right, in all we do.   65

   Reason's erroneous — honest instinct right —
Monkeys were made to grin and fleas to bite.
Using the spite by the Creator given,
We only tread the path that's mark'd by Heaven.
And sure with justice 'tis that we exclaim,   70
Such wrongs must e'en your modesty inflame;
While blockheads, court-rewards and honours share, ⎫
You, poet, patriot, and philosopher,   ⎬
No bills in pocket, nor no garter° wear.   ⎭

   When I see smoking on a booby's board,   75
Fat Ortolans and pye of Perigord,°
Myself am mov'd to high poetic rage,

---

50. *Subscribers:* "To the Translation of Homer" [*Works*].
74. *garter:* A badge of honor; in other words, Bolingbroke was not rewarded (with, say the garter of knighthood) for his work.
76. *Fat Ortolans and pye of Perigord:* Delicacies. An ortolan is a small bird; a Perigord pie is a meat pie flavored with truffles from Pèrigord.

(The Homer and the Horace of the age)
Puppies who have the insolence to dine
With smiling beauties, and with sparkling wine.   80
While I retire, plagu'd with an empty purse,
Eat broccoli, and kiss my ancient nurse.°
But had we flourish'd when stern Harry reign'd,°
Our good designs had been but ill explain'd;
The axe had cut your solid reas'nings short,   85
I, in the porter's lodge, been scourg'd at court.
To better times kind Heav'n reserv'd our birth,
Happy for you such coxcombs are on earth!
Mean spirits seek their villany to hide;
We show our venom'd souls with nobler pride,   90
And in bold strokes have all mankind defy'd.
Past o'er the bounds that keep mankind in awe,
And laugh'd at justice, liberty, and law.
While our admirers stare with dumb surprize,
Treason and scandal we monopolize.   95
Yet this remains our more peculiar boast,
You 'scape the block, and I the whipping-post.

JONATHAN SWIFT

From "A Letter from Capt. *Gulliver,* to his Cousin *Sympson*"

Swift (1667–1745) and Pope became good friends during the years of Harley's ministry, 1710–1714. Both were founders of the Scriblerus Club and collaborated on (as well as read) each other's works. On Anne's death in 1714, Swift lost all chance of preferment which would have allowed him to stay in London, so he returned to Dublin as dean of St. Patrick's cathedral. Though separated, the two remained in close correspondence.

---

82. *Eat broccoli, and kiss my ancient nurse:* Pope was known for his ambitious garden, and broccoli was a favorite. He had never concealed his affection for his old nurse, Mary Beach, who died in 1723.
83. *when stern Harry reign'd:* Henry VIII (?).

In this excerpt from the preface to *Gulliver's Travels* (1726) Lemuel Gulliver rants to his cousin Sympson (who had urged him to publish his adventures) that seven months after their publication human nature has not in the least reformed. Gulliver's final model for virtue and decency is the idealized race of horses, the Houyhnhnms; Gulliver's final conclusion about human nature sees us all as Yahoos, the filthy, violent, degenerate herd of human beasts.

The text and notes are from the Bedford case study in contemporary criticism edited by Christopher Fox (1995).

I do in the next Place complain of my own great Want of Judgment, in being prevailed upon by the Intreaties and false Reasonings of you and some others, very much against mine own Opinion, to suffer my Travels to be published. Pray bring to your Mind how often I desired you to consider, when you insisted on the Motive of *publick Good*; that the *Yahoos* were a Species of Animals utterly incapable of Amendment by Precepts or Examples: And so it hath proved; for instead of seeing a full Stop put to all Abuses and Corruptions, at least in this little Island, as I had Reason to expect: Behold, after above six Months Warning, I cannot learn that my Book hath produced one single Effect according to mine Intentions: I desired you would let me know by a Letter, when Party and Faction were extinguished; Judges learned and upright; Pleaders honest and modest, with some Tincture of common Sense; and *Smithfield*[1] blazing with Pyramids of Law-Books; the young Nobility's Education entirely changed; the Physicians banished; the Female *Yahoos* abounding in Virtue, Honour, Truth and good Sense: Courts and Levees of great Ministers thoroughly weeded and swept; Wit, Merit and Learning rewarded; all Disgracers of the Press in Prose and Verse, condemned to eat nothing but their own Cotten, and quench their Thirst with their own Ink. These, and a Thousand other Reformations, I firmly counted upon by your Encouragement; as indeed they were plainly deducible from the Precepts delivered in my Book. And, it must be owned, that seven Months were a sufficient Time to correct every Vice and Folly to which *Yahoos* are subject; if their Natures had been capable of the least Disposition to Virtue or Wisdom: Yet so far have you been from answering mine Expectation in any of your Letters; that on the contrary, you are loading our Carrier every Week with Li-

[1] Smithfield: Site in London of Bartholomew Fair and various popular entertainments.

bels, and Keys,[2] and Reflections, and Memoirs, and Second Parts; wherein I see myself accused of reflecting upon great States-Folk; of degrading human Nature, (for so they have still the Confidence to stile it) and of abusing the Female Sex. I find likewise, that the Writers of those Bundles are not agreed among themselves; for some of them will not allow me to be Author of mine own Travels; and others make me Author of Books to which I am wholly a Stranger.

JOHN GAY

From *Fables*
"The Council of Horses"

Poet and playwright John Gay was a close friend of Pope and Swift and a member of the Scriblerus Club. In 1713 he published *The Fan*, a mock-heroic modeled on *The Rape of the Lock*, and in 1716 *Trivia*, a mock-georgic on London. With Pope and John Arbuthnot he wrote the comedy *Three Hours After Marriage* (1717). He speculated disastrously in 1720, and was continually disappointed of preferment. "The Council of Horses" is part of a volume of *Fables* he wrote for the young son of Princess Caroline, published the same year she became queen, 1727. The *Fables* were enormously popular; Gay's patron, the Duke of Queensberry, issued a second series in 1738. Gay was passed over again despite his reknown, as Walpole had a powerful hold over government appointments. His best-known work, the comedy *The Beggar's Opera* (1728), hits back at Walpole through the characters of highwayman and thief-taker. Gay was known for his good humor but also for his ironic grasp of the folly and vice of human nature. He composed his own epitaph, which is engraved on his monument in Westminster Abbey: "Life is a jest, and all things show it, / I thought so once, but now I know it."

Gay may well have had Gulliver's Houyhnhnms in mind for "The Council of Horses," but the moral of the story corresponds more closely to Pope's view of the universe in the *Essay on Man*. The sage old horse sees order and balance, reason and reciprocity in the arrangement of things, and urges the rebellious young colt to resignation. We might ask whether there's any irony in that prescription given the way the last couplet, like the colt, is so sharply harnessed.

---

[2] *Keys:* Commentaries.

The text is from the first edition, with engravings from designs by Wootton and Kent (London: Printed for J. Tonson and J. Watts, 1727).

J. Wootton. in.   B. Baron. scul.

Fable XLIII.

Upon a time a neighing steed,
Who graz'd among a num'rous breed,
With mutiny had fir'd the train,
And spread dissention through the plain.
On matters that concern'd the State   5
The council met in grand debate.
A colt, whose eye-balls flam'd with ire,
Elate with strength and youthful fire,
In haste stept forth before the rest,
And thus the list'ning throng addrest.   10
    Good Gods! how abject is our race,
Condemn'd to slav'ry and disgrace!
Shall we our servitude retain,
Because our sires have born the chain?
Consider, friends, your strength and might;   15

'Tis conquest to assert your right.
How cumb'rous is the gilded coach!
The pride of man is our reproach.
Were we design'd for daily toil,
To drag the plough-share through the soil,   20
To sweat in harness through the road,
To groan beneath the carrier's load?
How feeble are the two-legg'd kind!
What force is in our nerves combin'd!
Shall then our nobler jaws submit   25
To foam and champ the galling bit?
Shall haughty man my back bestride?
Shall the sharp spur provoke my side?
Forbid it Heav'ns! Reject the rein,
Your shame, your infamy disdain.   30
Let him the lyon first controul,
And still the tyger's famish'd growle:
Let us, like them, our freedom claim,
And make him tremble at our name.
     A general nod approv'd the cause,   35
And all the circle neigh'd applause.
     When, lo, with grave and solemn pace
A steed advanc'd before the race,
With age and long experience wise,
Around he cast his thoughtful eyes,   40
And, to the murmurs of the train,
Thus spoke the *Nestor*° of the plain.
     When I had health and strength, like you,
The toils of servitude I knew;
Now grateful man rewards my pains,   45
And gives me all these wide domains;
At will I crop the year's encrease,
My latter life is rest and peace.
I grant to man we lend our pains,
And aid him to correct the plains;   50
But doth not he divide the care,
Through all the labours of the year?
How many thousand structures rise,

42. Nestor: "The name of a Homeric hero, famous for his age and wisdom, ap-
plied allusively to, or used as a designation of, an old man" [OED].

To fence us from inclement skies!
For us he bears the sultry day,   55
And stores up all our winter's hay;
He sows, he reaps the harvest's gain,
We share the toil and share the grain.
Since ev'ry creature was decreed
To aid each other's mutual need,   60
Appease your discontented mind,
And act the part by Heav'n assign'd.
  The tumult ceas'd. The colt submitted,
And, like his ancestors, was bitted.°

ALEXANDER POPE

Epistle to Miss Blount, with the Works of Voiture

This poem first appeared in Lintot's *Miscellany* in 1712 as *To A Young Lady, With the Works of Voiture.* (Vincent de Voiture [1598–1648] was a French postcard letter-writer.) It is not clear whether Teresa or Martha Blount was the original recipient. Maynard Mack speculates that Pope wrote this poem in 1709 or 1710 when Teresa Blount may have been considering an offer of marriage; but when the title was altered in 1735 to read *To Miss Blount*, Pope would have meant Martha, to whom he had become very close. The poem looks carefully at the social and cultural constraints on women and argues that the greatest tyrant may be a husband, who appears at first to promise the liberty of adulthood and social status. The poem anticipates and perhaps sanctions Clarissa's advice in *The Rape of the Lock* as the narrator uses the reputation of the beloved French poet Voiture to advise: "*Good Humour* only teaches Charms to last, / Still makes new Conquests, and maintains the past" (ll. 61–62).

The text is from the Reduced Twickenham edition.

In these gay Thoughts the Loves and Graces shine,
And all the Writer lives in ev'ry Line;
His easie Art may happy Nature seem,
Trifles themselves are Elegant in him.

---

64. *bitted*: Made accustomed to the bit, the mouthpiece of the bridle.

Sure to charm all was his peculiar Fate,   5
Who without Flatt'ry pleas'd the Fair and Great;
Still with Esteem no less convers'd than read;
With Wit well–natur'd, and with Books well–bred;
His Heart, his Mistress and his Friend did share;
His Time, the Muse, the Witty, and the Fair.   10
Thus wisely careless, innocently gay,
Chearful, he play'd the Trifle, Life, away,
'Til Fate scarce felt his gentle Breath supprest,
As smiling Infants sport themselves to Rest:
Ev'n Rival Wits did *Voiture*'s Death deplore,   15
And the Gay mourn'd who never mourn'd before;
The truest Hearts for *Voiture* heav'd with Sighs;
Voiture was wept by all the brightest Eyes;
The *Smiles* and *Loves* had dy'd in *Voiture*'s Death,
But that for ever in his Lines they breath.   20
    Let the strict Life of graver Mortals be
A long, exact, and serious Comedy,
In ev'ry Scene some Moral let it teach,
And, if it can, at once both Please and Preach:
Let mine, an innocent gay Farce appear,   25
And more Diverting still than Regular,
Have Humour, Wit, a native Ease and Grace;
Tho' not too strictly bound to Time and Place:
Criticks in Wit, or Life, are hard to please,
Few write to those, and none can live to these.   30
    Too much *your Sex* is by their Forms confin'd,
Severe to all, but most to Womankind;
Custom, grown blind with Age, must be your Guide
Your Pleasure is a Vice, but not your Pride;
By nature yielding, stubborn but for Fame;   35
Made Slaves by Honour, and made Fools by Shame.
Marriage may all those petty Tyrants chace,
But sets up One, a greater, in their Place;
Well might you wish for Change, by those accurst,
But the last Tyrant ever proves the worst.   40
Still in Constraint your suff'ring Sex remains,
Or bound in formal, or in real Chains;
Whole Years neglected for some Months ador'd,
The fawning Servant turns a haughty Lord;
Ah quit not the free Innocence of Life!   45

For the dull Glory of a virtuous Wife!
Nor let false Shows, or empty Titles please:
Aim not at Joy, but rest content with Ease.
    The Gods, to curse *Pamela* with her Pray'rs,
Gave the gilt Coach and dappled *Flanders* Mares,   50
The shining Robes, rich Jewels, Beds of State,
And to compleat her Bliss, a Fool for Mate.
She glares in *Balls*, *Front-boxes*, and the *Ring*,
A vain, unquiet, glitt'ring, wretched Thing!
Pride, Pomp, and State but reach her outward Part,   55
She sighs, and is no *Dutchess* at her Heart.
    But, Madam, if the Fates withstand, and you
Are destin'd *Hymen*'s willing Victim too,
Trust not too much your now resistless Charms,
Those, Age or Sickness, soon or late, disarms;   60
Good Humour only teaches Charms to last,
Still makes new Conquests, and maintains the past:
Love, rais'd on Beauty, will like That decay,
Our Hearts may bear its slender Chain a Day,
As flow'ry Bands in Wantonness are worn;   65
A Morning's Pleasure, and at Evening torn:
This binds in Ties more easie, yet more strong,
The willing Heart, and only holds it long.
    Thus *Voiture*'s early Care° still shone the same,
And *Monthausier*° was only chang'd in Name: 70
By this, ev'n now they live, ev'n now they charm,
Their Wit still sparkling and their Flames still warm,
    Now crown'd with Myrtle, on th' *Elysian* Coast,
Amid those Lovers, joys his gentle Ghost,
Pleas'd while with Smiles his happy Lines you view,   75
And finds a fairer *Ramboüillet* in you.
The brightest Eyes of *France* inspir'd his Muse,
The brightest Eyes of *Britain* now peruse,
And dead as living, 'tis our Author's Pride,
Still to charm those who charm the World beside.   80

---

    69. Voiture*'s early care:* "Madamoiselle Paulet" [P]. "Daughter of Charles Paulet, Secretary of the King's Bed-Chamber" [T].

    70. Monthausier: "Julie Lucine d'Angennes, Duchesse de Monthausier (1607–1671), eldest daughter of the Marquise de Rambouillet, one of Voiture's principal correspondents" [T].

CHARLES JERVAS

Portrait of Martha and Teresa Blount

The portrait of the sisters on page 294 shows us two of the most influential women in Pope's early life, whom Maynard Mack speculates inspired, as much as or more than Arabella Fermor, the "deep currents of affection and sexual attraction, not to mention [the] finely observed particulars both teasing and admiring" of *The Rape of the Lock* (257).

Valerie Rumbold persuasively reads Jervas's portrait of the two sisters as a couplet, balancing in their natures and their forms the various attractions of fair and dark and the various virtues of poetry and love.

[The portrait displays] visually something of the tension between similarity and difference from which Pope's couplet art draws its power: the sisters stand together, strikingly similar although one is fair, one dark. Teresa reaches her arms towards Patty [Martha] yet looks out of the picture, while Patty's gaze is on her sister and her arms lead the eye away from the group. The composition has a centrepiece which, like the rhyme in a couplet, ties its elements together: Teresa holds a wreath entwined with ribbon, on which is the legend, 'Martha Teresa Blount, Sic positae quoniam suaves'. . . . The allusion, which Mack convincingly attributes to Pope rather than to Jervas, is to lines from Virgil's *Eclogues* in which the shepherd Corydon gathers laurel and myrtle because their perfumes are complementary. . . . In the picture, Patty holds laurel [for poetry], Teresa myrtle [for love]. . . . Pope's fascination is more than the sum of its parts: were the girls not 'sic positae' as sisters it would be impossible to hover teasingly between them, to proclaim that he was alternately in love with each, to use one as insurance against a courtship of the other which could only lead to humiliation. (115)

Portrait of Martha and Teresa Blount (c. 1716) by Charles Jervas.

JOHN GAY

From *Fables*
"The Lady and the Wasp"

This poem figures another young woman at her dressing table. Her beauty, like Belinda's, attracts a buzz of admirers; her vanity, like Belinda's, contributes to her getting stung.

See the headnote to "The Council of Horses," pp. 287, for more information on Gay and his *Fables*.

The text is from the first edition, with engravings from designs by Wootton and Kent (London: Printed for J. Tonson and J. Watts, 1727).

FABLE VIII.

What whispers must the Beauty bear!
What hourly nonsense haunts her ear!
Where-e'er her eyes dispense their charms

Impertinence around her swarms.
Did not the tender nonsense strike,   5
Contempt and scorn might look dislike,
Forbidding airs might thin the place,
The slightest flap a fly can chase.
But who can drive the num'rous breed?
Chase one, another will succeed.   10
Who knows a fool, must know his brother;
One fop will recommend another;
And with this plague she's rightly curst,
Because she listen'd to the first.

    As *Doris*, at her toilette's duty,   15
Sate meditating on her beauty,
She now was pensive, now was gay,
And loll'd the sultry hours away.
    As thus in indolence she lyes,
A giddy wasp around her flies,   20
He now advances, now retires,
Now to her neck and cheek aspires;
Her fan in vain defends her charms,
Swift he returns, again alarms,
For by repulse he bolder grew,   25
Perch'd on her lip and sipt the dew.
    She frowns, she frets. Good Gods, she crys,
Protect me from these teazing flys!
Of all the plagues that heav'n hath sent
A wasp is most impertinent.   30
    The hov'ring insect thus complain'd.
Am I then slighted, scorn'd, disdain'd?
Can such offence your anger wake?
'Twas beauty caus'd the bold mistake.
Those cherry lips that breathe perfume,   35
That cheek so ripe with youthful bloom
Made me with strong desire pursue
The fairest peach that ever grew.
    Strike him not, *Jenny*,° *Doris* crys,
Nor murder wasps, like vulgar flys,   40
For though he's free (to do him right)

---

39. *Jenny:* Doris's waiting-woman; like Belinda's Betty.

The creature's civil and polite.
   In ecstasies away he posts,
Where-e'er he came the favour boasts,
Brags how her sweetest tea he sips,   45
And shows the sugar on his lips.
   The hint alarm'd the forward crew.
Sure of success away they flew;
They share the daintys of the day,
Round her with airy musick play,   50
And now they flutter, now they rest,
Now soar again, and skim her breast,
Nor were they banish'd, 'till she found
That wasps have stings, and felt the wound.

JONATHAN SWIFT

"The Progress of Beauty"

"The Progress of Beauty" was first published in *Miscellanies In Prose and Verse*, a collection of works by Swift and Pope edited by Pope and printed for Benjamin Motte in three volumes during 1727 and 1728. Esther Johnson, or "Stella," Swift's close friend, transcribed this poem and dated its composition 1719. Like *The Rape of the Lock* and "The Lady and the Wasp," "The Progress of Beauty" watches a young beauty at her dressing table, and like the *Epistle to a Lady*, admires the mingling of art and nature, painting and poetry. But in this case, the efforts at cosmetic self-construction "progress" into cancerous or venereal destruction.

The text is taken from *The Poems of Jonathan Swift*, ed. Harold Williams (Oxford: The Clarendon Press, 1937), vol. 1.

When first Diana° leaves her Bed
Vapors and Steams her Looks disgrace,
A frouzy dirty colour'd red
Sits on her cloudy wrinckled Face.

---

1. *Diana:* The goddess of the moon; the moon, of course, appears to grow whiter as it rises in the night sky.

But by degrees when mounted high   5
Her artificiall Face appears
Down from her Window in the Sky,
Her Spots are gone, her Visage clears.

'Twixt earthly Femals and the Moon
All Parallells exactly run;   10
If Celia should appear too soon
Alas, the Nymph would be undone.

To see her from her Pillow rise
All reeking in a cloudy Steam,
Crackt Lips, foul Teeth, and gummy Eyes,   15
Poor Strephon, how would he blaspheme!

The Soot or Powder which was wont
To make her Hair look black as Jet,
Falls from her Tresses on her Front
A mingled Mass of Dirt and Sweat.   20

Three Colours, Black, and Red, and White,
So gracefull in their proper Place,
Remove them to a diff'rent Light
They form a frightfull hideous Face,

For instance; when the Lilly slipps   25
Into the Precincts of the Rose,
And takes Possession of the Lips,
Leaving the Purple to the Nose.

So Celia went entire to bed,
All her Complexions safe and sound,   30
But when she rose, the black and red
Though still in Sight, had chang'd their Ground.

The Black, which would not be confin'd
A more inferior Station seeks
Leaving the fiery red behind,   35
And mingles in her muddy Cheeks.

The Paint by Perspiration cracks,
And falls in Rivulets of Sweat,
On either Side you see the Tracks,
While at her Chin the Conflu'ents met.   40

A Skillfull Houswife thus her Thumb
With Spittle while she spins, anoints,

And thus the brown Meanders come
In trickling Streams betwixt her Joynts.

But Celia can with ease reduce   45
By help of Pencil, Paint and Brush
Each Colour to it's Place and Use,
And teach her Cheeks again to blush.

She knows her Early self no more,
But fill'd with Admiration, stands,   50
As Other Painters oft adore
The Workmanship of their own Hands.

Thus after four important Hours
Celia's the Wonder of her Sex;
Say, which among the Heav'nly Pow'rs   55
Could cause such wonderfull Effects.

Venus, indulgent to her Kind
Gave Women all their Hearts could wish
When first she taught them where to find
White Lead, and Lusitanian Dish.°   60

Love with White lead cements his Wings,
White lead was sent us to repair
Two brightest, brittlest earthly Things
A Lady's Face, and China ware.

She ventures now to lift the Sash,   65
The Window is her proper Sphear;
Ah Lovely Nymph be not too rash,
Nor let the Beaux approach too near.

Take Pattern by your Sister Star,
Delude at once and Bless our Sight,   70
When you are seen, be seen from far,
And chiefly chuse to shine by Night.

In the Pell-mell° when passing by,
Keep up the Glasses of your Chair,°

---

60. *White Lead, and Lusitanian Dish:* A lead-based cosmetic paste, known even
then to be poisonous, stored in a beautiful Portuguese container (recall the expensive
cosmetic imports of Belinda's dressing table).
73. *Pell-mell:* Pall Mall, a wealthy and fashionable London street near St. James's
Park.
74. *the Glasses of your Chair:* The windows of a sedan chair.

Then each transported Fop will cry,   75
G — d d — m me Jack, she's wondrous fair.

But, Art no longer can prevayl
When the Materialls all are gone,
The best Mechanick Hand must fayl
Where Nothing's left to work upon.   80

Matter, as wise Logicians say,
Cannot without a Form subsist,
And Form, say I, as well as They,
Must fayl if Matter brings no Grist.

And this is fair Diana's Case   85
For, all Astrologers maintain
Each Night a Bit drops off her Face
When Mortals say she's in her Wain.

While Partridge° wisely shews the Cause
Efficient° of the Moon's Decay,   90
That Cancer with his pois'nous Claws°
Attacks her in the milky Way:

But Gadbury° in Art profound
From her pale Cheeks pretends to show
That Swain Endymion° is not sound,   95
Or else, that Mercury's her Foe.°

But, let the Cause be what it will,
In half a Month she looks so thin
That Flamstead° can with all his Skill
See but her Forehead and her Chin.   100

Yet as she wasts, she grows discreet,
Till Midnight never shows her Head;
So rotting Celia stroles the Street
When sober Folks are all a-bed.

---

89. *Partridge:* John Partridge, a contemporary astrologer.
89–90. *the Cause Efficient:* The immediate source or proximate cause of change.
91. *Cancer with his pois'nous Claws:* Cancer the Crab in the zodiac, but also breast cancer ("in the milky Way").
93. *Gadbury:* John Gadbury, another contemporary astrologer.
95. *Endymion:* The mortal youth with whom the moon goddess fell in love.
96. *Mercury's her Foe:* Mercury is the planet closest to the sun, and also the element used to treat venereal disease, often with disastrous side effects.
99. *Flamstead:* John Flamsteed (1646–1719), first Astronomer Royal.

For sure if this be Luna's Fate,°   105
Poor Celia, but of mortall Race
In vain expects a longer Date
To the Materialls of Her Face.

When Mercury her Tresses mows
To think of Oyl and Soot, is vain,   110
No Painting can restore a Nose,
Nor will her Teeth return again.

Two Balls of Glass may serve for Eyes,
White Lead can plaister up a Cleft,
But these alas, are poor Supplyes   115
If neither Cheeks, nor Lips be left.

Ye Pow'rs who over Love preside,
Since mortal Beautyes drop so soon,
If you would have us well supply'd,
Send us new Nymphs with each new Moon.   120

JUDITH DRAKE

From *An Essay in Defense of the Female Sex*

Judith Drake is presumed to be the sister of the physician and Tory pamphleteer James Drake (b. 1667); she apparently practiced medicine herself. *An Essay in Defense of the Female Sex* was often attributed to Mary Astell (1666–1731), an author of feminist and religious tracts, but various textual and historical evidence has led recent scholars to believe the essay is Drake's (see Ruth Perry, *The Celebrated Mary Astell*). The essay addresses the issue of intellectual and spiritual equality between men and women, and as in *Epistle to a Lady* when the poet observes that women are "by Man's oppression curst" to be "seen in Private life alone," it condemns the cultural, constructed conditions of inequality that discourage or silence women: "if any Histories were anciently written by women, Time, and the Malice of Men have effectually conspir'd to suppress 'em."

---

105. *Luna's Fate:* Luna is another name for the moon, which like Celia is doomed to wane.

The text is taken from the first edition, printed in London for A. Roper, R. Clavel, and E. Wilkinson, 1696.

The defence of our Sex against so many and so great Wits as have so strongly attack'd it, may justly seem a Task too difficult for a Woman to attempt. Not that I can, or ought to yield, that we are by Nature less enabled for such an Enterpize, than Men are; which I hope at least to shew plausible Reasons for, before I have done: But because through the Usurpation of Men, and the Tyranny of Custom (here in *England* especially) there are at most but few, who are by Education, and acquir'd Wit, or Letters sufficiently quallified for such an Undertaking. For my own part I shall readily own, that as few as there are, there may be and are abundance, who in their daily Conversations approve themselves much more able, and sufficient Assertors of our Cause, than my self; and I am sorry that either their Business, their other Diversions, or too great Indulgence of their Ease, hinder them from doing publick Justice to their Sex. The Men by Interest or Inclination are so generally engag'd against us, that it is not to be expected, that any one Man of Wit should arise so generous as to engage in our Quarrel, and be the Champion of our Sex against the Injuries and Oppressions of his own. Those Romantick days are over, and there is not so much as a *Don Quixot* of the Quill left to succour the distressed Damsels. 'Tis true, a Feint of something of this Nature was made three or four Years since by one;[1] but how much soever his Eugenia may be oblig'd to him, I am of Opinion the rest of her Sex are but little beholding to him. For as you rightly observ'd, *Madam*, he has taken more care to give an Edge to his Satyr, than force to his Apology; he has play'd a sham Prize; and receives more thrusts than he makes; and like a false Renegade fights under our Colours only for a fairer Opportunity of betraying us. But what could be expected else from a Beau? An Annimal that can no more commend in earnest a Womans Wit, than a Man's Person, and that compliments ours, only to shew his own good Breeding and Parts. He levels his Scandal at the whole Sex, and thinks us sufficiently fortified, if out of the Story of Two Thousand Years he has been able to pick up a few Examples of Women illustrious for their Wit, Learning or Vertue, and Men infamous for the contrary; though I think the

---

[1] *a Feint of something of this Nature was made three or four Years since by one:* William Walsh (1663–1708) published *A Dialogue Concerning Women, Being a Defence of the Sex. Written to Eugenia* in 1691.

most inveterate of our Enemies would have spar'd him that labour, by granting that all Ages have produc'd Persons famous or infamous of both Sexes; or they must throw up all pretence to Modesty, or Reason.

I have neither Learning, nor Inclination to make a Precedent, or indeed any use of Mr. W's. labour'd Common Place Book;[2] and shall leave Pedants and School-Boys to rake and tumble the Rubbish of Antiquity, and muster all the *Heroes* and *Heroins* they can find to furnish matter for some wretched Harangue, or stuff a miserable Declamation with instead of Sense or Argument.

Some advantages to be allow'd to the disparity of Education.

I shall not enter into any dispute, whether Men, or Women be generally more ingenious, or learned; that point must be given up to the advantages Men have over us by their Education, Freedom of Converse, and variety of Business and Company. But when any Comparison is made between 'em, great allowances must be made for the disparity of those Circumstances. Neither shall I contest about the preheminence of our Virtues; I know there are too many Vicious, and I hope there are a great many Virtuous of both Sexes. Yet this I may say, that whatever Vices are found amongst us, have in general both their source, and encouragement from them.

The Question I shall at present handle is, whether the time an ingenious Gentleman spends in the Company of Women, may justly be said to be misemploy'd, or not? I put the question in general terms; because whoever holds the affirmative must maintain it so, or the Sex is no way concern'd to oppose him. On the other side I shall not maintain the Negative, but with some Restrictions and Limitations; because I will not be bound to justifie those Women, whose vices and ill Conduct expose them deservedly to the Censure of the other Sex, as well as of their own. The Question being thus stated, let us consider the end and purposes, for which Conversation was at first instituted, and is yet desirable; and then we shall see, whether they may not all be found in the Company of Women. These Ends, I take it, are the same with those we aim at in all our other Actions, in general only two, Profit or Pleasure. These are divided into those of the Mind, and those of the Body. Of the latter I shall take no further

---

[2] *Common Place Book:* "A book in which 'commonplaces' or passages important for reference were collected" [OED].

Notice, as having no Relation to the present Subject; but shall confine my self wholly to the Mind, the Profit of which is the Improvement of the Understanding, and the Pleasure is the Diversion, and Relaxation of its Cares and Passions. Now if either of these Ends be attainable by the Society of Women, I have gain'd my Point. However, I hope to make it appear, that they are not only both to be met with in the Conversation of Women, but one of them more generally, and in greater measure than in Mens.

Our Company is generally by our Adversaries represented as unprofitable and irksome to Men of Sense, and by some of the more vehement Sticklers against us, as Criminal. These Imputations as they are unjust, especially the latter, so they favour strongly of the Malice, Arrogance and Sottishness[3] of those, that most frequently urge 'em; who are commonly either conceited Fops, whose success in their Pretences to the favour of our Sex has been no greater than their Merit, and fallen very far short of their Vanity and Presumption, or a sort of morose, ill-bred, unthinking Fellows, who appear to be Men only by their Habit and Beards, and are scarce distinguishable from Brutes but by their Figure and Risibility. But I shall wave these Reflections at present, however just, and come closer to our Argument. If Women are not quallified for the Conversation of ingenious Men, or, to go yet further, their friendship, it must be because they want some one condition, or more, necessarily requisite to either. The necessary Conditions of these are Sense, and good nature, to which must be added, for Friendship, Fidelity and Integrity. Now if any of these be wanting to our Sex, it must be either because Nature has not been so liberal as to bestow 'em upon us; or because due care has not been taken to cultivate those Gifts to a competent measure in us.

The first of these Causes is that, which is most generally urg'd against us, whether it be in Raillery, or Spight. I might easily cut this part of the Controversy short by an irrefragable Argument, which is, that the express intent, and reason for which Woman was created, was to be a Companion, and help meet to Man; and that consequently those, that deny 'em to be so, must argue a Mistake in Providence, and think themselves wiser than their Creator. But these Gentlemen are generally such passionate Admirers of themselves, and have such a profound value and reverence for their own Parts, that they are ready at any time to sacrifice their Religion to the Reputa-

---

[3] *Sottishness:* "Foolishness, folly, stupidity" [OED].

tion of their Wit, and rather than lose their point, deny the truth of the History. There are others, that though they allow the Story yet affirm, that the propagation, and continuance of Mankind, was the only Reason for which we were made; as if the Wisdom that first made Man, cou'd not without trouble have continu'd that Species by the same or any other Method, had not this been most conducive to his happiness, which was the gracious and only end of his Creation. But these superficial Gentlemen wear their Understandings like their Clothes, always set and formal, and wou'd no more Talk than Dress out of Fashion; Beau's that, rather than any part of their outward Figure shou'd be damag'd, wou'd wipe the dirt of their shoes with their Handkercher, and that value themselves infinitely more upon modish Nonsense, than upon the best Sense against the Fashion. But since I do not intend to make this a religious Argument, I shall leave all further Considerations of this Nature to the Divines, whose more immediate Business and Study it is to assert the Wisdom of Providence in the Order, and distribution of this World, against all that shall oppose it.

No *distinction of Sexes in Souls.*

To proceed therefore if we be naturally defective, the Defect must be either in Soul or Body. In the Soul it can't be, if what I have hear'd some learned Men maintain, be true, that all Souls are equal, and alike, and that consequently there is no such distinction, as Male and Female Souls; that there are no innate *Idea's*, but that all the Notions we have, are deriv'd from our External Senses, either immediately, or by Reflection. These Metaphysical Speculations, I must own Madam, require much more Learning and a stronger head, than I can pretend to be Mistress of, to be consider'd as they ought: Yet so bold I may be, as to undertake the defence of these Opinions, when any of our jingling Opponents think fit to refute 'em.

No *advantage in the Organization of their Bodies.*

Neither can it be in the Body, (if I may credit the Report of learned Physicians) for there is no difference in the Organization of those Parts, which have any relation to, or influence over the Minds; but the Brain, and all other Parts (which I am not Anatomist enough to name) are contriv'd as well for the plentiful conveyance of Spirits, which are held to be the immediate Instruments of Sensation, in Women, as Men. I see therefore no natural Impediment in the structure of our Bodies; nor does Experience, or Observation argue any: We use all our Natural Faculties, as well as Men, nay and our Rational too, deducting only for the advantages before mention'd.

. . . .

Women industriously kept in Ignorance.

It remains then for us to enquire, whether the Bounty of Nature be wholly neglected, or stifled by us, or so far as to make us unworthy the Company of Men? Or whether our Education(as bad as it is) be not sufficient to make us a useful, nay a necessary part of Society for the greatest part of mankind. This cause is seldom indeed urg'd against us by the Men, though it be the only one, that gives 'em any advantage over us in understanding. But it does not serve their Pride, there is no Honour to be gain'd by it: For a Man ought no more to value himself upon being Wiser than a Woman, if he owe his Advantage to a better Education, and greater means of Information, then he ought to boast of his Courage, for beating a Man, when his Hands were bound. Nay it would be so far from Honourable to contend for preference upon this Score, that they would thereby at once argue themselves guilty both of Tyranny, and of Fear: I think I need not have mention'd the latter; for none can be Tyrants but Cowards. For nothing makes one Party slavishly depress another, but their fear that they may at one time or other become Strong or Couragious enough to make themselves equal to, if not superiour to their Masters. This is our Case; for Men being sensible as well of the Abilities of Mind in our Sex, as of the strength of Body in their own, began to grow Jealous, that we, who in the Infancy of the World were their Equals and Partners in Dominion, might in process of Time, by Subtlety and Stratagem, become their Superiours; and therefore began in good time to make use of Force (the Origine of Power) to compell us to a Subjection, Nature never meant; and made use of Natures liberality to them to take the benefit of her kindness from us. From that time they have endeavour'd to train us up altogether to Ease and Ignorance; as Conquerors use to do to those, they reduce by Force, that so they may disarm 'em, both of Courage and Wit; and consequently make them tamely give up their Liberty, and abjectly submit their Necks to a slavish Yoke. As the World grew more Populous, and Mens Necessities whetted their Inventions, so it increas'd their Jealousy, and sharpen'd their Tyranny over us, till by degrees, it came to

that height of Severity, I may say Cruelty, it is now at in all the East-
ern parts of the World, where the Women, like our Negroes in our
Western Plantations, are born slaves, and live Prisoners all their
Lives. Nay, so far has this barbarous Humour prevail'd, and spread it
self, that in some parts of *Europe*, which pretend to be most refin'd
and civiliz'd, in spite of Christianity, and the Zeal for Religion which
they so much affect, our Condition is not very much better. And even
in *France*, a Country that treats our Sex with more Respect than most
do, We are by the *Salique Law*[4] excluded from Soveraign Power. The
French are an ingenious People, and the Contrivers of that Law knew
well enough, that We were no less capable of Reigning, and Govern-
ing well, than themselves; but they were suspicious, that if the Regal
Power shou'd fall often into the hands of Women, they would favour
their own Sex, and might in time restore 'em to their Primitive Lib-
erty and Equality with the Men, and so break the neck of that unrea-
sonable Authority they so much affect over us; and therefore made
this Law to prevent it. The Historians indeed tell us other Reasons,
but they can't agree among themselves, and as Men are Parties
against us, and therefore their Evidence may justly be rejected. To say
the truth Madam, I can't tell how to prove all this from Ancient
Records; for if any Histories were anciently written by Women,
Time, and the Malice of Men have effectually conspir'd to suppress
'em; and it is not reasonable to think that Men shou'd transmit, or
suffer to be transmitted to Posterity, any thing that might shew the
weakness and illegallity of their Title to a Power they still exercise so
arbitrarily, and are so fond of. But since daily Experience shews, and
their own Histories tell us, how earnestly they endeavour, and what
they act, and suffer to put the same Trick upon one another, 'tis nat-
ural to suppose they took the same measures with us at first, which
now they have effected, like the Rebels in our last Civil Wars, when
they had brought the Royal Party under, they fall together by the
Ears about the Dividend. The Sacred History takes no notice of any
such Authority they had before the Flood, and their Own confess that
whole Nations have rejected it since, and not suffer'd a Man to live
amongst them, which cou'd be for no other Reason, than their
Tyranny. For upon less provocation the Women wou'd never have
been so foolish, as to deprive themselves of the benefit of that Ease

---

[4] Salique Law: The law excluding women from the throne of France, which was
often used symbolically for the exclusion of women writers.

and Security, which a good agreement with their Men might have af-
forded 'em. 'Tis true the same Histories tell us, that there were whole
Countries where were none but Men, which border'd upon 'em. But
this makes still for us; for it shews that the Conditions of their Society
were not so easie, as to engage their Women to stay amongst 'em; but
as liberty presented itself, they withdrew and retired to the *Amazons*:
But since our Sex can hardly boast of so great Privileges, and so easie
a Servitude any where as in *England*, I cut this ungrateful Digression
short in acknowledgment; tho' Fetters of Gold are still Fetters, and
the softest Lining can never make 'em so easy, as Liberty.

ANNE FINCH, COUNTESS OF WINCHILSEA

"The Appology"

"Clarinda's Indifference at Parting with Her Beauty"

"On Myselfe"

Anne Finch, Countess of Winchilsea (1661–1720, born Anne
Kingsmill), was a poet, dramatist, and fable writer, and a friend of Pope,
Swift, Gay, and Rowe — who dubbed her "Ardelia." One contemporary
collection of her poems, *Miscellany Poems, On Several Occasions,* was
published in 1713 — though many of her poems (including those
reprinted here) remained in manuscript until this century. Sometime in
1714 Pope addressed an "Impromptu, To Lady Winchelsea, Occasion'd
by Four Satyrical Verses on Women-Wits, in The Rape of the Lock" (re-
ferring to the lines in Canto IV on the spleen: "Parent of Vapours and of
Female Wit, / Who give th' *Hysteric* or *Poetic* Fit, / On various Tempers
act by various ways, / Make some take Physick, others scribble Plays").
In this short stanza he exempts the countess from the general class of
scribbling female wits, in fact "blaming" her for outshining them:

> Fate doom'd the Fall of ev'ry Female Wit,
> But doom'd it then when first *Ardelia* writ. . . .
> To write their Praise you but in vain essay;
> Ev'n while you write, you take that Praise away:
> Light to the Stars the Sun does thus restore,
> But shines himself till they are seen no more.

Finch directly addresses the problems of women — and women writing — in a male-structured world. "The Appology" comments not only on the obvious — that she writes — but also on the less than obvious — her *right* to write; she demands to know "by what Rule / I am alone forbid to play the fool / To follow through the Groves a wand'ring Muse." "Clarinda's Indifference at Parting with Her Beauty" parallels Pope's and Swift's dismembering of beauty (and with beauty, traditional female "power"), but also points out ironically that such decay is not exactly something that needs so much pointing out. In "On Myselfe" Finch creates a space for a woman who is *not* temperamentally or educationally or culturally constrained by the social expectations of female vanity and emptiness: "I on my selfe can live, / And slight those aids, unequal chance does give."

These poems are reprinted from *The Poems of Anne Countess of Winchilsea*, ed. Myra Reynolds (Chicago: University of Chicago Press, 1903).

"The Appology"

'Tis true I write and tell me by what Rule
I am alone forbid to play the fool
To follow through the Groves a wand'ring Muse
And fain'd° Idea's for my pleasures chuse
Why shou'd it in my Pen be held a fault   5
Whilst Mira paints her face, to paint a thought
Whilst Lamia to the manly Bumper° flys
And borrow'd Spiritts sparkle in her Eyes
Why shou'd itt be in me a thing so vain
To heat with Poetry my colder Brain   10
But I write ill and there-fore shou'd forbear
Does Flavia cease now at her fortieth year
In ev'ry Place to lett that face be seen
Which all the Town rejected at fifteen
Each Woman has her weaknesse; mind [*sic*] indeed   15
Is still to write tho' hoplesse to succeed
Nor to the Men is this so easy found

---

4. *fain'd:* Invented, fashioned.
7. *Bumper:* "A cup or glass of wine, etc., filled to the brim" [OED].

Ev'n in most Works with which the Witts abound
(So weak are all since our first breach with Heav'n)
Ther's lesse to be Applauded then forgiven.   20

"Clarinda's Indifference at Parting with Her Beauty"

Now, age came on, and all the dismal traine
That fright the vitious,° and afflicte the vaine.
Departing beauty, now Clarinda spies
Pale in her cheeks, and dying in her eyes;
That youthfull air, that wanders ore the face,   5
That undescrib'd, that unresisted grace,
Those morning beams, that strongly warm, and shine,
Which men that feel and see, can ne're define,
Now, on the wings of restlesse time, were fled,
And ev'ning shades, began to rise, and spread,   10
When thus resolv'd, and ready soon to part,
Slighting the short repreives of proffer'd art°
She spake —
And what, vain beauty, didst thou 'ere atcheive,
When at thy height, that I thy fall shou'd greive,   15
When, did'st thou e're succesfully persue?
When, did'st thou e're th' appointed foe subdue?
'Tis vain of numbers, or of strength to boast,
In an undisciplin'd, unguided Host,
And love, that did thy mighty hopes deride,   20
Wou'd pay no sacrafice, but to thy pride.
When, did'st thou e're a pleasing rule obtain,
A glorious Empire's but a glorious pain,
Thou, art indeed, but vanity's cheife sourse,
But foyle to witt, to want° of witt a curse,   25
For often, by thy gaudy sign's descry'd
A fool, which unobserv'd, had been untry'd,
And when thou doest such empty things adorn,
'Tis but to make them more the publick scorn.

2. *vitious:* Those addicted to the social vices.
12. *the short repreives of proffer'd art:* Cosmetics.
25. *want:* Lack.

I know thee well, but weak thy reign wou'd be   30
Did n'one adore, or prize thee more then me.
I see indeed, thy certain ruine neer,
But can't affoard one parting sigh, or tear,
Nor rail at Time, nor quarrell with my glasse,
But unconcern'd, can lett thy glories passe.   35

"On Myselfe"

Good Heav'n, I thank thee, since it was design'd
I shou'd be fram'd, but of the weaker kinde,
That yet, my Soul, is rescu'd from the Love
Of all those Trifles, which their Passions move.
Pleasures, and Praise, and Plenty have with me   5
But their just value. If allow'd they be,
Freely, and thankfully as much I tast,
As will not reason, or Religion wast.
If they're deny'd, I on my selfe can Live,
And slight those aids, unequal chance does give.   10
When in the Sun, my wings can be display'd,
And in retirement, I can bless the shade.

ALEXANDER POPE

To Richard Temple, Viscount Cobham

The *Epistle to Cobham* was the third of the *Epistles to Several Persons* (or *Moral Essays*) to appear, first published January 16, 1733/4, although Pope always placed it first among the four. Subtitled "Of the Knowledge and Characters of Men," it supplies a useful context for understanding human traits that were often figured as distinctly *female*: "Our depths who fathoms, or our shallows finds, / Quick whirls, and shifting eddies, of our minds?" (ll. 29–30).

Cobham is Sir Richard Temple (1675–1749), soldier, politician, and leader of the opposition to Walpole in the 1730s. Pope contributed to the creation of Cobham's estate garden at Stowe, which celebrated classical and British patriots.

Pope rearranged the poem on the advice of Warburton in 1744, but F. W. Bateson, editor of the Twickenham edition of *Epistles to Several Persons*, argues that "the transpositions . . . were Warburton's, and Warburton's alone" (7); thus this text is taken from John Butt's Reduced Twickenham edition, which reproduces the earlier arrangements with Pope's later revisions. See Pat Rogers's argument in "Note on the Text" of *Alexander Pope: A Critical Edition of the Major Works* (xxvii–xxix) for reprinting the 1744 transpositions.

Of the Knowledge and Characters of Men

Argument of the First Epistle

That it is not sufficient for this knowledge to consider Man in the *Abstract: Books* will not serve the purpose, nor yet our own *Experience* singly, *v. I*. General maxims, unless they be formed upon *both*, will be but notional, *v. 10*. Some Peculiarity in every man, characteristic to himself, yet varying from himself, *v. 15*. The further difficulty of separating and fixing this, arising from our own Passions, Fancies, Faculties, *&c. v. 23*. The shortness of Life, to observe in, and the uncertainty of the *Principles of Action* in men, to observe by, *v. 29, &c.* Our *own* Principle of action often hid from ourselves *v. 41*. No judging of the Motives from the actions; the same actions proceeding from contrary Motives, and the same Motives influencing contrary actions, *v. 51*. Yet to form *Characters*, we can only take the strongest actions of a man's life, and try to make them *agree:* The utter uncertainty of this, from *Nature* itself, and from *Policy, v. 71. Characters* given according to the rank of men in the world, *v. 87*. And some reason for it, *v. 92. Education* alters the *Nature*, or at least *Character* of many, *v. 101*. Some few Characters plain, but in general confounded, dissembled, or inconsistent, *v. 122*. The same man utterly different in different places and seasons, *v. 130*. Unimaginable weaknesses in the greatest, *v. 140, &c.* Nothing constant and certain but *God* and *Nature, v. 154. Actions, Passions, Opinions, Manners, Humours*, or *Principles* all subject to change. No judging by *Nature, from v. 158 to 173*. It only remains to find (if we can) his RULING PASSION: That will certainly influence all the rest, and can reconcile the seeming or real inconsistency of all his actions, *v. 174*. Instanced in the extraordinary character of *Wharton, v. 179*. A caution against

mistaking *second qualities* for *first*, which will destroy all possibility
of the knowledge of mankind, *v. 210*. Examples of the strength of the
Ruling Passion, and its continuation to the last breath, *v. 222, &c.*

Yes, you despise the man to Books confin'd,
Who from his study rails at human kind;
Tho' what he learns, he speaks and may advance
Some gen'ral maxims, or be right by chance.
The coxcomb bird, so talkative and grave,   5
That from his cage cries Cuckold, Whore, and Knave,
Tho' many a passenger° he rightly call,
You hold him no Philosopher at all.
    And yet the fate of all extremes is such,
Men may be read, as well as Books too much.   10
To Observations which ourselves we make,
We grow more partial for th' observer's sake;
To written Wisdom, as another's, less:
Maxims are drawn from Notions, these from Guess.
    There's some Peculiar in each leaf and grain,   15
Some unmark'd fibre, or some varying vein:
Shall only Man be taken in the gross?
Grant but as many sorts of Mind as Moss.
    That each from other differs, first confess;
Next, that he varies from himself no less: 20
Add Nature's, Custom's, Reason's, Passion's strife,
And all Opinion's colours cast on life.
    Yet more; the diff'rence is as great between
The optics seeing, as the objects seen.
All Manners take a tincture from our own,   25
Or come discolour'd thro' our Passions shown.
Or Fancy's beam enlarges, multiplies,
Contracts, inverts, and gives ten thousand dyes.
    Our depths who fathoms, or our shallows finds,
Quick whirls, and shifting eddies, of our minds?   30
Life's stream for Observation will not stay,
It hurries all too fast to mark their way.
In vain sedate reflections we would make,
When half our knowledge we must snatch, not take.

    7. *passenger:* Passer-by.

On human actions reason tho' you can,   35
It may be reason, but it is not man:
His Principle of action once explore,
That instant 'tis his Principle no more.
Like following life thro' creatures you dissect,
You lose it in the moment you detect.   40
   Oft in the Passions' wild rotation tost,
Our spring of action° to ourselves is lost:
Tir'd, not determin'd, to the last we yield,
And what comes then is master of the field.
As the last image of that troubled heap,   45
When Sense° subsides, and Fancy sports in sleep,
(Tho' past the recollection of the thought)
Becomes the stuff of which our dream is wrought:
Something as dim to our internal view,
Is thus, perhaps, the cause of most we do.   50
   In vain the Sage, with retrospective eye,
Would from th' apparent What conclude the Why,
Infer the Motive from the Deed, and show,
That what we chanc'd was what we meant to do.
Behold! If Fortune or a Mistress frowns,   55
Some plunge in bus'ness, others shave their crowns:
To ease the Soul of one oppressive weight,
This quits an Empire, that embroils a State:
The same adust complexion has impell'd
Charles to the Convent, Philip to the Field.°   60
   Not always Actions show the man: we find
Who does a kindness, is not therefore kind;
Perhaps Prosperity becalm'd his breast,
Perhaps the Wind just shifted from the east:
Not therefore humble he who seeks retreat,   65
Pride guides his steps, and bids him shun the great:
Who combats bravely is not therefore brave,
He dreads a death-bed like the meanest slave:
Who reasons wisely is not therefore wise,

---

42. *spring of action:* Source or motive.
46. *Sense:* Consciousness.
60. *Charles to the Convent, Philip to the Field:* "Charles V (and) Philip II" [P].
Charles V (1500–1558), Holy Roman emperor, abdicated in 1555 to a monastery; his
son Philip II (1527–1598) succeeded him to the Spanish throne and involved Spain in
many wars.

His pride in Reas'ning, not in Acting lies.   70
 But grant that Actions best discover man;
Take the most strong, and sort them as you can.
The few that glare each character must mark,
You balance not the many in the dark.
What will you do with such as disagree?   75
Suppress them half, or call them Policy?
Must then at once (the character to save)
The plain rough Hero turn a crafty Knave?
Alas! in truth the man but chang'd his mind,
Perhaps was sick, in love, or had not din'd.   80
Ask why from Britain Cæsar would retreat?
Cæsar himself might whisper he was beat.
Why risk the world's great empire for a Punk?°
Cæsar perhaps might answer he was drunk.
But, sage historians! 'tis your task to prove   85
One action Conduct; one, heroic Love.
 'Tis from high Life high Characters are drawn;
A Saint in Crape is twice a Saint in Lawn;°
A Judge is just, a Chanc'lor juster still;
A Gownman,° learn'd; a Bishop, what you will;   90
Wise, if a Minister; but, if a King,
More wise, more learn'd, more just, more ev'rything.
Court-virtues bear, like Gems, the highest rate,
Born where Heav'n's influence scarce can penetrate:
In life's low vale, the soil the virtues like,   95
They please as Beauties, here as Wonders strike.
Tho' the same Sun with all-diffusive rays
Blush in the Rose, and in the Diamond blaze,
We prize the stronger effort of his pow'r,
And justly set the Gem above the Flow'r.   100
 'Tis Education forms the common mind,
Just as the Twig is bent, the Tree's inclin'd.
Boastful and rough, your first son is a 'Squire;
The next a Tradesman, meek, and much a lyar;
Tom struts a Soldier, open, bold, and brave;   105

---

83. *Punk:* Prostitute; in this case, Cleopatra.
88. *A Saint in Crape is twice a Saint in Lawn:* Crape and lawn are fabrics worn respectively by lower clergy and bishops.
90. *A Gownman:* An academic.

Will sneaks a Scriv'ner,° an exceeding knave:
Is he a Churchman? then he's fond of pow'r: ⎤
A Quaker? sly: A Presbyterian? sow'r: ⎥
A smart Free-thinker?° all things in an hour. ⎦
    True, some are open, and to all men known;   110
Others so very close, they're hid from none;
(So Darkness strikes the sense no less than Light)
Thus gracious CHANDOS° is belov'd at sight,
And ev'ry child hates Shylock,° tho' his soul
Still sits at squat,° and peeps not from its hole.   115
At half mankind when gen'rous Manly° raves,
All know 'tis Virtue, for he thinks them knaves:
When universal homage Umbra° pays,
All see 'tis Vice, and itch of vulgar praise.
When Flatt'ry glares, all hate it in a Queen,   120
While one there is who charms us with his Spleen.°
    But these plain Characters we rarely find;
Tho' strong the bent, yet quick the turns of mind:
Or puzzling Contraries confound the whole,
Or Affectations quite reverse the soul.   125
Or Falshood serves the dull for policy,
And in the Cunning, Truth itself's a lye:
Unthought-of Frailties cheat us in the Wise,
The Fool lies hid in inconsistencies.
    See the same man, in vigour, in the gout;   130
Alone, in company; in place, or out;
Early at bus'ness, and at Hazard° late;
Mad at a Fox-chace, wise at a Debate;
Drunk at a Borough, civil at a Ball,
Friendly at Hackney, faithless at Whitehall.°   135

---

106. *Scriv'ner:* A notary or money-lender.
109. *A smart Free-thinker:* An aetheist or deist in high society.
113. CHANDOS: James Brydges, first Duke of Chandos (1673–1744), a wealthy patron of the arts.
114. *Shylock:* A usurer.
115. *sits at squat:* Squats.
116. *Manly:* Hero of Wycherley's comedy *The Plain Dealer* (1676).
118. *Umbra:* A flatterer.
121. *one there is who charms us with his Spleen:* Swift.
132. *Hazard:* Gambling.
135. *Hackney, . . . Whitehall:* Political candidates for Middlesex (the county in which London is located) were nominated at Hackney and installed at Whitehall.

Catius° is ever moral, ever grave,
Thinks who endures a knave, is next a knave,
Save just at dinner — then prefers, no doubt,
A Rogue with Ven'son to a Saint without.
Who would not praise Patritio's high desert,   140
His hand unstain'd, his uncorrupted heart,
His comprehensive head! all Int'rests weigh'd,
All Europe sav'd, yet Britain not betray'd.
He thanks you not, his pride is in Picquette,°
New-market-fame,° and judgment at a Bett.   145
    What made (say Montagne, or more sage Charron!)°
Otho a warrior, Cromwell° a buffoon?
A perjur'd Prince° a leaden Saint revere,
A godless Regent° tremble at a Star?
The throne a Bigot keep, a Genius quit,   150
Faithless thro' Piety, and dup'd thro' Wit?°
Europe a Woman, Child, or Dotard rule,°
And just her wisest monarch made a fool?
    Know, God and Nature only are the same:
In Man, the judgment shoots at flying game,   155
A bird of passage! gone as soon as found,
Now in the Moon perhaps, now under ground.
    Ask men's Opinions: Scoto° now shall tell

---

136. *Catius:* An epicure.
144. *Picquette:* Piquet, a card game.
145. *New-market-fame:* Newmarket was England's horseracing center.
146. *(say Montagne, . . . Charron!):* Michel Eyquem de Montaigne (1533–1592), French moralist and essayist; Pierre Charron (1531–1603), admirer but modifier of Montaigne's skepticism.
147. *Otho . . . Cromwell:* M. Salvius Otho (A.D. 23–69), briefly Roman emperor; Oliver Cromwell (1599–1658), lord protector in the interregnum, portrayed by royalists as a buffoon.
148. *A perjur'd Prince:* "Louis XI of France wore in his Hat a leaden image of the Virgin Mary, which when he swore by, he feared to break his oath" [P].
149. *A godless Regent:* Philip, Duke of Orleans, regent of France during Louis XV's minority, believer in astrology but not religion.
150–151. *The throne . . . wit?:* "Philip V. of Spain [d. 1746], who, after renouncing the throne for Religion, resum'd it to gratify his Queen; and Victor Amadeus II. King of Sardinia [d. 1732], who resign'd the crown, and trying to reassume it, was imprisoned till his death" [P].
152. *Europe a Woman, Child, or Dotard rule:* Russian Czarina Anna Ivanovna (empress 1730–1740); Louis XV; Pope Clement XII (head of the church 1730–1741).
158. *Scoto:* Generic for Scotsman; in this case James Johnston (1655–1737), secretary of state for Scotland from 1692–1696 and a neighbor of Pope.

How Trade increases, and the World goes well;
Strike off his Pension, by the setting sun,   160
And Britain, if not Europe, is undone.
    That gay Free-thinker, a fine talker once,
What turns him now a stupid silent dunce?
Some God, or Spirit he has lately found,
Or chanc'd to meet a Minister that frown'd.   165
    Manners with fortunes, Humours turn with Climes,
Tenets with Books, and Principles with Times.
    Judge we by Nature? Habit can efface,
Int'rest o'ercome, or Policy take place:
By Actions? those Uncertainty divides: 170
By Passions? these Dissimulation hides:
Opinions? they still take a wider range:
Find, if you can, in what you cannot change.
    Search then the Ruling Passion: There alone,
The Wild are constant, and the Cunning known;   175
The Fool consistent, and the False sincere;
Priests, Princes, Women, no dissemblers here.
This clue once found, unravels all the rest,
The prospect clears, and Wharton° stands confest.
Wharton, the scorn and wonder of our days,   180
Whose ruling Passion was the Lust of Praise;
Born with whate'er could win it from the Wise,
Women and Fools must like him or he dies;
Tho' wond'ring Senates hung on all he spoke,
The Club must hail him master of the joke.   185
Shall parts so various aim at nothing new?
He'll shine a Tully and a Wilmot too.°
Then turns repentant, and his God adores
With the same spirit that he drinks and whores;
Enough if all around him but admire,   190
And now the Punk applaud, and now the Fryer.
Thus with each gift of nature and of art,
And wanting nothing but an honest heart;

179. *Wharton:* Philip, Duke of Wharton (1698–1731), ardent Jacobite, Catholic
convert, and president of the Hell-Fire Club.
187. *a Tully and a Wilmot too:* "John Willmot, Earl of Rochester, famous for his
Wit and Extravagancies in the time of Charles the Second" [P]. Wharton wants to be
known both as a parliamentary rhetorician like Cicero (Tully) and as a rake like the
notorious poet John Wilmot, Earl of Rochester (1646–1680).

Grown all to all, from no one vice exempt,
And most contemptible, to shun contempt;   195
His Passion still, to covet gen'ral praise,
His Life, to forfeit it a thousand ways;
A constant Bounty which no friend has made;
An angel Tongue, which no man can persuade;
A Fool, with more of Wit than half mankind,   200
Too quick for Thought, for Action too refin'd;
A Tyrant to the wife his heart approves;
A Rebel to the very king he loves;
He dies, sad out-cast of each church and state,
And (harder still) flagitious, yet not great!   205
Ask you why Wharton broke thro' ev'ry rule?
'Twas all for fear the Knaves should call him Fool.
     Nature well known, no prodigies remain,
Comets are regular, and Wharton plain.
     Yet, in this search, the wisest may mistake,   210
If second qualities for first they take,
When Catiline° by rapine swell'd his store,
When Cæsar made a noble dame a whore,°
In this the Lust, in that the Avarice
Were means, not ends; Ambition was the vice.   215
That very Cæsar, born in Scipio's° days,
Had aim'd, like him, by Chastity at praise.
Lucullus,° when Frugality could charm,
Had roasted turnips in the Sabin farm.
In vain th' observer eyes the builder's toil,   220
But quite mistakes the scaffold for the pile.°
     In this one Passion man can strength enjoy,
As Fits give vigour, just when they destroy.
Time, that on all things lays his lenient hand,
Yet tames not this; it sticks to our last sand.   225
Consistent in our follies and our sins,

---

212. *Catiline:* L. Sergius Catalina (c. 108–62 B.C.), a conspirator.
213. *a noble dame a whore:* Julius Caesar's mistress Servilia, mother of Marcus Brutus and sister of Cato.
216. *Scipio:* Scipio Africanus (c. 237–183 B.C.), Roman general who defeated Carthage.
218. *Lucullus:* L. Lucullus (c. 114–57 B.C.), Roman general known for his love of luxury.
221. *pile:* A pointed stake or post used to support a raised building.

Here honest Nature ends as she begins.
    Behold a rev'rend sire, whom want of grace
Has made the father of a nameless race,
Shov'd from the wall perhaps, or rudely press'd   230
By his own son, that passes by unbless'd;
Still to his wench he crawls on knocking knees,
And envies ev'ry sparrow that he sees.
    A salmon's belly, Helluo,° was thy fate,
The doctor call'd, declares all help too late.   235
Mercy! cries Helluo, mercy on my soul!
Is there no hope? Alas! — then bring the jowl.
    The frugal Crone, whom praying priests attend,
Still tries to save the hallow'd taper's end,
Collects her breath, as ebbing life retires,   240
For one puff more, and in that puff expires.
    'Odious! in woollen! 'twould a Saint provoke,
(Were the last words that poor Narcissa° spoke)
No, let a charming Chintz, and Brussels lace
Wrap my cold limbs,° and shade my lifeless face: 245
One would not, sure, be frightful when one's dead —
And — Betty — give this Cheek a little Red.'°
    Old Politicians chew on wisdom past,
And totter on in bus'ness to the last;
As weak, as earnest, and as gravely out,   250
As sober Lanesb'row° dancing in the gout.
    The Courtier smooth, who forty years had shin'd
An humble servant to all human kind,
Just brought out this, when scarce his tongue could stir,
'If — where I'm going — I could serve you, Sir?'   255

---

    234. *Helluo:* A glutton.
    243. *Narcissa:* The actress Anne Oldfield (1683–1730), who played Narcissa in Colley Cibber's *Love's Last Shift.*
    245. *Wrap my cold limbs:* After 1666 it became illegal to be buried in anything but British wool.
    242–247. *'Odious! . . . Red':* "This story, as well as the others, is founded on fact, tho' the author had the goodness not to mention the names. Several attribute this in particular to a very celebrated Actress, who, in detestation of the thought of being buried in woollen, gave these her last orders with her dying breath" [P]. *Betty:* A maid.
    251. *Lanesb'row:* James Lane, second Viscount Lanesborough (1650–1724). "An ancient Nobleman, who continued this practice long after his legs were disabled by the gout. Upon the death of Prince George of Denmark, he demanded an audience of the Queen, to advise her to preserve her health and dispel her grief by *Dancing*" [P].

'I give and I devise, (old Euclio° said,
And sigh'd) My lands and tenements to Ned.'
Your money, Sir? 'My money, Sir, what all?
Why, — if I must — (then wept) I give it Paul.'
The Manor, Sir? — 'The Manor! hold,' he cry'd,   260
'Not that, — I cannot part with that' — and dy'd.
    And you! brave COBHAM, to the latest breath
Shall feel your ruling passion strong in death:
Such in those moments as in all the past,
'Oh, save my Country, Heav'n!' shall be your last.   265

JOHN GAY

From *Fables*
"The Monkey Who Had Seen the World"

The monkey in this fable is dressed more or less as Sir Plume would
have appeared in *The Rape of the Lock*, complete with snuffbox, cane,
garters, and a mincing air. Like the young English gentleman, the aspir-
ing monkey embarks on a Grand Tour of his own to learn the ways of
other cultures; he comes back to the jungle imitating the ways of *men* in
foppery, flattery, scandal, and vice.

See the headnote to "The Council of Horses," pp. 287, for more in-
formation on Gay and his *Fables*.

The text is from the first edition, with engravings from designs by
John Wootton (London: Printed for J. Tonson and J. Watts, 1727).

FABLE XIV.

A Monkey, to reform the times,
Resolv'd to visit foreign climes;
For men in distant regions roam
To bring politer manners home:
So forth he fares, all toil defys;   5

256. *Euclio:* A miser.

Misfortune serves to make us wise.
   At length the treach'rous snare was laid;
Poor *Pug*° was caught, to town convey'd,
There sold; (How envy'd was his doom,
Made captive in a lady's room!)°   10
Proud as a lover of his chains,
He day by day her favour gains.
Whene'er the duty of the day,
The toilette calls; with mimic play
He twirles her knots, he cracks her fan,°   15
Like any other gentleman.
In visits too his parts and wit,
When jests grew dull, were sure to hit.
Proud with applause, he thought his mind
In ev'ry courtly art refin'd,   20

    8. *Pug:* A generic name for pets.
    10. *captive in a lady's room!):* Monkeys, like lap dogs and squirrels, were popular pets for young ladies.
    15. *He twirles her knots, he cracks her fan:* The monkey ties or plays with an ornamental bow or ribbon and snaps open her fan for her — typical pastimes of gentlemen attending ladies.

Like *Orpheus*° burnt with publick zeal,
To civilize the monkey weal;
So watch'd occasion, broke his chain,
And sought his native woods again.
    The hairy sylvans° round him press,   25
Astonish'd at his strut and dress,
Some praise his sleeve, and others glote
Upon his rich embroider'd coat,
His dapper perriwig° commending
With the black tail behind depending,   30
His powder'd back,° above, below,
Like hoary frosts, or fleecy snow;
But all, with envy and desire,
His flutt'ring shoulder-knot° admire.
    Hear and improve, he pertly crys,   35
I come to make a nation wise;
Weigh your own worth; support your place,
The next in rank to human race,
In citys long I pass'd my days,
Convers'd with men, and learnt their ways: 40
Their dress, their courtly manners see;
Reform your state, and copy me.
Seek ye to thrive? In flatt'ry deal,
Your scorn, your hate, with that conceal;
Seem only to regard your friends,   45
But use them for your private ends,
Stint not to truth the flow of wit,
Be prompt to lye, whene'er 'tis fit;
Bend all your force to spatter merit;
Scandal is conversation's spirit;   50
Boldly to ev'ry thing pretend,
And men your talents shall commend;
I knew the Great. Observe me right,
So shall you grow like man polite.
    He spoke and bow'd. With mutt'ring jaws   55

---

21. *Orpheus:* Son of Apollo and the Muse Calliope, renowned as musician, religious leader, and seer.
25. *sylvans:* Forest-dwellers.
29. *perriwig:* A fashionable wig for men, tied at the neck in back.
31. *His powder'd back:* Wigs were generally powdered white.
34. *shoulder-knot:* Ornamental ribbons (see the engraving on p. 322).

The wondring circle grinn'd applause.
  Now warm with malice, envy, spite,
Their most obliging friends they bite,
And fond to copy human ways,
Practise new mischiefs all their days.   60

  Thus the dull lad, too tall for school,
With travel finishes the fool,
Studious of ev'ry coxcomb's airs,
He drinks, games, dresses, whores and swears,
O'erlooks with scorn all virtuous arts,   65
For vice is fitted to his parts.

Their Appearances

[JOSEPH ADDISON]

From *The Spectator*, Nos. 127 and 145
["Unhoop the fair Sex"]

Mr. Spectator, having left London in order to cast his eye over the do-
ings in the country, finds on his return that women's hoopskirts have
swelled beyond reason, and an anxious male correspondent implores him
to correct the situation. A month later a female reader responds that she
"and other of your Female Readers, have conformed our selves to your

Opposite: "The Five Orders of Perriwigs," by William Hogarth, 1761. Ho-
garth loved to satirize what he considered the sartorial sillinesses of men and
women. Here, "The Five Orders of Perriwigs" are "measured architectoni-
cally" — that is, "with architectural fitness" (OED), referring to the five or-
ders of architecture outlined by Andrea Palladio (1508–1580), who adapted
classical Roman styles into the "Palladian" architecture that dominated
eighteenth-century British taste. Note the "Old Peerian or Aldermanic" style
(a peer is a member of the nobility; an alderman is a magistrate); the
"Queerinthian" (Corinthian) or "Queue de Renard" (ducktail); and the ad-
viso that this categorization of men's wigs will be complete "in about Seven-
teen Years" and in six large volumes.

Rules" about petticoats, but then points out that, as Hogarth's "The Happy Marriage" (p. 266) illustrates, men are equally guilty in "imitating" women's "Piramidical Form." So many members of early-eighteenth-century culture exposed their worries about the *lack* of gendered distinctions in their efforts to define and fix them.

Reprinted here are *The Spectator*, Nos. 127 (July 26, 1711) and 145 (August 16, 1711), ed. Donald F. Bond, vol. 2 (Oxford: Clarendon Press, 1965), 4–8 and 74.

No. 127

Thursday, July 26, 1711

. . . *Quantum est in rebus Inane?*[1]
—Pers.

It is our Custom at Sir ROGER's, upon the coming in of the Post to sit about a Pot of Coffee, and hear the old Knight read *Dyer*'s Letter,[2] which he does with his Spectacles upon his Nose, and in an audible Voice, smiling very often at those little strokes of Satyr which are so frequent in the Writings of that Author. I afterwards communicate to the Knight such Packets as I receive under the Quality of SPECTATOR. The following Letter chancing to please him more than ordinary, I shall publish it at his Request.

Mr. SPECTATOR,

'You have diverted the Town almost a whole Month at the Expence of the Country, it is now high time that you should give the Country their Revenge. Since your withdrawing from this Place, the fair Sex are run into great Extravagancies. Their Petticoats, which began to heave and swell before you left us, are now blown up into a most enormous Concave, and rise every Day more and more: In short, Sir, since our Women know themselves to be out of the Eye of the SPECTATOR, they will be kept within no Compass. You praised them a little too soon, for the Modesty of their Head-dresses; For as the Humour of a Sick Person is often driven out of one Limb into another, their Superfluity of Ornaments, instead of being entirely Ban-

---

[1] Quantum est in rebus Inane?: "How much emptiness is there in things?" (Persius, *Satires*).

[2] Dyer's *Letter*: John Dyer (d. 1713) published Dyer's *News-Letter*, a Tory favorite, read here by country squire Sir Roger de Coverley.

ished, seems only fallen from their Heads upon their lower Parts. What they have lost in Height they make up in Breadth, and contrary to all Rules of Architecture widen the Foundations at the same time that they shorten the Super-structure. Were they, like *Spanish* Jennits,[3] to impregnate by the Wind, they could not have thought on a more proper Invention. But as we do not yet hear any particular Use in this Petticoat, or that it contains any thing more than what was supposed to be in those in Scantier Make, we are wonderfully at a loss about it.

'The Women give out, in Defence of these wide Bottoms, that they are Airy, and very proper for the Season; but this I look upon to be only a Pretence, and a piece of Art, for it is well known we have not had a more moderate Summer these many Years, so that it is certain the Heat they complain of cannot be in the Weather: Besides, I would fain ask these tender-constitution'd Ladies, why they should require more Cooling than their Mothers before them.

'I find several Speculative Persons are of Opinion that our Sex has of late Years been very Saucy, and that the Hoop-Petticoat is made use of to keep us at a distance. It is most certain that a Woman's Honour cannot be better entrenched than after this manner, in Circle within Circle, amidst such a Variety of Outworks and Lines of Circumvallation. A Female who is thus invested in Whale-Bone is sufficiently secured against the Approaches of an ill-bred Fellow, who might as well think of Sir *George Etheridge*'s way of making Love in a Tub,[4] as in the midst of so many Hoops.

'Among these various Conjectures, there are Men of Superstitious Tempers, who look upon the Hoop-Petticoat as a kind of Prodigy. Some will have it that it portends the Downfall of the *French* King, and observe that the Farthingale[5] appeared in *England* a little before the Ruin of the *Spanish* Monarchy. Others are of Opinion that it foretells Battel and Bloodshed, and believe it of the same Prognostication as the Tail of a Blazing Star. For my part, I am apt to think it is a Sign that Multitudes are coming into the World, rather than going out of it.

'The first time I saw a Lady dressed in one of these Petticoats, I could not forbear blaming her in my own Thoughts for walking

---

[3] Spanish *Jennits:* Horses impregnated by the wind.
[4] *Love in a Tub:* Sir George Etherege's (1634?–1691) first play, *The Comical Revenge*, or *Love in a Tub* (1664).
[5] *Farthingale:* A hoop skirt.

abroad when she was *so near her Time*, but soon recovered my self
out of my Errour, when I found all the Modish Part of the Sex as *far
gone* as her self. It is generally thought some crafty Women have thus
betrayed their Companions into Hoops, that they might make them
accessary to their own Concealments, and by that means escape the
Censure of the World, as wary Generals have sometimes dressed two
or three dozen of their Friends in their own Habit, that they might
not draw upon themselves any particular Attacks from the Enemy.
The strutting Petticoat smooths all Distinctions, levels the Mother
with the Daughter, and sets Maids and Matrons, Wives and Widows,
upon the same bottom. In the mean while, I cannot but be troubled
to see so many well shaped innocent Virgins bloated up, and wad-
dling up and down like big-bellied Women.

'Should this Fashion get among the ordinary People our publick
Ways would be so crouded that we should want Street-room. Several
Congregations of the best Fashion find themselves already very much
streightned, and if the Mode encrease I wish it may not drive many
ordinary Women into Meetings and Conventicles. Should our Sex at
the same time take it into their Heads to wear Trunk Breeches (as
who knows what their Indignation at this Female Treatment may
drive them to) a Man and his Wife would fill a whole Pew.

'You know, Sir, it is recorded of *Alexander* the Great, that in his
Indian Expedition he buried several Suits of Armour which by his Di-
rections were made much too big for any of his Soldiers, in order to
give Posterity an extraordinary *Idea* of him, and make them believe
he had commanded an Army of Giants. I am persuaded that if one of
the present Petticoats happens to be hung up in any Repository of
Curiosities, it will lead into the same Error the Generations that lie
some Removes from us, unless we can believe our Posterity will think
so disrespectfully of their Great Grand-mothers, that they made
themselves Monstrous to appear Amiable.

'When I survey this new-fashioned *Rotonda*[6] in all its Parts, I can-
not but think of the old Philosopher, who after having entered into
an *Egyptian* Temple, and looked about for the Idol of the Place, at
length discovered a little Black Monkey enshrined in the midst of it,
upon which he could not forbear crying out, (to the great Scandal of
the Worshipers,) What a magnificent Palace is here for such a Ridicu-
lous Inhabitant!

---

[6] *Rotonda:* "A round or circular object" [OED; earliest example].

'Though you have taken a Resolution, in one of your Papers, to avoid descending to Particularities of Dress, I believe you will not think it below you, on so extraordinary an Occasion, to Unhoop the fair Sex, and cure this fashionable Tympany that is got among them. I am apt to think the Petticoat will shrink of its own Accord at your first coming to Town, at least a Touch of your Pen will make it contract it self, like the Sensitive Plant, and by that means oblige several who are either terryfied or astonished at this portentous Novelty, and among the rest,

Your Humble Servant, &c.'

No. 145

Thursday, August 16, 1711

Mr. SPECTATOR,
'I and several others of your Female Readers, have conformed our selves to your Rules, even to our very Dress. There is not one of us but has reduced our outward Petticoat to its ancient Sizable Circumference, tho' indeed we retain still a Quilted one underneath, which makes us not altogether unconformable to the Fashion, but 'tis on Condition, Mr. SPECTATOR extends not his Censure so far. But we find you Men secretly approve our Practice, by imitating our Piramidical Form. The Skirt of your fashionable Coats forms as large a Circumference as our Petticoats; as these are set out with Whalebone, so are those with Wire, to encrease and sustain the Bunch of the Fold that hangs down on each side; and the Hat, I perceive, is decreased in just Proportion to our Head-dresses. We make a regular Figure, but I defy your Mathematicks to give Name to the Form you appear in. Your Architecture is mere *Gothick,* and betrays a worse Genius than ours; therefore if you are partial to your own Sex, I shall be less than I am now

Your Humble Servant.

From *The Town Display'd, in a Letter to Amintor in the Country.*

This poem, printed in London in 1701 may be the work of John Gay. It offers a portrait gallery of society types, along the lines of Pope's *Epistle to Cobham.* The lines excerpted here spotlight the overdressed, underintelligent fop who, in dress as well as manners, blurs the boundaries of gender.

The next is *Cosmus*, who no trouble spares,
To put on killing Looks, and tender Airs:
He thinks his Coat bedawb'd with Gold, has Charms
To make a Countess take him in her Arms.
Then he affects a sort of Languishing,   5
You'd swear you never saw so soft a thing.
And if a Lady meets his Ogling Eyes,
He strait concludes for Love of him she Dies.
This tender Thing abhors a Naked Sword,
'Tis true, he Breeches wears, and has a Beard,   10
Has Travel'd, seen the *Louvre* and *Versailes*,°
Or I had plac'd the Beau among the *B'lls.*°

[JOSEPH ADDISON]

From *The Spectator,* No. 45 ["French Fopperies"]

Many of the faults of British society were blamed on French influence. Ever since Charles II had returned from exile in France in 1660, French clothes, French phrases, French manners, and French ideas had been extremely popular and vaguely threatening — they seemed infectiously effeminate or sexually suspect. This *Spectator* essay worries that English women are learning to dispense with the "proper" modesty and silence of the virtuous lady.

11. Louvre *and* Versailes: French palaces; the Louvre in Paris (now the famous art museum), and Versailles to the southwest.
12. B'lls: Belles.

Reprinted here from *The Spectator*, No. 45 (April 21, 1711), ed. Donald F. Bond, vol. 1 (Oxford: Clarendon Press, 1965), 191–95.

No. 45
Saturday, April 21, 1711

Natio Comœda est[1] . . .
— Juv.

There is nothing which I more desire than a safe and honourable Peace,[2] tho' at the same time I am very apprehensive of many ill Consequences that may attend it. I do not mean in regard to our Politicks, but to our Manners. What an Inundation of Ribbons and Brocades will break in upon us? What Peals of Laughter and Impertinence shall we be exposed to? For the Prevention of these great Evils, I could heartily wish that there was an Act of Parliament for Prohibiting the Importation of *French* Fopperies.

The Female Inhabitants of our Island have already received very strong Impressions from this ludicrous Nation, tho' by the Length of the War (as there is no Evil which has not some Good attending it) they are pretty well worn out and forgotten. I remember the time when some of our well-bred Country Women kept their *Valet de Chambre*, because forsooth, a Man was much more handy about them than one of their own Sex. I my self have seen one of these Male *Abigails* tripping about the Room with a Looking-Glass in his hand, and combing his Lady's Hair a whole Morning together.[3] Whether or no there was any Truth in the Story of a Lady's being got with Child by one of these her Hand-maids I cannot tell, but I think at present the whole Race of them is extinct in our own Country.

About the Time that several of our Sex were taken into this kind of Service, the Ladies likewise brought up the Fashion of receiving Visits in their Beds.[4] It was then looked upon as a piece of Ill Breeding, for a Woman to refuse to see a Man, because she was not

---

[1] Natio Comœda est: From Juvenal, *Satires* (3.100): "They are a nation of play actors" [Bond].
[2] *honourable Peace:* The War of the Spanish Succession (1701–1714) involved England, France, and much of the rest of Europe and its colonies.
[3] *combing his Lady's Hair a whole Morning together:* Cf. Gay's "The Monkey Who Had Seen the World," p. 321.
[4] *receiving Visits in their Beds:* A custom imported from France, called the *ruelle,* or "morning visit."

stirring; and a Porter would have been thought unfit for his Place, that could have made so awkward an Excuse. As I love to see every thing that is new, I once prevail'd upon my Friend WILL. HONEY-COMB[5] to carry me along with him to one of these Travell'd Ladies, desiring him, at the same time, to present me as a Foreigner who could not speak *English*, that so I might not be obliged to bear a Part in the Discourse. The Lady, tho' willing to appear undrest, had put on her best Looks, and painted her self for our Reception. Her Hair appeared in a very nice Disorder, as the Night-Gown which was thrown upon her Shoulders was ruffled with great Care. For my part, I am so shocked with every thing which looks immodest in the Fair Sex, that I could not forbear taking off my Eye from her when she moved in her Bed, and was in the greatest Confusion imaginable every time she stirred a Leg or an Arm. As the Coquets, who introduced this Custom, grew old, they left it off by degrees, well knowing that a Woman of Threescore may kick and tumble her Heart out, without making any Impressions.

Sempronia[6] is at present the most profest Admirer of the *French* Nation, but is so modest as to admit her Visitants no farther than her Toilet. It is a very odd Sight that beautiful Creature makes, when she is talking Politicks with her Tresses flowing about her Shoulders, and examining that Face in the Glass, which does such Execution upon all the Male Standers-by. How prettily does she divide her Discourse between her Woman and her Visitants? What sprightly Transitions does she make from an Opera or a Sermon, to an Ivory Comb or a Pin-Cushion? How have I been pleased to see her interrupted in an Account of her Travels, by a Message to her Foot man? and holding her Tongue, in the midst of a Moral Reflection, by applying the tip of it to a Patch.[7]

There is nothing which exposes a Woman to greater Dangers, than the Gaiety and Airiness of Temper, which are Natural to most of the Sex. It should be therefore the Concern of every Wise and Virtuous Woman, to keep this Sprightliness from degenerating into Levity. On the contrary, the whole Discourse and Behaviour of the *French* is to make the Sex more Fantastical, or (as they are pleased to term it,) *more awaken'd*, than is consistent either with Virtue or Discretion.

---

[5] WILL. HONEYCOMB: The dashing young man-about-town character in the *Spectator* essays.

[6] Sempronia: Based on the daring, "masculine" dancer described by Sallust in *Bellum Catilinae* (25.2) [Bond].

[7] *Patch*: An artificial beauty mark.

To speak Loud in Publick Assemblies, to let every one hear you Talk of Things that should only be mentioned in Private, or in Whisper, are looked upon as Parts of a refined Education. At the same time, a Blush is unfashionable, and Silence more ill-bred than any thing that can be spoken. In short, Discretion and Modesty, which in all other Ages and Countries have been regarded as the greatest Ornaments of the Fair Sex, are considered as the Ingredients of narrow Conversation, and Family Behaviour.

Some Years ago, I was at the Tragedy of *Macbeth*, and unfortunately placed my self under a Woman of Quality that is since Dead; who, as I found by the Noise she made, was newly returned from *France*. A little before the rising of the Curtain, she broke out into a loud Soliloquy, *When will the dear Witches enter*; and immediately upon their first Appearance, asked a Lady that sat three Boxes from her, on her Right Hand, if those Witches were not charming Creatures. A little after, as *Betterton*[8] was in one of the finest Speeches of the Play, she shook her Fan at another Lady, who sat as far on the left Hand, and told her with a Whisper, that might be heard all over the Pit, We must not expect to see *Balloon*[9] to Night. Not long after, calling out to a young Baronet by his Name, who sat three Seats before me, she asked him whether *Macbeth*'s Wife was still alive; and (before he could give an Answer) fell a talking of the Ghost of *Banquo*. She had by this time formed a little Audience to her self, and fixed the Attention of all about her. But as I had a mind to hear the Play, I got out of the Sphere of her Impertinence, and planted my self in one of the remotest Corners of the Pit.

This pretty Childishness of Behaviour is one of the most refined Parts of Coquetry, and is not to be attained in Perfection, by Ladies that do not Travel for their Improvement. A natural and unconstrained Behaviour has something in it so agreeable, that it is no wonder to see People endeavouring after it. But at the same time, it is so very hard to hit, when it is not Born with us, that People often make themselves Ridiculous in attempting it.

A very Ingenious *French* Author[10] tells us, that the Ladies of the Court of *France*, in his Time, thought it ill Breeding, and a kind of

---

[8] Betterton: Thomas Betterton (1635–1710), the most celebrated actor of the Restoration, famous for his Shakespearean roles.

[9] Balloon: Balon, a French dancer in London.

[10] French *Author*: Jean de La Bruyère (1645–1696), satiric moralist, author of *Les Caractères ou les moeurs de ce siècle* (1688), translated into English in 1699 as *The Characters, or Manners of the Age*.

Female Pedantry, to pronounce an hard Word right; for which Reason they took frequent occasion to use hard Words, that they might shew a Politeness in murdering them. He further adds, that a Lady of some Quality at Court, having accidentally made use of an hard Word in a proper Place, and Pronounced it right, the whole Assembly was out of Countenance for her.

I must however be so just to own, that there are many Ladies who have Travell'd several thousands of Miles without being the worse for it, and have brought Home with them all the Modesty, Discretion and good Sense, that they went abroad with. As on the contrary, there are great Numbers of *Travell'd* Ladies, who have lived all their Days within the Smoak of *London.* I have known a Woman that never was out of the Parish of St. *James*'s, betray as many Foreign Fopperies in her Carriage, as she could have Gleaned up in half the Countries of *Europe.*

JOHN HUGHES

From *The Tatler,* No. 113
["Inventory of a Beau"]

and

ADVERTISEMENT

From *The Tatler,* No. 113
["A Cosmetick for both Sexes"]

In *The Rape of the Lock*, the Baron's altar to Love is cluttered with French romances, garters, gloves, and *billet-doux* (II.37–42); Pope might well have been inspired by this *Tatler* satire on the accessories of a gentleman. The essay, in the form of an advertisement typical of the newspapers of the day, notifies the public of the sale by auction of the deceased's effects. The actual *Tatler* also printed genuine advertisements; one from this issue promises a cosmetic to purify the faces of "both Sexes in a very beautiful Manner."

The text is taken from *The Tatler*, ed. Donald F. Bond (Oxford: Clarendon Press, 1987), Vol. 2. The advertisement, for "Whitewashes for Men and Women," is not reprinted in Bond and is transcribed from the original issue.

"Inventory of a Beau"

No. 113
Thursday, December 29, 1709

Ecce iterum Crispinus![1]
— Juv.

Haymarket, December 23.

Whereas the Gentleman that behaved himself in a very disobedient and obstinate Manner at his late Tryal in *Sheer-Lane* on the 20th Instant, and was carried off dead upon the taking away of his Snuff-Box, remains still unburied; the Company of Upholders not knowing otherwise how they should be paid, have taken his Goods in Execution to defray the Charge of his Funeral. His said Effects are to be exposed to Sale by Auction at their Office in the *Haymarket* on the 4th of *January* next, and are as follow:

A very rich Tweezer-Case, containing Twelve Instruments for the Use of each Hour in the Day.

Four Pounds of scented Snuff, with Three gilt Snuff-Boxes; one of them with an invisible Hinge, and a Looking-glass in the Lid.

Two more of Ivory, with the Portraitures on their Lids of Two Ladies of the Town; the Originals to be seen every Night in the Side-Boxes of the Playhouse.

A Sword with a Steel Diamond Hilt, never drawn but once,[2] at *May-Fair.*

Six clean Packs of Cards, a Quart of Orange-Flower-Water, a Pair of *French* Scissors, a Tooth-pick Case, and an Eye-brow Brush.

A large Glass-Case, containing the Linnen and Clothes of the Deceased; among which are, Two embroidered Suits, a Pocket

---

[1] Ecce iterum Crispinus!: From Juvenal, *Satires* (4.1): "Once more Crispinus comes upon the stage" [Bond].

[2] *A Sword . . . never drawn but once:* Cf. the beau in *The Town Display'd* (p. 330), who "abhors a Naked Sword" — the sword is for ornament, not for defense or manly "honor."

"The Rape of the Lock," by William Hogarth, c. 1717. According to one of Pope's later editors, Joseph Warton, this "engraving of Sir Plume, with seven other figures, by Hogarth, was executed on the lid of a gold snuff box, and presented to one of the parties concerned" (*Works* 1: 317). A plump Sir Plume with cane and snuffbox leans toward the Baron, who dangles the lock in his hand, while Belinda weeps in the background.

Perspective,[3] a Dozen Pair of Red-heeled Shoes, Three Pair of Red Silk Stockings, and an Amber-headed Cane.

The strong Box[4] of the Deceased, wherein were found, Five Billet-doux, a *Bath* Shilling,[5] a crooked Sixpence,[6] a Silk Garter, a Lock of Hair, and Three broken Fans.

A Press for Books, containing on the Upper Shelf,

Three Bottles of Diet-Drink.
Two Boxes of Pills.
A Syringe, and other Mathematical Instruments.

[3] *Pocket Perspective:* A miniature instrument for looking at objects; both magnifying glasses and tiny telescopes were popular accessories at the time.
[4] *strong Box:* A storage trunk.
[5] *a* Bath *shilling:* Bath-metal is a copper-zinc alloy from the area near the resort city of Bath in western England; a Bath shilling could be a counterfeit coin or a cheap holiday memento. [?Not in OED]
[6] *a crooked Sixpence:* A token carried for good luck.

On the Second Shelf are several Miscellaneous Works; as,

Lampoons.
Plays.
Taylors Bills.
And an *Almanack* for the Year Seventeen Hundred.

On the Third Shelf,

A Bundle of Letters unopened, indorsed, (in the Hand of the Deceased) *Letters from the Old Gentleman.*
Lessons for the Flute.
Toland's Christianity not Mysterious.[7] And a Paper fill'd with Patterns of several fashionable Stuffs.[8]

On the Lowest Shelf,

One Shoe.
A pair of Snuffers.
A *French* Grammar.
A Mourning Hatband: And half a Bottle of Usquebaugh.[9]

There will be added to these Goods, to make a compleat Auction, a Collection of Gold Snuff-Boxes and Clouded Canes, which are to continue in Fashion for Three Months after the Sale.

The Whole are to be set up and prized by *Charles Bubbleboy*, who is to open the Auction with a Speech.

I find that I am so very unhappy, that while I am busie in correcting the Folly and Vice of one Sex, several Exorbitances break out in the other. I have not throughly examined their new-fashioned Petticoats, but shall set aside one Day in the next Week for that Purpose. The following Petition on this Subject was presented to me this Morning.

The Humble Petition of William Jingle, *Coach-maker and Chair-maker of the Liberty of* Westminster.
To *Isaac Bickerstaff* Esq; Censor of *Great-Britain.*
   SHEWETH,

---

[7] Toland*'s Christianity not Mysterious:* John Toland (1670–1722), an Irish freethinker, published the notorious *Christianity not Mysterious* in 1696; both Pope and Swift ridiculed him.
[8] *Stuffs:* Fabrics.
[9] *Usquebaugh:* Water of life, aqua vitae, whisky.

'That upon the late Invention of Mrs. *Catherine Cross-Stitch*, Mantoe-maker,[10] the Petticoats of Ladies were too wide for entring into any Coach or Chair which was in Use before the said Invention.

'That for the Service of the said Ladies, your Petitioner has built a round Chair, in the Form of a Lanthorn, Six Yards and an half in Circumference, with a Stool in the Centre of it; the said Vehicle being so contrived, as to receive the Passenger by opening in two in the Middle, and closing mathematically when she is seated.

'That your Petitioner has also invented a Coach for the Reception of one Lady only, who is to be let in at the Top.

'That the said Coach has been tryed by a Lady's Woman in one of these full Petticoats, who was let down from a Balcony, and drawn up again by Pullies, to the great Satisfaction of her Lady, and all who beheld her.

'Your Petitioner therefore most humbly prays, That for the Encouragement of Ingenuity and useful Inventions, he may be heard before you pass Sentence upon the Petticoats aforesaid.

And your Petitioner, *&c.*'

I have likewise received a Female Petition, signed by several Thousands, praying, That I would not any longer defer giving Judgment in the Case of the Petticoat, many of them having put off the making new Clothes, till such Time as they know what Verdict will pass upon it. I do therefore hereby certify to all whom it may concern, That I do design to set apart *Tuesday* next for the final Determination of that Matter, having already ordered a Jury of Matrons to be impannelled, for the clearing up of any difficult Points that may arise in the Tryal.

Being informed, That several Dead Men in and about this City do keep out of the Way and abscond, for Fear of being buried; and being willing to respite their Interrment, in Consideration of their Families, and in Hopes of their Amendment, I shall allow them certain Privileged Places, where they may appear to one another, without causing any Lett or Molestation to the Living, or receiving any in their own Persons from the Company of Upholders.[11] Between the Hours of Seven and Nine in the Morning, they may appear in Safety at St. *James*'s Coffeehouse, or at *White*'s, if they do not keep their Beds, which is more proper for Men in their Condition. From Nine to Eleven, I allow them to walk from *Story*'s to *Rosamond*'s Pond[12] in the *Park*, or in any

---

[10] *Mantoe-maker:* Mantua maker; that is, a dressmaker.
[11] *Upholders:* Undertakers.
[12] *from* Story's *to* Rosamond's Pond: From Story's Gate (at De La Way) at one end of Birdcage Walk in St. James's Park to Rosamond's Pond at the other (see Rocque's map, p. 375).

other publick Walks which are not frequented by the Living at that Time. Between Eleven and Three, they are to vanish, and keep out of Sight till Three in the Afternoon; at which Time, they may go to *'Change* till Five; and then, if they please, divert themselves at the *Hay-Market,* or *Drury-Lane*, till the Play begins. It is further granted in Favour of these Persons, That they may be received at any Table, where there are more present than Seven in Number; provided, that they do not take upon them to talk, judge, commend, or find Fault with any Speech, Action or Behaviour, of the Living, In which Case, it shall be lawful to seize their Persons at any Place or Hour whatsoever, and to convey their Bodies to the next Undertakers; any Thing in this Advertisement to the contrary notwithstanding.

"A Cosmetick for both Sexes"

No. 113
Thursday, December 29, 1709

This Chrystal Cosmetick, approv'd of by the Worthy Dr. Paul Chamberline, viz. by washing Morning or Evening, cures all red Faces, proceeding from what Cause soever: It takes off all Morphews,[13] Pimples, and Freckles; it's of a soft Nature, cleansing and adorning the Face and Hands of both Sexes in a very beautiful Manner; and may be us'd with as much Safety as Milk, having in it no Mercury (so frequently made Use of)[14] or any other Thing that may be prejudicial to the Body, being the best of this Nature now extant. The Price of the largest Bottle 6 s. the lesser 3 s. To be sold at Mr. Allcroft's at the Blue-Coat Boy, a Toyshop, against the Royal Exchange, Cornhil; at Mr. Jackson's in Cheapside near Wood-street; at Mrs. Stephens's, the Comb under St. Dunstan's street; at Mr. Brecknock's, Milliner over against St. James's street, Piccadilly. Note, to prevent Counterfeits, each single Bottle with Directions, is tied and sealed with this Coat of Arms, being a Frett, with a Lion Rampant in a Canton.[15]

---

[13] *Morphews:* "A leprous or scurfy eruption" [OED].

[14] *no Mercury (so frequently made Use of):* See Swift, "The Progress of Beauty," p. 297.

[15] *a Frett, with a Lion Rampant in a Canton:* Symbols of heraldry; roughly, a frett or fret is a figure formed by two interlacing bands, a lion rampant is a lion on its hind legs, and a canton is a square division, or field, in an upper corner of a shield.

Their Pleasures

[JOSEPH ADDISON]

From *The Spectator*, No. 323
["Clarinda's journal"]

Addison's satire — "Clarinda's" journal — exposes, even more than does *The Rape of the Lock*, the pleasurable vacuity that is the life of a fashionable young lady. Like Belinda, Clarinda fusses over her lap dog, gazes pensively into her mirror, plays cards, drinks her tea and chocolate, reads romances, and finds "an Earthly Lover lurking at her heart" (*Rape* III.144).

The following excerpt is taken from *The Spectator*, No. 323 (March 11, 1712), ed. Donald Bond, vol. 1 (Oxford: Clarendon Press, 1965), 181–85.

No. 323
Tuesday, March 11, 1712

... *modò Vir, modò Fœmina*[1] ...
— Virg.

The Journal with which I presented my Reader on *Tuesday* last, has brought me in several Letters with Accounts of many private Lives cast into that form. I have the *Rake's Journal*; the *Sot's Journal*; the *Whore-master's Journal*, and among several others a very curious Piece, Entituled, *The Journal of a Mohock*.[2] By these Instances I find that the Intention of my last *Tuesday*'s Paper has been mistaken by many of my Readers. I did not design so much to expose Vice as Idleness, and aimed at those Persons who pass away their Time rather in Trifle and Impertinence, than in Crimes and Immoralities. Offences of this latter kind are not to be dallied with, or treated in so ludicrous a manner. In short, my Journal only holds up Folly to the Light, and

---

[1] modò Vir, modò Fœmina: Ovid, *Metamorphoses* (4.280): "One while a Man, another while a Woman" [Bond]. Addison's mistaken attribution to Virgil is silently corrected in Bond's edition. The Virgil is *iuvenis quondam, nunc femina,* or "once a youth, now a woman" (4.448–49).

[2] Mohock: A member of a violent gang of upper-class young men.

shews the Disagreeableness of such Actions as are indifferent in them-
selves, and blameable only as they proceed from Creatures endow'd
with Reason.

My following Correspondent, who calls her self *Clarinda*, is such a
Journalist as I require: She seems by her Letter to be placed in a mod-
ish State of Indifference between Vice and Vertue, and to be suscep-
tible of either, were there proper Pains taken with her. Had her Jour-
nal been filled with Gallantries, or such Occurrences as had shewn
her wholly divested of her natural Innocence, notwithstanding it
might have been more pleasing to the Generality of Readers, I should
not have published it; but as it is only the Picture of a Life filled with
a fashionable kind of Gaiety and Laziness, I shall set down five Days
of it, as I have received it from the hand of my fair Correspondent.

Dear Mr. SPECTATOR,

'You having set your Readers an Exercise in one of your last
Week's Papers, I have perform'd mine according to your Orders, and
herewith send it you enclosed. You must know, *Mr.* SPECTATOR, that
I am a Maiden Lady of a good Fortune, who have had several
Matches offer'd me for these ten Years last past, and have at present
warm Applications made to me by a very pretty Fellow. As I am at
my own disposal I come up to Town every Winter, and pass my time
in it after the manner you will find in the following Journal, which
I began to write upon the very Day after your *Spectator* upon that
Subject.'

TUESDAY *Night*. Could not go to Sleep till one in the Morning for
thinking of my Journal.

WEDNESDAY. *From Eight till Ten*. Drank two Dishes of Chocolate
in Bed, and fell asleep after 'em.

From Ten to Eleven. Eat a slice of Bread and Butter, drank a Dish
of Bohea,[3] read the *Spectator*.

From Eleven to One. At my Toilet, try'd a new Head. Gave Or-
ders for *Veny*[4] to be combed and washed. *Mem*. I look best in Blue.

From One till half an Hour after Two. Drove to the *Change*.[5]
Cheapned[6] a couple of Fans.

[3] *Bohea:* Tea.
[4] Veny: Clarinda's lap dog, like Belinda's Shock.
[5] *the* Change: Either the New Exchange or the Royal Exchange (see "Places," the
final section of Part Two, Chapter 2).
[6] *Cheapned:* Bargained, haggled.

Till Four. At Dinner. *Mem.* Mr. *Froth* passed by in his new Liveries.

From Four to Six. Dressed, paid a Visit to old Lady *Blithe* and her Sister, having before heard they were gone out of Town that Day.

From Six to Eleven. At *Basset.*[7] *Mem.* Never set again upon the Ace of Diamonds.

THURSDAY. *From Eleven at Night to Eight in the Morning.* Dream'd that I punted[8] to Mr. *Froth.*

From Eight to Ten. Chocolate. Read two Acts in *Aurenzebe*[9] a-bed.

From Ten to Eleven. Tea Table. Sent to borrow Lady *Faddle*'s *Cupid* for *Veny.* Read the Play Bills. Received a Letter from Mr. *Froth. Mem.* Locked it up in my strong Box.

Rest of the Morning. Fontange,[10] the Tire-Woman, Her Account of my Lady *Blithe*'s Wash. Broke a Tooth in my little Tortoise shell Comb. Sent *Frank* to know how my Lady *Hectick* rested after her Monky's leaping out at Window. Looked pale. *Fontange* tells me my Glass is not true. Dressed by Three.

From Three to Four. Dinner cold before I sate down.

From Four to Eleven. Saw Company. Mr. *Froth*'s Opinion of *Milton.* His Account of the *Mohocks.* His Fancy for a Pin-cushion. Picture in the Lid of his Snuff-box. Old Lady *Faddle* promises me her Woman to cut my Hair. Lost five Guineas at Crimp.[11]

Twelve a Clock at Night. Went to Bed.

FRIDAY. *Eight in the Morning. A-bed*, read over all Mr. *Froth*'s Letters. *Cupid* and *Veny.*

Ten a Clock. Stay'd within all Day, not at home.

From Ten to Twelve. In Conference with my Mantua-Maker. Sorted a Suit of Ribbands. Broke my Blue China Cup.

From Twelve to One. Shut my self up in my Chamber, practised Lady *Betty Modely*'s Skuttle.[12]

---

[7] Basset: A card game.
[8] *punted:* A move in the card game of basset.
[9] Aurenzebe: John Dryden's tragedy *Aureng-Zebe* (1676).
[10] Fontange: Her French maid; a fontange was an elaborate headdress.
[11] *Crimp:* Another card game.
[12] *Skuttle:* "A quick pace; a short run; a pace of affected precipitation" [Johnson].

One in the Afternoon. Called for my flowered Handkerchief. Worked half a violet Leaf in it. Eyes aked and Head out of Order. Threw by my Work, and read over the remaining Part of *Aurenzebe.*

From Three to Four. Dined.

From Four to Twelve. Changed my Mind, dressed, went abroad, and play'd at Crimp till Midnight. Found Mrs. *Spitely* at home. Conversation: Mrs. *Brilliant*'s Necklace false Stones. Old Lady *Loveday* going to be married to a young Fellow that is not worth a Groat. Miss *Prue* gone into the Country. *Tom. Townley* has red Hair. *Mem.* Mrs. *Spitely* whispered in my Ear, that she had something to tell me about Mr. *Froth.* I am sure it is not true.

Between Twelve and One. Dreamed that Mr. *Froth* lay at my Feet, and called me *Indamora.*[13]

SATURDAY. Rose at Eight a Clock in the Morning. Sat down to my Toilet.

From Eight to Nine. Shifted a patch for half an Hour before I could determine it. Fixed it above my Left Eyebrow.

From Nine to Twelve. Drank my Tea, and dressed.

From Twelve to Two. At Chappel. A great deal of good Company. *Mem.* The third Air in the new Opera. Lady *Blithe* dressed frightfully.

From Three to Four. Dined. Miss *Kitty* called upon me to go to the Opera before I was risen from Table.

From Dinner to Six. Drank Tea. Turned off[14] a Footman for being rude to *Veny.*

Six a Clock. Went to the Opera. I did not see Mr. *Froth* till the beginning of the Second Act. Mr. *Froth* talked to a Gentleman in a black Wigg. Bowed to a Lady in the Front Box. Mr. *Froth* and his Friend clapt *Nicolini* in the third Act. Mr. *Froth* cryed out *Ancora.* Mr. *Froth* led me to my Chair, I think he squeezed my Hand.

Eleven at Night. Went to Bed. Melancholy Dreams. Methought *Nicolini* said he was Mr. *Froth.*

SUNDAY. Indisposed.

MONDAY. *Eight a Clock.* Waked by Miss *Kitty. Aurenzebe* lay upon the Chair by me. *Kitty* repeated, without Book, the Eight best

---

[13] Indamora: A character in *Aureng-Zebe.*
[14] *Turned off:* Fired.

Lines in the Play. Went in our Mobbs[15] to the Dumb Man,[16] according to Appointment. Told me, that my Lover's Name began with a *G*. *Mem*. The Conjuror was within a Letter of Mr. *Froth*'s Name. &c.

'Upon looking back into this my Journal, I find that I am at a loss to know whether I pass my Time well or ill; and indeed never thought of Considering how I did it, before I perused your Speculation upon that Subject. I scarce find a single Action in these Five Days, that I can thoroughly approve of, except the working upon the Violet Leaf, which I am resolved to finish the first Day I am at leasure. As for Mr. *Froth* and *Veny*, I did not think they took up so much of my Time and Thoughts, as I find they do upon my Journal. The latter of them I will turn off, if you insist upon it; and if Mr. *Froth* does not bring matters to a Conclusion very suddenly, I will not let my Life run away in a Dream.

Your Humble Servant
Clarinda.'

To resume one of the Morals of my First Paper, and to confirm *Clarinda* in her good Inclinations, I would have her consider what a pretty Figure she would make among Posterity, were the History of her whole Life published like these Five Days of it. I shall conclude my Paper with an Epitaph written by an uncertain Author[17] on Sir *Philip Sidney*'s Sister, a Lady who seems to have been of a Temper very much different from that of *Clarinda*. The last Thought of it is so very noble, that I dare say my Reader will pardon me the Quotation.

On the Countess Dowager of Pembroke.

> Underneath this Marble Hearse
> Lies the Subject of all Verse,
> *Sydney*'s Sister, *Pembroke*'s Mother;
> Death, ere thou hast Kill'd another,
> Fair and learn'd, and good as she,
> Time shall throw a Dart at thee.

---

[15] *Mobbs:* Loose dresses.
[16] *the Dumb Man:* Duncan Campbell, a deaf and dumb conjurer.
[17] *an uncertain Author:* Thought to be William Browne of Tavistock; the poem was first published in 1623.

JOHN MACKY

From *A Journey through England* ["The Theatres"]

John Macky (d. 1726), a Scottish writer and government agent (mainly noted for his *Memoirs of the Secret Services of John Macky, Esq., during the Reign of King William, Queen Anne, and King George I* [1733]), published a three-volume *Journey through England* that describes in colorful rhetoric the places and the customs of the English. As one might expect of a spy, Macky was a careful observer, and his opinionated guidebook supplies us with a very real sense of interiors, such as the description of the English playhouse excerpted here. As in *The Rape of the Lock*, we see a fashionable world that seems completely enchanted with the pleasures of seeing and being seen; Belinda acts her part in a world that celebrates spectacle.

The text is taken from the second edition of *A Journey through England. In Familiar Letters. From A Gentleman Here, to His Friend Abroad* (London, 1722), 1:170–71.

The Theatres here differ from those abroad; in those at *Venice*, *Paris*, *Brussels*, *Genoa*, and other Parts, you know, are composed of Rows of small Shut-Boxes, three or four Stories in a Semi-Circle, with a *Parterre* below; whereas here the *Parterre* (commonly call'd the *Pit*) contains the Gentlemen on Benches; and in the first Row of Boxes sit all the Ladies of Quality; in the second, the Citizens Wives and Daughters; and in the third, the common People and Footmen; so that between the Acts you are as much diverted by viewing the Beauties of the Audience, as while they act with the Subject of the Play; and the whole is illuminated to the greatest Advantage: Whereas abroad, the Stage being only illuminated, and the Lodge or Boxes close, you lose the Pleasure of seeing the Company; and indeed the *English* have reason in this, for no Nation in the world can shew such an Assembly of shining Beauties as here.

ANNE FINCH, COUNTESS OF WINCHILSEA

"The Spleen"

Although Pope did not in general approve of "Pindarik poems," finding them too irregular, he did admire "The Spleen," which first appeared in the 1713 edition of Finch's collected poems. In fact, he echoes the couplet on the jonquil and "Aromatick Pain" in *An Essay on Man* ("Or quick effluvia darting thro' the brain, / Die of a rose in aromatic pain?" [I.199–200]). The poem studies the tyrannical effects of the "English Malady" — that extreme melancholy, depression, peevishness, or hysteria that overwhelms Belinda in the Cave of Spleen, and that Finch sees tormenting humankind in every aspect of social, psychological, and spiritual life.

See the headnote to Finch's poems in "The Characters of Men and Women," p. 308, for biographical and bibliographical information.

The text is reprinted from *The Poems of Anne Countess of Winchilsea*, ed. Myra Reynolds (Chicago: University of Chicago Press, 1903).

A Pindarik Poem[1]

What art thou, *SPLEEN*, which ev'ry thing dost ape?
  Thou *Proteus*° to abus'd Mankind,
  Who never yet thy real Cause cou'd find,
Or fix thee to remain in one continued Shape.
  Still varying thy perplexing Form,   5
  Now a Dead Sea thou'lt represent,
  A Calm of stupid Discontent,
Then, dashing on the Rocks wilt rage into a Storm.
  Trembling sometimes thou dost appear,
  Dissolved into a Panick Fear;   10
  On Sleep intruding dost thy Shadows spread,
  Thy gloomy Terrours round the silent Bed,

---

[1] *A Pindarik Poem*: Pindaric odes are based on the form composed by the Greek poet Pindar and known to the seventeenth century primarily through Abraham Cowley's translations. The pattern, which can be repeated indefinitely, begins with a strophe, or turn, followed by an antistrophe, or counterturn, and an epode, or aftersong or stand.

2. Proteus: "A sea-god, son of Oceanus and Tethys, fabled to assume various shapes" [OED].

And croud with boading° Dreams the Melancholy
     Head;
    Or, when the Midnight Hour is told,
    And drooping Lids thou still dost waking hold,   15
    Thy fond Delusions cheat the Eyes,
    Before them antick Spectres dance,
Unusual Fires their pointed Heads advance,
    And airy Phantoms rise.
    Such was the monstrous *Vision* seen,   20
When *Brutus* (now beneath his Cares opprest,
And all *Rome*'s Fortunes rolling in his Breast,
    Before *Philippi*'s latest Field,
Before his Fate did to *Octavius* lead)°
    Was vanquish'd by the *Spleen*.   25
    Falsly, the Mortal Part we blame
    Of our deprest, and pond'rous Frame,
    Which, till the First degrading Sin
    Let Thee, its dull Attendant, in,
    Still with the Other did comply,   30
Nor clogg'd the Active Soul, dispos'd to fly,
And range the Mansions of it's native Sky.
    Nor, whilst in his own Heaven he dwelt,
    Whilst Man his Paradice possest,
His fertile Garden in the fragrant East,   35
    And all united Odours smelt,
    No armed Sweets, until thy Reign,
    Cou'd shock the Sense, or in the Face
    A flusht, unhandsom Colour place.
Now the *Jonquille* o'ercomes the feeble Brain;   40
We faint beneath the Aromatick Pain,
Till some offensive Scent thy Pow'rs appease,
And Pleasure we resign for short, and nauseous Ease.

    In ev'ry One thou dost possess,
    New are thy Motions, and thy Dress: 45
    Now in some Grove a list'ning Friend
    Thy false Suggestions must attend,

---

13. *boading:* Foreboding.
21–24. Brutus . . . Octavius: The Battle of Philippi (42 B.C.) led to the victory of
the second Roman triumvirate of Antony, Lepidus, and Octavian (Augustus) over Bru-
tus and Cassius, who had assassinated Julius Caesar. Brutus committed suicide follow-
ing the battle.

Thy whisper'd Griefs, thy fancy'd Sorrows hear,
Breath'd in a Sigh, and witness'd by a Tear;
   Whilst in the light, and vulgar Croud,   50
   Thy Slaves, more clamorous and loud,
By Laughters unprovok'd, thy Influence too confess.
In the Imperious *Wife* thou Vapours art,
   Which from o'erheated Passions rise
   In Clouds to the attractive Brain,   55
   Until descending thence again,
   Thro' the o'er-cast, and show'ring Eyes,
   Upon her Husband's soften'd Heart,
   He the disputed Point must yield,
Something resign of the contested Field;   60
Till Lordly *Man*, born to Imperial Sway,
Compounds for Peace, to make that Right away,
And *Woman*, arm'd with *Spleen*, do's servilely Obey.

   The *Fool*, to imitate the Wits,
   Complains of thy pretended Fits,   65
   And Dulness, born with him, wou'd lay
   Upon thy accidental Sway;
   Because, sometimes, thou dost presume
   Into the ablest Heads to come:
   That, often, Men of Thoughts refin'd,   70
   Impatient of unequal Sence,
Such slow Returns, where they so much dispense,
Retiring from the Croud, are to thy Shades inclin'd.
   O'er me alas! thou dost too much prevail:
   I feel thy Force, whilst I against thee rail;   75
I feel my Verse decay, and my crampt Numbers fail.
Thro' thy black Jaundice I all Objects see,
   As Dark, and Terrible as Thee,
My Lines decry'd, and my Employment thought
An useless Folly, or presumptuous Fault: 80
   Whilst in the *Muses* Paths I stray,
Whilst in their Groves, and by their secret Springs
My Hand delights to trace unusual Things,
And deviates from the known, and common way;
   Nor will in fading Silks compose   85
   Faintly th' inimitable *Rose*,
Fill up an ill-drawn *Bird*, or paint on Glass

The *Sov'reign's* blurr'd and undistinguish'd Face,
The threatening *Angel*, and the speaking *Ass.*

   Patron thou art to ev'ry gross Abuse,   90
      The sullen *Husband's* feign'd Excuse,
When the ill Humour with his Wife he spends,
And bears recruited Wit, and Spirits to his Friends.
     The Son of *Bacchus*° pleads thy Pow'r,
       As to the Glass he still repairs,   95
       Pretends but to remove thy Cares,
Snatch from thy Shades one gay, and smiling Hour,
And drown thy Kingdom in a purple Show'r.
When the *Coquette*, whom ev'ry Fool admires,
      Wou'd in Variety be Fair,   100
      And, changing hastily the Scene
      From Light, Impertinent, and Vain,
    Assumes a soft, a melancholy Air,
    And of her Eyes rebates the wand'ring Fires,
   The careless Posture, and the Head reclin'd,   105
      The thoughtful, and composed Face,
   Proclaiming the withdrawn, the absent Mind,
   Allows the Fop more liberty to gaze,
   Who gently for the tender Cause inquires;
   The Cause, indeed, is a Defect in Sense,   110
Yet is the *Spleen* alledg'd, and still the dull Pretence.
      But these are thy fantastic Harms,
      The Tricks of thy pernicious Stage,
      Which do the weaker Sort engage;
   Worse are the dire Effects of thy more pow'rful Charms.   115
      By Thee *Religion*, all we know,
      That shou'd enlighten here below,
      Is veil'd in Darkness, and perplext
With anxious Doubts, with endless Scruples vext,
And some Restraint imply'd from each perverted Text,   120
   Whilst *Touch* not, *Taste* not, what is freely giv'n,
Is but thy niggard Voice, disgracing bounteous Heav'n.
   From Speech restrain'd, by thy Deceits abus'd,
   To Deserts banish'd, or in Cells reclus'd,

---

94. Bacchus: The god of wine; a son of Bacchus is a drinker.

Mistaken Vot'ries to the Pow'rs Divine,   125
  Whilst they a purer Sacrifice design,
Do but the *Spleen* obey, and worship at thy Shrine.
  In vain to chase thee ev'ry Art we try,
    In vain all Remedies apply,
    In vain the *Indian* Leaf° infuse,   130
    Or the parch'd *Eastern* Berry° bruise;
Some pass, in vain, those Bounds, and nobler Liquors use.
    Now *Harmony*, in vain, we bring,
    Inspire the Flute, and touch the String.
    From Harmony no help is had;   135
Musick but soothes thee, if too sweetly sad,
And if too light, but turns thee gayly Mad.
    Tho' the Physicians greatest Gains,
    Altho' his growing Wealth he sees
    Daily increas'd by Ladies Fees,   140
  Yet dost thou baffle all his studious Pains.
    Not skilful *Lower* thy Source cou'd find,
  Or thro' the well-dissected Body trace
    The secret, the mysterious ways,
By which thou dost surprise, and prey upon the Mind.   145
  Tho' in the Search, too deep for Humane Thought,
    With unsuccessful Toil he wrought,
  'Till thinking Thee to've catch'd, Himself by thee
        was caught,
    Retain'd thy Pris'ner, thy acknowledg'd Slave,
And sunk beneath thy Chain to a lamented Grave.   150

130. *the* Indian *Leaf:* Tea.
131. *the parch'd* Eastern *Berry:* Coffee.

JOHN MACKY

From *A Journey through England*
["Of Coffee-houses"]

Macky's guide to London also takes us into the coffee houses and marks how deeply the "culture" of coffee — and who drinks it where — has settled into London life. Moreover, its explicit associations beyond the world of pleasure and into the world of commerce and politics reveal, as does *The Rape of the Lock*, the symbolic significance of the act of drinking coffee.

The text is taken from the second edition of *A Journey through England. In Familiar Letters. From A Gentleman Here, to His Friend Abroad* (London, 1722), 1:168–69, 174–75.

[T]he Parties have their different Places, where however a Stranger is always well received; but a *Whig* will no more go to the *Cocoa-Tree* or *Osinda's*, than a *Tory* will be seen at the Coffee-House of *St. James's*.

The *Scots* go generally to the *British*, and a Mixture of all sorts go to the *Smyrna*. There are other little Coffee-Houses much frequented in this Neighborhood, *Young-Man's* for Officers, *Old-Man's* for Stock-Jobbers,[1] Pay-Masters, and Courtiers, and *Little-Man's* for Sharpers: I never was so confounded in my Life, as when I enter'd into this last: I saw two or three Tables full at *Faro*,[2] heard the Box and Dice rattling in the Rooms above the Stairs, and was surrounded by a Set of sharp Faces, that I was afraid would have devoured me with their Eyes. I was glad to drop two or three Half-Crowns at *Faro*; to get off with a clear Skin, and was over-joy'd I was so got rid of them. . . .

The *Royal-Exchange* is the Resort of all the trading part of this City, Foreign and Domestick, from half an Hour after One till near Three in the Afternoon; but the better sort generally meet in *Exchange-Alley* a little before, at three celebrated Coffee-Houses, called *Garaway's*,[3] *Robin's*, and *Jonathan's*. In the first, the People of

---

[1] *Stock-Jobbers:* "A Member of the Stock Exchange who deals in stocks on his own account" [OED]. The OED cites a 1697 issue of the *London Gazette* that announces "An Act to Restrain the Number and Ill Practices of Brokers and Stock-Jobbers."

[2] Faro: Or Pharaoh, a gambling card game.

[3] Garaway's: The coffee-house opened by Thomas Garraway (or Garway).

Quality who have Business in the City, and the most considerable and wealthy Citizens frequent. In the second, the Foreign Banquiers, and often even Foreign Ministers. And in the third, the Buyers and Sellers of Stock.

When I enter'd into this last I was afraid I had got into *Little-Man's Coffee-House* again; for busy Faces run about here as there, with the same sharp intent Looks, with this Difference only, that here it is selling of *Bank-Stock*, *East-India*, *South-Sea*, and *Lottery-Tickets*,[4] and there is all Cards and Dice.

THE ROYAL SOCIETY

From *Philosophical Transactions*, No. 256, "A Discourse of Coffee"

The Royal Society was founded by Charles II in 1662 as an organization dedicated to the pursuit of various new scientific enterprises based on Baconian methods, or experiments verified by empirical rather than simply logical evidence. Isaac Newton, Christopher Wren, John Evelyn, Samuel Pepys, Robert Hooke, William Harvey, and Robert Boyle were early members. The *Philosophical Transactions* made available to a wide public the "Account[s] of the Present Undertakings, Studies and Labours of the INGENIOUS, in many Considerable Parts of the World." Although the society produced and published many exceptionally valuable discoveries, its various and, to some, esoteric interests were often satirized by writers such as Jonathan Swift, Aphra Behn, Thomas Shadwell, and Susanna Centlivre. The essay included here offers a straightforward history of coffee, a description of its properties, a prescription for its concoction, and speculations on its economic and political implications for Britain.

The text is taken from *Philosophical Transactions*, No. 256 (September 1699), pp. 311–17. Printed for *S. Smith* and *B. Walford*, Printers to the *Royal Society*, at the *Prince's Arms* in St. *Paul's* Church-yard. 1706.

---

[4] *selling of* Bank-Stock . . . Lottery-Tickets: Selling shares in various of England's trading companies and credit schemes.

Read at a Meeting of the *Royal Society*,
by Mr. John Houghton, F. R. S.

Several have written of this Plant, and particularly the Learned Mr. *Ray*, in his large History of Plants, pag. 1691, 2. 3. But for its Description, I shall only refer you to what was published by Dr. *Sloane*, in the 17th. Vol. of these Transactions, No. 208. pag. 63. where is the Figure, Description, &c.

At the beginning of the Transaction, is a Cut of the Branch, with its Leaves and Berries, only the Leaves are not set opposite one to another, as he tells me they ought to have been.

I cannot learn the use of any part of this Plant, except the Berries, of which boil'd in Water, a Drink is made, and drunk much among the *Arabians* and *Turks*, and also now in *Europe*.

. . . .

The general use of it quickly made it a Trade in great Towns, and the frequent use of it made it be desired stronger and stronger, till the excessive Drinkers would take whole spoonfuls of the Oyl that swims on the top, as our great Drinkers arrive from Wine to Brandy, and from thence to more burning Spirits.

Into these Publick-houses they would come by Hundreds, and among them Strangers would venture, where they learn't the Custom, and carried it to their own Countries; for one Mr. *Rastall* an *English* Merchant, whom I knew, went to *Leghorn* in 1651, and there found a Coffee-house. To the same House of Merchandise where this *Rastall* was, came Mr. *Daniel Edwards* a Merchant from *Smyrna* (where Coffee had been used immemorially) who brought with him, *Anno* 1652, a *Greek* Servant, named *Pasqua*, who made his Coffee, which he drank two or three Dishes at a time, twice or thrice in a Day.

The same Year *Edwards* came over Land into *England*, and Married the Daughter of one Alderman *Hodges* a Merchant, who lived I think in *Walbrook*. This *Hodges* used with great delight to drink Coffee with *Edwards*, so it is likely, that this *Edwards* was the first that brought Coffee into *England*, although I am inform'd that Dr. *Harvey*[1] the famous Inventer of the Circulation of the Blood, did frequently use it.

---

[1] *Dr.* Harvey: William Harvey (1578–1657), the English physician who published his findings on the heart and the circulation of the blood in 1628.

After this it grew more in use in several private Houses, which encouraged Mr. *Edwards* to set up *Pasqua* for a Coffee-man, who got a Shed in the Church-yard of St. *Michael Cornhil*, where he had great Custom, insomuch that the Ale-house keepers fearing it should spoil their Trade, Petitioned the Lord Mayor against him, alledging his not being a Freeman.[2] Upon this Alderman *Hodges* joyned as a Partner with *Pasqua* one *Bowman* his Coachman, who was made Free, upon which they lived unmolested in the same place, where Mr. *Rastall* found them in the Year 1654, but sometime after this *Pasqua* for some Misdemeanour run away, and *Bowman* had the whole Trade, and managed it so well, that by his Profit, and the Generosity of his Customers, who contributed Sixpence a piece, to the number of almost a Thousand; he turned his Shed into a House, and when he died left his Wife, who had been Alderman *Hodges*'s Cook-maid, pretty Rich, but she died Poor not many Years since.

John Painter was *Bowmans* first Apprentice, and out of his Time in 1664, *Bowman* died 1663, and after one Year his Wife let the House to one *Batler*, whose Daughter Married *Humphrey Hodskins* Bowman's second Apprentice, who was with him before *Monk*'s March,[3] Anno 1659. This *Humphrey* lived long in St. *Peter*'s-*alley* in *Cornhil,* and died not many Years since, and left there his Widow, *Batler*'s Daughter from whom I had this Account.

How long this has been in use in the World, is hard to say, but *Tavernier*'s Travels, the *English* Edition, says it had been in use but Twenty Years, although the Author said Six-score years.

I am inform'd that Dr. *Beveridge* has an *Arabick* Book, that says a Hermit drank it, and called it *Coffee* which signifies *Drink*, but the name is *Bun*.

This is what I can learn of the Original of Coffee, and Coffee-houses, but as for its Virtues, I think no body has Published any thing considerable about it. I shall give my Thoughts, which perhaps may provoke some that understands better to shew the Weakness of them, and in their room set forth better.

The best Coffee-berry is what is large and plump, with a greenish cast, and having on the thin parts a Transparency; the other has a yel-

---

[2] *Freeman:* A citizen of London, i.e., not an apprentice.

[3] Monk's *March:* George Monck, first Duke of Albemarle (1608–1670), who had been a firm supporter of Cromwell, marched to London on New Year's Day 1660 to protect Parliament against disaffected army commanders; it was General Monck who later received Charles II on the beach at Dover and restored the monarchy as England's only safeguard against anarchy.

lowish cast, and is more opaque, but when they are roasted, 'tis hard to distinguish.

I put some Berries into a Glass of Water about a Week since, to see if they will sprout, but as yet there is no appearance, altho' they are tollerably swell'd, and look white and bright.

I have made a Decoction of them, which has made them shoot.

The Common way of preparing the Berry for the Drink Coffee, is roasting it in a Tin Cylindrical Box full of holes, through the middle of which runs a Spit, under this is a semicircular Hearth, wherein is made a large Charcoal-fire: By the help of a Jack, the Spit turns swift, and so it Roasts, being now and then taken up to be shaken. When the Oyl arises, and it's grown of a dark brown colour, it's emptied into two Receivers made with large Hoops, whose bottoms are Iron-plates, these shut into, and there the Coffee is well shaken, and left till almost cold, and if it looks bright, Oyly, and shining, 'tis a sign 'tis well done.

Of this, when fresh, if an Ounce be ground, and boil'd in something more than a quart of Water, till it be fully impregnated with the fine Particles of the Coffee, and the rest is grown so ponderous, as it will subside, and leave the Liquor clear, and of a reddish Colour, it will make about a Quart of very good Coffee.

The best way of keeping the Berries when roasted, is in some warm place, where it may not be suffered to imbibe any Moisture, which will pall it; and take off it's briskness of Taste: It's best to grind it as used except it be ram'd into a Tin-pot, well covered and kept dry, and then I believe it will keep good a Month.

There will swim upon the Coffee an Oyl, which the *Turkish* great Coffee-drinkers will take in great plenty if they can get it. When the Coffee has stood some time to cool, the gross parts will subside, the briskness will be gone, and 'twill grow flat and almost clear again. . . .

It has been generally thought to be an Antihypnotick or Hinderer of Sleep, which I dare not gainsay; Dr. *Willis* and other learned Men having declared it so, but now it is come into frequent use, the contrary is often observ'd, although perhaps Custom as it does with *Opium* alters its natural Qualities. Could I meet with a satisfactory Theory of Sleep, perhaps at this I might give some better guesses.

As to the Political uses of Coffee, I am told, that our three Kingdoms spend about one hundred Tun a Year, whereof *England* spends about seventy Tun, which at fourteen Pounds a Tun (a middle price now a Days) will amount to 20586 Pound sterling, and if it were to be all sold in Coffee-houses, it would reach treble 61740 Pounds, which at ten Pounds a Head will find employments for 6174 Persons, although I believe all the People of *England* one with another do not spend five Pounds each.

Coffee when roasted loses about a fourth part; then there is spent about fifty two Tun and a half of roasted Coffee, which makes 117600 Pound or 1881600 Ounces or 15252800 Drachms, which if there be Eight Millions of People, it is not two Drachms or half a pint of Coffee a piece for a Year. How little is this Trade when thus considered, and how greatly may it be improved, although we spend as many Tuns in half a Year, as it has been Years with us. Besides what we use, we send a great deal abroad, and I doubt not but in short time the gain of what we send abroad will pay the first cost of all we shall spend at home, and I believe one of the best ways to make advantage of Foreign Trade is to use such Wares much at home, and that will teach all we trade with to follow our Example; it does thus in Silks, Calicoes, Pepper, Tobacco, and several other things.

Furthermore Coffee has greatly increased the Trade of Tobacco and Pipes, Earthen dishes, Tin wares, News-Papers, Coals, Candles, Sugar, Tea, Chocolate, and what not? Coffee house makes all sorts of People sociable, they improve Arts, and Merchandize, and all other Knowledge; and a worthy member of this Society (now departed) has thought that Coffee-houses have improved useful knowledge very much.

June 14 1699.

"The Coffee House, or News-mongers Hall"

In *The Rape of the Lock* it is "*Coffee*, (which makes the Politician wise, / And see thro' all things with his half-shut Eyes)" (III.117–18). This earlier broadside satirizes the whole realm of the coffee house as a sort of gossip garden in which every sort of social and political rumor circulates as truth. One of the pleasures of the coffee house was, of course, the chance it offered to mingle with others, hear the latest news, read the latest broadside, exchange the latest gossip, critique the latest poem.

The text is taken from a broadside in the British Library Luttrell Collection (*London*, Printed by *E. Crowch*, for *T. Vere*, at the Angel without *New-gate*, 1672).

In which is shewn their several sorts of Passions,
Containing News from all our Neighbour Nations

You that delight in Wit and Mirth,
   And long to hear such News,
As comes from all Parts of the *Earth*,
   Dutch, *Danes*, and *Turks*, and *Jews*,
I'le send yee to a Rendezvous,   5
   Where it is smoaking new;
Go hear it at a *Coffee-house*,
   It cannot but be true.

There Battles and Sea-Fights are Fought,
   And bloody Plots display'd,   10
They know more Things then ere was thought,
   Or ever was betray'd:
No Money in the Minting-house
   Is half so Bright and New;
And coining from a *Coffee-house*,   15
   It cannot but be true.

Before the *Navyes* fall to Work,
   They know who shall be Winner,
They there can tell ye what the *Turk*
   Last Sunday had to Dinner;   20
Who last did Cut *de Ruyters* Corns,°
   Amongst his jovial Crew;
Or who first gave the *Devil* Horns,
   This sounds as if 'twere true.

A *Fisherman* did boldly tell,   25
   And strongly did avouch,
He Caught a Shoal of Mackarel,
   That Parley'd all in *Dutch*,
And cry'd out *Yaw, Yaw, Yaw myn Heer*;
   But as the Draught they drew,   30
They stunk for fear, our Fleet being near,
   Which cannot but be true.

There's nothing done in all the World,
   From *Monarch* to the *Mouse*,

---

21. de Ruyters *Corns:* Michel Adriaanszoon de Ruyter (1607–1676), famous
Dutch admiral. A corn is a hard-centered or horny ingrowth of the toenail.

But every Day or Night 'tis hurld   35
   Into the *Coffee-house.*
What *Lillie* or what *Booker*° can
   By Art, not bring about,
At *Coffee-house* you'l find a Man,
   Can quickly find it out.   40

They'l tell ye there, what Lady-ware,
   Of late is grown too light;
What Wise-man shall from Favour fall,
   What Fool shall be a Knight;
They'l tell ye when our sayling Trade,   45
   Shall rise again, and Florish,
And when *Jack Adams* first was made
   Church-Warden of the Parish.

They know who shall in Times to come,
   Be either made, or undone,   50
From great St. *Peters-street* in *Rome,*
   To *Turnbul-street* in *London*;
And likewise tell, at *Clerkenwell,*
   What *Whore* hath greatest Gain;
And in that place, what Brazen-face   55
   Doth wear a Golden Chain.

At Sea their Knowledge is so much,
   They know all Rocks and Shelves,
They know all Councils of the *Dutch,*
   More then they know themselves;   60
Who 'tis shall get the best at last,
   They perfectly can shew
At *Coffee-house,* when they are plac'd,
   You'd scarce believe it true.

They know all that is Good, or Hurt,   65
   To Dam ye, or to Save ye;
There is the *Colledge,* and the *Court,*
   The *Countrey, Camp,* and *Navie*;

37. Lillie . . . Booker: (?) Sir Peter Lely (1618–1680), born in Westphalia, became a
leading portrait painter in England; A. Van Beeke was a seventeenth-century Dutch
still-life painter. On the other hand, Charles Lillie was a famous London perfumer (see
the advertisement for snuffboxes, p. 362) and Booker or Beeker could be someone in a
similar profession.

So great a *Universitie.*
   I think there ne're was any;   70
In which you may a Schoolar be
   For spending of a Penny.

A *Merchants Prentice* there shall show
   You all and every thing,
What hath been done, and is to do,   75
   'Twixt *Holland* and the *King*;
What *Articles* of *Peace* will bee,
   He can precizely show;
What will be good for *Them* or *Wee*,
   He perfectly doth know.   80

Here Men do talk of every Thing,
   With large and liberal Lungs,
Like Women at a Gossiping,
   With double tyre of Tongues;
They'l give a Broad-side presently,   85
   Soon as you are in view,
With Stories that, you'l wonder at,
   Which they will swear are true.

The Drinking there of *Chochalat,*
   Can make a *Fool* a *Sophie:*°   90
'Tis thought the *Turkish Mahomet*
   Was first Inspir'd with *Coffe,*
By which his Powers did Over-flow
   The Land of *Palestine*:
Then let us to the *Coffe-house* go,   95
   'Tis Cheaper far then Wine.

You shall know there, what Fashions are;
   How Perrywiggs are Curl'd,
And for a Penny you shall heare,
   All Novels in the World,   100
Both Old and Young, and Great and Small,
   And Rich, and Poor, you'l see:
Therefore let's to the *Coffe* All,
   Come All away with Mee.

90. *a* Sophie: Or sophy, a sage or wise man.

"A Broadside against Coffee;
or, the Marriage of the Turk"

Not everyone thought coffee and coffee houses were wonderful. Although some people approved of the way that coffee seemed to compete with, if not replace, alcohol in popularity, others believed that, coming from a "hot country," it aroused the passions. This broadside provides a kind of counterbalance to the subtle and largely celebratory treatment given to this social luxury in *The Rape of the Lock* — it damns the evil beverage outright, employing stereotypical images dealing with race, nationality, religion, gender, and class.

The text is taken from a broadside in the British Library Luttrell Collection (*London*, Printed for *J. L. Anno Dom.* 1672).

Coffee, a kind of *Turkish Renegade*,
Has late a match with *Christian water* made;
At first between them happen'd a Demur,
Yet joyn'd they were, but not without great *stir*;
For both so cold were, and so faintly met,   5
The *Turkish Hymen*° in his *Turbant*° swet.
Coffee was cold as *Earth*, *Water* as *Thames*,
And stood in need of recommending Flames;
For each of them steers a contrary course,
And of themselves they sue out a Divorce.   10
Coffee so brown a berry does appear,
Too swarthy for a Nymph so fair, so clear:
And yet his sails he did for *England* hoist,
Though cold and dry, to court the cold and moist;
If there be ought we can as love admit;   15
'Tis a hot love, and lasteth but a fit.
For this indeed the cause is of their stay,
Newcastle's bowels warmer are than they;°
The melting Nymph distills her self to do't,
Whilst the Slave *Coffee* must be *beaten* to't: 20
Incorporate him close as close may be,
Pause but a while, and he is none of he;
Which for a truth, and not a story tells,

6. Hymen: The god of marriage. Turbant: Turban.
18. Newcastle's *bowels warmer are than they*: Margaret, Duchess of Newcastle (1624–1674) was ridiculed in Charles II's promiscuous court for her strict chastity.

No Faith is to be kept with Infidels.
Sure he suspects, and shuns her as a Whore,   25
And loves, and kills, like the *Venetian Moor*;°
Bold Asian Brat! With speed our confines flee;
Water, though common, is too good for thee.
Sure *Coffee*'s vext he has the breeches loft,
For she's above, and he lies undermost;   30
What shall I add but this? (and sure 'tis right)
The Groom is *heavy*, 'cause the Bride is *light*.
This canting *Coffee* has his Crew enricht,
And both the *Water* and the *Men* bewitcht.
    A Coachman was the first (here) *Coffee* made,°   35
And ever since the rest *drive on* the trade;
Me no good Engalash! and sure enough,
He plaid the Quack to salve his Stygian stuff;°
Ver boon for de stomach, de Cough, de Ptisick,°
And I believe him, for it looks like Physick.°   40
Coffee a crust is charkt° into a coal,
The smell and taste of the Mock *China* bowl;°
Where huff and puff, they labor out their lungs,
Left *Dives*-like° they should bewail their tongues.
And yet they tell ye that it will not burn,   45
Though on the Jury Blisters you return;
Whose furious heat does make the water rise,
And still through the Alembicks of your eyes.°
Dread and desire, ye fall to't snap by snap,
As hungry Dogs do scalding porrige lap,   50
But to cure Drunkards it has got great Fame;

    26. Venetian Moor: Shakespeare's Othello, who kills his wife Desdemona out of jealousy.
    35. *A Coachman was the first (here)* Coffee *made:* See "A Discourse of Coffee," p. 352.
    38. *Stygian stuff:* Pertaining to the mythological River Styx, beyond which lay the underworld.
    39. Ptisick: "Phthisic, a wasting consumption of the lungs" [OED].
    40. *Physick:* Medicine.
    41. *charkt:* Charred.
    42. *the Mock* China *bowl:* Perhaps a reference to a chamber pot?
    44. Dives-*like:* "Dives" is a generic name for a rich man.
    48. *And still through the Alembicks of your eyes:* An alembic was an instrument for distilling; here, the hot coffee causes one's eyes to "still" or distill tears.

Posset° or *Porrige,* will't not do the same?
Confusion huddles all into one Scene,
Like *Noah*'s Ark, the clean and the unclean.
But now, alas! the Drench° has credit got,   55
And he's no Gentleman that drinks it not;
That such a *Dwarf* should rise to such a stature!
But Custom is but a remove from Nature.
A *little* Dish, and a *large* Coffee-house,
What is it, but a *Mountain* and a *Mouse?*   60
      From Bawdy-houses differs thus your hap;
They give their *tails, you* give their *tongues* a *clap.*°
      Mens humana novitatis avidisima.°

ADVERTISEMENT

From *The Spectator,* No. 138
["The Exercise of the Snuff-Box"]

   This is a genuine advertisement; Bond cites an eighteenth-century edi-
tor of *The Spectator* (Thomas Percy), who noted: "This Advertisement is
said to have brought Lillie into such notice, that he soon raised a fortune
from his trade" (*Spectator* 2: 46n4). What seems remarkable is the extent
to which the advertisement plays into Pope's satire: Lillie offers training
in the etiquette of formal gesture and predicts a metonymic battle be-
tween the snuffboxes and the fans, as Pope had imaged battles between
swordknots and swordknots, men's wits and Lady's Hair, Dapperwit
and Thalestris. Based on this advertisement, snuffboxes seem a fitting
container for Beaus' Wits (V.116).

---

   52. Posset: "A drink composed of hot milk curdled with ale, wine, or other liquor,
often with sugar, spices, or other ingredients; formerly much used as a delicacy, and as
a remedy for colds or other affections" [OED].
   55. *Drench:* To drink.
   62. clap: A pun, conjuring up both venereal disease and a sharp shock.
   63. Mens humana novitatis avidissima: "The human mind is most avid for nov-
elty" [trans. Gordon Braden, University of Virginia].

No. 138
August 8, 1711

The Exercise of the Snuff-Box, according to the most fashionable Airs and Motions, in opposition to the Exercise of the Fan, will be Taught with the best plain or perfum'd Snuff, at *Charles Lillie*'s, Perfumer, at the Corner of *Beauford-Buildings* in the *Strand*, and Attendance given for the benefit of the young Merchants about the Exchange for two Hours every Day at Noon, except *Saturdays*, at a Toy-Shop near *Garraway*'s Coffee-house. There will be likewise Taught *The Ceremony of the Snuff-Box*, or Rules for offering Snuff to a Stranger, a Friend, or a Mistress, according to the Degrees of Familiarity or Distance; with an Explanation of the Careless, the Scornful, the Politick, and the Surly Pinch, and the Gestures proper to each of them.

N.B. The Undertaker does not question but in a short time to have form'd a Body of Regular Snuff-Boxes ready to meet and make Head against all the Regiment of Fans which have been lately Disciplin'd, and are now in Motion.

Eighteenth-century snuffbox, by L. Pottin, 1738–1739. This sample of an eighteenth-century snuffbox from Paris is a likely example of what either the Baron or Sir Plume might have brandished. It is an elegant masculine ornament, made of gold, enamel, and onyx, and although we don't know whether Sir Plume's amber snuffbox had any particularly French association, the practice of taking snuff between words ("Plague on't! 'tis past a Jest — nay prithee, Pox!" [IV.129]) was associated with the "effeminizing" French customs so popular among upper-class fops.

ISAAC HAWKINS BROWNE

From *Four Poems in Praise of Tobacco*

Tobacco has long been a more or less licit social pleasure, although it had its enemies from the beginning. The earliest citation in the *Oxford English Dictionary* is from 1573 (in a text published 1588): "In these daies the taking-in of the smoke of the Indian herbe called Tabaco, by an instrument formed like a little ladell, wherby it passeth from the mouth into the hed & stomach, is gretlie taken up and used in England." Although taking tobacco in its ground-up version as snuff was generally more popular among the elegant set, smoking tobacco was becoming a common pastime as well.

The following selection combines, as does *The Rape of the Lock*, the pleasures of parody and the parody of pleasures — with Pope figuring more as model for this good-tempered imitation than as target. Isaac Hawkins Browne (1705–1760) imitated the styles of the leading poets of the day in his *A Pipe of Tobacco, in Imitation of Six Several Authors,* which appeared in the *London Evening Post* on December 2, 1735, and in 1736 was pirated by Pope's nemesis Edmund Curll as *Of Smoking: Four Poems in Praise of Tobacco.* Apparently Pope was amused by the poem: "Browne," he remarked to Spence in 1738, "is an excellent copyist in his imitations on tobacco, and those who take it ill of him are very much in the wrong" (Spence, 1: 214, #503).

The text is taken from Curll's edition, which prints "An Imitation of Mr. Pope's Style" as the fourth parody: *Of Smoking: Four Poems in Praise of Tobacco. An Imitation of the Style of Four Modern Poets, Viz. Alexander Pope, Esq; Ambrose Philips, Esq; Dr. Young, Mr. Thomson. With an ODE, on the same Subject, to Lord Bolingbroke.* London: Printed for E. Curll, at Pope's Head, in Rose Street, Covent Garden. 1736.

"An Imitation of Mr. Pope's Style"

Blest Leaf, whose aromatic Gales dispense
To Templars° Modesty; to Parsons Sense.
(So raptur'd Priests, at fam'd *Dodona*'s Shrine,°

---

2. *Templars:* "A barrister or other person who occupies chambers in the Inner or Middle Temple" [OED].
3. Dodona*'s Shrine:* The site in ancient Epirus of a famous oracle of Zeus.

Drink Inspiration from the Steam Divine);
Poison that cures, a Vapour that affords   5
Content more solid than the Smile of Lords;
Rest to the Weary, to the Hungry, Food;
The last kind refuge of the Wise and Good.
Inspir'd by thee, dull Cits° adjust the Scale
Of *Europe*'s Peace, when other Statesmen fail;   10
By thee protected; and thy Sister Beer,
Poets rejoyce, nor think the Bayliff near:°
Nor less the Critic owns thy genial Aid
While Supperless he plies the pidling Trade.
What tho' to Love and soft Delight a Foe,   15
By Ladies hated, hated by the Beau;
Yet social Freedom long to Courts unknown,
Your Health, fair Truth and Virtue are thy Own.
Come to thy Poet, come with healing Wings,
And let me taste thee, Unexcis'd° by Kings.

RICHARD STEELE

From *The Spectator,* No. 140
["Ladies at Ombre"]

The social pleasure that occupies the most number of lines in *The Rape of the Lock* is the long, symbolic game of ombre played by Belinda and the Baron. Throughout this chapter we have had many, many references to the various popular card games. This satirical little fragment from *The Spectator* almost foreshadows Clarissa's speech to Belinda on the virtues of losing gracefully.

The following excerpt is taken from *The Spectator,* No. 140 (August 10, 1711), ed. Donald Bond, vol. 2 (Oxford: Clarendon Press, 1965), 51–55.

9. *Cits:* Citizens of London; merchants and tradesmen.
12. *Poets rejoyce, nor think the Bayliff near:* The poverty of poets — here, on the brink of arrest for debt by bailiffs — was a favorite topic of satire.
20. *Unexcis'd:* Untaxed.

No. 140
August 10, 1711

SIR,

'I this Morning cast my Eye upon your Paper concerning the Expence of Time. You are very obliging to the Women, especially those who are not young and past Gallantry, by touching so gently upon Gaming: Therefore I hope you do not think it wrong to employ a little leisure time in that Diversion; but I should be glad to hear you say something upon the Behaviour of some of the Female Gamesters.

'I have observed Ladies who in all other respects are Gentle, Good-humoured, and the very Pinks of good Breeding, who as soon as the Ombre Table is called for, and set down to their Business, are immediately Transmigrated into the veriest Wasps in Nature.

'You must know I keep my Temper and win their Mony, but am out of Countenance to take it, it makes them so very uneasie. Be pleased, dear Sir, to instruct them to lose with a better Grace, and you will oblige

Yours,
Rachel Basto.'[1]

EDMUND WALLER

"Written on a Card that Her *Majesty* tore at Omber"

Waller's little stanza, a sort of fragment on a fragment, documents the early fashion of ombre; though taken from an edition published in Pope's time, the verse was written to Charles II's queen, Catherine of Braganza. It exemplifies the same kind of social gallantry that characterizes *The Rape of the Lock:* whether the queen tore the card by accident or from temper is not clear, but in either case the trivial act is transformed into the celestial.

The text is taken from *Poems, &c. written upon several Occasions, And to several Persons. By Edmond Waller, Esq. To which is Prefix'd The Author's Life* (London: Printed for Jacob Tonson, at Shakespear's Head over-against Catherine Street in the Strand, 1712).

---

[1] *Basto:* In ombre, the ace of clubs.

The Cards you tear in value rise,
So do the Wounded by your Eyes:
Who to Celestial Things aspire,
Are by that Passion rais'd the higher.

RICHARD SEYMOUR

From *The Court Gamester*

Richard Seymour's *The Court Gamester,* a manual for playing the most popular card and board games of the period, was first published in 1718 by Edmund Curll and went through at least five editions in Pope's lifetime alone. Included in this excerpt is Seymour's preface, in which he describes the popularity of gaming throughout the fashionable world, advertises the accessibility of his explanations, and offers a brief history of ombre with the order of cards. As if endorsing the attention ombre receives in *The Rape of the Lock,* Seymour emphasizes the "gravity" of the game and the consequent necessity for complete concentration, but in a later section (not included here) he can't resist a bit of tongue-in-cheek in his rationale for the strictness of the rules against equivocation: "As wise Lawgivers only consider the Publick Good, and tho sometimes the Inocent may suffer by the Severity of an Act, yet the greatest Evil must be consider'd and prevented." He concludes his discussion of ombre by "transcribing from Mr. POPE's *Rape of the Lock,* the beautiful Description he has given, of the Manner of playing this Game, in the following excellent Lines" (III.25–99).

The text is from the second edition, London, Printed for E. Curll next the *Temple*-Coffee-House in *Fleetstreet,* 1720.

THE
COURT-GAMESTER:
OR,
FULL and EASY
INSTRUCTIONS
FOR

Playing the GAMES now in Vogue,
after the best Method, as they are
Played at Court and in the Assem-
blees; *viz.*

OMBRE, PICQUET, and
the Royal Game of CHESS.

Wherein the Frauds in Play are detected,
and the Laws of each Game annexed, to
prevent Disputes.

Written for the Use of the Young PRINCESSES.

By RICHARD SEYMOUR Esq;

The SECOND EDITION Corrected.

LONDON,

Printed for E. CURLL *next the Temple*-Coffee-House in *Fleetstreet.*
1720.

Price 13.6d. Stitch'd, 20. Bound.

TO THEIR
Royal Highnesses THE Young Princesses; THIS
TREATISE
Is most Humbly Dedicated.

The PREFACE.

Gaming is become so much the Fashion among the *Beau-Monde*, that he who in Company should appear ignorant of the Games in Vogue, would be reckoned low-bred, and hardly fit for Conversation.

Therefore I have taken the pains to compile this little Treatise, in order to teach the Three Principal Games, viz. OMBRE, PICQUET, and the Royal Game of CHESS.

I think the Method is laid down so plain and easy, that a Person of a very common Capacity may quickly learn these three Entertaining Games.

First, As to OMBRE, this Game is variously played, according to the Humours of the Company, or the Stakes they play for; therefore, that the Reader may not be ignorant of any part of it, he will find it here described in all its Branches: and we have reduced it to Chapters, or Heads, that so the Reader might not find himself puzzled, by running from Article to Article, without Method.

It may be objected perhaps, that we enlarge in some Places upon Things that have been touched on before: but it must be considered, that this Essay is wrote in favour of those who have no Notion at all of the Game; and to these, we conceive, nothing can be made too plain. Besides, the Reader will find that we never speak of a Thing a second time, but where it has not been sufficiently explained before.

As for those who have already some Notion of the Game, this easy Method will soon make them Masters of it.

They who play it well, will find the Rules here laid down so exact, and with so much Justice, as readily to decide those frequent Disputes which happen about the Laws of the Game.

There is likewise, for the Use of Learners, a Table of all such Games as may with Prudence be played.

But because the Terms may sound a little barbarous to some Ears, and lest the Ignorant should think they are Terms of Magick, we have placed them all in a separate Table, with their Explanations.

Secondly, The Game of PICQUET is taught, as it is now played in the best of Companies: the Method is so easy, that I think nothing can be added here to explain it farther.

Thirdly, The Royal Game of CHESS, which some maintain to be as old as *Troy* and that it was invented by the *Grecian* Captains, to divert their tedious Evenings, at the Siege of that Famous City: It requires Art and Stratagem, and agreeably relieves the Mind, when wearied with the Fatigue of Business. In the Practice of this Game, a

Person meets with a great many odd Events, which give the same sort of agreeable Surprize, that we are moved with at the happy Incidents in a Comedy. By the short Abridgment we have given of it, any Person that once sees the Men placed upon the Board, may learn to play; but to be excellent in it requires a sutable Genius, and good Observation.

Of the Game of OMBRE.

This Game owes its Invention to the *Spaniards*, and has in it a great deal of the Gravity peculiar to that Nation. It is called *L'Hombra*, which in *Spanish* signifies Man: It was so named, as requiring Thought and Reflection, which are Qualities peculiar to Man. To play it well, requires a great deal of Application; and let a Man be ever so expert, he will be apt to fall into Mistakes, if he thinks of any thing else, or is disturbed by the Conversation of those that look on.

ATTENTION and Quietness are absolutely necessary, in order to play well. Therefore if the Spectators are discreet, they will be satisfied with the Pleasure of seeing it play'd, without distracting the Gamesters.

WHAT I have said, is not to persuade any, who have a mind to learn it, that the Pleasure is not worth the Pains: On the contrary, it will be found the most delightful and entertaining of all Games, to those who have any thing in them, of what we call the Spirit of Play.

THERE are many ways of playing *L'Ombre*; it is sometimes play'd with *Force Spadille*, or *Espadille Forcé*; sometimes two Persons, sometimes three, sometimes four, and sometimes five: but the general way is by three. Of this kind of Play we shall treat first; the rest we shall explain in their turns.

Of the Number of Cards.

This Game is played with forty Cards: You may buy from the Card-makers Packs made up on purpose for this Game; otherwise you may take an intire Pack, which consists of fifty-two Cards, and throw out all the Eights, Nines, and Tens, of the four Suits, which make twelve, there will remain forty: this is an *Ombre* Pack.

Of the Natural Order of the Cards.

What I call the natural Order of the Cards, is, their several Degrees when they are not Trumps.

THE Term *Trump* comes from a Corruption of the Word *Triumph*; for wherever they are, they are attended with Conquest.

OF Cards there are two Colours, *Red* and *Black*; the two Black are *Spades* and *Clubs*.

THE Order of *Spades* and *Clubs* is the fame as in other Games, in a natural Descent: King, Queen, Knave, Seven, Six, Five, Four, Three, Two.

IT is to be observed, That the two black Aces are not reckoned in the natural Order of the Cards among their own Suits, because they are always Trumps; as we shall explain hereafter.

THE two red Colours are *Hearts* and *Diamonds*, which in their Order are quite contrary to the Black; but this Difference is soon understood.

THE *King*, *Queen*, and *Knave* keep their natural Ranks, but the rest are quite revers'd, for the lowest Card still wins the highest.

To comprehend this at one Cast of an Eye and to see every Card's Value, turn to this Table.

Black	Red	
King	*King*	
Queen	*Queen*	
Knave	*Knave*	
Seven	*Ace*	
Six	*Two*	
Five	*Three*	
Four	*Four*	
Three	*Five*	
Two.	*Six*	
	Seven.	

Observe, that there are ten Cards in *Red*, and but nine in *Black*, by reason, as we have said before, the black Aces, which are always Trumps, are not to be reckon'd.

Their Places

JOHN GAY

From *Trivia; or, The Art of Walking the Streets of London*

Trivia is a mock-georgic poem, based on the form of Virgil's *carmina georgica*, or songs that explained and celebrated the art of agriculture. As a mock form, like *The Rape of the Lock*, Gay's poem simultaneously employs and up-ends the classical conventions. The narrator instructs the city walker how to dress and where to walk in London, depending on the time of day and time of year; his name for his primary goddess, Trivia, though alluding to the Roman word meaning the conjunction of three roads, also connotes trivialities (and he invokes a second goddess, Cloacina, she of the sewers and sewer-filth). But also like *The Rape of the Lock*, much of the tone seems affectionate, even genuinely admiring; most Londoners were proud of their prosperous, bustling, exciting city. The selections included here glance at some of the places mentioned in Pope's poem, giving us a closer look into the streets of the city that is an implicit but powerful context for *The Rape of the Lock*.

The text is taken from the first edition (London: Printed for Bernard Lintot, 1716).

BOOK I.

Of the Implements for walking the Streets, and Signs of the Weather.

Through winter streets to steer your course aright,
How to walk clean by day, and safe by night,
How jostling crouds, with prudence to decline,

Opposite: Detail of the city of London (*Plan of the Cities of London and Westminster,* by John Rocque, 1747), showing the Royal Exchange, home of the merchants (see *Rape* III.23), and Exchange Alley, home of Garraway's coffee house.

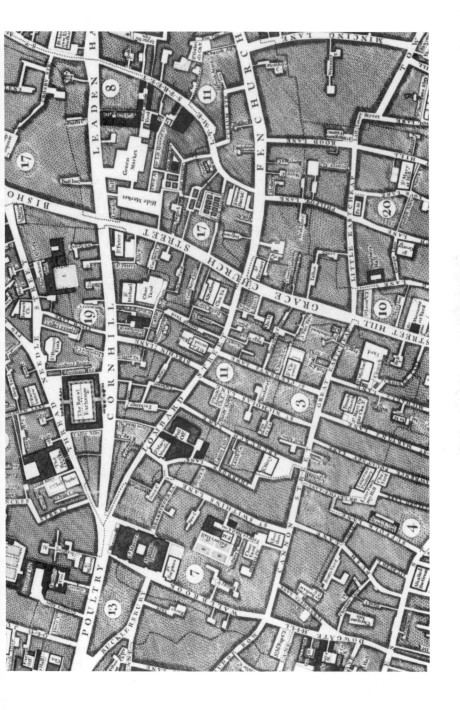

When to assert the wall, and when resign,
I sing: Thou, *Trivia*, Goddess, aid my song,   5
Thro' spacious streets conduct thy bard along;
By thee transported, I securely stray
Where winding alleys lead the doubtful way,
The silent court, and op'ning square explore,
And long perplexing lanes untrod before.   10
To pave thy realm, and smooth the broken ways,
Earth from her womb a flinty tribute pays;
For thee the sturdy pavior° thumps the ground,
Whilst ev'ry stroke his lab'ring lungs resound;
For thee the scavenger bids kennels° glide   15
Within their bounds, and heaps of dirt subside.
My youthful bosom burns with thirst of fame,
From the great theme to build a glorious name,
To tread in paths to ancient bards unknown,
And bind my temples with a Civic crown;°   20
But more, my country's love demands the lays,°
My country's be the profit, mine the praise.

· · ·

Nor do less certain signs° the town advise,
Of milder weather and serener skies.
The ladies gaily dress'd, the *Mall* adorn   145
With various dyes, and paint the sunny morn;

13. *pavior:* The street paver.
15. *kennels:* The open sewage drains that ran down the center of London streets.
20. *And bind my temples with a Civic crown:* Rather than choosing the myrtle of the lover or the bay leaves of the poet, this speaker prefers to be "crowned" with glory by the city.
21. *lays:* Verses.
143. *certain signs: Trivia* is largely a poem about how to read the "signs" of the city — in its weather, topography, and occupational hazards.

Opposite: St. James's Park, from *Plan of the Cities of London and Westminster,* by John Rocque, 1747. In *The Rape of the Lock,* this is the scene of the elegant Pall Mall, where the "Beau-monde" surveys and hails with music the ascent of the lock-turned-star (V. 133–34), and of Rosamond's Pond ("*Rosamonda's* Lake" [V. 136]), where forsaken lovers drowned themselves.

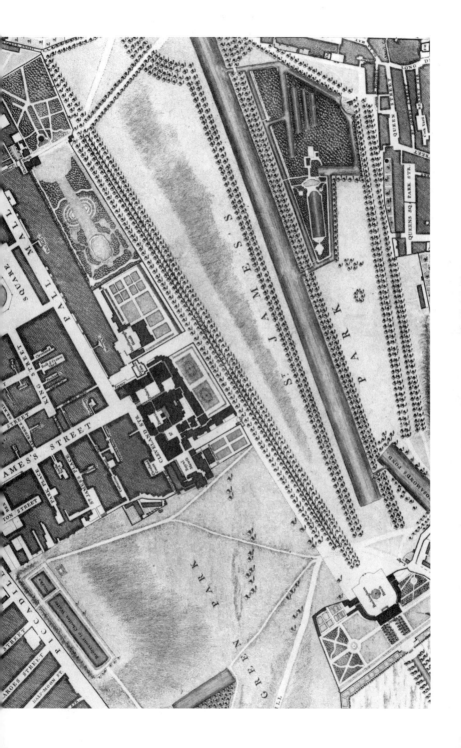

The wanton fawns with frisking pleasure range,
And chirping sparrows greet the welcome change:
   Not that their minds with greater skill are fraught,
Endu'd by instinct, or by reason taught,   150
The seasons operate on ev'ry breast;
'Tis hence that fawns are brisk, and ladies drest.
When on his box the nodding coachman snores,
And dreams of fancy'd fares; when tavern-doors
The chairmen idly croud; then ne'er refuse   155
To trust thy busie steps in thinner shoes.

. . .

BOOK II.

Of Walking the Streets by Day.

   O bear me to the paths of fair *Pell-mell,*
Safe are thy pavements, grateful is thy smell!°
At distance rolls along the gilded coach,
Nor sturdy carmen on thy walks encroach;   260
No lets would bar thy ways were chairs deny'd,°
The soft supports of laziness and pride;
Shops breathe perfumes, thro' sashes ribbons glow,
The mutual arms of ladies, and the beau.
Yet still even here, when rains the passage hide,   265
Oft the loose stone spirts up a muddy tide
Beneath thy careless foot; and from on high,
Where masons mount the ladder, fragments fly:
Mortar, and crumbled lime in show'rs descend,
And o'er thy head destructive tiles impend.°   270
   But sometimes let me leave the noisie roads,
And silent wander in the close abodes

---

   258. *grateful is thy smell!*: Given the stench of London's open sewers, spacious Pall Mall would have been a distinctive relief.
   261. *No lets would bar thy ways were chairs deny'd*: Perhaps redundant; an archaic meaning of "let" is hindrance or obstruction. The poet is suggesting that the sedan chairs and carriages get in the way of the more healthy and pleasurable form of leisure transportation: walking.
   270. *destructive tiles:* London's houses were roofed with tiles, which often blew off in storms.

Where wheels ne'er shake the ground; there pensive stray,
In studious thought, the long uncrouded way.
Here I remark each walker's diff'rent face,   275
And in their look their various bus'ness trace,
The broker here his spacious beaver wears,
Upon his brow sit jealousies and cares;
Bent on some mortgage (to avoid reproach)
He seeks bye-streets, and saves th' expensive coach.   280
Soft, at low doors, old letchers tap their cane,
For fair recluse, who travels *Drury lane*;
Here roams uncomb'd the lavish rake, to shun
His *Fleet-street* draper's everlasting dun.°

JONATHAN SWIFT

"A Description of the Morning"

Swift's vision of London is startlingly different from Gay's and Pope's.
Like *Trivia* and the *Rape*, this city poem uses familiar classical poetic
forms in order to upset or subvert a traditional, polite, or complacent
way of looking at things; in Swift, however, the upset is more shocking,
the city darker. "A Description of the Morning" first appeared in
Richard Steele's periodical *Tatler* (No. 9, April 28–30, 1709), datelined
"from Will's Coffee House." It is (very loosely speaking) an *aubade,* or a
lyric celebrating the dawn. In this case, the light spreading over the city
discovers a vast underworld of promiscuous masters, lazy servants, and
roaming prisoners shuffling to make themselves presentable. This poem
was reprinted in the 1711 *Miscellanies.*

The text is taken from *The Poems of Jonathan Swift,* ed. Harold
Williams (Oxford: Clarendon Press, 1937), vol. 1.

---

284. *His* Fleet-street *draper's everlasting dun:* The spendthrift rake tries to elude
his creditors, particularly his draper or tailor, in the side streets.

Now hardly here and there an Hackney-Coach°
Appearing, show'd the Ruddy Morns Approach.
Now *Betty* from her Masters Bed had flown,
And softly stole to discompose her own.
The Slipshod Prentice from his Masters Door,   5
Had par'd the Dirt, and Sprinkled round the Floor.°
Now *Moll* had whirl'd her Mop with dext'rous Airs,
Prepar'd to Scrub the Entry and the Stairs.
The Youth with Broomy Stumps began to trace
The Kennel-Edge, where Wheels had worn the Place.°   10
The Smallcoal-Man was heard with Cadence deep,
'Till drown'd in Shriller Notes of Chimney-Sweep,°
Duns at his Lordships Gate began to meet,
And Brickdust *Moll*° had Scream'd through half the Street.
The Turnkey now his Flock returning sees,   15
Duly let out a Nights to Steal for Fees.°
The watchful Bailiffs take their silent Stands,
And School-Boys lag with Satchels in their Hands.

ALEXANDER POPE

"A Farewell to London. In the Year 1715"

Pope circulated this playful tavern poem among his friends around the
end of May 1715, when he was preparing to leave London after a five-
month stay, during which he saw the first volume of the *Iliad* through
the press, published *The Key to the Lock*, and suffered a number of pam-

---

1. *Hackney-Coach:* A carriage for public hire.
6. *par'd the Dirt, and Sprinkled round the Floor:* Cleaned and watered the floor.
9. *The Youth . . . the Place:* The boy with the broom — the scavenger in Gay's
Trivia — is looking for old nails to sell, according to George Faulkner, the Dublin
bookseller and printer who published the first standard edition of Swift's works in
1735 (*Poems* 1: 124n).
11–12. *Smallcoal-Man . . . Chimney-Sweep:* Both tradesmen advertise their ser-
vices in traditional "London Cries," phrases sung or chanted.
14. *Brickdust* Moll: Powdered brick was sold for scouring purposes.
15–16. *The Turnkey . . . Fees:* Jailers extorted payment from prisoners for priv-
ileges — here a night furlough — and for basic subsistence.

phlet and newspaper attacks. He would return to Binfield to continue work on his translation of Homer. The poem reflects a typical personal and cultural ambivalence about that "damn'd, distracting Town," whisking through its irritations, its temptations, its pleasures. One of the main pleasures of this visit for Pope was meeting Richard Boyle, third Earl of Burlington, in 1714 or 1715 (line 47), who became one of his dearest friends and who apparently had a wonderful chef.

The poem is actually only attributed to Pope, for Pope never acknowledged it (there is a reference to the poem in a letter of Jervas to Pope); very few copies circulated, and it was not published until 1775. The text is taken from the Twickenham edition, which follows the first printing in 1775.

Dear, damn'd, distracting Town, farewell!
  Thy Fools no more I'll teize:

Pope's villa at Twickenham. The success of Pope's *Iliad* brought him lasting prosperity and enabled him to build this villa on the river Thames. He loved his modest Georgian house, carefully planning its gardens and grotto and reveling in its contrasts to the "damn'd, distracting Town." The illustration is taken from a 1747 engraving in *The Newcastle General Magazine*.

This Year in Peace, ye Critics, dwell,
   Ye Harlots, sleep at Ease!

Soft *B*— and rough *C*—*s*, adieu!   5
   Earl *Warwick* make your Moan,
The lively *H*——*k*° and you
   May knock up Whores alone.

To drink and droll be *Rowe* allow'd
   Till the third watchman toll;   10
Let *Jervase* gratis paint, and *Frowd*°
   Save Three-pence, and his Soul.

Farewell *Arbuthnot*'s Raillery
   On every learned Sot;
And *Garth*,° the best good Christian he,   15
   Altho' he knows it not.

Lintot, farewell! thy Bard must go;
   Farewell, unhappy *Tonson*!
Heaven gives thee for thy Loss of *Rowe*,
   Lean *Philips*, and fat *Johnson*.°   20

Why should I stay? Both Parties rage;
   My vixen Mistress squalls;
The Wits in envious Feuds engage;
   And *Homer* (damn him!) calls.

The Love of Arts lies cold and dead   25
   In *Hallifax's* Urn;°

5–7. *Soft B*— . . . *lively H*——*k*: Some of these identities are uncertain; *B*— is likely Hugh Bethel (1689–1747), member of Parliament and country gentleman, a close friend of Pope and Burlington; *C*—*s* is probably James Cragg (1687–1721), a politician implicated in the South Sea Bubble scandal; *Warwick* was Addison's son-in-law; *H*——*k* is Edward Richard, Viscount Hinchinbroke.

9–11. *Rowe* . . . *Frowd*: Nicholas Rowe (1674–1718), the dramatist, known for his wit and good humor; Charles Jervas, Pope's painter and friend (See Jervas's portrait of Pope, p. 88 and also his portrait of Martha and Teresa Blount, p. 294.); Philip Frowde (d. 1738), poet and friend of Swift, son of an improvident father.

13–15. *Arbuthnot's* . . . *Garth*: John Arbuthnot (1667–1735) and Sir Samuel Garth (1661–1732), both physicians, writers, and close friends of Pope and Swift.

17–20. *Lintot* . . . *Johnson*: Bernard Lintot (1675–1736), Pope's bookseller who was publishing the *Iliad*; Jacob Tonson (1656–1737), the major bookseller of his age; Nicholas Rowe; Ambrose Philips (1674–1749) ("Namby Pamby"); Charles Johnson (1679–1748), a corpulent dramatist.

26. *Hallifax's Urn*: Refers to Charles Montagu, Earl of Halifax (1661–1715), politician, poet, patron.

And not one Muse of all he fed,
 Has yet the Grace to mourn.

My Friends, by Turns, my Friends confound,
 Betray, and are betray'd: 30
Poor *Y—r*'s sold for Fifty Pound,
 And *B——ll°* is a Jade.

Why make I Friendships with the Great,
 When I no Favour seek?
Or follow Girls Seven Hours in Eight? —   35
 I need but once a Week.

Still idle, with a busy Air,
 Deep Whimsies to contrive;
The gayest Valetudinaire,°
 Most thinking Rake alive.   40

Solicitous for others Ends,
 Tho' fond of dear Repose;
Careless or drowsy with my Friends,
 And frolick with my Foes.

Laborious Lobster-nights, farewell!   45
 For sober, studious Days;
And *Burlington*'s delicious Meal,
 For Sallads, Tarts, and Pease!

Adieu to all but *Gay* alone,
 Whose Soul, sincere and free,   50
Loves all Mankind, but flatters none,
 And so may starve with me.

31–32. Y—r's . . . B——ll: Elizabeth Younger (1699?–1762), actress, friend, and
sister to M. Bicknell (1695?–1723), actress; both performed in Pope's and Gay's plays.
 39. *Valetudinaire:* An invalid or hypochondriac.

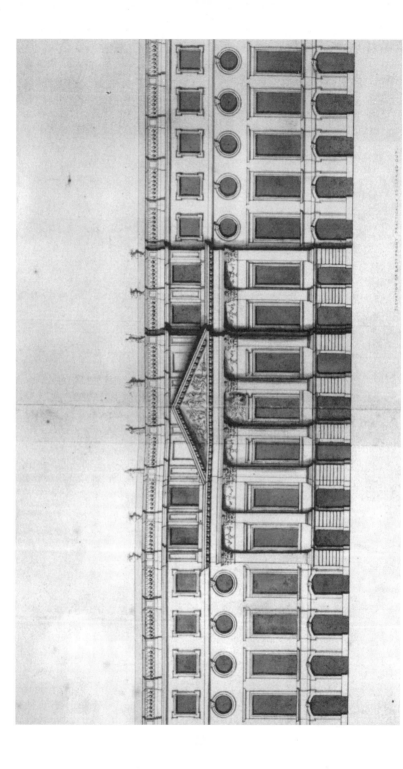

ALEXANDER POPE

"Epistle to Miss Blount, on her leaving the Town, after the Coronation"

This poem was originally addressed to Teresa Blount, the lively, lovely, impatient sister to Martha. Teresa had attended the coronation of George I, and Pope here imagines — perhaps exaggerates — the utter rural boredom dreaded by a young, attractive woman fresh from the glamour of London life.

The poem was written in 1714 and first published in the 1717 *Works*; Pope revised the poem in 1735 and 1739 and the Twickenham edition, from which this text is taken, includes those revisions.

As some fond virgin, whom her mother's care
Drags from the town to wholsom country air,
Just when she learns to roll a melting eye,
And hear a spark, yet think no danger nigh;
From the dear man unwilling she must sever,   5
Yet takes one kiss before she parts for ever:
Thus from the world fair *Zephalinda*° flew,
Saw others happy, and with sighs withdrew;
Not that their pleasures caus'd her discontent,
She sigh'd not that They stay'd, but that She went.   10
   She went, to plain-work,° and to purling brooks,

---

7. Zephalinda: Teresa's "pen name" in her correspondence with a Mr. H. More.
11. *plain-work:* Ordinary sewing, as opposed to embroidery or needlepoint.

Opposite: The East Front of the Wren palace at Hampton Court (detail) by Sir Christopher Wren, c. 1689–1702. The site of the "mighty Contests" in *The Rape of the Lock*, Hampton Court is situated several miles upstream from London. In 1689 William III commissioned Wren to reshape the old Tudor structure along the lines of Versailles. Work on the new palace stalled after William's death, but under Anne the palace was completed. This illustration shows a detail of Wren's elevation of the Park Front (the East Front facing the Great Fountain Garden) very much as it was carried out. The Park Front was intended to be the main part of the new palace and was thus lavishly decorated, its central area faced with stone, carved and ornamented.

Old-fashion'd halls, dull aunts, and croaking rooks,
She went from Op'ra, park, assembly, play,
To morning walks, and pray'rs three hours a day;
To pass her time 'twixt reading and Bohea,°   15
To muse, and spill her solitary Tea,
Or o'er cold coffee trifle with the spoon,
Count the slow clock, and dine exact at noon;
Divert her eyes with pictures in the fire,
Hum half a tune, tell stories to the squire;   20
Up to her godly garret after sev'n,
There starve and pray, for that's the way to heav'n.
    Some Squire, perhaps, you take a delight to rack;°
Whose game is Whisk,° whose treat a toast in sack,°
Who visits with a gun, presents you birds,   25
Then gives a smacking buss,° and cries — No words!
Or with his hound comes hollowing° from the stable,
Makes love with nods, and knees beneath a table;
Whose laughs are hearty, tho' his jests are coarse,
And loves you best of all things — but his horse.   30
    In some fair evening, on your elbow laid,
You dream of triumphs in the rural shade;
In pensive thought recall the fancy'd scene,
See Coronations rise on ev'ry green;
Before you pass th' imaginary sights   35
Of Lords, and Earls, and Dukes, and garter'd Knights;
While the spread Fan o'ershades your closing eyes;
Then give one flirt, and all the vision flies.
Thus vanish sceptres, coronets, and balls,
And leave you in lone woods, or empty walls.   40
    So when your slave, at some dear, idle time,
(Not plagu'd with headachs, or the want of rhime)
Stands in the streets, abstracted from the crew,
And while he seems to study, thinks of you:

15. *Bohea:* Tea.
23. *rack:* To torture or tease.
24. *Whisk:* Whist. *toast in sack:* Toast soaked in a rich white wine.
26. *buss:* A kiss.
27. *hollowing:* Shouting; bellowing hunting calls.

Just when his fancy points your sprightly eyes,   45
Or sees the blush of soft *Parthenia*° rise,
Gay pats my shoulder, and you vanish quite;
Streets, chairs,° and coxcombs rush upon my sight;
Vext to be still in town, I knit my brow,
Look sow'r, and hum a tune — as you may now.   50

46. Parthenia: A name for Martha Blount.
48. *chairs:* Sedan chairs.

The Apotheosis of Queene Anne, ceiling painting for the Queen's Drawing Room at Hampton Court by Antonio Verrio, 1702. Verrio's painting represents the queen as Justice, holding the scales in her left hand and the sword in her right, with a cornucopia of wealth at her side. On ascending to the throne, new monarchs were frequently apotheosized — represented as deities or as somehow otherworldly, when hopes for prosperous change still ran high — "Great *Anna*! whom three Realms obey" (Rape III.7).

3

The Political World

MERCHANTS AND JUDGES

The merchants and judges of London appear very briefly but very powerfully in *The Rape of the Lock*, poetically connecting death and cosmetics, hinting at how the demands and desires of the moment often negligently shape the future:

> The hungry Judges soon the Sentence sign,
> And Wretches hang that Jury-Men may Dine;
> The Merchant from th' *Exchange* returns in Peace,
> And the long Labours of the *Toilette* cease — (*Rape* III.21–24)

The mercantile City and the fashionable Town (shown toward the center and to the west in John Rocque's *Plan of the Cities of London and Westminster*) are linked socially as well as syntactically in these lines — the couplets pair the overworld and underworld, the merchant and the lady.

Along with the growing building boom in London, the bounding economic prosperity proved a source of cultural anxiety as well as of national pride. "Th' *Exchange*," or the Royal Exchange, was the architectural and symbolic seat of the new world of commerce, the center of wheeling and dealing among traders, merchants, shopkeepers, and con-artists. The ground plan from Maitland's *The History and Survey of London* (1760) shows the building organized around national and commercial interests: the Norway Walk, the Italian Walk, the Barbadoes Walk; the Clothiers Walk, the Grocers & Druggists Walk, the Brokers Walk. The excerpts from Defoe's *Tour* and *The Spectator* celebrate the beauty as well as the power of the Exchange, Defoe insisting it is "the greatest and finest of the Kind in the World," and the Spectator stoking his national pride in watching "so rich an Assembly of Country-men and Foreigners consulting together upon the private Business of Mankind, and making this Metropolis a kind of *Emporium*, for the whole Earth." Jonathan Swift in *The Examiner*, on the other hand, despises the blatant overemphasis on trade, which gives the nation "the Spirit of *Shop-keepers*."

New prosperities can mean new temptations for the criminally inclined, citizen and judge alike. The Baron himself, caught by the dazzling imperialized splendor of Belinda's self-creation, is tempted to steal her treasures. Power and prosperity ought to create a new sense of social obligation; too often they create new and easier ways to escape responsibility. Both Defoe and Ned Ward point out "the knaves of lesser magnitude" who haunt the alleys of commerce, Ward articulating and satirizing a number of the English xenophobic stereotypes about various trading nations. Hogarth's "The Bench" depicts a snoring judiciary and Defoe's *Review* chastises judiciary vices, while Henry Fielding and Jonathan Swift look with concern at the growing glamorization of a criminal death.

TRADE AND EMPIRE

I have suggested in the introduction to this edition that the game of ombre in *The Rape of the Lock* reflects the larger economic war that England is playing with the world, with "The *Club*'s black Tyrant" as Belinda's victim — as the figure of a black, "barbarian" prince of Africa or the Indies, he symbolizes the source *and* becomes the casualty of her dressing table spoils, of Britain's imperial expansion. Several documents included here capture the sometimes anxious, sometimes ambivalent, and often self-assured attitudes toward trade and empire permeating *The Rape of the Lock* and eighteenth-century England. Verrio's monumental painting of Queen Anne as Justice shows a rather typically exaggerated representation of a monarch's symbolic abilities. The illustration of the East India House, rebuilt in Pope's lifetime, features one of the most important economic buildings in London — the site of the East India Company, cornerstone of British trade in the East Indies and British rule in India. The first of Defoe's two *Review* essays shows on the one hand what many considered to be the great benefits of domestic and international trade — the economic as well as social profits accrued by *both* sides — and on the other suggests the dangers of unregulated trade and an unself-disciplined economy. The second addresses the target issue of the War of the Spanish Succession that preoccupied both Whigs and Tories in the debate about how to balance the political power of Europe and divide the spoils of victory. Pope's quick couplet "The Balance of Europe" is a neat little epigram on political, economic, and poetic balance that ties into the excerpt from *Windsor-Forest* in looking at the effects of conquest. Richard Steele's essay in *The Spectator* addresses the visual profits that spill into the shops of this "trading nation," as Defoe calls England, and includes an advertisement for maps and globes: increasingly popular consumer items in England, they offered visual representations of local, global, and universal habitations. The final documents give a glimpse of English versions of the "shining Sphere" where "midst the Stars" the poet's Muse "inscribe[s] *Belinda*'s Name!"

Merchants and Judges

DANIEL DEFOE

From *A Tour thro' the Whole Island of Great Britain* [On the Exchange]

In his *Tour* of London, Defoe enthusiastically details the various architectural and economic aspects of the flourishing state of British trade. This excerpt looks at the sites of importation and exchange — the sources of Belinda's toiletries and of Britain's growing imperialism: the Royal Exchange, the center of trade in the city; the East India House, site of the East India Company, incorporated in 1600 when Elizabeth I granted a charter to merchants trading with the East Indies and empowered it as the agent of the British government in India until 1858; the Bank of England, established in 1694; the Excise Office, which kept precise track of domestic taxes; the South-Sea House, home of the notorious South Sea Company (incorporated in 1711), which in 1719 promoted a highly speculative stock scheme that ended in the bursting of the South Sea Bubble in 1720–1722 (and in which Pope may have lost some of his earnings from the *Iliad* [Mack 388]); the Post Office, crucial to the smooth, swift running of trade; the Custom House, where ships would dock at the quay and pay customs on their goods; and the quays and wharves themselves, sites of import and export, "an Ornament to the City" and "a Testimony of the vast Trade carried on in it."

The text is taken from *A Tour thro' the Whole Island of Great Britain*, vol. 1, ed. G. D. H. Cole (London: Peter Davies, 1927), based on the first edition (1724).

The *Royal Exchange*, the greatest and finest of the Kind in the World, is the next publick Work of the Citizens, the Beauty of which answers for itself, and needs no Description here; 'tis observable, that tho' this *Exchange* cost the Citizens an immense Sum of Money rebuilding, some Authors say, Eighty Thousand Pounds, being finished and embellished in so exquisite a Manner, yet it was so appropriated to the grand Affair of Business, that the Rent or Income of it for many Years, fully answered the Interest of the Money laid out in Building it: Whether it does so still or not, I will not say, the Trade for Millenary Goods, Fine Laces, &c. which was so great above Stairs for many Years, being since scattered and removed, and the Shops, many of them, left empty; but those Shops, of which there were Eight double Rows above, and the Shops and Offices round it below, with the Vaults under the whole, did at first, yield a very great Sum.

. . .

The *East-India House*[1] is in *Leadenhall-Street*, an old, but spacious Building; very convenient, though not beautiful, and I am told, it is under Consultation to have it taken down, and rebuilt with addi-

---

[1] East-India House: Headquarters of the East India Company. The original building that Defoe describes, the mansion house of Sir William Craven, Lord Mayor of London in 1610, was rebuilt in 1726.

tional Buildings for Warehouses and Cellars for their Goods, which at present are much wanted.

The *African Company*'s House is in the same Street, a very handsome, well-built, and convenient House, and which fully serves for all the Offices their Business requires.

The *Bank* is kept in *Grocer's Hall,*[2] a very convenient Place, and, considering its Situation, so near the *Exchange*, a very spacious, commodious Place.

Here Business is dispatch'd with such Exactness, and such Expedition and so much of it too, that it is really prodigious; no Confusion, nobody is either denied or delayed Payment, the Merchants who keep their Cash there, are sure to have their Bills always paid, and even Advances made on easy Terms, if they have Occasion. No Accounts in the World are more exactly kept, no Place in the World has so much Business done, with so much Ease.

In the next Street (the *Old Jury*) is the *Excise Office*, in a very large House, formerly the Dwelling of Sir *John Fredrick,* and afterwards, of Sir *Joseph Hern,* very considerable Merchants. In this one Office is managed an immense Weight of Business, and they have in Pay, as I am told, near Four thousand Officers: The whole Kingdom is divided by them into proper Districts, and to every District, a Collector, a Supervisor, and a certain Number of Gaugers, called, by the vulgar Title Excise Men.

Nothing can be more regular, than the Methods of this Office, by which an Account of the whole Excise is transmitted from the remotest Parts of the Kingdom, once every Six Weeks, which is called a Sitting, and the Money received, or Prosecutions commenced for it, in the next Sitting.

Under the Management of this Office, are now brought, not only the Excise upon Beer, Ale, and other Liquors, as formerly, but also the Duties on Malt and Candles, Hops, Soap, and Leather, all which are managed in several and distinct Classes, and the Accounts kept in distinct Books; but, in many Places, are collected by the same Officers, which makes the Charge of the Collection much easier to the Government: Nor is the like Duty collected in any Part of the World, with so little Charge, or so few Officers.

---

[2] *The* Bank *is kept in* Grocer's Hall: From 1690 to 1734 the Bank of England, established in 1694, was housed in Grocer's Hall in Princes Street, first built in 1428, rebuilt in 1668/69, and enlarged to become the Lord Mayor's house in 1682.

Detail from "A New Plan of the City of London and Westminster," pub-
lished in John Stryne's updated 1720 edition of John Stow's 1598 *A Survey
of London*. This overview of the city conveys a sense of the topographical
contrasts between the irregular, densely webbed City, source of trade and
commerce, and the more open, ordered, baroque spaces of the Town and
Court to the west.

The *South-Sea House*[3] is situate in a large Spot of Ground, between *Broad-Street* and *Threadneedle-Street*, Two large Houses having been taken in, to form the whole Office; but, as they were, notwithstanding, straighten'd for Room, and were obliged to summon their General Courts in another Place, *viz.* At *Merchant-Taylors*

[3] South-Sea House: Home of the South Sea Company and another bustling meeting place of merchants.

Hall; so they have now resolved to erect a new and compleat Building for the whole Business, which is to be exceeding fine and large, and to this End, the Company has purchased several adjacent Buildings, so that the Ground is inlarged towards *Threadneedle-Street*; but, it seems, they could not be accommodated to their Minds on the Side next *Broad-Street*, so we are told, they will not open a Way that Way, as before.

As the Company are enlarging their Trade to *America*, and have also engaged in a new Trade, namely, That of the *Greenland* Whale Fishing, they are like to have an Occasion to enlarge their Offices. This Building, they assure us, will cost the Company from Ten to Twenty thousand Pounds, that is to say, a very great Sum.

The *Post Office*, a Branch of the Revenue formerly not much valued, but now, by the additional Penny upon the Letters, and by the visible Increase of Business in the Nation, is grown very considerable. This Office maintains now, Pacquet Boats to *Spain* and *Portugal*, which never was done before: So the Merchants Letters for *Cadiz* or *Lisbonne*, which were before Two and Twenty Days in going over *France* and *Spain* to *Lisbonne*, oftentimes arrive there now, in Nine or Ten Days from *Falmouth*.

Likewise, they have a Pacquet from *Marseilles* to *Port Mahone*, in the *Mediterranean*, for the constant Communication of Letters with his Majesty's Garrison and People in the Island of *Minorca*.

They have also a Pacquet from *England* to the *West-Indies*; but I am not of Opinion, that they will keep it up for much Time longer, if it be not already let fall.

This Office is kept in *Lombard-Street*, in a large House, formerly Sir *Robert Viner*'s, once a rich Goldsmith; but ruined at the shutting up of the *Exchequer*, as above.

The *Penny Post*, a modern Contrivance of a private Person, one Mr. *William Dockraw*,[4] is now made a Branch of the general Revenue by the *Post Office*; and though, for a Time, it was subject to Miscarriages and Mistakes, yet now it is come also into so exquisite a Management, that nothing can be more exact, and 'tis with the utmost Safety and Dispatch, that Letters are delivered at the remotest Corners of the Town, almost as soon as they could be sent by a Messenger, and that from Four, Five, Six, to Eight Times a Day, ac-

---

[4] *Mr* William Dockraw: Also Dockwra or Dockwray (d. 1716), merchant, projector, and controller of the penny post from 1697 to 1700; Dockwray was dismissed for mismanagement.

cording as the Distance of the Place makes it practicable; and you may send a Letter from *Ratcliff* or *Limehouse* in the *East,* to the farthest Part of *Westminster* for a Penny, and that several Times in the same Day.

Nor are you tied up to a single Piece of Paper, as in the *General Post-Office,* but any Packet under a Pound weight, goes at the same Price.

I mention this the more particularly, because it is so manifest a Testimony to the Greatness of this City, and to the great Extent of Business and Commerce in it, that this Penny Conveyance should raise so many Thousand Pounds in a Year, and employ so many poor People in the Diligence of it, as this Office employs.

We see nothing of this at *Paris,* at *Amsterdam,* at *Hamburgh,* or any other City, that ever I have seen, or heard of.

The *Custom House*[5] I have just mentioned before, but must take up a few Lines to mention it again. The Stateliness of the Building, shewed the Greatness of the Business that is transacted there: The *Long Room* is like an *Exchange* every Morning, and the Croud of People who appear there, and the Business they do, is not to be explained by Words, nothing of that Kind in *Europe* is like it.

Yet it has been found, that the Business of Export and Import in this Port of *London,* is so prodigiously increased, and the several new Offices, which they are bound to erect for the managing the additional Parts of the Customs, are such, that the old Building, though very spacious, is too little, and as the late Fire burnt or demolish'd some Part of the *West* End of the *Custom House,* they have had the Opportunity in rebuilding, to enlarge it very much, buying in the Ground of some of the demolished Houses, to add to the *Custom House,* which will be now a most glorious Building.

The Keys, or Wharfs, next the River, fronting not the *Custom House* only, but the whole Space from the *Tower* Stairs, or Dock, to the Bridge, ought to be taken Notice of as a publick Building; nor are they less an Ornament to the City, as they are a Testimony of the vast Trade carried on in it, than the *Royal Exchange* itself.

The Revenue, or Income, brought in by these Wharfs, inclusive of the Warehouses belonging to them, and the Lighters they employ,

---

[5] *The* Custom House: In Lower Thames Street. First built in 1275, it was rebuilt after the Fire by Sir Christopher Wren between 1669 and 1671, with two stories and wings running back to Thames Street; rebuilt again by Thomas Ripley from 1717 to 1725 after a store of gunpowder nearby exploded.

is said to amount to a prodigious Sum; and, as I am told, seldom so little as Forty thousand Pounds *per Annum:* And abundance of Porters, Watchmen, Wharfingers, and other Officers, are maintained here by the Business of the Wharfs; in which, one Thing is very remarkable, That here are Porters, and poor working Men, who, though themselves not worth, perhaps, Twenty Pounds in the World, are trusted with great Quantities of valuable Goods, sometimes to the Value of several Thousand Pounds, and yet 'tis very rarely to be heard, that any Loss or Embezzlement is made. The Number of these Keys extending, as above, from the Bridge to the *Tower Dock*, is Seventeen.

[JOSEPH ADDISON]

From *The Spectator*, No. 69
[The Royal Exchange; "This Grand Scene of Business"]

Mr. Spectator loves the Royal Exchange; in his usual invisible, shape-changing style he roams the walks and courtyard, mingling with merchants and speculating on the relationships of power and profit among the nations represented. Note how public and private concerns intersect here ("the private Business of Mankind" in this emporium for the world), as they do throughout *The Rape of the Lock* (as in the items on Belinda's dressing table, the strategies of ombre, and the ceremony of coffee). Note too the articulation of nationalism: Mr. Spectator's English pride shifts him from a contemplation of the profitable interdependence of a trading world and the relative barrenness of an isolated England to a prospect of the world at England's feet: "the Vineyards of *France* our Gardens; the Spice-Islands our Hot-Beds; the *Persians* our Silk-Weavers, and the *Chinese* our Potters."

No. 69
Saturday, May 19, 1711

> Hic segetes, illic veniunt felicius uvæ:
> Arborei fœtus alibi, atque injussa virescunt
> Gramina. Nonne vides, croceos ut Tmolus odores,
> India mittit ebur, molles sua thura Sabæi?
> At Chalybes nudi ferrum, virosaque Pontus

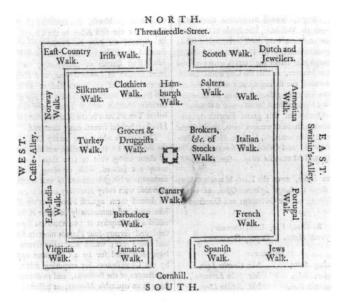

Plan of the Royal Exchange. "For the more easy expediting their Affairs, the Merchants dealing in the same Commodities have, by Custom, fixed on these different Parts of the *Exchange* to meet one another, called their Walks, which may be seen at one View by the following Sketch or Plan" (Maitland 2:901). As the plan shows, the "walks" were arranged not only by trade but also by country. The illustration is taken from William Maitland, *The History and Survey of London*, 3rd ed. (1760).

> Castorea, Eliadum palmas Epirus equarum?
> Continuo has leges æternaque fœdera certis
> Imposuit Natura locis . . .[1]

> — Vir.

---

[1] *Hic segetes . . . locis:* The motto is from Virgil (*Georgics* 1.54–61), translated by Dryden:

> This Ground with *Bacchus*, that with *Ceres* suits:
> That other loads the Trees with happy Fruits
> A fourth with Grass, unbidden, decks the Ground:
> Thus *Tmolus* is with yellow Saffron crown'd:
> *India,* black Ebon and white Ivory bears:
> And soft *Idume* weeps her od'rous Tears.
> Thus *Pontus* sends her Beaver Stones from far;
> And naked *Spanyards* temper Steel for War.

There is no Place in the Town which I so much love to frequent as the *Royal-Exchange*. It gives me a secret Satisfaction, and, in some measure, gratifies my Vanity, as I am an *Englishman*, to see so rich an Assembly of Country-men and Foreigners consulting together upon the private Business of Mankind, and making this Metropolis a kind of *Emporium* for the whole Earth. I must confess I look upon High-Change[2] to be a great Council, in which all considerable Nations have their Representatives. Factors in the Trading World are what Ambassadors are in the Politick World; they negotiate Affairs, conclude Treaties, and maintain a good Correspondence between those wealthy Societies of Men that are divided from one another by Seas and Oceans, or live on the different Extremities of a Continent. I have often been pleased to hear Disputes adjusted between an Inhabitant of *Japan* and an Alderman of *London*, or to see a Subject of the *Great Mogul* entering into a League with one of the *Czar* of *Muscovy*. I am infinitely delighted in mixing with these several Ministers of Commerce, as they are distinguished by their different Walks and different Languages: Sometimes I am justled among a Body of *Armenians*: Sometimes I am lost in a Crowd of *Jews*, and sometimes make one in a Groupe of *Dutch-men*. I am a *Dane*, *Swede*, or *French-Man* at different times, or rather fancy my self like the old Philosopher,[3] who upon being asked what Country-man he was, replied, That he was a Citizen of the World.

Though I very frequently visit this busie Multitude of People, I am known to no Body there but my Friend, Sir ANDREW,[4] who often smiles upon me as he sees me bustling in the Croud, but at the same time connives at my Presence without taking any further notice of me. There is indeed a Merchant of *Egypt*, who just knows me by sight, having formerly remitted me some Mony to *Grand Cairo*; but

---

       Epirus for th' *Elean* Chariot breeds,
       (In hopes of Palms,) a Race of running Steeds.
       This is the Orig'nal Contract; these the Laws
       Impos'd by Nature, and by Nature's Cause,
          On sundry Places.

[2] *High-Change:* The time of greatest activity at the Exchange.

[3] *the old Philosopher:* Either Diogenes the Cynic, according to Diogenes Laertius, or Socrates, according to Cicero (Bond 1: 294n).

[4] *Sir ANDREW:* Sir Andrew Freeport, a regular *Spectator* character, "a Merchant of great Eminence in the city of *London*" (*Spectator* 2, March 2, 1711).

as I am not versed in the Modern *Coptick*,[5] our Conferences go no further than a Bow and a Grimace.[6]

This grand Scene of Business gives me an infinite Variety of solid and substantial Entertainments. As I am a great Lover of Mankind, my Heart naturally overflows with Pleasure at the sight of a prosperous and happy Multitude, insomuch that at many publick Solemnities I cannot forbear expressing my Joy with Tears that have stolen down my Cheeks. For this reason I am wonderfully delighted to see such a Body of Men thriving in their own private Fortunes, and at the same time promoting the Publick Stock; or in other Words, raising Estates for their own Families, by bringing into their Country whatever is wanting, and carrying out of it whatever is superfluous.

Nature seems to have taken a particular Care to disseminate her Blessings among the different Regions of the World, with an Eye to this mutual Intercourse and Traffick among Mankind, that the Natives of the several Parts of the Globe might have a kind of Dependance upon one another, and be united together by their common Interest. Almost every *Degree* produces something peculiar to it. The Food often grows in one Country, and the Sauce in another. The Fruits of *Portugal* are corrected by the Products of *Barbadoes*: The Infusion of a *China* Plant sweetned with the Pith of an *Indian* Cane: The *Philippick* Islands give a Flavour to our *European* Bowls. The single Dress of a Woman of Quality is often the Product of an hundred Climates. The Muff and the Fan come together from the different Ends of the Earth. The Scarf is sent from the Torrid Zone, and the Tippet[7] from beneath the Pole. The Brocade Petticoat rises out of the Mines of *Peru*, and the Diamond Necklace out of the Bowels of *Indostan*.

If we consider our own Country in its natural Prospect, without any of the Benefits and Advantages of Commerce, what a barren uncomfortable Spot of Earth falls to our Share! Natural Historians tell us, that no Fruit grows originally among us, besides Hips and Haws, Acorns and Pig-Nutts, with other Delicacies of the like Nature; That our Climate of it self, and without the Assistances of Art, can make

---

[5] *the Modern* Coptick: The language of the Copts, or Egyptian Christians.

[6] *Grimace:* "'Grimace, in our author's times meant, simply, such a turn of the countenance as expressed acquaintance, or civility: but, because this air of complaisance was assumed, or was taken by our surly countrymen, to be assumed, without meaning, the word came to be used (as it is now) in an ill sense, for any *affected distortion of features*' (Hurd)" [Bond].

[7] *Tippet:* A shoulder-cape or muffler.

no further Advances towards a Plumb than to a Sloe,[8] and carries an Apple to no greater a Perfection than a Crab.[9] That our Melons, our Peaches, our Figs, our Apricots, and Cherries, are Strangers among us, imported in different Ages, and naturalized in our *English* Gardens; and that they would all degenerate and fall away into the trash of our own Country, if they were wholly neglected by the Planter, and left to the Mercy of our Sun and Soil. Nor has Traffick more enriched our Vegetable World, than it has improved the whole Face of Nature among us. Our Ships are laden with the Harvest of every Climate: Our Tables are stored with Spices, and Oils, and Wines: Our Rooms are filled with Pyramids of *China*, and adorned with the Workmanship of *Japan*: Our Morning's-Draught comes to us from the remotest Corners of the Earth: We repair our Bodies by the Drugs of *America*, and repose our selves under *Indian* Canopies. My Friend Sir ANDREW calls the Vineyards of *France*, our Gardens; the Spice-Islands our Hot-Beds; the *Persians* our Silk-Weavers, and the *Chinese* our Potters. Nature indeed furnishes us with the bare Necessaries of Life, but Traffick gives us a great Variety of what is Useful, and at the same time supplies us with every thing that is Convenient and Ornamental. Nor is it the least part of this our Happiness, that whilst we enjoy the remotest Products of the North and South, we are free from those Extremities of Weather which give them Birth; That our Eyes are refreshed with the green Fields of *Britain*, at the same time that our Palates are feasted with Fruits that rise between the Tropicks.

For these Reasons there are not more useful Members in a Commonwealth than Merchants. They knit Mankind together in a mutual Intercourse of good Offices, distribute the Gifts of Nature, find Work for the Poor, add Wealth to the Rich, and Magnificence to the Great. Our *English* Merchant converts the Tin of his own Country into Gold, and exchanges his Wooll for Rubies. The *Mahometans* are cloathed in our *British* Manufacture, and the Inhabitants of the Frozen Zone warmed with the Fleeces of our Sheep.

When I have been upon the 'Change, I have often fancied one of our old Kings standing in Person, where he is represented in Effigy,[10] and looking down upon the wealthy Concourse of People with which

---

[8] *Sloe:* A small plum.

[9] *Crab:* A crabapple.

[10] *Kings . . . in Effigy:* Statues of English monarchs were displayed in the courtyard niches of the Royal Exchange; a statue of Charles II by Grinling Gibbons stood in the center.

that Place is every Day filled. In this Case, how would he be surprized to hear all the Languages of *Europe* spoken in this little Spot of his former Dominions, and to see so many private Men, who in his Time would have been the Vassals of some powerful Baron, Negotiating like Princes for greater Sums of Mony than were formerly to be met with in the Royal Treasury! Trade, without enlarging the *British* Territories, has given us a kind of additional Empire: It has multiplied the Number of the Rich, made our Landed Estates infinitely more Valuable than they were formerly, and added to them an Accession of other Estates as Valuable as the Lands themselves.

EDWARD WARD

From *The London Spy*, No. 3
[A Different Exchange]

Ned Ward (1667–1731) was a so-called hack writer, one of Pope's dunces, famous (or infamous) for his ribald satiric sketches of London life and foreign travel. *The London Spy* was a series of eighteen essays published in 1698–1700, narrated by a country visitor to London who meets up with a city acquaintance. Together they roam the streets, wander into the public edifices, poke into the corners, and slither into the holes of London, uncovering all sorts of unpleasantness as they go, apparently with rich enjoyment. This excerpt shows a different side to the Royal Exchange — or rather, the Spies have a different perspective on it, seeing vice and hypocrisy in everyone they meet, and voicing disgust through hostile national stereotypes (that include the varieties of British).

The text is taken from *The London Spy*, ed. Paul Hyland, from the 4th edition of 1709 (East Lansing: Colleagues Press, 1993).

No. 3
1698

We then proceeded and went on to the 'Change, turned to the right, and jostled in amongst a parcel of swarthy buggerantoes[1] (preternatural fornicators, as my friend called them) who would ogle a handsome young man with as much lust as a true-bred English

---

[1] *buggerantoes:* Those who commit buggery (bestial or homosexual intercourse).

whore-master would gaze upon a beautiful virgin. Advertisements hung as thick round the pillars of each walk as bells about the legs of a morris dancer,[2] and an incessant buzz, like the murmurs of the distant ocean, stood as a diapason to our talk, like a drone to a bagpipe. The wainscot was adorned with quacks' bills, instead of pictures; never an empiric[3] in the town but had his name in a lacquered frame, containing a fair invitation for a fool and his money to be soon parted. Thus he that wants physic for a clap, or a wet-nurse for a child, may be furnished here at a minute's warning.

After we had squeezed ourselves through a crowd of bum-firking[4] Italians, we fell into a throng of strait-laced monsters in fur and thrum-caps, with huge logger heads, effeminate waists, and buttocks like a Flanders mare, with slovenly mien and swinish looks, whose upper lips were gracefully adorned with turd-coloured whiskers. These, with their gloves under their arms, and their hands in their pockets, were grunting to each other like hogs at their peas. These, my friend told me, were the water-rats of Europe, who love nobody but themselves, and fatten upon the spoils, and build their own welfare upon the ruin of their neighbours.

We had no sooner jostled through this cluster of Commonwealth's-men, but we were got amongst a parcel of lank-haired formalists, in flat crowned hats and short cloaks, walking with as much state and gravity as a snail o'er the leaf of a cabbage, with a box of tobacco-dust in one hand, and the other employed in charging their nostrils from whence it drops into their moustaches, which are always as full of snuff as a beau's wig is full of powder. Every sentence they spoke was graced with a shrug of the shoulders, and every step they took was performed with as much leisure as a cock strides. These, my friend told me, were Spaniards. Says he, 'you may know them by their smell, for they stink as strong of garlic as a Bologna sausage.'

These were confusedly jumbled among people of sundry nations such as our neighbouring antics the French, who talk more with their heads and hands than with their tongues. They commonly speak first and think afterwards, step a minuet as they walk, and sit as gracefully on an Exchange bench as if in a great saddle. Their bodies always dance to their tongues, and they are so great lovers of action that they

---

[2] *morris dancer*: A kind of English folk dancer.
[3] *empiric*: "An untrained practitioner in physic or surgery; a quack" [OED].
[4] *bum-firking*: Mincing, with a sexual pun.

were ready to wound every pillar with their canes as they passed by, either in tierce, carte, or seconde.

There, likewise, were the Lord's vagabonds, the Jews, who were so accursed for their infidelity that they are generally the richest people in all nations where they dwell. Like the wicked Spaniards, they were such great consumers of the wicked weed in snuff that their upper lips looked as if they excreted through their nostrils and had forgot to use bum-fodder. 'These,' says my friend, 'are the hawks of mankind, the spies of the universe, the only trade-politicians, subtle knaves, and great merchants.'

Here were also a few amber-necklace sellers, as my friend called them; men with fur caps, long gowns and grave countenances, seeming wise in their carriage, retaining something of the old Grecian grandeur in their comely deportment. Among them there was one very handsome young fellow, which my companion bid me take particular notice of, 'for,' says he, 'that spark in the red gown was very familiar with some of our sweet-lipped ladies of the City. He was very much admired and courted by several topping benefactresses at this end of the town, to receive their favours, till the fool, proud of his happiness, must needs boast of their kindnesses to the disreputation of his humble servants; so they all discarded him with such hatred and contempt that he is now become the scorn and ridicule of every woman in the City.'

'Pray,' said I, 'what tall, sober-looked gentleman is that, in so grave a dress, in the long black wig and formal hat that stands as level in the brim as a pot-lid? He seems to be wonderfully reverenced by a great many much finer than himself.' 'That man,' says my friend, 'is the greatest merchant we have in England, and those fellows that keep astern, and now and then come upon his quarter with their topsails lowered, are commanders of ships who are soliciting for employment. He that plies him so close, they call Honour and Glory, who lately bore command in the Service. He was originally a poor fisherman, but did a very notable exploit (by the help of his man Jack) that recommended him to a commission. But either for want of discretion or honesty, he is turned out, and I suppose rather than return to his nets, he is willing to enter into the merchant service.'

In the next walk we went into were a parcel of swordsmen in twisted wigs and laced hats, with broad faces and flattish noses, saluting one another commonly by the title of Captain. But they looked as if they had been a long while out of commission, for most of them were out of repair, some like gentlemen without estates, and others like footmen out of places, many of them picking their teeth, often plucking out large tobacco-boxes to cram a wad in their mouths, as if most of their food was minced meat.

The other sort were a kind of lean, carrionly creatures with reddish hair and freckly faces, being very much given to scratching and shrugging, as if they held lousiness no shame and the itch no scandal; stooping a little in the shoulders as if their backs had been used to a pedlar's pack. Amongst them was a poor parson who came to the wrong place to look for a benefice. These, I found, were a compound of Scotch and Irish, who looked as if they rather came to seek for business than dispatch any.

We now came to the back gate of the 'Change, on the east side of which sat a parcel of women, some looking like jilts who wanted cullies,[5] and others like servants who wanted places.

We passed by them, and squeezed amongst coasters and English traders, who were as busy in outwitting one another as if plain dealing was a crime and cozenage a virtue.

'Take notice,' says my companion, 'of that camel-backed spark. He is dignified with the title of My Lord and has as many maggots in his head as there are holes in a colander. Though the rickets have crushed him into that lump of deformity, he has the happiness, or curse, I know not which, to have a very handsome woman for a wife, whose prevailing glances have tempted such custom to her shop that he can afford to spend three or four hundred pounds a year in a tavern without doing himself a prejudice. This she very generously allows him to do out of her gettings, as some censorious people are apt to imagine as a gratuity for his toleration for her liberty of conscience. She is never without a shopful of admirers, whom she poisons with her eyes, and bubbles[6] as she pleases. Give her her due, she's as beautiful as an angel, but as subtle as the Devil; as courteous as a courtesan, but sharp as a needle; very free, but very jiltish; very inviting, yet some say very virtuous.'

'Now,' says my friend, 'we are got amongst the Plantation traders. This may be called Kidnappers' Walk, for a great many of these Jamaicans and Barbadians, with their kitchen-stuff countenances, are looking as sharp for servants as a gang of pickpockets for booty. But

[5] *jilts who wanted cullies:* Whores looking for gullible victims.
[6] *bubbles:* Cheats.

we have given these their characters already in the *Trip to Jamaica*,[7] therefore we shall speak but little of them here. I'll warrant you, if they knew the author was among them, they'd hustle him about, as the Whigs would a Jacobite at the election of a Lord Mayor, or the Quakers would a drunken Ranter that should disturb 'em at their Meeting.

'Pray,' said I, 'what is the meaning of this inscription in golden capitals over the passage, "My Lord Mayor's Court"?' My friend replied that it was the nest of City cormorants who, by scraping a little out of many men's estates, raise great ones to themselves, by which they teach fools wit, and bring litigious knaves to repentance.

Within that entry is an office of intelligence, pretending to help servants to places, and masters to servants. They have a knack of bubbling silly wenches out of their money, who loiter hereabouts, upon this expectancy, till they are picked up by the Plantation kidnappers and spirited away into a state of misery and whoredom.

'Now,' says my friend, 'let us walk on the middle of the 'Change and view the statue. This,' says he, 'is the figure of King Charles II, and those are stockjobbers who are hovering about him, and are, by report, a pack of as great knaves as ever he had in his dominions. The rest are a mixed multitude of all nations, and not worth describing. Now I'll conduct you upstairs, where we'll first take a view of the fair ladies, and so adjourn to the tavern and refresh ourselves with a bottle.'

Accordingly we went up, where women sat in their pinfolds[8] begging of custom with such amorous looks, and after so affable a manner, that I could not but fancy they had as much mind to dispose of themselves as the commodities they dealt in. My ears on both sides were so baited with 'Fine linen, sir!' 'Gloves and ribbons, sir!' that I had a milliner's and a sempstress' shop in my head for a week together. 'Well,' says my friend, 'what do you think of all these pretty ladies?' I answered, I thought of them as I did of the rest of their sex; I supposed they were all ready to obey the laws of nature and answer the end of their creation. Says he, 'You have guessed right, for this place is the merchants' seraglio,[9] a nursery of young wagtails for the private consolation of incontinent citizens; for most that you see here

---

[7] Trip to Jamaica: Published by Ward in 1698.
[8] *pinfolds:* Pens or stalls.
[9] *seraglio:* A harem.

come under Chaucer's character of a sempstress, and so we'll leave them.

> 'She keeps a shop for countenance
> And swyves for mountenance.'[10]

JONATHAN SWIFT

From *The Examiner*, No. 22
["The Spirit of Shop-keepers"]

The Examiner was a Tory periodical begun by Bolingbroke in 1710; Swift took charge in October, producing numbers 14 through 46; Delarivier Manley (author of *The New Atalantis, Rape* III.165) succeeded Swift in 1711. In this excerpt of No. 22 (which focuses primarily on the state of the clergy), Swift takes a very different and very dim view of merchants and the commercial spirit pervading London. He eyes with distrust the "leveling" or republican tendencies of commerce that blur national and cultural distinctions, threatening the hierarchy of the social system and the sacredness of religion.

The text is from the original *Examiner*, No. 22 (December 28, 1710) (London, Printed for J. Morphew, December 21–28, 1710).

No. 22
From Thursday December 21, to Thursday December 28, 1710

Whoever is a true Lover of our Constitution, must needs be pleas'd to see what successful Endeavours are Daily made to restore it in every Branch to its ancient Form, from the languishing Condition it hath long lain in, and with such deadly Symptoms.

. . .

In this deplorable State of the *Clergy*, nothing but the Hand of Providence, working by its glorious Instrument, the QUEEN, could have been able to turn the Peoples Hearts so surprizingly in their Favor. This Princess, destin'd for the Safety of *Europe*, and Blessing to Her Subjects, began Her Reign with a noble Benefaction to the

---

[10] *swyves for mountenance*: Sleeps for her keep.

Church; and it was hoped the Nation would have follow'd such an Example, which nothing could have prevented, but the false Politicks of a Set of Men, who form their Maxims upon those of every tottering Commonwealth, which is always strugling for Life, subsisting by Expedients, and often at the Mercy of any powerful Neighbour. These Men take it into their Imagination, that Trade can never flourish unless the Country becomes a common Receptacle for all Nations, Religions and Languages; a System only proper for small popular States, but altogether unworthy, and below the Dignity of an Imperial Crown; which with Us is best upheld by a Monarch in possession of his just Prerogative, a Senate of Nobles and of Commons, and a Clergy establish'd in its due Rights with a suitable Maintenance by Law. But these Men come with the Spirit of *Shop-keepers* to frame Rules for the Administration of Kingdoms; or, as if they thought the whole Art of Government consisted in the Importation of *Nutmegs*, and the curing of *Herrings*. Such an Island as ours can afford enough to support the Majesty of a Crown, the Honor of a Nobility, and the Dignity of a Magistracy; we can encourage Arts and Sciences, maintain our Bishops and Clergy, and suffer our Gentry to live in a decent, hospitable manner; yet still there will remain Hands sufficient for Trade and Manafactures, which do always indeed deserve the best Encouragement, but not to a degree of sending every living Soul into the *Warehouse* or the *Workhouse*.

This Pedantry of Republican Politicks hath done infinite Mischief among us; To this we owe those noble Schemes of treating Christianity as a System of *Speculative Opinions*, which no Man should be bound to believe; of making the *Being* and the Worship of God, a *Creature* of the State.

DANIEL DEFOE

From *A Review*, Nos. 85 and 90
[On the Vices of the Justices of the Peace]

In 1704 Defoe started a periodical called *A Weekly Review of the Affairs of France*, which by 1707 became *A Review of the State of the British Nation* and which was published through 1713. It was written almost entirely by Defoe as a nonpartisan discussion of economic, political, and social topics. Number 85 (December 26, 1704) attacks the kinds of judges who lurk in the *Rape* and stand (or sit) exposed in Hogarth's engraving. The *Review* also featured "Scandal Club" stories that made use of real or fictional contributions from the general public, on the model of Addison and Steele's *Spectator* and Manley's *The Female Tatler*. From *Review*, No. 90 (January 13, 1705) we have some "Advice from the Scandal Club" on the pervasive drunkenness and general viciousness of justices.

The text is taken from the original edition.

No. 85

Tuesday, December 26, 1704.

Purg'd from the Errors and Partiality of *News-Writers* and *Petty-Statesmen,* of all Sides.

The digression of the last two *Reviews,* had ended with them, had not some new Advocates appear'd to Vindicate our Workhouses, as useful Steps to our *Reformation of Manners,* by being Houses of Correction, and Punishment to Stroulers,[1] Rogues, Whores, and all sorts of Vagrants.

I would be very forward to yield up any Point in their Favour, and shall, I hope, never be guilty of saying any thing to Dishonour, or Discourage the Needful Work of *Reformation of Manners.*

But it has been long in vain, that I have been an Impertinent Fellow in Preaching this Doctrine, *viz.*

> For shame your *Reformation Clubs* give o'er,
> And jest with Men, and jest with Heaven no more:
> But if you would Avenging Heaven appease,
> Avert his Plagues, and heal the Vile Disease:
> Impending Ruine avoid, and calm the Fates,
> Ye Hyppocrites, Reform your Magistrates.
>   — Reform. of Man. a Satyr, p. 42.[2]

The punishing Vices in the Poor, which are daily practis'd by the Rich, seems to me to be, setting our Constitution with the wrong end upward, and making Men Criminals because they want Money.

'Tis now 8 Years since I first had the Misfortune to Anger my Masters the Magistrates, by Writing a little Book, call'd, *The Poor*

---

[1] *Stroulers:* "A vagabond, vagrant; itinerant beggar or pedlar" [OED].
[2] *Reform. of Man. a Satyr:* Defoe, *Reformation of Manners, A Satyr* (1702).

"The Bench," by William Hogarth, 1758, showing four judges — pompous, callous, or fast asleep — listening to a case in the Court of Common Pleas. These figures are meant to be "characters" rather than overly exaggerated caricatures, and they have been identified as real historical figures (Shesgreen, Pl. 92n). The upper row of heads was an addition Hogarth was working on the day before he died.

Man's Plea,[3] against all the Proclamations, or Acts of Parliament for *Reformation*; wherein the Honest Poor Man protests against being set in the Stocks by a Drunken Justice; or Fin'd for Swearing, by a Magistrate, with a *G—d D—n him, let the Dog pay for it?* Nay, and tho' an Honest, Learned, and Judicious Clergyman, was pleased to do that Book more Honour than its Author deserv'd, by taking it into the Pulpit with him, 'tis plain he has been Censur'd for the Sermon,

---

[3] The Poor Man's Plea: Defoe, *The Poor Man's Plea, in relation to all the proclamations, declarations, acts of Parliament, &c., which have been, or shall be made, or publish'd for a reformation of manners, and for suppressing immorality in the nations* (London, 1698).

and is hated to this Day, by all the Leading Men of the Parish of
St. J———, not far from the City of *London.*

And yet I must still take the Liberty, against the Rule of Authors,
to Quote my self, and say to our Gentlemen of Justice and
Correction.

> Our Modes of Vice from high Examples came,
> And 'tis Example only, must reclaim.
> You'll eas'ly Check the Vices of the Town,
> When e'er you please but to suppress your own:

From hence, I confess, I have long ago left off Complaining of the
Prophaneness and Immoralities of our People, and the Lewdness,
Drunkenness, and Ill Language of our Streets; and if ever I meddle
with our Vices, I place it chiefly on those who practice it in the very
Chair and Bench of Authority; where they have (Heavens regard their
Impudence) not stuck to punish with one Hand the Crimes they com-
mit with the other.

For this I am ill treated by the Guilty, or their Friends, as a Re-
proacher of Magistrates, a Reviler of the Rulers of the People, and a
Medler with what is not my Business; and a certain Noble Person de-
scended so much below the Honour of his Quality, as well as Office,
as to tell me, in Defence of these things, That *if I saw a Man Lie with
another Man's Wife, in the middle of the Street, I had no Right to
publish the scandal, nor unless I was a Magistrate, to meddle with the
Matter:* Had his Lordship told me, *If I saw my Neighbour's House on
Fire, I had no Right to* cry out, *because it would raise a Tumult,* I
might have given Credit to it, but to the other, I can never agree.

Every Man who is subject to the Law, and punishable by it, has a
Right in the Execution of the Law upon all Offenders equally with
himself; and if one is punish'd for a Crime, and another goes free, the
first Man is Injur'd, because he has not Equal Justice with his Neigh-
bours. Again, I have a Right of Complaint, when any Offender is not
brought to Justice, because it is an Encouragement to the Offence;
and I may one time or other find the Effect of it.

But to avoid these Reasons, the Reproach to Justice, the Scandal to
the Nation, the Encouragement to Vice, by Example is what we are
all concern'd in; and I am, and ever shall be concern'd to hear us talk
of Reformation, when those who should Reform us, practice all the
Crimes they ought to punish.

What a noise has a poor Author about him, if he tells a Story of a
Drunken Justice: ——— All the Drunken Justices in the Town, *and*

Lord, how many are they! Think themselves concern'd, if a poor Author tells of a Magistrate Bound-over to the Peace for Fighting, throwing Brick-bats, and the like, and Fin'd for Swearing; all the Fighting, Swearing Justices, that stand Bound-over to the Peace, of whom our Records can easily tell the Number, are abusing me for calling it to mind: What have I to do, *say they*, with Swearing Mayors, Drunken Aldermen, and Justices, keeping the Peace? Why, that's true, Gentlemen, but then pray don't Talk of Reformation; Societies that can't bear a Sermon, because 'twas Preach'd in *Plain English*. Talk no more of well Govern'd Cities with Aldermen, and Great Folks in 'em, amongst whom are Crimes Black as the Robes they wear; whose Feasts are Debauches and Drunkenness; whose Houses are fill'd with all manner of Excesses; their Heads with Wine, in their Hands is Bribery and Oppression, and their Mouths are full of Cursings, and Blasphemy.

Shall fear of the powerful Injury of Man, stop the Just Exclamation of my Pen, at the flagrant Abuses of the Nations Laws; may those Writers be for ever D — d to Silence, who seeing the Laws broke, Good Manners Invaded, Justice Abus'd, the Innocent Punish'd, and the Guilty sit in the Chair of Authority, are afraid to let the World know who is the Villain, that the Honest Man may be Distinguish'd.

I am charg'd with promoting Scandal, say some of my Friends, and Well-wishers, I boldly affirm, I never charg'd Person, Party, Members, or Body of high or low Quality, or Degree, with one Fact either obliquely or directly, which I was not able to bring untainted undeniable Testimony to the Truth of, and by God's Grace I never will: If I am Impos'd upon in any particular Relation, I'll do effectual Justice to any Injur'd Person; of which, I shall soon give the World a satisfactory Example.

From hence I say also, our *Scan. Club* Stories,[4] tho' they have some Mirth in 'em, have all their Morals; and this serious sad Reflection goes with most of them, That as to Vices of every kind, *the Lord have Mercy upon the Magistrates and Clergy of this Nation.*

On this score, fewer Houses of Correction would serve; if none of the Poor are to be punish'd till the Magistrates, and Rich People are Reform'd; *Bridewell*, and *New-Prison* was large enough before; and

---

[4] Scan. Club *stories:* "Advice from the Scandal Club," a feature of the *Review* that included letters from the public (real and fictional).

the Usefulness of another House of Correction, in *Bishopsgate-street*, remains to be prov'd.[5]

No. 90
January 13, 1705

The Great Misfortune of our Society has been, that when they happen to have a Vicious Story to tell, there are so many Gentlemen put in for a Claim to the Character, that they have ten Accusers to one Fact; they therefore humbly crave of all the J————s[1] that are Men of the Bottle, or that now and then take occasion to Divert themselves a little with another Man's Wife, or the like, that they would not pretend the following Picture was drawn for them, unless they can prove they were actually Drunk at the Sign of the *King's-Head* some where or other, within the compass of six Months last past.

> Gentlemen,
>   You told us, in one of your *Reviews*, of three Bullies, that could not be Drunk in three Nights sitting; sure their Brains were Impregnable: For two of our Justices sate at the *Kings-Head Tavern*, but from *11* in the Forenoon, till *5* next Morning, and were both so Drunk, that they fell foul upon a Butcher's Wife: First they snatch'd away her Nosegay, then would have hall'd[2] her into Drink. The Woman not yielding, they fell to Damning her for a Bitch, and swore they knew her to be a Whore, and to *Bridewell*[3] she should go: But her Husband coming in the Interim, threatned their Worships for Swearing, and for being Drunk, and Rescu'd his Wife out of their Clutches; the Justices Reel'd away towards C————*ell* Church. Pray, *Gentlemen*, are not these fit tools to Correct Vice? If you question the Truth of this, I will tell you their Names and Places of Abode.

Upon reading this Letter, the Society declar'd, they would have nothing to do with it; for that it was the way to bring half the J————ces in the Nation upon their Backs; and they had long since had their Bellies full of Publick Resentment.

---

[5] Bridewell . . . *remains to be prov'd:* In the *Tour*, twenty years later, Defoe writes: "There are in London, notwithstanding we are a nation of liberty, more public and private prisons, and houses of confinement, than any city in Europe, perhaps as many as in all the capital cities of Europe put together."
[1] *J————s:* Justices.
[2] *hall'd:* Hauled.
[3] *Bridewell:* Women's prison.

HENRY FIELDING

From *An Enquiry into the Causes of the Late Increase of Robbers*
["Of the Manner of Execution"]

"And Wretches hang that Jury-Men may Dine" (*Rape* III.22). Pope's poem tucks the wretches out of sight, so to speak, tossing them lightly into a lighthearted poem. Yet the very callousness of the casualness satirizes the way that the judicial system abused its privileges and produced snoring Hogarthian judges. In the following excerpt from novelist and magistrate Henry Fielding's treatise exploring the contemporary world of crime and punishment, we see a different aspect of the criminal justice system: its ineffectiveness in discouraging crime. Executions were public affairs in eighteenth-century Britain, and many writers worried about the growing sense of glamour that seemed to attend the condemned criminal. In Gay's *The Beggar's Opera* (1728), the heroine Polly imagines her lover, the highwayman Macheath, on his way to the gallows: "Methinks I see him already in the cart, sweeter and more lovely than the nosegay in his hand! I hear the crowd extolling his resolution and intrepidity! What vollies of sighs are sent from the windows of Holborn, that so comely a youth should be brought to disgrace! I see him at the tree! The whole circle are in tears! Even butchers weep!" (I.xii). Fielding and his half-brother Sir John Fielding, deploring this attitude, worked steadily against corruption on the bench and crime in the streets.

The text is taken from the original edition (London: Printed for A. Millar, 1751).

SECT. XI.

Of the Manner of Execution.

But if every Hope which I have mentioned fails the Thief: If he should be discovered, apprehended, prosecuted, convicted, and refused a Pardon; what is his Situation then? Surely most gloomy and dreadful, without any Hope, and without any Comfort. This is, perhaps, the Case with the less practised, less spirited, and less dangerous Rogues; but with those of a different Constitution it is far otherwise. No Hero sees Death as the Alternative which may attend his Undertaking with less Terror, nor meets it in the Field with more imaginary Glory. Pride, which is commonly the uppermost Passion in both, is in both treated with equal Satisfaction. The Day appointed by Law for the Thief's Shame is the Day of Glory in his own Opinion. His Procession to *Tyburn*,[1] and his last Moments there, are all triumphant; attended with the Compassion of the meek and tender-hearted, and with the Applause, Admiration, and Envy of all the bold and hardened. His Behaviour in his present Condition, not the Crimes, how atrocious soever, which brought him to it, are the Subject of Contemplation. And if he hath Sense enough to temper his Boldness with any Degree of Decency, his Death is spoke of by many with Honour, by most with Pity, and by all with Approbation.

How far such an Example is from being an Object of Terror, especially to those for whose Use it is principally intended, I leave to the Consideration of every rational Man; whether such Examples as I have described are proper to be exhibited must be submitted to our Superiors.

JONATHAN SWIFT

"Clever Tom Clinch *going to be hanged"*

Swift satirizes in poetry what Fielding protests in prose: the inflated popularity of public executions, the popular valorization of the criminal. Where *The Rape of the Lock* suggests that the social world takes trivial things far too seriously, "Clever Tom Clinch" sees a culture taking terrible things far too lightly.

The text is taken from *The Poems of Jonathan Swift*, ed. Harold Williamson (Oxford: Clarendon Press, 1937), which is reprinted from Faulkner's edition, 1735.

Written in the Year 1726.

As clever *Tom Clinch*, while the Rabble was bawling,
Rode stately through *Holbourn*,° to die in his Calling;
He stopt at the *George*° for a Bottle of Sack,°

---

[1] *Tyburn:* Site of London's gallows, at the northeast corner of Hyde Park (now Marble Arch).

2. Holbourn: A street on the route to Tyburn gallows.

3. *the* George: A tavern. *Sack:* A rich white wine.

And promis'd to pay for it when he'd come back.
His Waistcoat and Stockings, and Breeches were white,   5
His Cap had a new Cherry Ribbon to ty't.
The Maids to the Doors and the Balconies ran,
And said, lack-a-day! he's a proper young Man.
But, as from the Windows the Ladies he spy'd,
Like a Beau in the Box, he bow'd low on each Side;   10
And when his last Speech the loud Hawkers° did cry,
He swore from his Cart, it was all a damn'd Lye.
The Hangman for Pardon fell down on his Knee;
Tom gave him a Kick in the Guts for his Fee.
Then said, I must speak to the People a little,   15
But I'll see you all damn'd before I will *whittle*.°
My honest Friend *Wild*,° may he long hold his Place,
He lengthen'd my Life with a whole Year of Grace.
Take Courage, dear Comrades, and be not afraid,
Nor slip this Occasion to follow your Trade.   20
My Conscience is clear, and my Spirits are calm,
And thus I go off without pray'r-Book or Psalm.
Then follow the Practice of clever *Tom Clinch*,
Who hung like a Hero, and never would flinch.

11. *his last Speech the loud Hawkers did cry:* Hawkers were street-sellers; gallows confessions were frequently printed and sold.
16. whittle: "'A Cant Word for confessing at the Gallows.' — Faulkner" [Williamson].
17. Wild: Jonathan Wild (1683–1724), was simultaneously a gang leader and a thief-taker in London: That is, he informed on his own men for reward money. Both Defoe and Fielding wrote "biographies" of Wild.

Trade and Empire

DANIEL DEFOE

From *A Review*, No. 3
["Of the English Trade"]

Daniel Defoe was a tradesman and shopkeeper as well as a political
and prose fiction writer (not to mention a spy, a builder, a projector, and
a gardening consultant to King William), and he was always very much
concerned with the status of both trade and tradesmen in London. He
wrote frequently on the advantages of foreign and domestic trade both
for the nation itself and for all its various individual inhabitants. In later
Review essays Defoe explores in detail the dangers of declining trade that
he mentions in this issue; here he sets out the general topics. He defines
England as "a *Trading Nation*," distinguishing it from other European
countries that sharply divide their nobility and gentry from trading pro-
fessions. The benefits of trade are not only economic but social: The
landed classes intermarry and intermix with the merchant classes and, ac-
cording to Defoe, mutually strengthen each other, much the way the cir-
culation of domestic trade keeps all parts of England commercially
strong.

Defoe was not a complete propagandist for England's trade; or rather,
he would often articulate the dangers — economic, social, and politi-
cal — that attended indiscriminate or unregulated trade and a credit
economy. But for the most part his was one of the strongest voices in the
early eighteenth century favoring the development and expansion of
world commerce.

The text is taken from the original edition.

Vol. II, No. 3
Tuesday, March 6, 1705.

England may, without any Reproach to her, be said to be a *Trad-
ing Nation*. Some Nations value themselves upon abstracted Nobility,
and make it Criminal, as we may call it, to their Characters, to Mix
with the Trading part of the People, as in *Spain*, *Italy*, and some Parts
of *Germany*, *Hungary*, and *Poland*.

Will:ᵐ Overley Joyner at the Sign of the Eaſt India Houſe *in* Leaden-hall Street LONDON Makes all ſorts of Sea Cheſts in Deal or Wainſcot. Ruff or ſmooth Packing Cheſts or Caſes, and Caſes of Bottles, & Boxes of all Sizes, Preſſes in Deal or Wainſcot, & Bedſtds, Tables, Desks, Book Caſes, Burous & Writing Desks, Letter holes, & Drans for Shops. Allſo Counters and all ſorts of Joyners worke done —— at Reaſonable Rates ——

The Old East India House, c. 1714–1716. The Leadenhall Street site of the East India Company was originally the mansion house of Sir William Craven, Lord Mayor of London in 1610, richly detailed with the British lion and unicorn dominating a globe and British ships filling a muralled sea. The Old East India House is from William Overley's Trade Card in the British Museum.

But *England* cannot make these Distinctions; her Numerous Gentry, her Illustrious Nobility, and most, if not all her best Families, owe their Wealth and Rise, first or last, to the Oppulence and Profits of Trade.

Nor is it any Dishonour to them to do so, since the Exceeding Wealth of our Merchants, having Qualified them for Gentlemen, Noblemen, or Statesmen, they have made it appear, that those Characters have suited them, and sate as well upon their Posterity, as upon those of the best Blood in the Nation; and if there has been any Difference, the Trading Branches have had it with Advantage.

In these latter Ages of the World, great Families have risen more upon Casual Wealth,[1] than upon the Inheritances of Ancestors; Pride, Luxury, and Time, have made great Depredations upon Noble Families, which Trade has frequently restor'd, and added Families, to make good the Deficiencies of those Decayed and Extinct.

It is not the Business of this Paper, to Examine into the real Difference between Ancient and Modern Nobility, or Gentry; a Nicety very few in *England* can Distinguish; but to lay down the Fact, in order to draw their Inference from it, That

England is a Trading Nation, that the Wealth and Oppulence of the Nation, is owing to Trade, that the Influence of Trade is felt in every Branch of its Government, in the Value of its Land, and the Blood of Trade is mix'd and blended with the Blood of Gallantry, so that Trade is the Life of the Nation, the Soul of its Felicity, the Spring of its Wealth, the Support of its Greatness, and the Staff on which both King and People lean, and which (if it should sink) the whole Fabrick must fall, the Body Politick would sicken and languish, its Power decline, and the Figure it makes in the World, grow by degrees, most Contemptibly Mean.

Trade Employs the People, raises the Price of Wages, and that of Provisions, and that of Lands, and that encreases the Estates of the Gentry; their Estates encreasing, they Live Splendidly, Entertain Servants, keep Plentiful Tables, wear Fine Cloaths, ride in Coaches, &c. and that again makes Trade.

By this Circulation, Demands of Goods are made from us; by this our Manufactures are Encreas'd, our Merchants build Ships, and employ Seamen and Multitudes of Artizans, Labourers, Tradesmen, &c. in the Equipment and Navigating those Ships. Thus the Merchant

---

[1] *Casual Wealth:* Unexpected, accidental, or earned wealth, not to be calculated (as opposed to inherited wealth, which could be depended upon).

grows Rich, lays up vast Sums and being able to give great Portions, his Daughter Marries my Lord Duke's Son, and in time becomes a Duchess; and his Son Marries my Lord's Eldest Daughter; and thus the Tradesman's grandson becomes a Duke, and my Lord's Grandson goes Prentice to a Merchant; their Coats of Arms are Quarter'd *Parte per Pale*,[2] and Posterity knows no Difference.

Again, Trade thus Encreasing, pays vast Customs and Taxes; this Enables the Government to raise Armies, fit out great Navies, and become formidable to the World; and thus the Figure of this whole Nation is deriv'd from Trade; and I think, I have made it out, that we are *a Trading Nation.*

Whoever can read this, and not own with me, That to see Trade Sinking, Declining, and in the way to Ruine, ought sensibly to afflict us, must have less Concern for his Native Country, than, I hope, all Men have that think it worth their while to read this Paper.

To Examine a little therefore, why, and for what Reason I assume the Argument, That Trade is Sinking and Declining, and what I mean by it? 'Tis necessary to enter a little into the History of Trade, and tell the World what I mean by it.

I allow, we drive as Great a Trade as ever this Nation did, I mean, as we did at the beginning of this last War.[3]

The *English* Trade consists in Three large Branches, in which are generally Included all the rest; and which, I suppose, to contain in general, our Whole Trade.

I. Our Home-Trade from Town to Town, Circulating within our selves.

II. Our Export.

III. Our Import.

1. Our Home-Trade consists chiefly of the several Woollen Manufactures made in *England*, and which being made in several Counties, are (generally speaking) sent to *London*, as the Center of Trade, and from thence retail'd back again to such respective Counties where they are wanted, several Counties making some particular Manufactures, but *London* only being capable to furnish all Parts.

This I call the Circulation of our Trade, and this makes it plain, that a certain Worthy Kt.[4] who Published a Draught for an Act of

---

[2] Parte per Pale: In heraldry, "said of the shield when divided by a vertical line through the middle" [OED].

[3] *this last War:* The War of the Spanish Succession (1701–1714).

[4] *Kt.:* Knight. (Work untraced.)

Parliament to Settle and Employ the Poor, understood very little of Trade, when he propos'd to set up the Woollen Manufacture in every Parish in *England*, which enabling the Inhabitants of every Parish, to make within themselves the Manufactures they should want, would immediately put an End to the Circulation of Trade, confound the Manufactures, and cause our Home-Trade to cease of it self.

But as this is a Capital Grievance in Trade, I shall endavour to Expose it more plainly, when I have first gone thro' the Generals.

2. Our Exports consist chiefly in our Manufactures, and the Growth of the Country and Colonies; in which last Article, I include Provisions, Metals, Sugars, Tobacco's, Spices, Furs, Drugs, *&c.*

3. Our Imports, consist chiefly of Linen, Silk, Wine, Brandy, Oyl, Fruit, Drugs, Dyers Stuffs, *East-India* Wares, Naval Stores, Gold, Silver, Jewels, Slaves and Souls of Men.

I shall go on to Examine these Articles, or General Heads of Trade, in their present Posture and Misfortunes; and having search'd to the bottom the Grievances of Trade, shall humbly propose, what, I think, may remedy those Evils; and then I think I have done: For my Business is not to force People to accept of Deliverance, but to shew them which way they may split the Ship, or save it.

He that will hang himself, must Die, Nature can't save him, and Providence will not —— . I shall so far act the Pilot, as to place a Mark upon the Dangerous Shoal; if the Rash Traders will run upon it, they must split, I can do no more.

DANIEL DEFOE

From *A Review*, No. 65
["We do not fight for Conquest, but for Peace"]

In this excerpt from the *Review* Defoe writes about the precarious balance of power in Europe, arguing on the one hand that the War of the Spanish Succession is vital to maintaining that balance, and on the other that Britain must not get so caught up in its victories that it becomes the very tyrant it is fighting to restrain. The essay reveals a wider political context of debate about the balance of power and the love of conquest that inhabit the social realm of *The Rape of the Lock*.

Briefly, the War of the Spanish Succession (1701–1714) was fought to determine the succession to the Spanish throne on the death of Charles II of Spain. Britain entered the war in 1701, alarmed at the rapid growth of French power at the union of French and Spanish crowns when Charles II's successor, Philip of Anjou, became Philip V of Spain in 1700. Britain formed the Grand Alliance with the Holy Roman Empire and the Netherlands; France and Spain united against the Alliance with Bavaria, Savoy, and Portugal; fighting began in Italy and Bavaria. "Arguments in England about the war or, more strictly, about the conduct and conclusion of the war, were a major factor in the party strife which was such a feature of the age of Anne" (Downie 64). The Whigs, celebrating the victories of the Duke of Marlborough at Blenheim (1704) and elsewhere, wanted to press the war and Britain's power much further, demanding the surrender of the entire Spanish monarchy by the end; the Tories, who comprised a number of country gentlemen whose taxes were paying for this costly war, were eager to sue for peace, which was finally but controversially concluded with the Peace of Utrecht in 1713/14. The peace reorganized political lines in Europe, confirmed Philip V's succession, and won Britain major territorial concessions in Canada from the French.

Vol. III, No. 65
Saturday, June 1, 1706

Whoever they are that wish this War to end in any thing but a firm and solid peace, have either little to lose, get Money by, or depend upon the War, or do not understand the Interest and true Benefit of their native Country.

We do not fight for Conquest, but for Peace; 'tis *Peace* only can restore the Breaches War has made upon our Commerce; *Peace only* can make our Wealth flow like a high Spring Tyde. Indeed there are Circumstances by which we must say, we shall *thrive with the War*, and of which I shall speak by its self; but 'tis a Sort of thriving we ought not to court, in Competition with a settled Conclusion of the War; nor can it be compar'd to the Prosperity and Encrease, which the Advantages of Trade, open'd and settled by Peace, must bring to such a Trading Nation as this.

The End of this War is to reduce exorbitant Power to a due Pitch, to run it quite down, would be to erect some *other Exorbitant* in its Room, and so set up our selves as publick Enemies to *Europe*, in the room of that publick Enemy we pull down.

Every Power, which over ballances the rest, *makes its self a Nusance* to its Neighbours. *Europe* being divided into a great Variety of

separate Governments and Constitution; the Safety of the whole con-
sists in a due Distribution of Power, so shar'd to every Part or Branch
of Government, that no one may be able to oppress and destroy the
rest.

And 'tis evident from Experience, that whenever it has been other-
wise, the Consequence has been, potent Confederacies among the
weaker Powers by Joint Assistance to reduce the encroaching grow-
ing Part to such Terms of Reason, and preserve and secure the Tran-
quility of the rest.

When that Power is reduc'd, it ceases to be any more the Object ei-
ther of Jealousie or Resentment of the rest; but if any of the united
Powers erect themselves upon the Ruin of that; or by any other
method set themselves up too high; the Nusance is transpos'd to that
Power, which before it was thought convenient to assist, and it be-
comes as necessary to the rest to reduce that Power or Prince, as it
was before to reduce the other.

Thus the *Spanish* Power in Queen *Elizabeth*'s Time[1] grew for-
midable to *Europe*, and all the Princes, who took Umbrage at their
Greatness, confederated with *France* and *England* to reduce it.

The *Austrian* Power in the Emperor *Ferdinand* II.[2] became for-
midable to *Europe*; whereupon all the Protestant Princes agreed to
call in, and assist the King of *Sweden*, in bringing the *Germans* to due
Bounds, and to hearken to Reason, and *England*, *France*, and *Hol-
land* joyntly concurr'd.

France from these Fractions and Quarrels among the Protestants,
establish'd its Greatness, and raised her self on the Ruin of its so po-
tent Neighbours, till the most exquisite Conduct of the present King[3]
has brought that Greatness to a too formidable Height; and thereby
plac'd her in the envied Seat of Power, which standing without the
Circle of Mediocrity makes her uneasie to all the rest.

Should any of the Branches of the present Confederacy push at a
Conquest, and by the Advantage of the falling Greatness of the
French power, engross to themselves a Dominion too large, or any
Superiority of Power above his proper Sphere, that very Power or

---

[1] *Queen* Elizabeth's *Time:* Elizabeth I, reigned 1558–1603; the Spanish Armada
was destroyed by the English fleet in 1588.
[2] *Emperor* Ferdinand *II:* Ferdinand II (1578–1637), king of Bohemia and Hungary;
Holy Roman Emperor, 1619–1637. His reign was marked by the Thirty Years' War.
[3] *the present King:* Louis XIV, reigned 1643–1715.

Prince would in his Degree become equally obnoxious to the rest, and the Ballance of Power being thereby broken, would be as much the publick Enemy as the *French* are now.

General Safety consists in *Peace*; *Peace* is the Bond of Property, the Root of Commerce, the Fountain of Wealth, the Blessing of Mankind, the Emblem of Heaven, and the Joy of the World.

PEACE is the only End of just War, the only justifiable Article of the present Undertakings; *If this* were not the ultimate Extent of the Wish or Desire of *England* in this War, the Prosecution of it would make us a Den of Thieves, a meer Nest of Algerines,[4] Rovers and Robbers of other Men's Right, Murtherers of Nations, Pursuers of the Innocent, and Bloodhounds bent for Destruction, and born to disturb the World.

ALEXANDER POPE

"The Balance of Europe"

Pope manages to make a political statement about the balance of international affairs in the small balanced space of one closed couplet. Both adversaries had by now conceded territories to the other. Britain had gained a number of victories under Marlborough, but in 1711 it withdrew from the Grand Alliance because the new Holy Roman Emperor, Charles VI, was a claimant to the Spanish throne, and any allied victory over France would have joined Spain to the Holy Roman Empire — an unacceptable solution, from Britain's point of view, to the balance of power in Europe.

The couplet (or epigram) first appeared at the end of a letter to John Caryll, July 19, 1711 (Correspondence 1: 130). Pope later included it, without his name, in *Miscellanies, The Last Volume* (1727). The text, from the Twickenham edition, follows the 1727 version.

> Now *Europe's* balanc'd, neither Side prevails,
> For nothing's left in either of the Scales.

---

[4] *Algerines:* Algerians, specifically pirates from Algiers.

ALEXANDER POPE

From *Windsor-Forest*

Pope published *Windsor-Forest* at the signing of the Peace of Utrecht in 1713; the poem, modeled on Virgil's *Georgics*, anticipates a new Golden Age under Anne: "At length great *ANNA SAID* — Let Discord cease! / She said, the World obey'd, and all was *Peace*!" (lines 327–28). On the one hand, this poem heralds Britain's new imperial power:

> Behold! *Augusta*'s glitt'ring Spires increase,
> And Temples rise, the beauteous Works of Peace.
> I see, I see where two fair Cities Bend
> Their ample Bow, a new *White-Hall* ascend!
> There mighty Nations shall inquire their Doom,
> The World's great Oracle in Times to come;
> There Kings shall sue, and suppliant States be seen
> Once more to bend before a *British* QUEEN. (ll. 377–84)

But the following excerpt (ll. 93–134) shows the complexity of Pope's vision of conquest and peace: He sees matters from the perspective of the victim, from the view of the conquered, through his vivid metaphoric depiction of the hunted.

Pope's note to the text says: "This poem was written at two different times: the first part of it which relates to the country, in the year 1704, at the same time with the Pastorals: the latter part was not added till the year 1713, in which it was publish'd." The work was published as *Windsor-Forest: To the Right Honourable George Lord Lansdowne*, London: Printed for Bernard Lintott at the Cross-Keys in Fleet-Street, 1713. The text is taken from the Twickenham edition.

Ye vig'rous Swains! while Youth ferments your Blood,
And purer Spirits swell the sprightly Flood,
Now range the Hills, the gameful Woods beset,   95
Wind the shrill Horn, or spread the waving Net.
When milder Autumn Summer's Heat succeeds,
And in the new-shorn Field the Partridge feeds,
Before his Lord the ready Spaniel bounds,
Panting with Hope, he tries the furrow'd Grounds,   100
But when the tainted Gales the Game betray,

Couch'd close he lyes, and meditates the Prey;
Secure they trust th'unfaithful field, beset,
Till hov'ring o'er 'em sweeps the swelling Net.
Thus (if small Things we may with great compare)   105
When *Albion*° sends her eager Sons to War,
Some thoughtless Town, with Ease and Plenty blest,
Near, and more near, the closing Lines invest;
Sudden they seize th'amaz'd, defenceless Prize,
And high in air *Britannia*'s Standard flies.   110
    See! from the Brake the whirring Pheasant springs,
And mounts exulting on triumphant Wings;
Short is his Joy! he feels the fiery Wound,
Flutters in Blood, and panting beats the Ground.
Ah! what avail his glossie, varying Dyes,   115
His Purple Crest, and Scarlet-circled Eyes,
The vivid Green his shining Plumes unfold;
His painted Wings, and Breast that flames with Gold?
    Nor yet, when moist *Arcturus*° clouds the Sky,
The Woods and Fields their pleasing Toils deny.   120
To Plains with well-breath'd Beagles we repair,
And trace the Mazes of the circling Hare.
(Beasts, urg'd by us, their Fellow Beasts pursue,
And learn of Man each other to undo.)
With slaught'ring Guns th'unweary'd Fowler roves,   125
When Frosts have whiten'd all the naked Groves;
Where Doves in Flocks the leafless Trees o'ershade,
And lonely Woodcocks haunt the watry Glade.
He lifts the Tube,° and levels with his Eye;
Strait a short Thunder breaks the frozen Sky.   130
Oft, as in Airy Rings they skim the Heath,
The clam'rous Lapwings feel the Leaden Death:
Oft as the mounting Larks their Notes prepare,
They fall, and leave their little Lives in Air.

106. Albion: A name for England.
119. Arcturus: The brightest star in the constellation Bootes, or the Great Bear;
seen in autumn skies.
129. *Tube:* A gun.

[RICHARD STEELE]

From *The Spectator,* No. 552
["The Industrious Part of Mankind"]

Steele's essay celebrates several aspects of British nationalism, imperialism, and scientific discovery. Just as Defoe in the *Review* sees the strength of England emerging from the intermingling of the landowners and the merchants, Steele points to the ways in which trade not only influences but infiltrates daily English life in the shop and warehouses of the writer Peter Motteux. Organ builder Renatus Harris proposes a project for St. Paul's that would honor "the *British* Name." And John Rowley's globes bring the known universe into the visual field of the almost-ordinary Briton — like Pope's *Iliad,* the globes were an expensive undertaking, financed by subscription. But also like Pope's Homer, globes, like local and world maps, were fast becoming popular commodities and affordable to a wider, and more curious, consumer public.

No. 552
Wednesday, December 3, 1712

. . . Qui prægravat artes
Infra se positas extinctus amabitur idem.[1]
— Hor.

As I was tumbling about the Town the other Day in an Hackney-Coach, and delighting my self with busy Scenes in the Shops of each side of me, it came into my Head, with no small Remorse, that I had not been frequent enough in the Mention and Recommendation of the industrious Part of Mankind. It very naturally, upon this Occasion, touched my Conscience in particular, that I had not acquitted my self to my Friend Mr. *Peter Motteux.*[2] That industrious Man of Trade, and formerly Brother of the Quill, has dedicated to me a Poem upon Tea. It would injure him, as a Man of Business, if I did not let the World know that the Author of so good Verses writ them before

---

[1] Qui prægravat . . . idem: From Horace's *Epistles* (2.1.13–14): "'For those are hated that excell the rest, / Altho when dead they are belov'd, and blest.' CREECH" [Bond].

[2] Peter Motteux: Peter Anthony Motteux (1663–1718), French poet, playwright, librettist, and translator, came to England in 1685; his *Poem upon Tea* was published in July 1712.

he was concerned in Traffick. In order to expiate my Negligence towards him, I immediately resolved to make him a Visit. I found his spacious Warehouses filled and adorned with Tea, China, and Indian Ware. I could observe a beautiful Ordonnance[3] of the Whole, and such different and considerable Branches of Trade carried on in the same House, I exulted in seeing disposed by a Poetical Head. In one Place were exposed to view Silks of various Shades and Colours, rich Brocades, and the wealthiest Products of foreign Looms. Here you might see the finest Laces held up by the fairest Hands; and there examined by the beauteous Eyes of the Buyers the most delicate Cambricks, Muslins, and Linnens. I could not but congratulate my Friend on the humble, but, I hoped, beneficial use he had made of his Talents, and wished I could be a Patron to his Trade, as he had been pleased to make me of his Poetry. The honest Man has, I know, that modest Desire of Gain which is peculiar to those who understand better Things than Riches; and I dare say he would be contented with much less than what is called Wealth in that Quarter of the Town which he inhabits, and will oblige all his Customers with Demands agreeable to the Moderation of his Desires.

Among other Omissions of which I have been also guilty with relation to Men of Industry of a superiour Order, I must acknowledge my Silence towards a Proposal frequently enclosed to me by Mr. *Renatus Harris, Organ-Builder.*[4] The Ambition of this Artificer is to erect an Organ in St. *Paul*'s Cathedral over the West Door at the Entrance into the Body of the Church, which in Art and Magnificence shall transcend any Work of that Kind ever before invented. The Proposal in perspicuous Language sets forth the Honour and Advantage such a Performance would be to the *British* Name, as well as that it would apply the Power of Sounds in a Manner more amazingly forcible than, perhaps, has yet been known, and I am sure to an End much more worthy. Had the vast Sums which have been laid out upon Opera's without Skill or Conduct, and to no other Purpose but to suspend or vitiate our Understandings, been disposed this Way, we should now, perhaps, have had an Engine so formed as to strike the Minds of half a People at once in a Place of Worship with a Forgetfulness of present Care and Calamity, and an Hope of endless Rapture, Joy, and Hallelujah hereafter.

---

[3] *Ordonnance:* "Plan or method of composition" [OED].
[4] Renatus Harris: One of a family of organ builders, Harris was involved in disputes and contract competitions with rivals; his proposal for a new organ at St. Paul's apparently came to nothing.

Geography Rectified:

OR, A

DESCRIPTION

OF THE

WORLD,

In all its Kingdoms, Provinces, Countries,
Iſlands, Cities, Towns, Seas, Rivers, Bayes, Capes,
Ports; Their Ancient and Preſent Names, Inhabitants,
Situations, Hiſtories, Cuſtoms, Governments, &c.
As alſo their Commodities, Coins, Weights, and
Meaſures, Compared with thoſe at *LONDON.*

Illuſtrated with Seventy eight MAPS.

The Third Edition, Enlarged. To which is added a Compleat Geographical Index
to the Whole, Alphabetically digeſted.

The whole Work performed according to the more Accurate Obſervations
and Diſcoveries of Modern Authors.

By *ROBERT MORDEN.*

LONDON

Printed for *Robert Morden* and *Thomas Cockerill,* at the *Atlas*
in *Cornhill,* and at the *Three Legs* in the *Poultrey,* over-againſt
the *Stocks-Market.* MDCXCIII.

Geography Rectified: Or, A Description of the World, by Robert Morden,
1720, offering the reader a description of the world in its various relations to
London. Morden (d. 1703), a popular map and globe maker, began his busi-
ness shortly after the Great Fire of 1666 destroyed most of the map-stock of
the city and started a cartographic flurry in London. Morden's maps of Great
Britain and continental Europe catered to a growing market of people inter-
ested in visualizing the scope and boundaries of their city, their country, their
geographical position in the world. The title page (above) and "General Map
of the Earth" (opposite) are taken from Robert Morden, *Geography Recti-
fied: Or, A Description of the WORLD* (LONDON: Printed by R. R. for
Robert Morden and *Thomas Cockerill,* at the *Atlas* in *Cornhill,* and at the
Three Legs and *Bible* in the *Poultrey,* against *Grocers-Ally,* MDCC).

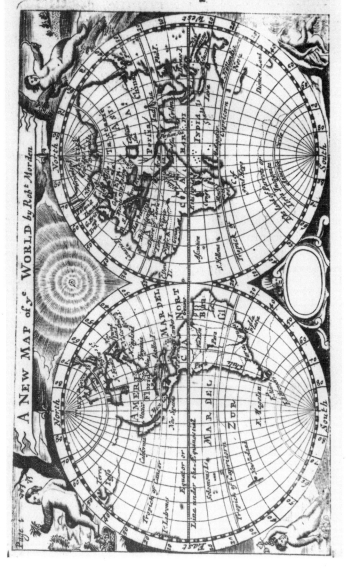

When I am doing this Justice, I am not to forget the best Mechanick of my Acquaintance, that useful Servant to Science and Knowledge, Mr. *John Rowley*; but think I lay a great Obligation on the Publick, by acquainting them with his Proposals for a pair of new Globes.[5] After his Preamble, he promises in the said Proposals that,

In the Celestial Globe,

'Care shall be taken that the Fixed Stars be placed according to their true Longitude and Latitude, from the many and correct Observations of *Hevelius, Cassini*, Mr. *Flamsteed*, Reg. Astronomer, Dr. *Halley, Savilian* Professor of Geometry in *Oxon*; and from whatever else can be procured to render the Globe more exact, instructive, and useful.[6]

'That all the Constellations be drawn in a curious, new, and particular Manner; each Star in so just, distinct, and conspicuous a Proportion, that its true Magnitude may be readily known by bare Inspection, according to the different *Light* and *Sizes* of the Stars. That the Tract or Way of such Comets as have been well observed, but not hitherto expressed in any Globe, be carefully delineated in this.

In the Terrestrial Globe.

'That by reason the Descriptions formerly made, both in the *English* or *Dutch* great Globes, are Erroneous, *Asia, Africa*, and *America* be drawn in a Manner wholly new; by which Means it is to be noted, that the Undertakers will be obliged to alter the Latitude of some Places in 10 Degrees, the Longitude of others in 20 Degrees: Besides which great and necessary Alterations, there be many remarkable Countries, Cities, Towns, Rivers, and Lakes, omitted in other Globes, inserted here according to the best Discoveries made by our late Navigators. Lastly, That the Course of the Trade-Winds, the

[5] John Rowley: An instrument builder (d. 1728), often attributed with the invention of the orrery, a device designed to show the motions of the planets around the sun using clockwork. The orrery was actually invented by George Graham about 1700 for Charles Boyle, fourth Earl of Orrery, but Rowley produced and marketed the instrument.

[6] Hevelius . . . Halley: Hevelius (1611–1687), Polish astronomer, catalogued 1,500 stars; Giovanni Domenico Cassini (1625–1712), director of the observatory at Paris; John Flamsteed (1646–1719), first Astronomer Royal; Edmond Halley (1656–1742), predicted the return of the comet that now bears his name; he succeeded Flamsteed as Astronomer Royal in 1720.

Monsoons, and other Winds periodically shifting between the Trop-
icks, be visibly expressed.

'Now in Regard that this Undertaking is of so universal Use, as the
Advancement of the most necessary Parts of the Mathematicks, as
well as tending to the Honour of the *British* Nation, and that the
Charge of carrying it on is very expensive, it is desired that all Gentle-
men who are willing to promote so great a Work, will be pleased to
subscribe the following Conditions.

'I. The Undertakers engage to furnish each Subscriber with a Ce-
lestial and Terrestrial Globe, each of 30 Inches Diameter, in all Re-
spects curiously adorn'd, the Stars gilded, the Capital Cities plainly
distinguished, the Frames, Meridians, Horizons, Hour-Circles and In-
dexes so exactly finished up and accurately divided, that a Pair of
these Globes will really appear, in the Judgment of any disinterested
and intelligent Person, worth Fifteen Pounds more than will be de-
manded for them by the Undertakers.

'II. Whosoever will be pleased to Subscribe, and pay Twenty Five
Pounds in the Manner following for a Pair of these Globes, either for
their own Use, or to present them to any College in the Universities,
or any publick Library or School, shall have his Coat of Arms, Name,
Title, Seat, or Place of Residence, *&c.* inserted in some convenient
Place of the Globe.

'III. That every Subscriber do at first pay down the Sum of Ten
Pounds, and Fifteen Pounds more upon the Delivery of each Pair of
Globes perfectly fitted up: And that the said Globes be delivered
within Twelve Months after the Number of Thirty Subscribers be
compleated; and that the Subscribers be served with Globes in the
Order in which they subscribed.

'IV. That a Pair of these Globes shall not hereafter be sold to any
Person but the Subscribers under Thirty Pounds.

'V. That if there be not thirty Subscribers within four Months after
the first of *December,* 1712, the Money paid shall be return'd on De-
mand by Mr. *John Warner,* Goldsmith, near *Temple-Bar,* who shall
receive and pay the same according to the above-mentioned Articles.'

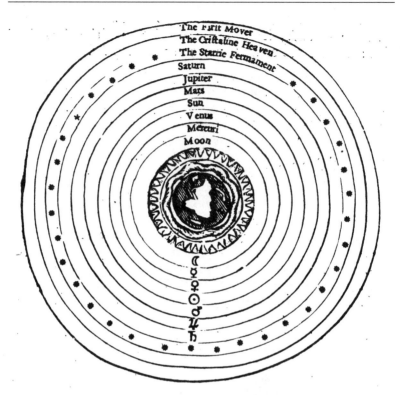

"The Composition of the Whole Frame of the World," by Joseph Moxon, 1699. Moxon (1627–1700) authored, translated, printed, and sold in his own shop a number of works on printing, architecture, mathematics, geography, and astronomy, including *A Tutor to Astronomy and Geography*, in which this illustration appeared. Moxon, along with many others of Pope's time, made visible to many what could be seen through "*Galileo*'s Eyes" as Belinda's Lock "pursue[s] its Progress thro' the Skies" (*Rape* V.138, 132). The illustration is taken from Joseph Moxon, *A Tutor to Astronomy and Geography; or, An Easie and Speedy Way to Know the Use of Both the Globes, Celestial and Terrestial* [*sic*], 5th ed. (1699).

EARL OF CASTLEMAINE

From *Philosophical Transactions*, No. 139
["The English Globe"]

Roger Palmer, Earl of Castlemaine (1634–1707), was a diplomat and author, husband of Charles II's mistress Barbara Villiers. He was also a devout Catholic, a mathematician, a linguist, and a shaper of the world with his invention of the "English Globe," which, as this description in *Philosophical Transactions* boasts, is literally "a fix'd and immoveable one." The phrase could almost be taken as metaphor for the British Empire's tightening hold on trade and other nations, seeing itself central, to whom "Kings shall sue, and suppliant States be seen / Once more to bend before a *British* QUEEN" (*Windsor-Forest*, ll. 383–84). Castlemaine's globe is advertised as simultaneously more simple to use than previous kinds of globes, and more comprehensive; moreover, it is accessible to "any one" no matter how "unacquainted with Mathematicks," thus putting the world into the figurative grasp of any Briton who could afford to buy it.

The text is taken from The Royal Society, *Philosophical Transactions*, No. 139 (April, May, June 1678): 988.

Being a Stabil and Immobil one, performing what the Ordinary Globes do, and much more

There is invented by the Right Honourable the Earl of *Castlemaine* a new kind of Globe, called (for distinctions sake) the *English Globe*; being a fix'd and immoveable one, performing what the Ordinary ones do, and much more, even without their usual Appendancies, as *Wooden Horizons, Brazen Meridians, Vertical Circles, Horary Circles*, &c.[1] For it composes it self to the Scite and Position of the World, without the *Mariners Compass* or the like Forein help; and besides, other useful and surprizing operations (relating both to the *Sun* and *Moon*, and performed by the Shade alone,) we have by it not

---

[1] *usual Appendancies . . . Horary Circles, &c.:* Globes often had various mechanical attachments or mathematical supplements; the following are much-simplified explanations of highly technical concepts: *Wooden Horizons:* The wooden ring in which a globe is fixed; *Brazen Meridians:* A brass circle or semicircle in which a globe is suspended and revolves; *Vertical Circles:* Great circle perpendicular to the horizon; *Horary Circles:* Metal circle on a globe, marked with the hours, showing the time differences between meridians.

only the constant proportion of Perpendiculars to their Shades, with several Corollaries thence arising, but also an easy new and most compendious way of describing *Dials* on all Planes, as well Geometrically as Mechanically, most of which may be taught any one in few hours, though never so unacquainted with mathematicks.

To this is added on the *Pedestal* a Projection of all the appearing *Constellations* in this Horizon, with their Figures and Shapes. And besides, several new things in it differing from the common *Astrolabe*[2] (tending to a clearer and quicker way of operating) the very Principles of all *Steriographical Projections*[3] are laid down and Mathematically demonstrated, as is every thing else of moment throughout the whole Treatise.

These *Globes* will be made and exposed to Sale about *August* next (God willing) against which time the Book for its use will also be printed, and sold by *Joseph Moxon* on *Ludgate-Hill* at the Sign of the *Atlas*.

[2] Astrolabe: An instrument used to measure altitudes and solve other problems of practical astronomy; often mechanically complicated, with moving circles representing the circles of the heavens.

[3] Steriographical Projections: Representations of solid bodies on a plane.

Selected Bibliography

The bibliography is divided into two parts, "Works Cited" and "Suggestions for Further Reading." The first part contains all primary and secondary works quoted or discussed in the general and section introductions, headnotes, and notes to documents, with the exception of the documents themselves reprinted in the edition. The second part is a selective list of materials for the student interested in knowing more about Pope's life, work, and culture. Some of the works cited also appear as suggested readings.

WORKS CITED

Boswell, James. *Life of Johnson.* Ed. R. W. Chapman. Intro. Pat Rogers. Oxford: Oxford UP, 1953, 1970, 1980.

Brown, Laura. *Alexander Pope.* Oxford: Blackwell, 1985.

Carretta, Vincent. "A Note on Money." In Equiano, Olaudah. *The Interesting Narrative and Other Writings.* Ed. Vincent Carretta. New York: Penguin, 1995.

Colley, Linda. *Britons: Forging the Nation, 1707–1837.* New Haven: Yale UP, 1992.

Deutsch, Helen. "'The Truest Copies' and the 'Mean Original': Pope, Deformity, and the Poetics of Self-Exposure." *Eighteenth-Century Studies* 27.1 (Fall 1993): 1–26.

Downie, J. A. *To Settle the Succession of the State: Literature and Politics, 1678–1750*. London: Macmillan, 1994.

Fox, Christopher. *Locke and the Scriblerians: Identity and Consciousness in Early Eighteenth-Century Britain*. Berkeley: U of California P, 1988.

Gordon, I. R. F. *A Preface to Pope*. 2nd ed. London: Longman, 1976, 1993.

Hagstrum, Jean. *The Sister Arts: The Tradition of Literary Pictorialism and English Poetry from Dryden to Gray*. Chicago: U of Chicago P, 1958.

Halsband, Robert. *The Rape of the Lock and Its Illustrations 1714–1896*. Oxford: Clarendon, 1980.

Handover, P. M. *Printing in London from 1476 to Modern Times*. Cambridge, MA: Harvard UP, 1960.

Hazlitt, William. *Lectures on the English Poets*. London: Printed for Taylor and Hessy, 1818.

Hobbes, Thomas. *The Elements of Philosophy*. In *The English Works of Thomas Hobbes of Malmesbury*. Ed. Sir William Molesworth. London: J. Bohn, 1839–45.

Hogarth, William. *Engravings by Hogarth*. Ed. Sean Shesgreen. New York: Dover, 1973.

Hume, David. *A Treatise of Human Nature*. Ed. L. A. Selby-Bigge. 2nd ed. P. H. Nidditch. Oxford: Clarendon, 1978.

Hunter, J. Paul. *Before Novels: The Cultural Contexts of Eighteenth–Century English Fiction*. New York: Norton, 1990.

Johnson, Samuel. *Lives of the English Poets*. Vol. 3. Oxford: Clarendon, 1935.

Locke, John. *An Essay Concerning Human Understanding*. Ed. Peter H. Nidditch. Oxford: Oxford UP, 1975.

Mack, Maynard. *Alexander Pope: A Life*. New York: Norton, and New Haven: Yale UP, 1985.

Nash, Roy. *Hampton Court: The Palace and the People*. London and Sydney: Macdonald, 1983.

Nussbaum, Felicity. *The Brink of All We Hate: English Satires on Women 1660–1750*. Lexington: U of Kentucky P, 1984.

Perry, Ruth. *The Celebrated Mary Astell: An Early English Feminist*. Chicago: U of Chicago P, 1986.

Pincus, Steve. "'Coffee Politicians Does Create': Coffeehouses and Restoration Political Culture." *Journal of Modern History* 67 (Dec. 1995): 807–34.

Pope, Alexander. *Alexander Pope: The Oxford Authors Series*. Ed. Pat Rogers. Oxford and New York: Oxford UP, 1993.

———. *The Correspondence of Alexander Pope*. Ed. George Sherburn. 5 vols. Oxford: Clarendon, 1956.

————. *Epistles to Several Persons (Moral Essays)*. Ed. F. W. Bateson. In *Poems of Alexander Pope*. Twickenham Edition. Vol. III-ii. 2nd ed. London: Methuen, and New Haven: Yale UP, 1961.

————. *The Iliad of Homer*. Ed. Maynard Mack. In *Poems of Alexander Pope*. Twickenham Edition. Vols. VII–VIII. London: Methuen, and New Haven: Yale UP, 1967.

————. *Selected Prose of Alexander Pope*. Ed. Paul Hammond. Cambridge: Cambridge UP, 1987.

————. *Works, Complete*. Ed. Joseph Warton. London: Printed for B. Law, 1797.

Rumbold, Valerie. *Women's Place in Pope's World*. Cambridge: Cambridge UP, 1989.

Sacheverell, Henry. *The Political Union*. London: Printed by Leonard Lichfield, for George Clements, 1702.

Spence, Joseph. *Observations, Anecdotes and Characters of Books and Men, Collected from the Conversation of Mr. Pope and Other Eminent Persons of His Time*. Ed. J. M. Osborn. 2 vols. Oxford: Clarendon, 1966.

Strutt, Joseph. *A Biographical Dictionary: Containing an Historical Account of All the Engravers, from the Earliest Period of the Art of Engraving to the Present Time*. London, 1785. Geneva: Minkoff Reprint, 1972.

Weinbrot, Howard. "Fine Ladies, Saints in Heaven, and Pope's *Rape of the Lock*: Genealogy, Catholicism, and the Irenic Muse." *Augustan Subjects: Essays in Honor of Martin C. Battestin*. Ed. Albert J. Rivero. Newark, DE: U of Delaware P, 1997.

SUGGESTIONS FOR FURTHER READING

Other Editions

Pope, Alexander. *The Poems of Alexander Pope*. Ed. John Butt. Twickenham Edition. Vol. 2. New Haven: Yale UP, 1963.

————. *Alexander Pope: The Oxford Authors Series*. Ed. Pat Rogers. Oxford and New York: Oxford UP, 1993.

————. *The Rape of the Lock*. Ed. J. S. Cunningham. Oxford: Oxford UP, 1966.

————. *The Rape of the Lock*. Ed. Elizabeth Gurr. Oxford: Oxford UP, 1990.

————. *The Rape of the Lock. Contexts Series: Selected Literary Works in their Historical Settings*. Ed. William Kinsley. Hamden, CT: Archon, 1979.

————. *The Rape of the Lock.* Ed. David Lougee and Robert McHenry, Jr. Columbus, OH: Charles Merrill, 1969.

————. *The Rape Observed: An Edition of Alexander Pope's Poem "The Rape of the Lock."* Ed. Clarence Tracy. Toronto: U of Toronto P, 1974.

————. *Works, Complete.* Ed. Joseph Warton. London: Printed for B. Law, 1797.

Articles and Special Issues

Brooks, Cleanth. "The Case of Arabella Fermor." *The Well-Wrought Urn.* New York: Harcourt, 1947.

Brückmann, Patricia. "Virgins visited by angel powers: *The Rape of the Lock,* platonick love, sylphs and some mysticks." *The Enduring Legacy: Allexander Pope Tercentenary Essays.* Ed. G. S. Rousseau and Pat Rogers. Cambridge: Cambridge UP, 1988.

The Eighteenth Century: Theory and Interpretation 29.2 (Spring 1988). A Special Issue on Alexander Pope. Ed. David B. Morris.

New Orleans Review 15:4 (Winter 1988). Special Edition on *The Rape of the Lock.*

Nicholson, C. E. "A World of Artefacts: *The Rape of the Lock* as Social History." *Literature and History* 5.2 (Autumn 1979).

Weinbrot, Howard. "*The Rape of the Lock* and the Contexts of Warfare." In *The Enduring Legacy: Alexander Pope Tercentenary Essays.* Ed. G. S. Rousseau and Pat Rogers. Cambridge: Cambridge UP, 1988.

Pope's Life and Work

Aden, John. *Pope's Once and Future Kings: Satire and Politics in the Early Career.* Knoxville: U of Tennessee P, 1978.

Barnard, John, ed. *Pope: The Critical Heritage.* London: Routledge, 1973.

Battestin, Martin C. *The Providence of Wit: Aspects of Form in Augustan Literature and the Arts.* Oxford: Clarendon, 1974. Charlottesville: U of Virginia P, 1989.

Bogel, Fredric V. *Acts of Knowledge in Pope's Later Poems.* Lewisburg, PA: Bucknell UP, 1981.

Brower, Reuben Arthur. *Alexander Pope: The Poetry of Allusion.* Oxford: Clarendon, 1959.

Damrosch, Leopold. *The Imaginative World of Alexander Pope.* Berkeley: U of California P, 1987.

Deutsch, Helen. *Resemblance & Disgrace: Alexander Pope and the Deformation of Culture.* Cambridge, MA: Harvard UP, 1996.

Dixon, Peter. *The World of Pope's Satires.* London: Methuen, 1968.

Doody, Margaret. *The Daring Muse: Augustan Poetry Reconsidered.* Cambridge: Cambridge UP, 1985.

Fairer, David. *Pope's Imagination.* Manchester: Manchester UP, 1984.

Foxon, David F. *Pope and the Eighteenth-Century Book Trade.* Oxford: Oxford UP, 1991.

Goldberg, S. L. "Integrity and Life in Pope's Poetry." *Studies in the Eighteenth Century.* Ed. R. F. Brissenden and J. C. Eade. Toronto: U of Toronto P, 1973.

Goldgar, Bertrand A. *Literary Criticism of Alexander Pope.* Lincoln: U of Nebraska P, 1965.

Griffin, Dustin H. *Alexander Pope: The Poet in the Poems.* Princeton: Princeton UP, 1978.

Guerinot, J. V. *Pamphlet Attacks on Alexander Pope 1711–1744: A Descriptive Bibliography.* London: Methuen, 1969.

Hagstrum, Jean. *The Sister Arts: The Tradition of Literary Pictorialism and English Poetry from Dryden to Gray.* Chicago: U of Chicago P, 1958.

Hunter, J. Paul. "Pope and the Ideology of the Couplet." *Ideas* 4.1 (1996): 22–29.

———. "From Typology to Type: Agents of Change in Eighteenth-Century English Texts." *Cultural Artifacts and the Production of Meaning.* Ed. Margaret J. M. Ezell and Katherine O'Brien O'Keeffe. Ann Arbor: U of Michigan P, 1994.

Kenner, Hugh. "Pope's Reasonable Rhymes." *ELH* 41 (1974): 74–88.

Mack, Maynard. *The Garden and the City: Retirement and Politics in the Later Poetry of Pope, 1731–1743.* Toronto: U of Toronto P, 1969.

———, and James Winn, eds. *Pope: Recent Essays by Several Hands.* Brighton, Sussex: Harvester, 1980.

Morris, David B. *Alexander Pope: The Genius of Sense.* Cambridge, MA: Harvard UP, 1984.

Nicolson, Marjorie Hope, and G. S. Rousseau. *"This Long Disease, My Life": Alexander Pope and the Sciences.* Princeton: Princeton UP, 1968.

Pollak, Ellen. *The Poetics of Sexual Myth: Gender and Ideology in the Verse of Swift and Pope.* Chicago: U of Chicago P, 1985.

Price, Martin. *To the Palace of Wisdom: Studies in Order and Energy from Dryden to Blake.* Garden City, NY: Doubleday, 1964.

Rogers, Pat. *Hacks and Dunces: Pope, Swift, and Grub Street.* London: Methuen, 1980.

Rumbold, Valerie. *Women's Place in Pope's World.* Cambridge: Cambridge UP, 1989.

Sherburn, George. *The Early Career of Alexander Pope.* Oxford: Clarendon, 1934.

Spacks, Patricia Meyer. *An Argument of Images: The Poetry of Alexander Pope.* Cambridge, MA: Harvard UP, 1971.

———. "Imaginations Warm and Tender: Pope and Lady Mary." *South Atlantic Quarterly* 83.2 (Spring 1984).

Wall, Cynthia. "Editing Desire: Pope's Correspondence with (and without) Lady Mary." *Philological Quarterly* 71 (Spring 1992): 221–37.

Wimsatt, William K. *The Portraits of Alexander Pope.* New Haven: Yale UP, 1965.

Winn, James. *A Window in the Bosom: The Letters of Alexander Pope.* Hamden, CT: Archon, 1977.

The Social and Political World

Brown, Laura. *Ends of Empire: Women and Ideology in Early Eighteenth-Century English Literature.* Ithaca: Cornell UP, 1993.

Castle, Terry. *Masquerade and Civilization.* Stanford: Stanford UP, 1986.

Colley, Linda. *Britons: Forging the Nation 1707–1837.* New Haven: Yale UP, 1992.

Downie, J. A. *To Settle the Succession of the State: Literature and Politics, 1678–1750.* London: Macmillan, 1994.

Erskine-Hill, Howard. *The Social Milieu of Alexander Pope: Lives, Examples, and the Poetic Response.* New Haven: Yale UP, 1975.

Fox, Christopher. *Locke and the Scriblerians: Identity and Consciousness in Early Eighteenth-Century Britain.* Berkeley: U of California P, 1988.

Hunter, J. Paul. *Before Novels: The Cultural Contexts of Eighteenth–Century English Fiction.* New York: Norton, 1990.

Keay, John. *The Honourable Company: A History of the English East India Company.* New York: Macmillan, 1991.

Novak, Maximilian. *English Literature in the Age of Disguise.* Berkeley: U of California P, 1977.

Stallybrass, Peter, and Allon White. *The Politics and Poetics of Transgression.* Ithaca, NY: Cornell UP, 1986.

Weinbrot, Howard. *Britannia's Issue: The Rise of British Literature from Dryden to Ossian.* Cambridge: Cambridge UP, 1993.

Text Acknowledgments

The text of *The Rape of the Lock* and of all other poems by Alexander Pope are reprinted from the "reduced version" of the Twickenham edition of *The Poems of Alexander Pope,* edited by John Butt (1963), by permission of Routledge Press.

Excerpts from *The Correspondence of Alexander Pope,* edited by George Sherburn (1956), reprinted by permission of Oxford University Press.

Excerpts from *The Spectator,* edited by Donald Bond (1965) and *The Tatler,* edited by Donald Bond (1987), are both reprinted by permission of Oxford University Press.

Daniel Defoe, excerpts from *A Tour thro' the whole island of Great Britain,* edited by G. D. H. Cole (1927), reprinted by permission of the University of Virginia Library.

Samuel Johnson, excerpts from *Lives of the English Poets,* vol. 3, edited by George Birkbeck Hill (1945), reprinted by permission of Oxford University Press.

Joseph Spence, excerpts from *Anecdotes, Observations, and Characters of Books and Men,* edited by Samuel Weller Singer (1964), reprinted by permission of Oxford University Press.

Jonathan Swift, excerpts from *The Poems of Jonathan Swift,* edited by Harold Williams (1958), reprinted by permission of Oxford University Press.

Ned Ward, excerpts from *The London Spy,* edited by Paul Hyland (1993), reprinted by permission of the editor.

Illustration Credits

Pages 48, 49, 58, 64, 72, 80, frontispiece engraving, title page, and engravings for Cantos 1–5, from *The Rape of the Lock: An Heroi-Comical Poem. In Five Canto's.* Written by Mr. Pope. With original illustrations by Louis du Guernier. (1714) By permission of The British Library. [Identification no. C70bb1(1)]

Page 88, portrait of Alexander Pope by Charles Jervas (1714). Reproduced by permission of The Bodleian Library, University of Oxford. [Poole Portrait 243]

Page 128, portrait of Arabella Fermor. Undated painting. Artist unknown.

Pages 132–164, facsimile copy of *The Rape of the Locke* (1712 edition), 2 canto version, Printed for Bernard Lintott in *Miscellaneous Poems and Translations by Several Hands.* Photos courtesy of the Newberry Library.

Page 199, caricature of Alexander Pope. "His/HOLINESS/and his/PRIME MINISTER./THE PHIZ AND CHARACTER OF _____ the Hyper-critic & Comentator. . . . Sold by the Print-sellers of London and Westminster." Anonymous engraving. Courtesy Beverly Chew Bequest, Print Collection, Miriam and Ira D. Wallach Division of Art, Prints, and Photographs, The New York Public Library, Astor, Lenox, and Tilden Foundations. Reproduced with permission.

Page 202, caricature of Alexander Pope by William Hoare after Condé. Copyright © The British Museum. Reproduced with permission.

Page 245, portrait of Lady Mary Wortley Montagu attributed to Charles Jervas. Date unknown. Present location unknown.

Page 253, shield of Achilles: rough sketch from Pope's Homer MS [BM Add. 4808 folio 81v]. By permission of The British Library.

Page 266, "The Happy Marriage," engraving from *The Analysis of Beauty* by William Hogarth (1753). Courtesy of the Print Collection, Lewis Walpole Library, Yale University.

Page 288, "The Council of Horses" (Fable XLIII); page 295, "The Lady and the Wasp" (Fable VIII); page 322, "The Monkey Who Had Seen the World" (Fable XIV) from *Fables* by John Gay with illustrations by John Wootton (1727). Special Collections Department, University of Virginia Library. Reproduced with permission.

Page 294, portrait of Martha and Teresa Blount by Charles Jervas, c. 1716. Mapledurham Collection; Mr J J Eyston. Photograph Courtauld Institute of Art. Reproduced with permission.

Page 325, "The Five Orders of Perriwigs" by William Hogarth. First state, November 1761. Courtesy of the Print Collection, Lewis Walpole Library, Yale University.

Page 336, "The Rape of the Lock," small oval engraving by William Hogarth. Date unknown. Courtesy of the Print Collection, Lewis Walpole Library, Yale University.

Page 363, Gold, enamel, and onyx snuffbox by L. Potter, Paris, 1738–39. The Wallace Collection. [#52 G2 snuffbox.]

Page 373, Royal Exchange and page 375, St. James's Park, details from *A Plan of the City of London*, etc. (1746) by John Rocque, Surveyor. Courtesy of The New York Public Library, Astor, Lenox and Tilden Foundations.

Page 379, a contemporary view of Pope's villa at Twickenham. Courtesy of the Print Collection, Lewis Walpole Library, Yale University.

Page 382, Sir Christopher Wren, drawing from his architectural plans for Hampton Court Palace: detail for centre of Park front (East), Wren Palace, Hampton Court. Courtesy Sir John Soane's Museum.

Page 386, "The Apotheosis of Queene Anne" by Antonio Verrio. Ceiling painting in the Queen's Drawing Room at Hampton Court. Copyright © The Warburg Institute. Photograph supplied by National Monuments Record.

Pages 392–93, detail from *A Plan of the Cities of London and Westminster*, etc. (1720) by John Strype. By permission of The British Library. [Crace Collection of Plans, Portfolio II(85)]

Page 397, plan of the Royal Exchange from *The History and Survey of London*, 3rd ed. (1760) by William Maitland. By permission of The British Library. [Identification no. 578l19]

Page 409, "The Bench," engraving by William Hogarth (1758). Courtesy of the Print Collection, Lewis Walpole Library, Yale University.

Page 417, The Old East India House, from William Overley's trade card, c. 1714–26. Copyright © British Museum.

Page 428, title page, and page 429, map from *Geography Rectified, or a Description of the World* (1720) by Robert Morden. Special Collections Department, University of Virginia Library. Reproduced with permission.

Page 432, "The Composition of the Whole Frame of the World" from *A Tutor to Astronomy and Geography; or, an Easie and Speedy Way to Know the Use of Both the Globes, Celestial and Terrestial* [sic], 5th ed. (1699) by Joseph Moxon. Special Collections Department, University of Virginia Library. Reproduced with permission.